Thomas W. Knox
Civil War Correspondent in Missouri

Very Truly Yours,
Tho. W. Knox

Thomas W. Knox

Civil War Correspondent in Missouri

Robert G. Schultz

Camp Pope
2018

Copyright © 2018 by Robert G. Schultz

Library of Congress Control Number: 2018961613

ISBN: 978-1-929919-85-7

Camp Pope Publishing
PO Box 2232
Iowa City, Iowa 52244
www.camppope.com

Frontispiece: Thomas W. Knox from his book
Backsheesh! Or Life and Adventures in the Orient

Contents

Preface ix

Introduction xii

1. First Reports from Missouri 1
2. The Dance Begins 33
3. The Battle of Boonville 44
4. Missouri in the Spotlight 66
5. Waiting for News 81
6. Seeking Action – Forsyth 95
7. Dug Springs 112
8. Wilson's Creek 127
9. Retreat and Repercussions 148
10. Knox Afield 174
11. Frémont's Troubles 183
12. Jefferson City 207
13. On to Springfield 221
14. Farewell to Springfield 246
15. Halleck in Charge 264
16. Winter Quarters 294
17. A New Year 323
18. "Third Time's A Charm" 365
19. Battle of Pea Ridge 378
20. Other Times, Other Places 407
    Appendix 412

Endnotes 452

Bibliography 537

Index 550

Appendix

I. Proclamation 412

II. Military Department of the West 413

III. The Harney Price Agreement 415

IV. General Price's Address 416

V. Governor Jackson's Proclamation of June 12, 1861 418

VI. Proclamation of General Lyon, June 15, 1861 421

VII. Proclamation of General Lyon, June 18, 1861 424

VIII. Proclamation of John Ross, Chief of the Cherokee Nation. 426

IX. Proclamation of General Ben McCulloch 427

X. General Sweeny's Proclamation at Springfield 428

XI. Judge Catron's Charge 429

XII. Franc Wilkie's Report on the Forsyth Action 430

XIII. Frémont's Proclamation 436

XIV. Martial Law in Missouri: The Fall of Lexington 438

XV. Frémont's Staff, October, 1861 439

XVI. Frémont-Price Treaty 443

XVII. McClellan's Instructions to Halleck 445

XVIII. Hamilton Gamble, Calling State Militia into Service 447

XIX. Letters Exchanged Between Generals Price and Halleck, January, 1862 448

Thomas W. Knox
Civil War Correspondent in Missouri

Preface

"News is the First Draft of History."[1]

The American Civil War has been a source of continuing fascination for more than 150 years. Almost as soon as the war was over, and even sooner in some cases, book publication began. That flow of books, magazines and articles continues to this day. A particular flood of books appeared during the 150th anniversary celebrations, 2011–2015. And it seems that all phases of the Civil War were covered, from sweeping vistas of four years of war to studies of particular battles, biographies, unit histories, the effects of the war on given states and towns, intimate diaries from soldiers and the home front, slavery and abolition, politics, technology, reprints of older books, and many more areas.

For the state of Missouri and the city of St. Louis, Civil War era coverage has also been extensive over the years.[2] St. Louis newspapers like the *Democrat* (actually a Republican paper) and the *Republican* (a Democrat newspaper) are available on microfilm. This book, however, takes a different view, focusing on one reporter, Thomas W. Knox, an easterner, born in New Hampshire, but with some western experience in the Colorado gold fields. Knox was assigned by the *New York Herald* to report on the war from St. Louis. He approached this assignment with gusto and not only covered events in the city, but also took to the field with the Union armies in Missouri. His reports, therefore, are filled with many small tidbits of information often missing from official reports and later books. They provide a novel wartime level of richness of phrase and detail. In 1865 Knox wrote of his experiences throughout the war in *Camp-fire and Cotton-field*. But there was much more to the story than recorded in his book. This is Knox's more comprehensive story as he told it, not only in the pages of his overview book, but especially in the *New York Herald* and in the newspapers that reprinted his *Herald* articles. Much of what follows has not been seen since its original publication. At the same time, this account is not a complete report on the activities in Missouri in the first year of the Civil War, but rather a report on what Knox, himself, actually experienced. Today, he would called an embedded reporter, covering the major engagements in Missouri. The state's other notable battles and skirmishes like Carthage, Lexington, Belmont, and Fredericktown, receive scant mention.

There were two prefaces to his book, one for the correspondents:[3]

TO
THE REPRESENTATIVES OF THE PRESS,
WHO FOLLOWED THE
FORTUNES OF THE NATIONAL ARMIES,
AND RECORDED
THE DEEDS OF VALOR THAT SECURED THE PERPETUITY OF THE REPUBLIC,
𝔗𝔥𝔦𝔰 𝔙𝔬𝔩𝔲𝔪𝔢
IS SYMPATHETICALLY INSCRIBED.

And one for the reader:

TO THE READER

A PREFACE usually takes the form of an apology. The author of this volume has none to offer.

The book owes its appearance to its discovery of a publisher. It has been prepared from materials gathered during the Campaigns herein recorded, and from the writer's personal recollections.

Whatever of merit or demerit it possesses remains for the reader to ascertain. His judgment will be unprejudiced if he finds no word of promise on the prefatory page.

New York September 15th, 1865.

Knox deserves to be heard again. The richness of detail within his work provides a small look at the human side of the war that shattered so many lives and brought about so many changes, large and small. Many of the tales he tells are found nowhere else in Civil War literature. My purpose in compiling this book is to act as an amanuensis for him and to provide annotation and connective tissue for his work. Much of Knox's reports are presented verbatim, but some material has been omitted for the sake of brevity. Where this has been done, the omissions are noted and the omitted material is to be found in the endnotes.

Robert G. Schultz.

Introduction

War correspondents have fascinated American readers over the years, from the Revolution to the most recent "dust-up" overseas. Often, they put themselves in harm's way to accurately inform their reading public. In the early years of the Republic, war news traveled only as fast as a horse could gallop or a ship could sail. A classic example of this communication problem arose at the end of the War of 1812. The Treaty of Ghent, ending the war, was signed December 24, 1814, in the Netherlands, and ratified by the British Parliament on December 30, but the news was slow in reaching America. Senate ratification did not take place until February 18, 1815. In the meantime, the British were defeated at the Battle of New Orleans on January 8, 1815 – neither side having known of the peace treaty.

By the time the Civil War began, communications had radically changed. The telegraph had spread its wires to most major cities and beyond. (The telegraph had reached San Francisco and the first message from the new State of California was sent to President Abraham Lincoln on October 24, 1861.[1]) Railroads from many eastern cities had extended their lines to Chicago by 1852, St. Louis by 1855, and Memphis by 1861. With this enhanced speed of communication, news reports were often in print within two days of the event. It was widely known that President Lincoln spent hours at the Washington telegraph office awaiting battle reports.

A new kind of newspaper also emerged before the war with the advent of steam-powered, high-speed presses. Newspaper prices dropped to one or two cents per issue. Content also changed. While shipping reports, prices current, advertisements and government documents remained, new kinds of news stories appeared – crime, politics, and human-interest stories. Increasingly lurid prose lured readers. Larger cities hosted several daily newspapers, often of opposing political persuasion and in fierce competition. Smaller towns, especially county seats were served by weekly papers. There were also many foreign language papers, often in German,

Introduction

and papers specifically devoted to religious issues. Reports from one paper were often copied by other papers, usually with credit given. Articles from German language newspapers were translated and printed as "from the German Press" to give readers a sense of what the great number of German immigrants were thinking.

Readers were excited by a new type of weekly publication, which appeared within the decade preceding the Civil War, the weekly illustrated newspaper. *Harper's Weekly* (subtitled *A Journal of Civilization*), which began in 1857, *Frank Leslie's Illustrated Newspaper* (1852), the *New York Illustrated News* (1859) and others carried news, illustrated reports of events and people, serialized novels, and cartoons. The illustrations were woodcuts or engravings, sometimes reproduced from photographs. Photography was beginning to come into its own, but the process was slow, and "action" photographs were far in the future. Photographs themselves could not yet be reproduced in print, rather it was necessary for artists and engravers to convert, or redraw, the images.

Similar publications appeared in Europe. The *London Illustrated News* (1842), *Punch; or The London Charivari* (1841), and the Paris *Le Monde Illustré* (1857) are examples. During the Civil War, there was considerable European interest in American events. In general, European sympathy tended to be with the Confederacy, and President Lincoln was often caricatured harshly.

With all this new technology and publishing changes, a new type of reportage and reporter appeared in the 1850s. The preferred method for filing their reports was the telegraph. Only if the wire were not available or the report too long to be telegraphed were letters used. In either case a new style of reporting developed in which the most important information was placed first with elaboration following (the pyramid style). War correspondents were hired by newspapers to provide the news from the field. They sometimes were on a salary and at other times they were paid by the inches of column produced from their reports. Correspondents called themselves the "Bohemian Brigade." One of these Bohemians, Junius Henri Browne, described the correspondents:

> The war correspondent is a hybrid, neither a soldier nor a

citizen; with the Army, but not of it; is present at battles, and often participating in them, yet without any rank or recognized existence, has mystified not a few, and rendered his position as anomalous as undesirable.[2]

Browne goes on to explain the high ideals of truth and nobility of motive of the correspondent. He describes the pressures from officers that their units be seen in the very best light and bravest. But then he admits:

The Bohemians have faults not a few, as has been stated; but they are the best abused class of which I have any knowledge. They are too much inclined to publish their information before prudence and patriotism permit; but that is the fault of their employers, and ought to be wholly discouraged. The man who can forget the duty he owes his country in his desire to serve the journal he represents, ought to be disgraced and punished.[3]

These high-sounding words often seemed to be honored in the breach in the Bohemian's desire to be first with the story. J. Cutler Andrews, in his *The North Reports the Civil War* described their characteristics:

Although they competed fiercely for news, the Western army correspondents were generally on friendly terms with each other; they usually ate, slept, traveled, smoked together, and not infrequently drank from the same flask with equal relish. On the other hand, the Eastern correspondents of the New York papers with the Army of the Potomac competed so sharply that they hesitated to let others know of their movements.[4]

The Bohemians were an interesting lot, for as fast friends they were also enemies, fiercely competing to scoop each other for the story. Since army campaigns often required much delay and waiting, the Bohemians found alternate "amusements." Drinking, gambling, horse racing and horseplay were common, and initiation of newcomers was often raucous. The campaigns they followed were often far from city comforts, and

Introduction

Bohemians were often forced to accept very rude accommodations. Woe to the innkeeper who was forced to accept their presence. Damages could be considerable and reparations were rare. This was the milieu in which Thomas W. Knox operated.

As the Civil War progressed, two distinct theaters of operation developed, Eastern (at first, mainly Virginia), and Western (trans-Appalachian extending to the Pacific). The Eastern Theater was relatively small and compact. The Western Theater, on the other hand, was vast with early operations centered mainly in Missouri and Kentucky. Distances were greater than in the East and communications more difficult and less reliable. St. Louis became a major nexus of communications, and St. Louis became correspondent Knox's first base of operations.

Then and now the question is often asked: why should we be interested in newspaper reports of the first year of the Civil War in Missouri? And why reports from Thomas W. Knox of the *New York Herald*? There are several possible answers to these questions:

1. The usual articles and books on this early period in the Civil War in Missouri rely on the dry *Official Records* and a few early and often prejudiced books. Many of these reports are short and lack much color. The two largest St. Louis newspapers both had local and political axes to grind and lacked a strong national perspective.
2. As a reporter, Thomas W. Knox was an engaging writer, filling his reports with local color, anecdotes, and human-interest stories. While a few writers cite Knox in their studies, it is usually from his book *Camp-fire and Cotton-field*, published in 1865. Not cited were his contemporaneous reports in the *New York Herald* that contained much more extensive information. The present study is probably the first time most of them have reappeared in print.
3. Missouri, a hotly contested border state, is interesting because in the early months of the war, a significant portion of the war news came from the action there. Many different military organizations, Union and secessionist, were established that became prototypes for future units.
4. Thomas W. Knox was one of the very few reporters actually on the

scenes of the early action. There were only two reporters at the early skirmishes at Boonville and Forsyth; Knox was the only reporter at Dug Springs, and one of maybe three or four at Wilson's Creek. In fact, in the first four months of the war in Missouri, Knox was the only reporter from the Eastern part of the country. Franc B. Wilkie, of Davenport, Iowa, reported for an Iowa newspaper and was later hired by the *New York Times*. Most other Eastern newspapers, other than Knox's *New York Herald*, recycled reports from the Missouri *Democrat* or the Missouri *Republican*.

5. As a reporter, Knox had the ability to get close to various important people like General Nathaniel Lyon and Colonel Frank Blair. Readers loved that kind of "inside" reporting. As a strong Union supporter, Knox used his reporting to help mold public opinion early in the conflict.
6. As an example of this influence, Knox's reports in the *New York Herald* were picked up and reprinted widely in other eastern (and Midwestern) newspapers and also in *Harpers Weekly*. There his reporting was influential in forming public opinion about the people and situations involved in the actions in Missouri.

Missouri Military Organizations

Missouri military organizations in the Civil War carried a very confusing mixture of names that separated Union (Federal), State (Secessionist), and Confederate units. They were:

- The original *Missouri State Militia* (or Missouri Volunteer Militia, MVM) that operated under the Militia Act of 1858 was the organization called into training sessions in May 1861, including the units at Lindell's Grove in St. Louis (called Camp Jackson).
- After the Camp Jackson "massacre" of May 10, Governor Claiborne Fox Jackson called the State Legislature into special session, where it enacted the 1861 Military Bill, which created a new, reorganized militia called the *Missouri State Guard* (MSG) which clearly was secessionist in nature.

Introduction xvii

- To counteract this secessionist State Guard, Home Guard regiments and smaller units were created, informally, throughout the State. Federal authority was given to Brigadier General of Volunteers Nathaniel Lyon to organize, arm, and support these Home Guards. Many were not in full-time service, but could be called up as needed during their enlistment period. Most of the Home Guard soldiers had enlisted for three months and by August had been replaced by six-month militia. Some of these units were called *Regiments of Infantry, Missouri Volunteers*.
- On November 6, 1861, Provisional Governor Hamilton R. Gamble reached an agreement with the Federal Government to form a new, full-time state militia that was equipped and financed by the Federals but under the control of the governor who had the power to appoint officers for the organization. This new organization, the *Missouri State Militia* (MSM), was mainly comprised of mounted units that were not to be subjected to service outside the state of Missouri.
- As for the secessionist *Missouri State Guard*, on March 17, 1862, after the Battle of Pea Ridge, Arkansas, it was merged into the *Confederate Army of the West*.

THOMAS W. KNOX

Who then, was this influential Civil War correspondent Thomas W. Knox? Thomas Wallace Knox was born in Pembroke, NH, on June 26, 1835, son of Nehemiah Knox (1797–1837) and Jane Wallace Critchett (1806–1840). He had one older sister, Emily, (1829-1915).[5] Thomas and Emily were orphaned at an early age. In the 1850 Census, Thomas Knox, age 15, is living in Epsom, NH, in the household of William Brackett, farmer, age 36 and his wife, Betsy Critchett Brackett, age 30. Also living with them is Sally Critchett, age 58. This Critchett connection through his mother may explain why Thomas Knox is there.[6] We know nothing of his education, but it must have been a solid one. There are mentions of his attendance at the Kingston (NH) Academy and the Deerfield (NH) Academy, but no records have been uncovered. He is next reported to be teaching and/or the principal at the Kingston Academy in Kingston, NH, sometime in the 1850s.[7] No records have been found, but it is unlikely that a twenty-year-old youth (in 1855) could have been a principal. Again, there is mention of his living with a relative in Boston, but no records of his education have been identified.

The decade of the 1850s provided significant changes for Thomas W. Knox. Forsaking teaching for the life of a newspaper correspondent, he wrote for the *Boston Atlas and Bee*, and then the 1859 Pikes Peak (Colorado) gold rush exerted its call on him and fellow newspaperman from the east Albert D. Richardson, who at that time represented Horace Greeley's *New York Tribune*, but earlier had written for the *Boston Journal*. The fact that both Knox and Richardson had been newspapermen in Boston at the same time probably accounts for their comradeship on the plains. Together they traveled to Denver, leaving from St. Joseph, Missouri in May 1860. Richardson's letters written along the way appeared in the Lawrence *Republican*.[8] Knox and Richardson reached Denver and Golden, Kansas Territory[9] by mid-June. There they plied their craft, not as prospectors or miners, but as newspapermen. They joined the staff of the short-lived *Western Mountaineer* of Golden.[10] They had a small house built for them on the outskirts of Denver.

"Our House in Denver," Richardson, *Beyond the Mississippi*, 295.

Introduction

In the autumn of 1860, Knox wrote for the *Rocky Mountain News* and also for eastern newspapers.[11] In one of these pieces he described the practice of journalism at the *Rocky Mountain News* rather dramatically:

> Journalism at Pike's Peak, like the course of true love, does not run smooth.
>
> Repeated shots have been fired at the *News* office by indignant "roughs"; the editors have been assaulted at various times, and on a few occasions their lives have been in great jeopardy. In July last, as the senior editor was quietly seated in his sanctum, several ruffians entered, and two of them presenting cocked revolvers at his head, requested him to take a pleasant walk with them to a gambling-saloon a few squares distant. As their invitation was *pressing*, he accepted it, and proceeded to the place designated. He was saved from being there shot down only by a stratagem of the saloon-keeper. Every few weeks a threat of cleaning out the *News* office is made by its enemies, and the whole corps, from the "devil" upward, is prepared to resist such a purifying process. The sanctum abounds in guns and revolvers, always at hand; and in squally times each man in the composing-room has a "six-shooter" by the side of his copy. The foreman sports a huge "navy" at his belt, and the roller-boy is ready to support the honor of the establishment with the weapon of his branch of trade. Pleasant business, publishing newspapers at Pike's Peak![12]

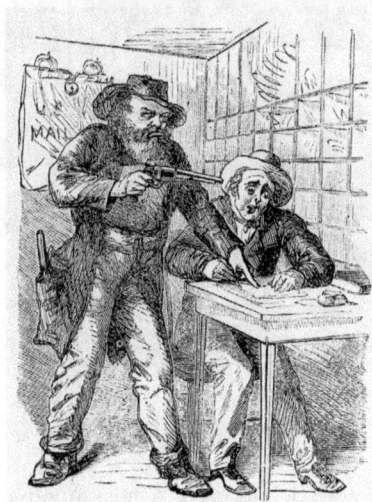

A VOLUNTARY RETRACTION.

Richardson, *Beyond the Mississippi*, 306.

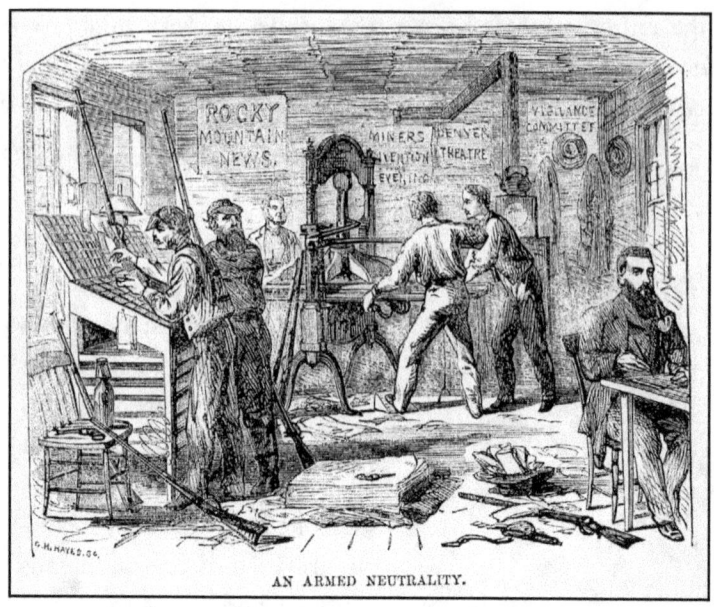

Richardson, *Beyond the Mississippi*, 291.
The person on the far right may be Thomas W. Knox.

Knox's tenure in Colorado was short, as was Richardson's. After Lincoln's election in 1860, newspapers' interest turned from news of gold and silver mining and the wild-west to the threatening war clouds developing in the east. Seeing this trend in journalism, Knox noted:

> During my stay in that region I supplied several Eastern journals with letters from Colorado and New Mexico. One after another, the editors of these journals informed me that letters from the territories had lost their interest, owing to the troubles growing out of the election. Wishing to take part in the drama about to be enacted, I essayed a midwinter journey across the plains, and, in February, stood in the editorial room of *The Herald*.[13]

His trip eastward again took him to Missouri and St. Joseph, a trading center, one of the major jumping-off places for westward travel and the western terminus of the Hannibal and St. Joseph Railroad. Arriving there on the day of the historic election for delegates to the Missouri State

Introduction xxi

Convention that would decide on union or secession (February 18, 1861), Knox found St. Joseph relatively quiet:

> There was no disorder, more than is usual on election days in small cities. Little knots of people were engaged in discussion, but the discussions partook of no particular bitterness. The vote of the city was decidedly in favor of keeping the State in the Union.[14]

In New York, Knox met the editor in chief of the *Herald* (probably Frederick Hudson) who predicted:

> A long and bloody war is upon us, in which the whole country will be engaged. We shall desire you to take the field, probably in the West. It may be several weeks before we need you, but the war cannot be long delayed.[15]

At that time, the *New York Herald*, under the leadership of James Gordon Bennett, Sr., emerged as one of the leading papers in the city and one deeply involved in presenting the sensational aspects of the news. With many correspondents throughout the South the *Herald* was well-positioned to understand the Southern mentality and heart as the Civil War loomed.

Visiting friends back in New Hampshire, Knox found the spirit for war rising and the presence of strangers suspicious and threatening. Back in New York, he found the *Herald* offices busy with arrangements for wide coverage of the impending war. Overall, some ninety correspondents were dispatched at one time or another by the *Herald*.[16] Thomas W. Knox was assigned to report from St. Louis and was exceptionally fortunate in this assignment. Missouri would prove to be one of the most active theaters in the first year of the Civil War and a fertile field for his reportage.

The correspondent for the Dubuque *Herald* and later the *New York Times*, Franc B. Wilkie, first met Thomas W. Knox in Springfield in August, 1861 and closely described him:

> The first of the more noted of the correspondents I met was Thomas W. Knox, representing the *New York Herald*. It was

at Springfield, Mo., a few weeks before the battle of Wilson's Creek, that I made his acquaintance. He was a large, heavy man, rather clumsy in movement and ungainly in form. He was dark, with small, keen brown eyes, a large head, and had an expression of great sagacity with an intermingling of a trace of the sardonic. He drawled a little in his speech, and was given to sarcastic utterances. He had been, I understood, a teacher somewhere in New England before the war.[17]

It is possible that the "drawl" that to Wilkie's Iowa ears was a New England accent. Wilkie's description seems to fit the figure at the right in the image on page xx.

While this book covers just the one year that Knox reported on the war in Missouri, he went on to a distinguished career in Civil War reportage. One singular achievement was his arrest and trial for treason. General William T. Sherman brought these charges based on unflattering reportage of Sherman's attack at Chickasaw Bayou December 26–29, 1862. Knox was acquitted and returned to reporting from General Ulysses S. Grant's forces, but remained excluded from Sherman's camp. (See Chapter 20.)

Knox's Articles

Thomas W. Knox's articles from the field were written in pencil in notebooks. These he probably transcribed for telegraphers or into letters mailed to the *Herald*. His St. Louis letters were produced under less pressure and probably written in ink. Once they reached the *Herald*, they were subjected to editorial scrutiny and typesetting. All of these processes could introduce errors into Knox's prose. No effort has been made to try to elucidate these changes – with one exception. In Knox's long articles some additional paragraphing beyond what was present in the *Herald* article has been introduced for the sake of clarity. Parts of these long articles of lesser interest have been reproduced in the endnotes rather than in the main text to maintain readability and flow.

Chapter 1

First Reports from Missouri

It was spring 1861 when Thomas Knox began his odyssey reporting on the situation in Missouri for *Herald* readers. He met his friend from Denver, Albert D. Richardson, now reporting for the *New York Tribune*, and they decided to travel together. Both Knox and Richardson described their trip.[1] Their travels took them via Niagara Falls to Chicago. There, banking was suffering. Many banks held southern paper, (both state bonds and business loans) that they feared would be worthless. Southern trade had also fallen steeply. On their trip from Chicago to St. Louis, Richardson described the patriotic fervor he observed:

> Our train from Chicago to St. Louis was crowded with Union troops. Along the route booming guns saluted them; handkerchiefs fluttered from windows; flags streamed from farm-houses and village streets; old men and boys at the plow huzzaed themselves hoarse.[2]

They arrived in St. Louis in early May, probably a few days before the Camp Jackson "Massacre" on May 10.[3] Although the city remained "far from quiet, though there was nothing to lead a stranger to consider his personal safety in danger,"[4] he also noted, "There were many loyal men in St. Louis… Revolvers were at a premium."[5] As in Chicago, the newsmen found the commercial situation problematic. Southern debts were being repudiated and many southerners of suspected loyalty to the Confederacy were driven north. Richardson decided to go to Cairo to seek news, while Knox settled into a St. Louis hotel and began to make his rounds meeting people of importance and reporting on the situation in St. Louis. Knox's first report on May 10, was published in the *Herald* on May 17:

> There is evidently a good deal of truth in the old maxim, "Go away from home to learn news." If we are to judge by the various telegraphic reports and newspaper items floating around the country, St. Louis has been for some time in a state of anarchy, although we here are entirely unconscious of the fact; and I very much question whether there is a city in the Union where there has been so little excitement, much less anything bordering on mob rule. I also see it is stated in the telegraphic news of yesterday that the Unionists here were in danger of being overcome by the secessionists, and had called upon the government for protection. This report was regarded by the Unionists as an exceedingly good joke. They are, and ever have been, abundantly able to take care of themselves; they have always largely preponderated in numbers, and from present appearances are likely to continue to do so.[6]

CAMP JACKSON

Knox was wrong. His long letter must have been placed into the mails in the morning of May 10, just before the storm at Camp Jackson broke. Captain Nathaniel Lyon (not yet promoted to brigadier general of Union volunteers) surrounded the training camp of General Daniel M. Frost's pro-secession Missouri State Militia and forced their surrender. As the captured militia was being marched to the St. Louis Arsenal as prisoners, rioting broke out in the streets and twenty-eight civilians were killed by Lyon's men.[7]

On May 12, the *New York Herald* carried a commentary on Camp Jackson and in praise of "Colonel Lyons" [sic], and also referred to other events. It certainly was not written by Knox.[8] (This discrepancy between words and facts may also account for the apparent delay in publishing Knox's letter.) His May 10 letter recounted the formation of the Union volunteer units and their growing strength:

> The Union men in the city, in case of an emergency, could easily muster from eight to ten thousand, and there are at least that many drilling now night and day. The city has furnished five regiments for the United States service now stationed in the Arsenal, barracks and Marine Hospital, besides two regiments in command of Cols. McNeal and Brown, to serve as a Home Guard.[9] It is confidently predicted that in less than two weeks there will be in the city and county, twelve thousand men enrolled to uphold the Federal Government a sufficient force to defy all the secessionists in the State. How idle then, to talk of the Union men here being frightened at the blustering and braggadocio of a few thousand secessionists, one half of whom are Northern men with Southern principles, whose hearts are not in the cause, but are solely actuated by ambition for place and power. Such an insinuation is a reflection upon their patriotism, and, an insult to their courage. The vast majority of the citizens of St. Louis have ever been loyal to the constitution and the Union, and, if ever occasion requires, they will prove it on the battle field.

While this statement might have seemed to be a bit blustery, Knox was probably correct. Most of the secessionist comments came from the "old line" residents who had come from the South and had relatives there. While less wealthy, those who had come to St. Louis more recently, from northern states and from Germany and Ireland, were firmly on the side of the Union. In his May 10 letter, Knox ventured an assessment on the political situation in Missouri and on the Southwest Battalion:

> The Legislature, as your readers are doubtless aware, is now deliberating with closed doors. A majority of the members are avowed secessionists and politicians of desperate fortunes, and there is no conjecturing to what infamous moves they many resort to precipitate the State out of the Union. They have already passed a bill postponing the apportionment of the school fund for the present year, and to let it remain

in the treasury, subject to the order of the Legislature. This fund amounts to about $250,000, and is for the purpose of educating the children of the State. The next thing they attempt will doubtless be to raise means by direct taxation. It is also rumored that they contemplate passing an ordinance of secession and enforcing its ratification after the style of Virginia, in other words, at the point of the bayonet. But this is too absurd to obtain credence. They have the will, but not the courage to try it on, for, notwithstanding they are secession blind, they know they would meet with an overwhelming defeat. So far as I can observe, however, the Unionists appear perfectly indifferent as to the course the Legislature may pursue, having the most implicit confidence in their ability to wipe them out either at the ballot box or the cannon's mouth. They are contending for a glorious cause. It is not whether we shall have a system of revenue approximating absolute free trade or prohibition; not whether slavery shall be prohibited or protected in the Territories; but whether the American Union – which even traitors tell us is the "best government ever devised by the wisdom of man" – shall be perpetuated; and move on in its unparalleled career of glory, grandeur and power; and they will enter into the struggle with their lives in the hollow of their hands, with the determination of meeting death with the serenity and fortitude becoming American citizens, conscious they could not ascend to Heaven in defense of a purer or nobler cause.

The Southwest battalion, which was sent out to the border to protect the settlers in that section from the depredations of Montgomery and his band returned to the city on Tuesday last, and is now at Camp Jackson.[10] It is composed of two companies – Captain McDonald's mounted riflemen, fifty-three in number, and Captain Jackson's corps of artillery, numbering seventy-two.

They were enlisted for six months and their time will

expire on the 10th of June next. A great deal of curiosity was manifested by their friends to know how they stood in regard to the Union. It was ascertained that they were about equally divided, from which fact it is thought they will be immediately disbanded, and reorganized with men who consider treason to the American government a political virtue

The Southwest Battalion Knox mentions was indeed at Camp Jackson at the time of the May 10 events, but it is not known how many of the men from these units were in camp with the other militia units. The actual number of prisoners taken by Lyon was far smaller than the number that should have been in the camp if all were present for duty. It is unclear whether the absentees were merely away visiting or left because of Union sentiments. On May 13, Knox filed another report, published by the *Herald* May 14, 1861 titled "Details of the Riot at St. Louis." In it he described the carnage in some detail:

> An official statement published this morning says the first firing at Camp Jackson, on Friday evening, was some half dozen shots near the head of the column of the First regiment, heralded by a volley of stones and a pistol shot from the crowd. No one was hurt at this point.
>
> The second firing occurred from the rear of the column guarding the prisoners. The crowd here was large and very abusive, and one man discharged three barrels of a revolver at Lieutenant Faron, of the regular service, many of the mob cheering him and drawing their revolvers and firing at the troops.
>
> The man who commenced the attack then laid his pistol across his arm, and was taking deliberate aim at Lieutenant Faron, when he was thrust through with a bayonet and fired upon at the same time, and instantly killed.[11]

This report of the bayoneting may be the source of the drawing that appeared in the *New York Illustrated News,* May 25, 1861, (next page), eleven days after the *Herald* report. That drawing has been called, "A popular but inaccurate view of the Federal troops at Camp Jackson."[12]

"Terrible Tragedy at St. Louis."(*New York Illustrated News,* May 25, 1861).

Knox's May 13 letter continued:

> A thousand people left the city yesterday afternoon in consequence of the reports of insubordination among the German troops and their threats to burn and sack the city; but the appearance of General Harney's proclamation in a great measure restored confidence, and many of those who left will probably return today.[13]

The day after the Camp Jackson affair, May 11, troubles continued. The Fifth Reserve Corps of volunteers under Colonel Charles G. Stifel,[14] a group that had not taken part at Camp Jackson, was armed at the Arsenal and then marched back into St. Louis. Knox described the resulting confrontation between the Reserve Corps and citizen secessionists for his *Herald* readers:

First Reports from Missouri 7

About six o'clock (on 11th) a large body of Home Guards entered the city through Fifth Street from the Arsenal, where they had been enlisted during the day, and furnished with arms. On reaching Walnut Street the troops turned westward, a large crowd lining the pavement to witness their progress. At the corner of Fifth Street parties among the spectators began hooting, hissing, and otherwise abusing the companies as they passed, and a boy about fourteen years old discharged a pistol into their ranks. Part of the rear company immediately turned and fired upon the crowd, and the whole column was instantly in confusion, breaking their ranks and discharging their muskets down their own line and among the people on the sidewalks. The shower of balls for a few minutes was terrible, and bullets flying in every direction, entering the doors and windows of private residences, breaking shutters, and smashing bricks in the third story.

The utmost confusion and consternation prevailed, spectators fleeing in all directions, and but for the random firing of the troops scores of people must have been killed. As most of the firing was directed down their own ranks the troops suffered most severely, four of their number being instantly killed and several wounded. Intense indignation was expressed against the Germans. Mayor Taylor addressed the excited crowd and induced them to disperse under the promise that no further violence should be done. The city was comparatively quiet during the evening and night, a heavy rain preventing the assembling of large crowds.[15]

Interestingly, the *Harper's Weekly* of June 1, 1861 carried this story, verbatim from Knox's report in the *Herald*, while not citing the *Herald*, saying, "The tragedy was thus described by a spectator." It also included the drawing by M. Hastings.[16]

"United States Volunteers Attacked by the Mob, Corner of Fifth and Walnut Streets, St. Louis, Missouri." (*Harper's Weekly*, June 1, 1861).

Later in his article on the shooting at Fifth and Walnut, Knox added:

> Considerable lawlessness has prevailed for the last few days, and several innocent Germans have been shot in the streets. The feeling against the Germans is most intense, the regular volunteers and Home Guard being composed mainly of that class of citizens, and through their acts so many innocent people have been killed. Several persons charged with firing on the troops and shooting in the streets, have been arrested, and the police are on the alert.[17]

Thomas W. Knox must have been shocked! He had experienced the rough and tumble of the gold mining districts around Denver, but now, in civilized St. Louis, blood was in the streets and passions were aroused. He had arrived and written a piece on the calm in St. Louis on the morning of the Camp Jackson Affair. And now the Camp Jackson Affair had changed everything.

Herald reporter Knox began to look at the St. Louis region differently. On May 15, he reported on the Coroner's jury returned verdict:

> That the several victims of the events which took place at Camp Jackson on the 10th of May came to their deaths from gunshot wounds inflicted by musket balls discharged by certain United States volunteers under the command of General N. Lyon, Colonels F. P. Blair, H. Boernstein and others.[18]

And on May 18, he sent a piece by telegraph that told of Union military confiscation of arms held by southern sympathizers:

> Two pieces of cannon, several hundred muskets and rifles and a number of pistols and ammunition were taken from the custody of the Police Commissioners today by order of the United States authorities. Sixty Colt's heavy revolvers were also seized while in the hands of the American Express Company. All these arms have been sent to the Arsenal.
>
> The State Tobacco Warehouse was also visited yesterday by the United States authorities and a considerable quantity of arms, munitions of war, &c., taken therefrom.[19]

The finding of such "arms, munitions of war &c" was an indication of considerable unrest below the surface. These materials could not have been accumulated overnight, but were the result of a process beginning at least by the time of Lincoln's election. A similar accumulation on the Union side was probably also occurring in St. Louis. From his observations, Knox could describe the defensive precautions that had been undertaken.

ST. LOUIS DEFENSES

> The city is now environed by a line of military posts, extending from the river below the Arsenal, around the western outskirts, to the river again on the north. The object of these posts is to prevent any hostile troops, munitions of war, &c., from entering the city, protect the public peace, and

give complete security to every peaceful citizen. The forces comprising these encampments belong to regiments under the command of Colonels Blair, Boernstein and Sigel.[20]

In a long description of the area on May 19, Knox wrote of the extensive waterfront and its geographical advantages and size:

> The city of St. Louis now numbers some 145,000 inhabitants, of whom, a very large proportion are Germans, and what are known here as "Free Democrats," and consequently have strong free soil tendencies. It is from this class that most of the government troops are drawn.[21]

Describing the Arsenal, its strength, its resources and its capacity for producing Minié balls (20,000 per day), Knox reported the total number of Union troops around St. Louis at 11,000. Then he turned perceptively to the political feelings in the city:

> It would be out of the question to depict the state of political feeling here, though of the citizens, I should judge, fully four-fifths are for Union unconditionally, while those who favor secession are busy as bees fomenting discord, and not a few would be ready at a moment's notice to renew the riots of last Friday week irrespective of consequences. A great change seems to be coming over the spirits of the people; those who a week ago were loud for "Governor Jackson and secession" being now daily and hourly enlisted in the government's service, and especially is this true of the Irish population.
>
> The most striking changed I have noticed, in coming here from the East, is the almost entire absence of flags and bunting; except upon the Arsenal grounds and regimental headquarters I saw but one banner of any kind in the whole city, and that upon Keevil's Corinthian Hall Buildings,[22] on Broadway.[23]

Finally, Knox opined, "It is idle to think that the troubles in Missouri are over, and it would not be surprising if within two weeks scenes should transpire more startling than any that have yet occurred."[24] The steamboat

First Reports from Missouri

Iatan was chartered for government service on May 14 and shortly thereafter put into service.[25] Knox reported on May 22 that:

> The steamer *J. C. Swon* was seized yesterday at Harlow's Landing, thirty miles below this city, and brought to the Arsenal, by order of General Lyon. This is the steamer that brought the arms from Baton Rouge, which were captured by General Lyon at Camp Jackson. Measures will be taken to effect the legal confiscation of the boat.[26]

A day later, the St. Louis *Missouri Republican* revealed that the *Iatan*, with 100 men under Captain Franz had carried out the capture.[27] Twelve days later on May 26, another steamboat, the *City of Louisiana* was put under charter by the military authorities.[28] Two days later on May 24, Knox expanded on steamboat stories with a quote from General Lyon:

> "One blank cartridge, hereafter, Captain, will be sufficient; that being given, you can fire with ball; ammunition is just now rather expensive," said Gen. Lyon yesterday to one of his captains after four blank shots had been fired to bring about a steamboat that was passing the Arsenal without answering the summons of the river guard. So for the future only one un-shotted gun can be expected. All boats passing the Arsenal, whether bound up or down the Mississippi, are carefully searched by the officers in charge of that post. Day before yesterday the *J. C. Swon*, the boat which brought from Baton Rouge the munitions of war for Camp Jackson, which were seized by General Lyon, was captured thirty-six miles below the city by a detachment of federal forces, and now lies at the Arsenal. She will doubtless be confiscated, and enter the service of the United States.[29]

THE HARNEY-PRICE AGREEMENT

On May 21 the "Harney-Price Agreement" had been produced. This short note pledged restoration of peace and good order for the people of Missouri. But the *definition* of "peace and good order" was missing. To some, it meant cessation of enlistments on both sides and an end to depredations against dissenting citizens. But these phrases were not put to paper, and good wishes were smothered by rising passion. General William S. Harney, then commander of the U.S. Army's Department of the West, wrote to Washington enclosing copies both of the agreement between himself and General Sterling Price, commander of the Missouri State Guard, and his proclamation to the people of Missouri.[30] Reports of problems rapidly arose, prompting a note expressing President Lincoln's concern saying, "The professions of loyalty to the Union by the State authorities of Missouri are not to be relied upon."[31] On May 29, Harney wrote reassuringly to Washington, "Missouri is rapidly becoming tranquilized....I entertain the conviction that the agreement between myself and General Price will be carried out in good faith."[32]

Sterling Price and William S. Harney (*Wikipedia*)

Surprisingly, there was no report from St. Louis that could be attributed to Knox about the Harney-Price Agreement of May 21. In this agreement, Generals Price and Harney pledged themselves to keep the peace and maintain order with violations to be reported to both generals.

The news of the agreement was widely telegraphed and perhaps Knox saw no reason for further comment at that time. The news did appear in the *New York Herald* as part of a section entitled "The Situation of Affairs" on May 22.[33] The full agreement is to be found in the Appendix.

Insider Reports, Lyon and Blair

As Knox settled into his assignment in St. Louis as was his custom, he called upon many of the power figures in the region. And he seems to have been accepted into their circles. Two men in particular were of special interest to him.

General Nathaniel Lyon was in effective command of the Union troops. He was promoted to brigadier general of volunteers on May 17,[34] and assumed command of the Department of the West, succeeding General William S. Harney on May 31.[35]

Colonel Frank Blair, one of Missouri's pro-Union political leaders, had organized Missouri Unionists into volunteer "home guard" units, but of even more importance were his close political connections in Washington. He was a member of the U. S. House of Representatives. His father was Francis Preston Blair, one of the founders of the Republican Party in 1854 and an advisor to Lincoln. His brother, Montgomery Blair, served as postmaster general in Lincoln's cabinet. Frank Blair, with his connections, was acutely aware of the need for favorable reports in the national press and welcomed Knox into the Arsenal command center.

Knox reciprocated the favor. On May 21, he wrote of the growing strength of Unionists and ebbing fortunes of secessionists and prominently mentioned Frank Blair:

> The Arsenal is in the hands of the federal forces, and cannot be easily taken. Governor Jackson is reported to have not more than three thousand men with him at Jefferson City, and is in constant fear of an attack. Rebellious movements in various parts of the State have been stopped, and the only place now making any show of resistance, apart from Jefferson City is St. Joseph. Ex-Governor R. M. Stewart and Major Joshua P. Bruce, editor of the *Journal*, were forced to leave that city a few days since, on account of their well-known Union sentiments. Frank Blair thinks they won't be obliged to stay away long. It was reported here yesterday that the rebels had seized upon the Hannibal and St. Joseph Railroad at the

western terminus and were fortifying it at several points. Men from that vicinity say that St. Joseph stands in too great fear of the volunteers of Kansas to do anything very aggressive.[36]

In the same article, Knox told of the arrival in St. Louis of a long-time resident of Holly Springs, Mississippi, who was "suspected and barely escaped with his life." Holly Springs, the Mississippian said, was in fear of a slave revolt and had greatly increased its police force and at the same time disbanding a military company of local residents, some originally from the north who were forced to leave town.

Knox's May 24 letter was a long one covering many other fronts. There was news from Jefferson City. Governor Jackson's pro-southern state troops had refused to disband and go back to their home counties as ordered, and instead were "spilin for a fight." Knox added:

> The troops say that they came to fight and they will fight, and General Lyon and Colonel Blair being anxious to please them, meditate sending federal forces to Jefferson City to assist the State militia to disperse and go home. The movement will probably be made in a few days, unless Missouri's brave defenders think better of their condition and separate quietly.[37]

Out in St. Joseph, reports of men attacking the St. Joseph post office, hauling down the United States flag and running up the state flag came in. Knox briefly noted, "General Harney threatens to pay them a complementary visit, if these eccentricities are persisted in."[38]

General Lyon received another favorable note:

> Some five thousand pounds of lead destined to aid the rebels in Arkansas, were seized two days ago at Ironton, a town on the Iron Mountain Railroad, about sixty miles distant. The seizure was made by order of General Lyon, and several prominent secessionists of that region were arrested at the same time and brought to St. Louis.[39]

Knox's reports were not always positive – there was one final sad note in his letter:

> Captain Blandowski, who was shot in the leg on the day of the taking of Camp Jackson, was last evening obliged to undergo amputation of the wounded limb. He was struck below the knee by a Minié ball; gangrene commencing rendered amputation above the knee necessary. His recovery is doubtful.

Constantin Blandowski died on May 26 and was buried with military honors he next day.[40]

MISSOURI'S MOOD

Several days later, Knox returned to the "overview" reporting he did so well. On May 25, Knox related two stories that were typical of the State of Missouri and also of the thinking of the people in the state:

> Those who sympathize with the recent attempts to get Missouri out of the Union, and are anxious to keep up the Camp at Jefferson City, are not backward in furnishing aid and comfort to the State forces there assembled. Last week several boxes of contraband goods were started for that point in some of the boats bound up the Missouri river, and were labeled "soap," in order to insure their safe conduct, as the forwarders wisely thought that to furnish them an article so much needed and so little used would be more like a missionary than a belligerent act. So much soap going to Western Missouri excited suspicion, and the property was duly examined and seized. The Pacific Railroad was then taken as a route of transportation, and drays were heard last night and the night previous at the witching hours of one and two o'clock AM carrying goods to the depot of that line. That business was at once stopped, and the depot in this city is now carefully watched and nothing can depart therefrom that is not "all right." The

secessionists find themselves watched at every point and will soon consider it best to yield with as good grace as possible.[41]

In the same letter to the *Herald*, Knox commented on the situation in the southwestern part of Missouri where Union sentiment among both the general public and slaveholders was strong. Again, Knox mentioned Blair favorably:

> Apropos of this is a remark made by Col. Blair. I yesterday made a call on him at the Arsenal, and while I was there a gentleman from the western part of the State entered the room to give the news from that locality. In the course of the conversation he stated that he was a Union man, but was at the same time, pro-slavery, as he owned niggers. "Well," replied Blair, quietly, as he twisted his mustache, "a man can be for the Union and be pro-slavery too; we don't object to it, but if you fellows that favor slavery take Missouri out of the Union, you will be in six months from now one of the most niggerless set of men in America." A good many others here think the same.[42]

In the same May 25 letter he commented, "Advices today from Jefferson City do not give much promise of an adherence to the compact lately agreed upon."[43] In an additional letter written on the same day Knox expanded upon the problems of the Harney-Price agreement as he saw them:

> You have heard of the arrangement made between General Harney and General Price, to the effect that the latter stipulated that the State troops shall be disbanded, and that the Union men of the State be protected by the State authorities, but I have seen no account published of the cause of that arrangement. I have received some information which leads to its explanation. Some two weeks ago, under the new State Militia act, the Governor ordered out the State militia and a large body of them began to gather at Jefferson City,

under the Southern confederacy flag. News of this movement reached the United States authorities here, and a week ago last Thursday General Harney dispatched a messenger to Governor C. F. Jackson, with an ultimatum to this effect:

Sir – The government desires peace and will have it. The forces under your command are openly working in connection with the enemies of the government – are menacing and threatening the friends of the government, and committing outrages such as the government cannot tolerate. The people must be protected in their constitutional rights, and hostile forces must be disbanded if the State authorities are inadequate to render the protection sought, then the Federal Government and the forces under my command will relieve the State of Missouri and its officers of the responsibility and with sufficient force will secure the people from molestation, injury and insult. I desire your immediate answer.

This brought General Sterling Price to the city on Sunday last and on Monday, "the arrangement" was made. There is nothing like determination in making "arrangements." But as yet, Governor Jackson and General Price have not secured the safety of the people, for the Unionists are pouring into the city and crossing over to Illinois and Iowa in droves, having been driven from the State by border ruffians. I saw last night and conversed with Mr. J. B. Brown, formerly proprietor of the Arcade Hotel in Philadelphia – a brother in law of Dr. Jayne, and a nephew of Commodore Stewart and ex-Governor Pollock – who with his family and those of twenty-five others – in all one hundred and forty persons – had been driven from their farms one hundred and fifty miles west of here, between the Gasconade and Osage rivers, by the secessionists. The families were all from Pennsylvania formerly, and removed from Union and Lycoming counties.

Their offense consisted in not signing the following paper, which I send you as a specimen of Far West literature. It is verbatim &c.

ARTICLES OF CONFEDERATION
[BY MILLER COUNTY SECESSIONISTS]

1. Resolved, That wee the sitezens of Miller and adjoining counties. In the Stait of Missouri, do hereby enter into a firm league of friendship with each other for the common defence and security of their liberties and their constitutional rights, mutual and general welfare, binding themselves to assist each other against all force offered or attacks made upon them or any of them, on account of wanting to maintane our constitutional rights which has been given us by the Dred Scott decision.
2. We also further pledge our lives, our fortunes and our sacred honor to put down all marauding bands that may infest our and repel the assaults, let them come from what quarter they may.
3. We are opposed to coercing those States that have ceceded, believing that no such power is delegated to the President, but let them went off in peace.
4. We highly appreciate the action of our Governor C. F. Jackson, in resisting the call of the President for volunteers from Missouri to coerce the seceding States. We further agree to defend the rights of Missouri to defend against Northern aggression, if she dissolves her connection with the federal union or remove or change our residence from the State. To this article we subscribe our names, this 16th day of May, 1861.

Knox then continued his commentary on the plight of the refugees:

They left behind them over two hundred thousand dollars' worth of improvements and personal property which is ere this either confiscated or destroyed. Mr. Brown goes today to see Gen. Harney to obtain if possible a company of solders to return with him to escort the families which are left behind.[44]

He also commented on the powder keg situation within the city of St. Louis and reported an example that was a far cry from his May 10 letter:

> There is no use in disguising the fact that St. Louis is resting now upon the very vortex of a slumbering volcano, politically and socially, which will require but a spark – but one inadvertent act on the part of either party – to set into a state of fearful eruption. To be sure there can be but one issue, but one result to any tumultuous outbreak. The governed authorities have all the war machinery, enginery, and appliances; have full twelve thousand men under arms at all times, well disciplined and fully equipped; nevertheless one who has any knowledge of human nature cannot remain long here, moving about in political circles and witnessing the fever of intense feeling at what they consider "outraged rights" on the part of the friends of secession, without realizing that, whether armed or not, such men will not long brook the restraint thus felt to be forced upon them. One sees, if he be a keen observer, many little things to justify him in this last conclusion. Let me mention one of the many which are constantly occurring.
>
> Last night two soldiers passed by my hotel, having in charge an intoxicated, uniformed recruit. A small crowd began to gather about the trio, and word reached the hotel that the soldiers had arrested a secessionist. Immediately a score of men rushed to their rooms, and as quickly reappeared, each with a revolver or bowie knife, and started for the street; but upon learning the true state of facts, and finding that the uniformed man was not a secessionist, they returned. When all was quiet I thought I would sound the guests, and learn, if possible, their feelings; and

conversation revealed the fact that two out of every three of them were at heart opposed to the general government.[45]

Knox's description signaled just how on edge St. Louis was. Too many men were all too willing to take offense at any real or imagined insult. More and more men began carrying guns and knives. Knox predicted:

> There can be no doubt but that active work is soon to be commenced in the west and along the course of the Mississippi river. I am credibly informed, and my information comes from an officer of the army here, and is corroborated by my own observation, that a large number of troops will be dispatched within a week from this point on steamers that can run up the Missouri. The government have a number of large sized boats already chartered, and already wooded, at the levee here.[46]

In the Capital

Knox could stand it no longer – he had to see for himself. He took the Pacific Railroad train to Jefferson City and he wrote from there on May 27:

> I left St. Louis yesterday morning for this place, coming via Pacific Railroad. At the depot in that city was a company of volunteers from the United States Arsenal, who searched the train thoroughly, to prevent the transportation of goods contraband of war. This is done at the departure of every train on all the roads diverging into Missouri.[47]

Most of the State troops (Missouri State Guard, MSG) that had gathered in Jefferson City had been sent home in apparent compliance with the Harney-Price "treaty." There were only two MSG companies remaining in Jefferson City, commanded by Captains Duke and Kelly, of St. Louis.[48] These men were ordered to remain there permanently to act as a bodyguard for the governor, "and as a check to the Union men of the County, in case they should have the temerity to assert their rights."

Knox revealed and perhaps also warned how sympathies were developing:

> The Confederate flag is kept flying at Camp Frost, from the staff on the Governor's home, and from one other staff in the town. The whole affair is as much a secession movement as are any of the demonstrations which have occurred in South Carolina the past year, and yet the leaders deny any intention of taking the State out of the Union, and fall back upon the dignity of the State and of State rights.[49]

In Jefferson City, the word on the street was that a Confederate agent was closeted with Governor Jackson and offering men, arms and ammunition if he would take Missouri out of the Union. Supposedly, the governor had accepted the offer and planned to effect secession by autumn. Another rumor was that the State Guards (MSG):

> are to be supplied with several thousand stand of arms immediately by way of Arkansas, as the route through St. Louis and up the Missouri is completely blockaded. Twenty wagons started three days ago from Sedalia, a town some thirty miles west of here bound for Little Rock or some point near there, where they will be loaded with guns and powder.[50]

The next day, Knox filed an additional report from Missouri's capital with more news and observations:

> The troops that have lately gone to their homes became, before their departure, much disaffected towards Gov. Jackson. "It's an ill wind that blows nobody any good," and the truce of Price and Harney may be looked upon as a blast of the unbeneficial order. It displeased the Union men of St. Louis, as it prevented their carrying out their intention of putting the State thoroughly under a Union rule. It annoys the rank and file of the rebel forces, as it hinders their immediate indulgence in a fight. To the rebel leaders, it will prove a great

assistance, as they will gain time for perfecting all their arrangements.⁵¹

Then there was the problem of Missouri's lead mines. In the east, near Potosi, and in the west, near Carthage and Granby, profitable lead mines were in operation. Those in the east were under Union control, but those in the west had been appropriated for rebel use:

> A quantity of lead belonging to the Granby Mining Company, of which Henry T. Blow, of St. Louis, is the managing agent, was seized by the rebels near Sedalia a few days since while it was in transit.⁵² Application has been made to purchase a large amount to send to Arkansas and Texas, and as high as seven cents per pound has been offered for it at the mines, notwithstanding it is worth but five cents in St. Louis. Mr. Blow refuses to sell a single pound there, and not even in St. Louis unless he knows it is not going to the confederacy, and takes special care to have his transporting wagons provided with a suitable guard. The quantity of bullet material that will find its way into secession hands from the Granby mines will be quite small.⁵³

Native Americans were also becoming a concern. Both Union and Confederate governments sent representatives to treat with tribal leaders:

> Negotiations are now going on between John Ross, President of the Choctaw Nation,⁵⁴ and emissaries of Gov. Jackson, with the view to engage the services of a large number of Choctaw Indians, to aid in subjugating the Union men of Missouri. Should these red men be employed, it is sure to bring on a bloody war.⁵⁵

Knox scored somewhat of a coup. Although from New York and a suspected "Yankee," he landed a short interview with Governor Jackson. Whatever the governor said to Knox, it did not turn out well for the governor. Knox's report on their meeting included a bit of sarcasm:

> I have just had the pleasure of a quarter hour's interview with Governor Jackson. Our introduction took place in a barroom, and after it his Excellency accepted an invitation to drink at the expense of the *Herald* correspondent. If I should forward you a bill containing the charge, "Whiskey, one dime," know that you are mulcted to that amount for the benefit of the State brains of Missouri.
>
> The governor is a shrewd talker, and one cannot "make much out of him." His face is indicative of treachery, and no one ever so insane would select Claib Jackson as a model of all the masculine virtues. He affects a deep regret at the recent occurrences and hopes all difficulties will soon be settled.[56]

AGAIN FROM ST. LOUIS

Back in St. Louis, Knox, in his letter of May 29 to the *Herald*, described the formation of a regiment of American Zouaves, "to consist entirely of Americans,"[57] the continuing enrollments in villages along the railroad lines, and the formation of Union Home Guard companies.[58] In the same correspondence he noted enthusiasm for Union activities:

> The departure of the Fourth regiment for Bird's Point[59] last evening was witnessed by a large crowd of spectators. The troops were marched on board the *City of Louisiana* and slowly started down the stream, while the bands played various popular airs, and the crowd on shore joined in singing the "Star Spangled Banner." The utmost enthusiasm was manifested by all. Two companies additional were taken on board at Jefferson Barracks.[60]

Knox wryly described a typical incident of Civil War "commerce":

> Two hundred kegs of butter were lately shipped down the river from this point to Memphis, which were found to contain ball cartridges instead of pure Goshen. They did not reach their destination.[61]

Most newsworthy to the Union cause in Missouri was the "relief" of General Harney. Frank Blair, in particular had been working with his Washington contacts to secure the general's removal, and had such orders on hand for some time.[62] Knox described the reaction in the city and his own feelings:

> The great excitement of this city at the present time is the announcement that General Harney has been relieved, and that General Lyon takes command in his place. It is difficult to say exactly how the public is impressed with this move, in consequence of the diversity of opinion on the subject. My belief is that the Union men are generally well pleased, and the secessionists disgusted and angry. In most of his course, General Harney has shown a commendable promptness and energy, but in the case of the armistice between himself and General Price he has not received the sanction of Unionists at home nor of the Department at Washington. The document signed by the two "high contracting parties" was very obscurely and ambiguously written and admitted of several constructions.
>
> From the first it was evident that Governor Jackson and those with him did not intend to keep the treaty, as the continuance of the camp at Jefferson City and the sending home of the troops under arms and in pay of the State well attested. It was General Harney's duty to attend to the full and faithful carrying out of every stipulation, and he was strongly urged thereto by many Union men but an immense outside pressure from friends and relatives was brought to bear upon him in the opposite direction. He hesitated to put a stop to Governor Jackson's illegal proceedings, and for this neglect he was removed from his command. His successor, General Lyon, will not let the treasonable proceedings go on much further without investigation and thorough ventilation. Governor Jackson, Jeff Thompson, Colonel Reynolds, and some other prominent ones may soon find themselves in durance vile without the benefit of a writ of habeas corpus.[63]

Enrollment of State (MSG) troops continued beyond St. Louis in violation of the Harney-Price Agreement. The state's "Military Bill" was, in theory, to have been suspended and no State Guard enlistments made. Using his valuable connection with General Lyon, Knox noted in the same June 1 letter "a handbill given me this morning by General Lyon":

PUBLIC MEETING

All persons in favor of forming a military company in Chillicothe Township under the military law of the State are requested to meet at the Court House, in Chillicothe, on Saturday, June 1, at one PM

General Slack will explain the law, and there will be addresses by other persons.[64]

At the time of the Camp Jackson affair, the steamship *J. C. Swon* had supposedly brought "eleven hundred Minié rifles" which were never found. With unconcealed criticism, Knox wrote in the same letter at the end of May:

Yesterday [May 31], a body of troops surrounded and searched the house of Dr. McDowell, a prominent physician of St. Louis, and a notorious secessionist. Their examination was unrewarded by any discovery, and the troops returned to their quarters.[65]

As a reporter, Knox was not above making a bit of fun of one of his rivals, the St. Louis *Missouri Republican*, a paper of Democratic politics with distinct states' rights tilt:

The *Republican* of this morning attempts to show that the statement that a Confederate flag is kept flying from the staff in front of the Governor's house, at Jefferson City, is untrue. I made the statement a few days since in a letter, not from information but actually seeing it and gazing upon the three-striped rag for a full and sufficient time. The *Republican* was a few weeks since a warm advocate of secession, but came around on the other side when it found what the prevailing sentiment was in and around St. Louis. It now "talks Union" in a most enthusiastic manner, but at the same time omits no opportunity to ridicule and vilify every movement made by the Union men of the State, and to hide the treason and make pure the character of Governor Jackson and his associates. It reminds me of the anecdote of the Irishman making his pig believe he was driving him to Fermoy, while all the time he had him on the road to Cork.[66]

An updated report on St. Louis business was troubling:

As an illustration of the manner in which the war affects the business of St. Louis in a region where the route is not closed, I can mention that two years ago there were eighty boats engaged in the Missouri river trade, all hailing from St. Louis and doing a good business. The number of boats now engaged in the same traffic is but five, and they have considerable difficulty in getting full freights.

The opening of the Hannibal and St. Joseph railroad has been partly the cause of this falling off of business, but it is owing chiefly to the war. The trade to the upper Mississippi is nearly, but not quite as dull; and that to the lower Mississippi has been completely stagnated.[67]

AT A POINT OF NO RETURN

The newsman's response to a letter from General Price to his brigadier generals of the Missouri State Guard published in the St. Louis *Missouri Republican*, the *New York Herald*, and other papers was vitriolic.[68] (Its content may be found in the Appendix.) He spared neither Price nor Harney, in his June 5 letter, but reserved particular criticism for Price:

General Price's proclamation, published in the papers of this morning, has taken all parties by surprise. It is far more gratifying to the Union men of St. Louis, than to the secessionists, as it shows the hostile position of Governor Jackson and his Jefferson City associates, and leaves them an opportunity to take decided steps to meet the Gubernatorial treachery. The stipulation between Harney and Price was principally of a verbal nature; and the portion of it that was committed to paper, signed and published, was as obscurely worded as the most abstruse productions of Thomas Carlyle or Great Incomprehensible Emerson. It admitted of many different modes of construction; but the two heroes, with whom the pen is far less mighty than the sword, and much more difficult to handle, made a verbal agreement, in the presence of witnesses, to all the debatable points of the unique document. General Harney, at the conclusion of the treaty, retired to his quarters, satisfied that he had done a good work by not making it necessary to fight a good fight; and, following the theoretical beautiful, but practically fallacious doctrine of considering all other men as honest as himself, supposed the State authorities would stick to their promises as well as he stuck to his own.

After castigating General Harney in a sarcastic and sardonic manner, Knox turned to Sterling Price with a litany of his perfidy, then went back to General Harney and his gullibility, and finally he made a prediction of trouble:

> General Price returned to Jefferson City, and, while very slightly keeping the word of promise to Harney's ear, most emphatically broke it to his hope.
> Pretending to disperse troops, he sent them home to drill; pretending to protect men of all parties in the enjoyment of their rights, he allowed secessionists to have full sway and flout their banners on the breeze, while Union men were daily threatened and driven from their homes; pretending to disarm the State, he procured powder and military stores in as

large quantities as possible; and, if not aiding the movement, at least conniving at the seizure of lead belonging to Union men; professing to ignore the military bill, he has allowed formation of companies under it, and has issued direct and emphatic orders to the contrary. While agreeing to a position of neutrality, he, with Governor Jackson, has been conferring with agents of the confederacy and of the Southwest Indians, with reference to engaging forces to aid Missouri to get out of the Union. And to the representation of all of these things by Union men, General Harney remained inactive, trusting too much to those who had shown themselves traitors at the outset, and confiding in the advice of those who were his personal, though not his political friends. Consequently his removal and the appointment of General Lyon to fill his place. The latter gentleman will before long make a vigorous demonstration in some direction, where the rebels will be likely to feel it. The proclamation of yesterday, giving the Jeffersonian interpretation to the armistice, will call down upon the heads of the State authorities a shower of something harder and heavier than manifestoes and paper pellets. Look out for some movements of importance within the next week.[69]

Knox was correct. He noted the Planter's House meeting in two short telegraphic reports that appeared on June 13.[70] Knox's full report, his long letter from St. Louis dated June 12, along with a separate report of General Lyon's actions dated June 15 appeared in the June 16 issue of the *Herald*, evincing once again Knox's closeness to Lyon and the reporter's ability to ferret out details of the critical Planter's House proceedings and of Lyon's mindset.[71]

> The conference yesterday between General Lyon and Colonel Blair on the part of the government and Governor Jackson and General Price on behalf of the State authorities, terminated about four PM without anything being arrived at in the shape of an agreement. The interview took place, as announced

yesterday, at the instance of the State authorities, and was not by request or desire of either Lyon or Blair, as the *Republican* of this morning falsely states. I have my information from General Lyon himself. Governor Jackson sent to General Lyon offering to come to St. Louis if he could be protected while on the way hither, and could be free from arrest while here, for it seems that his Excellency was in mortal dread of a writ being issued with his name prominent upon it, and which might cause him some unhappy detention, and perhaps a very disagreeable trial. General Lyon sent him a pass to protect him *en route*, and to make him proof against sheriff's officers while here. Armed with this document Claiborne F. found no trouble whatever, but he appeared somewhat uneasy during the whole period of his visit. General Lyon requested to see him at the Arsenal, but the Governor objected to going there, thinking, doubtless, that a journey to St. Louis was a sufficient "letting down," without being required to beard the lion in his den. The conference accordingly took place at the Planter's House, there being present General Lyon, Colonel Blair, Governor Jackson and General Price. Major Conant was present as Secretary to General Lyon and Governor Jackson's Private Secretary[72] was also in the room.

The Governor opened the convention in much the same manner as the chief of a hostile tribe of Indians opens a council – that is by making numerous professions of peace and amity, saying that the United States troops must leave the State and not enter it, and he would then disband his own troops, after which we could not have trouble. This remark he threw in at various times during the interview, using it as a sort of piece de resistance. The Governor soon talked himself out, and then put forward General Price, who commenced bolder than he put out. It has turned out that Gen. Harney required of Price, before he would meet him with a view to negotiation, that the latter should acknowledge the Military

Bill to be in fact a secession ordinance, and should agree to ignore it entirely, and forbid its being carried out. To this Price agreed, and the meeting was held, from which emanated the "Peace proclamation." At the interview yesterday, Gen. Price stated that his course had been in the most exact accordance with the terms of the treaty with Harney, and that in no instance had he violated it. In answer to a question of Gen. Lyon, he said he made no agreement whatever with Harney about the enforcement or suspension of the Military bill, and repeated his statement with considerable emphasis. General Lyon then produced the correspondence that passed at the time, showing the agreement I have above mentioned, and giving the lie direct to General Price. Hereupon both Price and Jackson illustrated the power attributed to the chameleon, and appeared as if they could be exceedingly

> *Happy with neither.*
> *Were both their dear charmers away.*[73]

General Lyon was firm in refusing Jackson's request to send the troops away, giving as his reasons that there was no assurance that Union men in the rural districts would meet with any better protection than had hitherto been given them, a very sorry protection to say the least. As Jackson did not seem prepared to make any stipulation unless the federal troops were withdrawn from the State, General Lyon brought the conference to a close, by remarking that there was no prospect of an agreement. Governor Jackson wished to carry on the negotiations by a correspondence, to which General Lyon objected, on the ground that it would be too voluminous. He offered that each party might briefly put down his views, but the Governor was averse to this mode of proceeding. They then separated, Lyon and Blair returning to the Arsenal, and Jackson and Price sending to the depot to have a special train ready to take them to Jefferson. They started back in less than an hour from the time of separation.

With additional details of the meeting and the reactions of bystanders Knox reported that:

> While they were in session, a large crowd, principally of secessionists, gathered in the basement of the hotel and on the sidewalk in front. When it was whispered around that nothing had been effected, many of the assembled faces were the blankest kind of expression imaginable. They had had strong hopes of getting ahead of General Lyon in the same manner that they had circumvented Harney, but were doomed to sad disappointment. The organization of home guards will go on with increased vigor, and secession will be put down. By the terms of protection given to Governor Jackson by General Lyon the former was not to be exempt from arrest after June 12th, and in a few days a forward movement from St. Louis may be safely looked for.[74]

In the same letter Knox also called to task the administration at Fort Leavenworth. His criticism, in light of subsequent events, was well justified:[75]

> St. Joseph has been taken possession of by federal troops from Fort Leavenworth, and the Stars and Stripes are now waving on the breezes that sweep across the "Big Muddy." There is some complaint about some of the officers in the Department of the West, that they wait for word from the Circumlocution Department in Washington before taking any steps a single inch ahead of their elders, however much the public safety may demand it. For instance, the officer in command at Fort Leavenworth has arms sufficient for all the Federal volunteers in Kansas, but refuses to give them out until he has authority from government, although he knows the troops stand in

great need of them, and is perfectly well aware that he will get instructions to distribute the weapons.[76]

General Lyon was promoted for taking Camp Jackson, although he had no orders to that effect, and some of these younger epaulette wearers had better follow his example.

Affairs in Missouri had now come to the point of no return. The time for talk and posturing was over. In a little more than a month after the Camp Jackson Affair, Missouri began its descent in a bloody maelstrom of violence that would last for four years. For the first year of this war, Thomas W. Knox was at its center, reporting to the *Herald's* readers.

Chapter 2

The Dance Begins

It was war. There was no longer any doubt. The severing of communications by burning railroad bridges and cutting telegraph wires were attempts to slow opponents' pursuit. On the State's side, there were calls to action in Jefferson City by Missouri's Governor Jackson and State Guard Major General Price. Similar calls for rapid movements by General Lyon and others in St. Louis were made. The Planter's House Conference collapsed on June 11 and Governor Jackson and General Price returned to Jefferson City. The next day, June 12, Governor Jackson issued a long proclamation (found in full in the Appendix) that was essentially a declaration of war, but was also hedged in tone.[1] He laid out a litany of offenses committed by the Federal Government.

With Jackson calling out 50,000 troops to "repel invasion," the course for General Lyon was clear and expected – attack! Union troops were called up, put aboard steamboats, and the advance up the Missouri River began. In May, three steamboats had become General Lyon's "fleet." They were the *J. C. Swon*, confiscated (seized) on May 21, the *Iatan*, chartered May 14, and the *City of Louisiana*, chartered May 26.[2] Reporter Knox was able to gain a "ringside" seat on the *Swon* along with General Lyon and his staff.

Between Jefferson City and Hermann the telegraph lines had been cut and the bridge over the Gasconade River burned. However, both rail and telegraph service were maintained to the east from Hermann.[3]

St. Ambert,[4] (nine miles from Jefferson City), June 14, 8 PM.
A special agent who was sent down from Jefferson City with the mail has just returned here, having left [t]here this

afternoon. He says the Governor and all State officers left there yesterday, and that the last of the soldiers left today at 2 PM, taking with them all the locomotives (of which I understand there were five), and cars, and burning the bridge at Grey's Creek, three miles west of Jefferson City. Also, one above these, after they had passed over them.

It is supposed the Governor has ordered his forces to concentrate either at Boonville or Arrow Rock, probably the latter.

It is thought that General Lyon will push after him and, should he meet with no detention, he will not be more than twenty-for hours behind him.

The Moreau Bridge, forty-one miles this side of Jefferson City, is unharmed, but the western span of the Osage bridge, nine miles this side is burned.

Knox added an additional report from Hermann:

Herman[n], Mo. June 14, 1861.
A gentleman from Jefferson City says the steamer *White Cloud*[5] was loading at that place yesterday with canon and military stores. It was said that Governor Jackson and all State officers were to embark in her for Arrow Rock, a strong point sixty miles above, on the Missouri River.

Captain Kelly's guard of one hundred men was the only troops at Osage bridge or Dodd's Island.[6]

JEFFERSON CITY OCCUPIED

Knox announced the occupation of Jefferson City, sending a short telegram one day later.[7] His detailed and lengthy letter on the advance to Jefferson City appeared on June 20 in the *Herald*. His unique description of river travel and confrontation was widely read and discussed in the East.[8]

Note: subheadings, in brackets, have been added here and in subsequent articles to break up the narrative.

The Dance Begins

Jefferson City, Mo., June 15, 1861. Immediately on hearing of the burning of the bridges over the Gasconade and Osage, by order of Governor Jackson, General Lyon issued orders for Colonel Sigel's regiment (the Second Missouri Volunteers) to proceed up the Pacific Railroad and occupy the line as far as the former stream, in order to prevent further damage by the rebels.[9] They left the Arsenal at 5 PM on the 12th, and took possession of the road without opposition from the traitors in that section. On the following day the *Iatan* and the *J. C. Swon* left the Arsenal, destined for Jefferson City, the former having on board five companies of the First Regiment of Missouri Volunteers, under Lieutenant Colonel Andrews, and Captain Totten, with 400 regulars. Colonel Blair, commanding the First Regiment, was on the *J. C. Swon*, with the remaining five companies. On the *Swon* were also Lieutenant Lathrop, with 100 artillerymen and fifty infantry, and General Lyon's company of regulars, nearly eighty strong. The *Iatan* took one six-pound piece and one twelve-pound howitzer, under the command of Captain Totten, with the complement of shot and shell. The *Swon* was provided with two field pieces, one a twelve-pounder and one a six-pounder, and an eight-inch siege howitzer, with a liberal supply of shells, round and canister shot. The steamer *Louisiana* was ordered to proceed to Jefferson Barracks, take on board Colonel Boernstein's regiment (the Third), and follow in the wake of her predecessors. General Lyon, on board the *Swon*, commanded the expedition. The *Iatan* left the Arsenal landing at twelve o'clock PM on the 13th and the *Swon* got away about two o'clock PM, having been delayed till that time by sticking to the river bank. I was fortunate by securing passage on the latter boat, and thus far we have progressed under the guidance of Captain Bart Able,[10] formerly commander of the *Iatan*. To him, as well as General Lyon, Colonel Blair and other officers of the expedition, I am under obligation for many acts of courtesy, in extending to me the facilities as a looker on in Vienna;[11] and I trust that Heaven and the Federal Government will be alike profuse in favors to them all.

[DEPARTURE]

As we steamed up the river past St. Louis, crowds at various points on the levee saluted us with hearty and enthusiastic cheering, and a most liberal display of linen handkerchiefs. Leaving the city behind, and taking our course up the middle of the stream, Captain Able kept the boat for a long time exactly on the line which separates the chocolate colored water of the Missouri from the far purer aqueous fluid of the Mississippi. The foliage on the banks was of the deep green summer tint, and formed a pleasing contrast with the fields of wheat which were just assuming the golden color which betokens that "their greatness is a ripening."[12] At various points on the shore, the natives came down to gaze at us as we passed, most of whom displayed their loyalty by demonstrations of delight.

Occasionally would be see a few who would look on in sullen silence, showing that though their bodies were present on the banks of the "Big Muddy," their hearts were far away in the sunny South with J. D. and his bosom friends. About twenty miles above the point where we entered the Missouri, we tied up to the bank to wait for the approach of the *Sam Gaty*, from St. Louis, bound up, which was reported to have a supply of powder on board for one of the secessionists.

On her arrival she was peremptorily ordered to heave to, but a careful search revealed nothing contraband. She was, however, compelled to fall behind us to prevent her from conveying intelligence of our being on the way. At Washington, Hermann, and several other places, the crowds on shore displayed the Stars and Stripes and cheered us most vociferously. The ladies were out in abundance and I was told at

Washington that twenty five of the fair sex had that morning walked five miles to carry breakfast to one hundred Home Guards who were protecting a railroad bridge. Newport, between Washington and Hermann, the only place on the lower Missouri where the confederacy fast was observed, was as silent as a country cemetery on a rainy Sabbath.[13]

[NEWS FROM JEFFERSON CITY]

At dusk on the 14th, as we were wooding up at a point some thirty miles below Jefferson City, and about fifteen miles below the mouth of the Osage, a skiff appeared coming down the river, and was ordered to drop astern of the *Swon*. It proved to contain W. H. Lusk, formerly editor of the Jefferson City *Inquirer*, now Deputy Postmaster of that place, in charge of the mail on its way to Hermann, the point which the cars now run from St. Louis. Mr. Lusk came on board, and the mail passed on to its destination. From him we learned that Jefferson City had been deserted by the civil and military authorities of the State of Missouri, and there was no body of men there to oppose its occupation by federal troops. This information acted as a damper to the ardor of some of our officers, who had been looking with considerable enthusiasm for a brush with the enemy at the capital. Someone in St. Louis telegraphed to Gov. Jackson, via St. Joseph and Leavenworth, at the time of our departure from the Arsenal, that we were on the way. Immediately the business of evacuation commenced, a portion of the packing up and removing of the public property had been done at the time of the scare of last week. The employee of the railroad managed to disable one locomotive and to put a few cars out of running order. One of the engineers positively refused to afford any assistance in moving the rebels, and after some time spent in vain attempts to persuade him to change his determination, they concluded to let him have his own way. The lost labor of making ready for a westward movement was ended by daylight on the 14th, and soon after sunrise but few of the rebels were found to be in the town. Orders were given by Governor Jackson for the destruction of the Moreau Bridge, four miles down the Missouri, and Gen. Price attended to the demolition of the telegraph. With his own hands he cut down several posts above the city and severed the wires at intervals of two or three rods for a mile or more. All the cars and locomotives that could be used were taken by the rebels

In their flight and as fast as they crossed streams, they secured themselves from pursuit by burning the bridges. Some of the notables and many of fugitives went by the steamer *White Cloud*. They were quite cautious in concealing their place of destination from the loyal men of Jefferson, but certain remarks made it pretty certain they were bound for Boonville, forty miles above, and one of the strongest secession towns in the State.

The progress of the expedition up the Missouri was somewhat slow, owing to the *Swon* several times getting aground. This boat is one of the St. Louis and New Orleans packets, and was built expressly for service on the lower Mississippi. She was seized by the government a few weeks since for bringing from Baton Rouge the guns seized at Camp Jackson. She is an excellent and well-constructed boat, with engines of enormous power. No craft of her size has ever before been up the Missouri, that river in many places being quite shallow.

At several of these points General Lyon ordered the men to march around by land, thus reducing the draft of the *Swon* nearly a foot. At the mouth of the Osage they made a detour through the forest, and at a stone house near the ruins of the railroad bridge. Captain Yates of Company B, First regiment made a seizure of four kegs of gunpowder, a portion of the quantity sent down from Jefferson City to destroy the bridge.

It had been reported that the rebels had erected a masked battery on an island at this point, but nothing of the kind was discovered, and the proofs were everywhere apparent of almost precipitous flight towards the Kansas border.

[AT JEFFERSON CITY]

On the morning of the 15th, ten miles below Jefferson City, Captain Lyon transferred his regulars to the *Iatan*, and proceeded with that boat, leaving the *Swon* to follow in his wake. As we approached the city, crowds gathered on the levee and saluted us with prolonged and oft repeated cheering. Colonel Thomas L. Price (no relative to the rebel, Sterling Price), a prominent Unionist of Jefferson City, was the first to greet General Lyon as he stepped on shore. A bar has formed at the regular landing and so [we] were obliged to run out our gangplank below the penitentiary, at a point where the railway company has placed a large quantity of loose stone, preparatory to forming a landing of its own. The steep rough bank prevented the debarkation of our artillery, but the infantry scrambled up in fine style. First was the company of regulars formerly commanded by General Lyon, but now led by Lieutenant Hare. Those were set to occupy a high hill or bluff near the railroad depot and commanding the town. They went forward in fine style, ascending the steep acclivity at the "double quick step." In one minute from reaching the summit they were formed in a hollow square, ready to repel all attacks from foes, whether real or imaginary. Next came the left wing of the First Volunteer regiment, under Lieutenant Colonel Andrews, five hundred strong. These soldiers were formed by sections and marched to the tune of "Yankee Doodle," with the Stars and Stripes conspicuous, through the principal streets to the State House, of which they took possession amid the cheers of the people of the town. After some delay in finding the keys, which had not been very carefully hid, Lieutenant Colonel Andrews with a band, color bearer and guard, accompanied by Col. Thos. L. Price, W. H. Lusk, former editor of the Jefferson City *Inquirer*, and the St. Louis *Democrat* and *New York Herald* correspondents ascended to the cupola and displayed the American flag, while the band played the "Star Spangled Banner" and the populace and the troops below gave round after round of enthusiastic applause. Thus was the "sacred soil" of Missouri's capital invaded by federal troops and the bosom of "the pride of the Big Muddy" desecrated by the footprints of the volunteer soldiers of St. Louis. She rather seemed to like it.

The capital being occupied, Gen. Lyon took possession of the railroad depot, and sent a detachment to seize the steamer *McDowell*,[14] on the opposite side of the river, the boat which brought up a supply of powder for the secessionists a few weeks since and aided in the transportation of the State troops to and from Jefferson City. Very soon a dense column of smoke was seen issuing from her chimneys and two hours afterwards the boat left her moorings and took up her position near the *Swon* and *Iatan*. Next the Governor's mansion, which was unoccupied, though well furnished, was taken in hand and surrounded by a guard. It will doubtless be used as the headquarters of the officer who remains in charge of Jefferson City. As the last sad relics of Jackson's rebel soldiery had left the city about an hour before our arrival, all our victories were bloodless.

Major Conant, Private Secretary to General Lyon, paid a visit to the Penitentiary. The prisoners cheered lustily from their cells when they somehow got the word that United States soldiers had entered the building, and the officials found it impossible to stop the tumult. Some of them cheered for Jeff. Davis, some for Jackson and some for both those worthies. Lincoln and Scott were not forgotten by these servants of the State, and most of them seemed to be favorable to the Union, and would no doubt, be willing to follow the flag. Captain Cole of the First regiment was sent out to look for secession flags, but after a vigorous search of two hours returned with not a single striped rag to reward his efforts.

   Mr. Simpson of the Jefferson *Inquirer* called upon General Lyon, stated that his sheet was not a secessioner, and professed his willingness to hoist the Union flag at the head of his columns. This paper had been one of the most vituperative opponents of the course of the Federal Government, but came in all right at the eleventh hour. The Mayor has closed all the whiskey shops, cutting off nearly the entire trade of its merchants, and expresses himself as anxious to cooperate with Gen. Lyon in maintaining the peace and honor of the city. Everything is quiet, and there is no immediate prospect of difficulty with the rebels in the vicinity.

Knox then shifted to military matters, opining on the relative defensive situation in Jefferson City compared to the terrain at Boonville.

Gov. Jackson and the whole military and civil government of the State have fled to Boonville, forty miles above this place. I have just seen a man who left that place this morning. He says there are not far from fifteen hundred men now there, the most of them armed with their own rifles and shotguns. They have six or eight iron cannon. They are throwing up earthworks to protect the town from attack both by river and by land. It was a sad mistake by the rebels – sad for them but glorious for us – that they did not stay in this city. Jefferson is situated on a cluster of low but steep hills, on the right [south] bank of the Missouri, and with very little labor could be made almost impregnable.

   These hills are higher than those around, which would make them exceedingly difficult to take possession of, provided the holders had a decent supply of the proper means of defense. Boonville, on the contrary, is on a level grade on the south side of the river, and is quite easy of approach. General Lyon's plans are not fully made, or if made are not revealed; but he will probably wait for Colonel Boernstein's regiment, now coming on the *Louisiana*, take two or three companies from that to hold Jefferson City, and push on with the whole force on the *Iatan* and *Swon*, and the remainder of Colonel Boernstein's regiment. Thirty hours from now, something will have happened.

Mail facilities between Jefferson City and the East since the bridge burning below are quite irregular. There has been no mail up for a week, and but one down during that time. This letter goes down in a skiff to Hermann, fifty miles below here, and from there goes by rail. The boatman who takes it is now waiting for the precious document.

General Lyon's rapid response and movement was, as can be seen by the multiple short notes and also Knox's full report in the *Herald,* were of great interest to the American public. Other newspapers picked up Knox's story, but only the *Herald* and the St. Louis *Democrat* were able to print first-hand accounts. The news spread rapidly and by June 17–18 the news of the capture of Missouri's capital city appeared in newspapers as far apart as Milwaukee; Lowell, MA; Omaha; Cleveland; Washington, DC; and Bellows Falls, VT – a good example of the telegraph's effect on the wide and rapid dissemination of the news. However, for the longer, more complete story, the less expensive postal service was still used.

The first illustrated story of the event came from the *Harper's Weekly* of July 6. The story accompanying the illustration begins, "A correspondent thus describes the landing at Jefferson City." This text is a direct quotation of Knox's *Herald* letter without attribution to either Knox or the *Herald*.

Later, in his book, Knox reflected on his feelings as he approached his first battle:

> So on the eve of that first battle in Missouri, as I reclined in the cabin of our flag boat, I saw the surgeons busy with their preparations for the coming day; as I saw them bring to light

all the dreadful instruments of their trade, and arrange them in readiness for sudden use – a coldness crept over me, and I fully realized we had earnest work before us. Since that time I have witnessed many a battle, many a scene of preparation and bloody work with knife and saw and bandage, but I have never experienced a chill like the one I felt on that early day of the Rebellion.[15]

Speculation was rampant about General Lyon's next move, but the consensus was that he would follow the retreating secessionists to Boonville. The newsworthy success at Jefferson City piqued the interest of more correspondents. Soon, there would be more correspondents in Missouri, but for the assault on Boonville, Knox and the St. Louis *Democrat* correspondent remained on their own.

"Landing of United States Volunteers, Under General Lyon, at Jefferson City, Missouri." Sketched by Orlando C. Richardson[16]. (*Harper's Weekly*, July 6, 1861).

Chapter 3

The Battle of Boonville

It was time for the next step in General Lyon's campaign up the Missouri River, but first a change was made in the transports being loaded. The *Augustus McDowell*,[1] captured at Jefferson City, replaced the *Swon*, which was sent back downriver to St. Louis. Built for Mississippi River service the *Swon* had a greater draft than other boats that were better adapted for service on the Missouri, with its shifting sandbars and currents.

On June 17, Lyon's boats began the attack up the river. While the ultimate target was Boonville, there were bluffs at the town that would make an assault difficult. The troops landed near Merna on a bottom land site about eight miles below Boonville, where there were no impeding bluffs. They waded ashore and advanced, throwing out probing skirmish lines. After an advance of about a mile, they encountered and drove in State Guard advance pickets. Lyon's men brought up their artillery and shelled the State Guard's line of defense and a nearby house holding rebels. They swept away the rebel line of defense and easily marched through the rebel camp and into Boonville. Colonel Marmaduke's men, new to war, fled in disarray. Casualties were few and the headline-making rout was complete.

Fragmentary notes of State Guard buildup at Boonville,[2] and of a battle there[3] appeared and were confirmed.[4] Knox sent a short note from Boonville about the battle on June 20, with what he called "Additional Particulars" that appeared on June 22.[5] His initial report, an extensive and detailed letter, with flamboyant headlines was published on June 23, 1861:[6]

The Battle of Boonville

> **IMPORTANT FROM MISSOURI.**
>
> **THE BATTLE OF BOONEVILLE.**
>
> **THE DETAILS OF THE FIGHT.**
>
> **Four Thousand Rebels Routed, and the Field Occupied in Twenty Minutes After the Opening Gun.**
>
> **Capture of a Camp and Fixtures.**
>
> **BOONEVILLE OCCUPIED.**
>
> **A Parson with Four Men Capture Twenty-four Rebels.**
>
> **THE NUMBER OF THE KILLED AND WOUNDED.**
>
> **The Rebels Probably Making A Stand At Independence,**
>
> &c., &c. &c.
>
> SPECIAL REPORT TO THE NEW YORK HERALD.

Booneville, Cooper County, Mo., June 18, 1861.[7]

On the morning of the 16th last, the steamer *Louisiana*, having on board Colonel Boernstein's (Second) regiment, arrived at Jefferson City, and about noon, General Lyon, having transferred the men and lading of the *Swon* to the *A. McDowell*, and leaving three hundred men to hold the city, the three boats, *Iatan, Louisiana* and *McDowell* moved forward up the river. Before leaving, a squad of men, headed by Captain Yates, visited the house of the State Paymaster General, J. R. Rogers, and arrested that gentleman, seizing his private person.

The arrest was made to obtain possession of the money appropriated to pay the officers and men of the celebrated "Southwest Expedition" of last autumn.[8] In his valise were found checks for $45,000, drawn by the State Auditor and countersigned by the State Treasurer. Mr. Rogers was in the village at the time of the visit, and his wife attempted to conceal the valise by carrying it to the negro quarters in rear of the house, thus awakening suspicion that it contained something of value. Among his papers was a letter from Warwick Hough, Adjutant General of Missouri, advising Mr. Rogers to refuse to pay any money to the purpose for which it was appropriated and devote it to arming the State.

The boats moved up to a landing eight miles below Booneville on the south side of the river. Here they fastened to the shore, and the troops were debarked. A farmer at work in a field near the landing stated that the enemy was in camp four and a half miles from the spot, or three and a half miles below Booneville. The level bottom land of the Missouri was here half a mile in width to the back, but is gradually narrowed as it extended up the river, until it terminated where the bluff came to the water's edge, two miles from the boat landing. The road followed for a mile and a half along the bottom, and then ascended the bluff. The latter is a range of low hills or ridges, about two hundred feet in height, which are separated by ravines, some of them with quite precipitous sides. The order of proceeding was as follows: Ten mounted men, the only cavalry in the expedition, led the advance; scouting parties from the Second regiment, were thrown out for half a mile on the left and to the river on the right; General Lyon's company of regulars, led by Sergeant Griffin, and company B of the Second regiment, commanded by Captain Schutte, followed the cavalry; Captain Totten's battery and his company of regulars, the latter led by Lieutenant Lathrop, came next, followed by Colonel Blair's (First) regiment; the rear was brought up by a battalion of Colonel Boernstein's regiment, led by Colonel Schaffer. On board the boat was Captain Richardson with Company B, First regiment and Captain Boester,[9] with twenty men and a siege (eight inch) howitzer.

The troops landed and began their advance. The rebels had formed a ragged line to oppose Lyon's advance. Knox continued: [Note: The following two paragraphs, part of Knox's *Herald* article, were reprinted verbatim in the *Harper's Weekly* July 13, 1861 article on the Battle of Boonville.]

At just three minutes before seven AM, on June 17, the order was given to move. The morning was cloudy, with occasionally a few drops of rain, but before the battle was over the sun shone out clear and bright as ever. As the column ascended the bluff the pickets of the enemy were seen and driven in. After an advance of three-fourths of a mile one of the advanced guard rode hastily back to the head of the column and informed General Lyon that the whole body of the State troops was drawn up a few hundred yards in front. General Lyon at once ordered the regulars under Sergeant Griffin to the left, and Captain Schultez's[10] riflemen to the right. Captain Totten's battery was ordered to the front to occupy the road.

The enemy were drawn up about three hundred yards in advance, on the crest of a hill, or rather a long swell or ridge, over which the road passed at the highest point. The road was occupied by Colonel Marmaduke, with a small body of horsemen and a battalion of infantry. Immediately on his left was a brick house filled with rebel troops, and back of this, toward the river, was a narrow lane, where his left wing was posted. To their rear was a wheat field, and this was miscellaneously scattered small crowds of men, apparently without order or regularity. To his right was another wheat field, separated from an adjacent corn field by a "worm fence,"[11] and behind this fence his right wing was posted. Soon as our men were in position Captain Totten unlimbered a twelve-pounder and a six-pounder, and sent a shell from the former into the midst of the men occupying the road. A puff of smoke rising from among them showed that the gunner's aim had been true. The next shell was directed upon the squads of men in the wheat field and caused them to make a hasty retreat. The fire now became general along the whole line, the regulars on the right, and the German troops on the left, advancing in good order.[12] Our line was formed on a ridge similar to that occupied by the enemy and parallel to it, separated from the latter by a valley with a gentle descent on either side. To our left was a corn field and on our right a copse or grove of scattered oaks. The regulars advanced in the corn field, to the crest of the ridge, creeping up the latter and firing when opportunity occurred, taking for their motto that of an Irishman at Donnybrook Fair,[13] "Whenever you see a head hit it." The hollow between the ridges was full of scattered oaks, and these served as a cover to our men. Captains Stone, Cole, and Cavender were sent to support the right of the regulars, and in this way they all advanced to the fence where the enemy were at first posted. The battalion from the Second, supported by Captains Maurice's, Burke's, and Yates's companies, were at the same time doing good work on the right; and in twenty minutes from the time Captain Totten fired the first shell the rebels were in full retreat, and our men occupying the line first held by the enemy. The house on the right had been completely riddled by the last shots front the battery, and one shell burst in the very center of the building, at a time when it was full of soldiers. Several dead bodies of the rebels were found in the wheat field near the lane, showing that our fire had been effective. In fact, at the first volley from the right wing several saddles were emptied of their riders, and two horses galloped over to our lines. The correspondents of the New York *Herald* and St. Louis *Democrat* entered the battle on foot, by the side of the battery, but were very soon mounted, having succeeded in capturing these runaway steeds.

[FORWARD AGAIN]

From this point the Union troops proceeded, still in line, nearly a mile, over ground somewhat uneven, but not rough. In a grove at the entrance to Camp Vest,[14] the rebels made a brief stand, but two shells and a few rounds of Minié balls dislodged them, and they fled in tumultuous haste towards Booneville. Captain Cole, supported by Captain Miller, entered and took possession of the camp, capturing a large quantity of provisions, ammunition, rifles and camp equipage. He secured one secession flag, one lone star flag, and one State flag with fifteen stars.

The breakfasts of the men were cooking on the fires at the time we landed, as the half-baked bread, the partially fried pork still in the pans, and the unboiled coffee plainly told. A huge ham was found lying on the ground, with one slice partially severed and the knife still sticking in the meat. Captain Cole's company was left to take care of the camp, while the main column moved on towards the town. At the Fair Grounds, a mile below Booneville, was the camp of a body of rebels; but a shell from Captain Totten's battery and one from the *McDowell* – that boat having moved up the stream – at the same time, sent them flying to the westward. General Lyon then advanced to the edge of the town, halted, and awaited the approach of the Mayor, O'Brien, and several leading citizens. Mr. O'Brien assured General Lyon that there should be no trouble entering and occupying Booneville, and offered to ride with the commanding officer at the head of the column through the principal streets. His proposition was accepted, and we entered the town, the people cheering as we passed, and from numerous windows showing the Stars and Stripes. The Court House was at once taken possession of, and occupied as the headquarters of the officers. Suspected houses were searched, and a large quantity of war munitions were seized. At the foundry, the molds were still hot from casting Minié bullets.

The men who remained on the boats desperately wanted to get into the fight. As the *McDowell* began to steam up the river, shells fired from the battery left on the boat had some effect:

> Captain Richardson received his command to stay on the boats with much regret, and some of his men even shed tears because they were unable to join the battle. After the troops had marched to the bluff, Captain Richardson advanced, with the *McDowell*, and with Captain Boester's[15] howitzer captured a battery of two iron six-pounders about five miles below the town. He also secured at the same time one caisson, full of ammunition; eight horses, with military saddles, and twenty prisoners. After this exploit they advanced and threw a shell into the Fair grounds. At night, when I saw him, with his men, on board the *McDowell*, he seemed in better spirits than in the morning. He was confident he had had his share of the fun.

[CASUALTIES]

The number of killed and wounded on the part of the rebels has not and probably will not be accurately ascertained. Many of those fighting on the rebel side were "loose men," not enrolled in any company, and fled in large numbers, not to any rallying point, but directly home, thinking, doubtless, there was some mistake about the popular belief that Union troops are cowards. Out of one company (Captain McCulloch's Cooper County Rifles) thirteen are known to be killed and several wounded. The number of dead already brought into Boonville or taken to friends in the country can not fall much short of fifty, and the wounded now heard of are as many more. Several shells were burst directly in their midst and the Minié balls flew thick and fast from the rifles of our soldiers, so that the mortality list must have been quite large. On the side of the Union troops, there were three killed, ten wounded, and one missing. Capt. Yates's company lost one killed and six wounded, owing partially to a withholding of their fire upon an advancing party, which delivered a volley quite near, our men supposing the latter to be friends. Captain Burke of Company K, First regiment, was saved by his scabbard, a Minié ball striking it near the top with such force as nearly to cut it through, but not injuring the wearer. An Artilleryman was hit upon the left breast, the ball striking a rib, passing around under his arm, and being cut out on his back below his shoulder. I have the ball in my possession. It is flattened out to nearly the shape of a half coffee bean, and must have "hit hard."

Prisoners were rounded up during the engagement (hardly much of a "battle"). In general, the rebel soldiers had shown little training and it appeared that many had not even been placed in organized units. Correspondent Knox listed their numbers and told some anecdotes:

> We took eighty prisoners, nineteen of whom have been released, and the remaining sixty-one put on board the *Louisiana*. During the engagement, Rev. W. A. Pile, of St. Louis, chaplain to the First regiment, was furnished with a detail of four men to look after the wounded. Descending to a ravine he came suddenly upon a party of twenty-four rebels and peremptorily ordered them to stop and surrender. They evidently considered discretion the better part of valor, and at once threw up the sponge, i. e., took off their hats and laid down their arms. The parson soon after reported himself to Gen. Lyon, with his twenty-four prisoners, guarded by four men and himself. The story is pretty well circulated among our boys, and the chaplain

is looked upon (if his clerical neck choker will allow the expression) as a perfect trump, a decided brick.[16]

Capt. Boester,[17] who managed the siege howitzer on the *McDowell* at the time the battery was taken, last evening asked Gen. Lyon to furnish him with harnesses for his eight horses captured yesterday, so that he can take his howitzer into action. The captain is an old artillerist and has seen service in Europe. Gen. Lyon will probably grant his request.

During the skirmish at Camp Vest, a mounted man rode up to Capt. Yates and said that Gen. Parsons had sent orders for all his infantry to come into Booneville, as there were two steamers ready to take them up the river. After talking with him a few moments, they communicated to him the pleasing information that he was conversing with Union troops and must be made prisoner. He came in rather reluctantly.

[FUGITIVE REBELS]

General Price, commander of the State forces, left for up the river the day before the battle, his health not permitting him to remain. Colonel J. S. Marmaduke had command on the day of the engagement, and Horace T. Brand of Cooper County acted as Lieutenant Colonel.[18] The latter is reported killed. The rebels, in their flight through the town, left behind them many of their guns and much of their personal property. A few wagons took away small quantities of their camp equipage, but the greater part of it is aboard our boats. They fled up the river in the steamer *H. D. Bacon*[19] and along its banks by land, and are reported to have made a stand twelve miles above. They have been reinforced by General Parsons, who arrived here during the engagement, and is said to have a few pieces of artillery, but has no men qualified to work them. The number of men here at the time of the battle was about four thousand, one half of whom were in the engagement. They were variously armed, with Minié and hunting rifles, shotguns and pistols, but made a poor use of them. Nine hundred of them were mounted but could hardly be called cavalry. The number that have fled homeward will probably be made up by reinforcements, so that at the next engagement we shall have about the same number to contend with. But few of those taken prisoner are in uniform, the most of them being fresh from the country. They express great astonishment at the efficiency of our troops, and think the Dutch portion of them is not so bad after all.

General Parsons's private papers, including his commission, are in the hands of General Lyon.

Governor Jackson is reported to have made splendid time on his retreat. With Union troops behind him, he could doubtless eclipse the famous riders of the pony express.

General Price's papers, muster rolls, and correspondence to June 13, fell into the hands of General Lyon. Several prominent men in the State are implicated and will be speedily brought to justice.

Among the prisoners are several who were captured at Camp Jackson on May 10. At that time they gave their parole of honor, taking oath never again to appear in arms against the government. They will doubtless be executed.[20]

At no time during the action were more than six hundred men engaged on the side of the Unionists. At the commencement the rebels had not far from two thousand men on the field, a large number of whom were mounted. Their horses greatly facilitated their departure. Above Booneville, on their retreat, they pressed into service all the guns, pistols and ammunition they could find at the houses on the road, and took considerable quantities of provisions.

Boonville had fallen and was now searched for any war materials. The rebels had told lurid tales of what would befall women and children if the "Dutch" were to take the town. Apprehensions were rapidly relieved:

This morning files of men were moving in various directions

in and around the town, making searches of houses suspected of containing contraband goods. A large lot of provisions, ammunition and camp equipage were seized, several wagon loads of it at a house four miles from town on the route of the fleeing rebels. The reportorial corps – the *Herald* and *Democrat* correspondents – by their native inquisitiveness, got trace of various contraband property. Procuring a squad of men, they made several searches, securing a rebel flag thirty feet in length, eight rifles, and nearly two thousand dollars worth of rebel provisions. The boats *Sunshine, War Eagle, White Cloud*[21] and the Booneville ferry boat, have all been seized for their complicity with the rebels.

Booneville's four thousand inhabitants appear agreeably astonished that the Union troops do not pillage the town and slaughter the inhabitants. The report that they would burn every home and kill all women and children included, had been industriously circulated by the rebel leaders.

During the engagement, Dr. Cornyn, surgeon to the First regiment,[22] saw a soldier with a wound on the side of his neck, just below the ear, from which the blood flowed profusely. Fearing his throat had been injured, the doctor gave him some brandy, and asked him to try to swallow it. Taking a hearty draught, the soldier said,

"I can swallow first rate, can't I?"

"Oh yes," said the Doctor, "your throat is all right, but where is the ball?" "I don't know," was the cool reply, "I spit the d—d thing out."

We hear tonight that the rebels are at Arrow Rock, fifteen miles above, and are to move on towards Lexington, there to make a stand. No orders have been issued from General Lyon, but we expect to move up the river tomorrow.

The telegraph is broken in several places above and below. The repairer of the line came in tonight, and stated that the wire is broken behind him as soon as he repairs it, and men tell him it is no use to attempt putting it in order.

Dr. William Quarles, of this town, was among the killed on the side of the rebels. M. W. Coolidge, of Boston, was killed in Captain Yates' company, Colonel Blair's regiment. Jacob Kiburtz, a German, was killed in Company B, Colonel Boernstein's regiment.

The prisoners taken yesterday were all released on parole a few minutes since, with the exception of those who were among the captured at Camp Jackson.

In his book, Knox augmented his newspaper reports with some personal anecdotes of his experiences at Boonville:

General Lyon was my personal friend, but he very nearly did me great injustice. Seeing myself and a fellow-journalist on a distant part of the field, he mistook us for scouts of the enemy, and ordered his sharp-shooters to pick us off. His chief-of-staff looked in our direction, and fortunately recognized us in time to countermand the order....A civilian's dress on the battle-field (a grey coat formed a part of mine) subjects the wearer to many dangers from his friends, as most war correspondents can testify.

While approaching the town, I stopped to slake my thirst at a well. A group of our soldiers joined me while I was drinking. I had drank very freely from the bucket, and transferred it to a soldier, when the resident of a neighboring house appeared, and informed us that the well had been poisoned by the Rebels, and the water was certain to produce death. The soldiers desisted, and looked at me with much pity. For a moment, I confess, the situation did not appear cheerful, but I concluded the injury, if any, was already done, and I must make the best of it. The soldiers watched me as I mounted my horse, evidently expecting me to fall within a hundred yards. When I met one of them the following day, he opened his eyes in astonishment at seeing me alive. From that day, I entertained a great contempt for poisoned wells.[23]

General Lyon was now famous for his victory at Boonville. When the report of the battle appeared in the *Harper's Weekly* of July 13, his portrait was on the front page.

"General Nathaniel Lyon."
(*Harper's Weekly*, July 13, 1861).

The battle was illustrated on an inner page.

"The Battle of Boonville, Missouri." Sketched by Orlando C. Richardson.
(*Harper's Weekly*, July 13, 1861).

In addition, the battle provided a field day for cartoonists. Puns were made about both Lyon (favorable, Lion) and Jackson (unfavorable, Jack or jackass).

From the author's collection

General Price's illness and absence from the battlefield were also alluded to. Others said Price was moving west to counter incursions from Kansas.

General Lyon issued a proclamation in Boonville on June 18 that was widely reprinted. Its text is reproduced in full in the Appendix. In essence, he offered both an olive branch and a club to the rebellious Missourians. On June 21, the *New York Herald* added an editorial comment:

> General Lyon has issued a very sensible and firm proclamation to the people of Missouri after the late brilliant battle at Booneville, which we give in full today. He states that the prisoners that he captured are mostly immatured [sic] youths who confessed themselves duped and misled by their leaders, and that he liberated them upon promising not to take any part against the government. He reminds people, however, that the clemency of the government cannot be too far relied upon in the case of persons taken in array against its authority. He assures them that his mission is not to invade their private

rights as citizens, or to interfere with their business occupations, and he implores all loyal citizens to return to their ordinary avocations, in which they will be protected.[24]

Captain Totten was placed in command of some six hundred men and ordered to Syracuse, south of Boonville. Knox went with them and wrote two observation reports from Syracuse:

[ON TO SYRACUSE]

Syracuse, Mo., June 21, 1861.

Five companies of the First regiment Missouri Volunteers, two companies of regulars and Capt. Totten's battery of four pieces of artillery, the whole in command of Capt. Totten, left Booneville on the 19th at half-past nine o'clock PM for this place, reaching here at nine o'clock on the morning of the 20th, after a fatiguing march of twenty-four miles. Governor Jackson, with about 700 rebels, had left Syracuse but four hours before, taking the road to Warsaw by way of Florence, ten miles distant and remain[ed] till late this afternoon. With a view of attacking the rebels in camp, Capt. Totten early this morning proceeded to Florence, but found himself four hours too late for that purpose, Jackson having moved on towards Warsaw, forty-five miles from Syracuse. The command returned to Syracuse, and at the moment of writing are coming to a halt near the depot. The day has been very hot, and the men have suffered much from their twenty mile march over prairie road. Many of them have sore and blistered feet, and two are prostrated from the effects of *coup de soliel*.

On Wednesday morning last, just at daybreak, the rebels, five hundred strong, made an attack on Captain Cooke's command, at Coal [Cole] Camp, twenty two miles west of here.[25] Captain Cooke had not far from nine hundred men, five hundred of them without arms, and the rest armed with rifles and double and single barreled shotguns. Captain Cooke retreated after losing fifteen men having six wounded. His men are now scattered in the forest around. He arrived in Syracuse this afternoon, having come alone, by a circuitous route. In the engagement, he was wounded in the head by a musket ball. The leaden missile has just been extracted by Dr. Cornyn, surgeon to the First regiment. The rebels lost thirty-five men killed and fourteen wounded. They left Coal Camp immediately after the fight, and proceeded towards Warsaw, where their forces appear to be concentrating, and where they will probably make a stand. On their way, they impress all the guns they can find, take possession of the best horses, in some instances stealing them outright and in others giving State scrip for their value to the owners. It is thought that if not attacked soon at Warsaw, they will press on to the southwestern portion of the State, and concentrate in the neighborhood of Springfield.

The troops that were collected at Coal Camp were home guards and recruits raised in the vicinity. They were waiting for arms from the St. Louis Arsenal. The rebels were generally armed with rifles and shot guns, a few of them having Minié muskets.[26]

Two days later, Knox reported again from Syracuse with little real news. The most interesting item was the arrival of Iowa troops. They had been guarding the Hannibal & St. Joseph Railroad, but now were assigned to Lyon's force and likely to see some real action.[27] The letter is given in its entirety is in the endnotes.

After the Syracuse expedition, Knox decided to return to St. Louis to await further action. He took the steamer *D. A. January* down the river and while on board wrote his last letter from the Boonville expedition, again a long detailed account.[28]

> Steamer *D. A. January*,
> Missouri River, June 26, 1861.
> I returned to Booneville from Syracuse, with Captain Totten's

command, on the 24th. Captain Totten had no skirmish whatever with the rebels on the entire trip, either going or returning, as Gov. Jackson fled altogether too fast for us to overtake him. He had, on his arrival at Warsaw, made a stand there. With the intention of giving battle in case the Union forces should come up, but abandoned that determination, and fled toward Springfield. It is reported that he received an awful "scare" at Warsaw. While his forces were crossing the Osage at that point, preparatory to going southward, a runner came up announcing that General Lyon was within a mile and a half of the town. Governor Jackson immediately sank the ferry boats (there is no bridge over the Osage at Warsaw) leaving two hundred of his men on the north side of the stream. Bidding these two hundred take care of themselves he continued on his way with the major portion of his command.

Some of the two hundred attempted to swim the river, but lost seven horses in the attempt. The others made tumultuous haste to a point eight miles above, where they found a steam ferry which took them over in safety. General Lyon did not molest them, as at that identical time he was more than sixty miles away.

Governor Jackson's followers are not at all scrupulous about the appliances they make use of to hasten their flight. Everything which can aid them in their progress becomes the prey of these Arabs of the New World. At Warsaw, the inhabitants were plundered of their horses, provisions, clothing and whatever else was of any importance to our fugitive Governor [Claiborne Jackson], with but little regard to whether its owner was for or against the Union.[29]

After Boonville, Lyon's plans changed. He had planned to move on Lexington to attack Price there, but on getting word that Price had, with his main force, moved south, he decided to pursue Price overland. This created a major problem. Lyon had moved to Boonville by steamboat and now had only the minimal number of wagons for an overland movement. Delay was necessary:

> In my last, from Syracuse, I incorrectly gave the name of the colonel of the Iowa regiment. That efficient body of troops is under the command of Colonel J. F. Bates, a gentleman by instinct, an able officer. His regiment has joined the command of General Lyon, and, with the regulars and the volunteers of the Missouri river expedition, increases the force to not far from twenty-five hundred men. Last Friday, preparations were nearly completed for moving upon Lexington to attack the rebel forces gathered there; but on learning of the evacuation of that place, General Lyon changed his determination for a move in that direction and decided to march upon Springfield, in the hope of preventing the rebels from making a junction with Ben McCulloch.
>
> On Sunday he convened the Common Council and leading citizens of Booneville, and stated to them his desire of procuring a hundred wagons, with their compliment of mules or horses. He said is was the usual custom of military commanders to press teams into service wherever found, but he did not wish to do this and intended to buy or hire all the teams needed, and thought the citizens could furnish them with far less inconvenience to the owners than his own men collect them. As a consequence of this course, the wagons, horses and mules were gathered at the Fair Grounds in less than forty-eight hours from the time the order for them was issued. They are now being loaded and prepared for the trip.
>
> The command was expect[ed] to start tonight, but may not get away before tomorrow, and will proceed toward Springfield, one hundred twenty miles distant, at the rate of from fifteen to twenty-five miles per day. No fighting is expected before reaching that point, and the prospect of a brush even there are not very brilliant. It is hoped that either Colonel Sigel or Colonel Solomon, acting under General Sweeny, will

intercept the rebels in their march towards Arkansas, and, if not able to effect a battle, will retard their progress until General Lyon can come upon them in the rear.

Governor Jackson has become prodigiously frightened that he will not be very likely to make a halt till he reaches the Arkansas line. When he has crossed into that lovely and refined state, he will doubtless "thank God and take courage," and bid defiance to the pursuing Union troops.[30]

Knox ended his letter with some "housekeeping" items. He described arrangements to protect the river towns, conditions on the Pacific Railroad, and the strict discipline enforced by General Lyon. The balance of his letter is to be found in the endnotes.[31]

Back in St. Louis

Thomas Knox returned to St. Louis on June 27 and filed a short telegraphic report on the general state of affairs in Missouri, as seen from the River City:[32]

St. Louis, June 27, 1861.

Gentlemen who came down the Pacific Railroad tonight report that General Lyon left Booneville today with his command and Colonel Bates's Iowa regiment for Springfield, where he will form a junction with the Kansas troops under Major Sturgis, and Colonel Sigel's command from here.

Hon. Mr. Phelps,[33] wife and son, arrived here last night, from Springfield on Thursday. She reports all quiet there; that the rebels have left; that the people do not credit the threatened invasion from Arkansas, and thinks that the Union troops will find no enemies to fight on the southern border.

Four companies of Colonel Stevens's[34] Seventh regiment, under Major Curry, left for Booneville this evening, where they go into camp.

Two companies of Colonel Sliefer's[35] regiment, destined for Jefferson City, left on the same train.

Nothing new received from the west. It is understood, however, that General Lyon has not left Booneville, as previously reported.

Although Knox remained in St. Louis for a while and reported on events in the region, his appetite for action had been whetted and he was anxious to resume his field reports. Nevertheless his involvement in the affairs of state was, for a time, a less active one, more that of an observing reporter than a participant. Knox's report on June 28 on communication problems and the attitudes of Missourians was especially cogent:

> My last letter was dated on board the *D. A. January*, when on my way down from Booneville. The boat came to Hermann, eighty miles from St. Louis, and there connected on the train on the Pacific Railroad, by which I came to this city. Colonel White (Lieutenant Colonel of the Second regiment)[36] was in command of her with two companies of volunteers on board. On the morning after I left the boat was to return up the river to Booneville, thence to Lexington, one hundred and twenty five miles beyond. His mission to Lexington is to blow up the foundry there, leaving not one stone upon another. The foundrymen in that town have been particularly active in aiding the rebels, and quite lately have cast some sixteen cannon for their use. Since the rebel forces evacuated Lexington for their march southward the labor of love still goes on, cannon and balls are yet in process of construction. When Colonel White commences the work of leveling that foundry he will be pretty certain to make it complete, and we can all rest assured "that that machine won't never do duty any more." About the time you receive this letter Colonel White will probably be engaged in the demolishing business.[37]
>
> The *J. C. Swon* went, two days ago, to Cape Girardeau, Missouri, a town on the river some sixty miles below here,

taking five companies of volunteers. The object of the trip was to look after the operations of several rebels of note in that locality. She was expected to return yesterday, but up to this morning, nothing had been heard from her. No one has any fear that she has fallen into the hands of the rebels, but, on the contrary, all have fullest confidence that the expedition is busy in putting affairs at Cape Girardeau on a good footing. You will likely to hear occasionally of similar trips undertaken for the good of the Union cause.

It has not yet been ascertained that General Lyon has actually started from Booneville for Springfield, but he doubtless commenced his march on Wednesday or Thursday evening.

It is impossible to keep up telegraphic communication above Jefferson City. The wires are constantly cut by those in league with the rebels, and no repairs made to the line are of any avail for more than a few hours. When the expedition was passing up the Missouri, Governor Jackson had an operator named Tracy (the only rebel operator on the whole line) stationed in the woods near the river's bank provided with telegraphing instruments, to give notice of General Lyon's approach, and state what force he had. At one office an operator cut out his instrument by disengaging the wires where they entered the garret of the building, and though he made the utmost efforts to get a communication when the rebel officers were present, not a sound could be obtained. Governor Jackson threatened to hang the telegrapher if he did not manage to run the machine; but after repeated assertions from the latter that the line was down, and that hanging him would not put it up, his humane Excellency let the operator go. After the departure of the Governor from the office, the recent prisoner took his instruments up stairs, and found where the line was down.

The excitement in St. Louis with reference to the battle

of Booneville, has by no means subsided. The affair is still discussed with vehemence at street corners and in the places of public resort, and occasionally a fight of the duel order, in which a little claret is drawn, grows out of the agitation of the subject.

The chivalry of this city has experienced a grievously letting down by the result of the Booneville transactions, and there is an end to the boasting that the brave and intelligent sons of Missouri can whip four times their number of Union soldiers. A prestige for the Union forces has been established, and it will be likely to remain through the war. The name of General Lyon is, to the rebels, synonymous with all words that cause terror to the heart and weakness to the knees. Missourians may be brave, but once they have taken a "scare" it is impossible to rally them. In the Kansas wars, Jim Lane was feared in the same manner that General Lyon is now, and for two year after these troubles ended, Missouri mothers used his name to frighten their children to sleep.

Nothing has been heard for some days from General Sweeney's command. He is expected to make a junction with General Lyon soon.[38]

By now, in June, the war in Missouri had garnered considerable attention.[39] Other correspondents were beginning to take notice. Albert D. Richardson, of the New York *Tribune*, who had arrived in St. Louis with Knox but then had gone to Cairo, returned to St. Louis in mid-June.[40] Richardson apparently followed in the footsteps of Knox and Lucien J. Barnes of the *Democrat* and visited Jefferson City, where he was hosted by Colonel Boernstein and shown the "sights." He then went on to Booneville where on June 21 he reported the arrival of the First Iowa Infantry.[41] But Richardson did not stay in Missouri, instead he went to Chicago and Cincinnati in search of news.

Chapter 4

Missouri in the Spotlight

On Monday, July 8, the *New York Herald* ran a series of articles, beginning on the front page with a map of Missouri titled, "The Seat of the War in the West."¹ The map was sub-titled, "The Important Points of the War in Missouri, Showing the Object of the Advance of Union and Rebel Troops Towards the Southwest."

New York Herald, July 8, 1861

In addition, a long article appeared on the front page. Several more Missouri articles appeared on page 2, including two letters from Knox, making this Monday *Herald* into a major tutorial-like explanation of the situation in Missouri for its readers. It also contained a biography of General Lyon and reports from other newspapers.

THE SEAT OF THE WAR IN THE WEST.

Locality of the Missouri Lead Mines in the Southwest.

Sarcoxie, Where The Rebel Legislature is to Assemble.

The Position Held By Governor Claiborne Jackson And His Forces

The Union Forces Surrounding Him on All Sides

THE WHEREABOUTS OF BEN. McCULLOCH

His Proclamation To The Rebels of Arkansas

The Movements of Gen. Lyon and the Missouri Volunteers

&c.,   &c.   &c.

Said the *Herald*:

> The map which we give today will be found of great use to our readers, as it portrays the whole of the present seat of the war in the West, which field of enterprise may in the course of history be as great in importance to the Union cause as in Virginia. We have already shown that the object of the rush of Union and rebel troops to the Southwest is to gain possession of the Granby lead mines, the location of which can be perceived by referring to the left hand lower corner of the map. The Indian Territory borders on this portion of the State, and it is supposed that the rebels, under Ben McCulloch, may have the aid of about two thousand of the aborigines. This help to their wretched cause may prove of little avail, as doubtless when the Indians perceive they are fighting against United States troops they will fear the loss of their annuities and back out, if they have not already done so, on ascertaining the nature of John Ross' proclamation.[2] But the fact must still be borne in mind that until we know to the contrary, these two thousand are arrayed against us. Then we have to recollect that Ben McCulloch and his horde are reported as being along the Arkansas border of the State; that they had been in full force at Pocahontas, and had also been observed along the White river, which leads to within a comparatively few miles of the lead mines. A report has also reached us that Ben McCulloch had been in Bentonville, in consultation with the Indians. All these point will be found on reference to the lower portion of the map. By the proclamation which will be elsewhere found, it has been ascertained that Ben McCulloch was at Little Rock, in the center of the State of Arkansas, on July 1.[3]

Continuing, the *Herald* took up the politics and geography of Missouri, not necessarily with any great clarity for Eastern readers. This whole exposition was certainly not written by the *Herald's* man on the spot, Knox, but probably by some scrivener in the bowels of the *Herald* building:

> The next important fact to be attended to is the position of Governor Claib. Jackson and his rebel force. According to a recent dispatch, he was on Clear Creek, eight miles south of Osceola, on the 26th of June, with one thousand men, six thousand muskets, and three hundred horses and mules. Osceola is situated about midway between Springfield and the western terminus of the Pacific Railroad, and on the Little Osage river. Gen. Price, with two hundred and fifty men, was in the same neighborhood. It was also reported that several companies were *en route* to join Jackson's forces in that neighborhood. By our St. Louis correspondence, published in another column of this day's issue, it will be perceived that Doniphan and Houston, important points in the neighborhood of the copper region,[4] and near the southern or lower border of the State are likely to become scenes of lively interest, as the rebel forces are there organizing.
>
> A gentleman from Springfield on the 2nd inst. said that about fifteen hundred of Jackson's troops are encamped in Benton County. Without commenting on the chances of the truth of this report, we will state that Benton County occupies a space including Camp Cole, Warsaw, &c., and is immediately in the neighborhood of the southern side of the Pacific Railroad.
>
> The positions of the Union forces are now matters of consideration. Rolla, the terminus of the southwestern branch of the Pacific Railroad, is in the possession of Colonel McNeil's reserve corps of Missouri Union Volunteers. This regiment could be divided at that place into two battalions, and marched down upon Houston by one road and Doniphan by another, uniting, if necessary, at Thomasville. Or they might proceed in one body to Harmony, and, there

dividing, as before, and take the right and left roads from that place to those country towns.[5] This force will doubtless check the rebel excitement in that neighborhood, unless the rebel forces have already reached Pocahontas.

At Springfield it appears that Col. Solomon has half his regiment of Missouri Union Volunteers, and Col. Brown his regiment of Missouri Union reserve corps.[6] The First Iowa regiment is reported moving from Booneville toward this point.

By dispatches and correspondence we learn that Col. Sigel, at the head of his own regiment and a battalion of half Colonel Solomon's regiment of Missouri Union Volunteers, has advanced from Springfield in a southwesterly direction to Mount Vernon, and even to Neosho. This movement will help protect the lead mines, which strategic point must always be borne by our readers. About four hundred rebels, who were assembled at Oliver's Prairie, fled on hearing of Sigel's approach. Oliver's Prairie is situated between Neosho and McDonald.

Next came a listing of all the various units scattered throughout the region (see the table left.) The supposed location of rebel forces was also noted.

TROOPS IN MISSOURI AND NEIGHBORHOOD.

CHIEF OFFICERS.

Major General Commanding in the West	J. C. Fremont.
Major General Commanding in Missouri	Nath'l Lyon.
Brig. Gen of Missouri Reserve Corps	T. W. Sweeny.
Brigadier General at Cairo	B. M. Prentiss.
Brigadier General Iowa Volunteers	S. R. Curtis.

MISSOURI VOLUNTEERS.

Regiment	Colonel	Location.
First Union Vol.	F. P. Bair, Jr.,	En route for S. W.
Second Union Vol.	H. Boernstein	En route for S. W.
Third Union Vol.	F. Sigel	Mount Vernon, &c.
Fourth Union Vol.	N. Schutner	Cairo.
Fifth Union Vol.	C. E. Salomen	Springfield, &c.
Sixth Union Vol, First battalion.	P. E. Bland	St. Louis.
Sixth Union Vol., Second battalion.	P. E. Bland	Cape Girardeau.
Seventh Union Vol.	J. D. Stevenson	Missouri river.
First U.S. R. Corps	—— Almstedt	St. Louis, &c.
Second U.S R Corps	—— Kallman	St. Louis, &c.
Third U S R Corps	J. McNeil	Rolla.
Fourth U S. R. Corps	B. G. Brown	Springfield.
Fifth U.S R Corps	—— Stifel	Booneville, &c.

IOWA VOLUNTEERS.

First Volunteers.	J. F. Bates	En route for Spfi'd.
Second Volunteers.	Lt. Col. Tuttle com.	H. & St. J. R. R.
Third Volunteers.	—	Keokuk.

ILLINOIS VOLUNTEERS.

Seventh Vol.	J. Cook	Mound City.
Eighth Vol.	R. J. Oglesby	Cairo.
Ninth Vol.	E. A. Paine	Cairo.
Tenth Vol.	J. D. Morgan	Cairo.
Eleventh Vol.	W. H. L. Wallace	Bird's Point.
Twelfth Vol.	J. McArthur	Cairo
Thirteenth Vol.	J. B. Wyman	Caseyville.
Fourteenth Vol.	J. M. Palmer	Hannibal.
Fifteenth Vol.	T. J. Turner	Alton.
Sixteenth Vol.	B. F. Smith	Palmyra&Railroad.
Seventeenth Vol.	L. F. Ross	Alton.
Eighteenth Vol.	M. K. Lawler	Cairo.
Nineteenth Vol.	C. C. Marsh	En route for Alton.
Twentieth Vol.	S. S. Goode	Quincy.
Twenty-first Vol.	M. Dougherty	Caseyville.
Twenty-second Vol.	J. R. Scott	Quincy.
Irish Brigade.	J. A Mulligan	Caseyville.
German Jaegers	—— Hecker	Alton.

This list is independent of six regiments of militia at Chicago and elsewhere, besides a number of artillery and rifle companies (detached) located at Cairo, Chicago, &c.

KANSAS VOLUNTEERS.

First Vol.	J. Montgomery	En route thro' Mo.
Second Vol.	—— Phillips	Do.
Third Vol.	—— Weer	Do.

In addition to these volunteers are several bodies of regular troops under Majors Sturgis, Sully, Captains Prince, Totten and other officers of the United States Army. The last news from the First Kansas volunteer regiment states that they were at Harrisonville, which will be found on the map a short distance south of Kansas City.

New York Herald, July 8, 1861

Along that portion of the border between Missouri and Kansas, and extending between the lead mines and Kansas City, on the Missouri River, the outlets are guarded by regular troops, under Captain Prince, U.S.A., and Kansas volunteers, a portion of which are under Captain Prince, and others under James Montgomery &c. Latterly these bodies have not been heard of, but they will doubtless suddenly turn up in the foremost of the fight. Regular troops and volunteers are located at Fort Leavenworth and neighborhood, while home guards protect such points as Kansas City, Independence, &c. The Missouri River is guarded from Kansas City to its mouth, near Alton, by the Irish brigade of Missouri under Colonel Stevenson.[7] The railroad running from St. Joseph to Hudson is guarded by the Second (Iowa) Volunteers under Lieutenant Colonel Tuttle; while at St. Joseph itself, it is believed there are four companies of regulars under Major Sully. From Hudson to Palmyra and Hannibal the railroad is protected by the Fourteenth and Sixteenth Illinois Volunteers, while at Quincy, the northern terminus of the Palmyra branch, the Twentieth and Twenty-second Illinois are encamped with open communication through Illinois to Chicago &c. At Keokuk, some short distance further north, are encamped the Third Iowa Volunteers. This regiment has received orders to move to the railroad now occupied by the Second regiment, and the latter will go into camp at St. Joseph. Passing down the Mississippi to Alton, we find an encampment of three Illinois regiments, the Fifteenth, Seventeenth, and Hecker's German Jaeger Volunteers. At St. Louis is stationed a battalion of the Sixth Missouri Union Volunteers, Colonel Bland, the First and Second regiments of the Union Reserve Corps of Missouri, with regulars &c. The Thirteenth and Twenty-first regiments of Illinois Volunteers, from Caseyville are expected at this point, and a railroad communication is open with Ohio. At Jefferson Barracks are regulars and companies of volunteers not yet organized. At Cape Girardeau is a battalion of Colonel Bland's command, while at Cairo, a short distance farther south, we have Gen. Prentiss's command of great strength. At Bird's Point are two regiments – the Eleventh and Eighteenth regiments, Illinois Volunteers.

Having given the particulars of the troops on the borders, a few words will be said about the center of the State. Jefferson City is the capital, and here are located detachments of the First and Second Iowa Volunteers, Home Guards, and regulars. The railroad running west to Sedalia and east to St. Louis is guarded by volunteers and Home Guards, each important point being held by a strong force. The bridges crossing the Gasconade and Osage rivers, between Jefferson City and St. Louis, were destroyed by the rebels, but have since been rebuilt. The railroads running from St. Louis to Hudson (northwesterly) and to Rolla (southwesterly) are similarly protected. Booneville, the recently important place – it being the camp of Gen. Lyon – is situated on the Missouri a short distance to the northwest of Jefferson City. A short time since there were stationed at this point a body of regulars under Captain Totten and others, the First and Second regiments of Missouri Union Volunteers, four companies of Colonel Stevenson's Missouri Union Volunteers and four companies of Colonel Stifel's Union reserve corps of Missourians. A portion, if not the whole of this body of troops, estimated at 3,500, is now *en route* for the southwestern portion of the State.

The following telegraphic dispatch from Leavenworth, July 6, will account for the movement:

Governor Jackson's secretary has called a session of the Missouri Legislature, to meet at Sarcoxie, seventy miles southeast of Fort Scott, for the purpose of passing an ordinance of secession.

The rebels in western Missouri were concentrating at that point. This Sarcoxie is situated between Mount Vernon and Neosho, in the vicinity of the lead mines. Fort Scott is on the Kansas border.

Ben McCulloch's proclamation, calling for rebel troops to locate at Fayetteville, brings that place into the arena of Western warfare. Fayetteville is situated at about twenty miles south of Bentonville and about thirty from the Missouri border. A good road unites the two places.

At this point after listing the troops in Missouri, the *Herald's* tutorial continued with two letters from Knox dated July 1 and July 3. The first contains interesting comments on the Pacific Railroad, St. Louis newspapers, parole procedures, and Knox's view of this "Wild, Wild West:"

St. Louis, Mo., July 1, 1861.

In a letter from Syracuse, Mo., bearing the date of June 21, I referred to the arrest of H. B. Franklin, an employee of the Pacific Railroad Company, who has been conspicuous in the bridge burning affairs. In the heading to my letter occurs the phrase, "The Pacific Railroad officials aiding the rebels." Mr. Franklin is, as far as I know, is the only one connected with the line who has willingly afforded any facilities to the rebels at Jefferson City or elsewhere. Mr. Taylor, the President, and Mr. McKissock, the Superintendent, are as staunch Union men as are to be found in Missouri, and with the exception of Mr. Franklin I do not know a person in their employ who advocated the cause of Gov. Jackson and his great father, Jeff. Davis. I make this statement as it is unjust to go abroad that the Pacific Railroad officials favor the rebels. The rebels have caused a destruction or damage to the company's property to upwards of $100,000, and in several instances the injury has been purely wanton. This fact alone would cause the corporation to look with no friendly eye upon the movements of the rebels, and would not tend to prepossess Gov. Jackson in their favor.

We hear as yet of no fighting in the Southwest. It is reported, though not on satisfactory authority, that Col. Sigel, with his own regiment and part of Col. Solomon's regiment, had occupied Springfield without opposition, getting beyond the rebels who were between Warsaw and that place. Should this be true, as we all devoutly pray, there is some hope of catching Jackson, or at any rate of capturing his command, hemmed in as it is by United States troops on every side. There is no fear that Jackson's forces will go towards the Kansas border, as they have a mortal horror of Montgomery, and evince a most unequivocal desire to keep out of his reach. "A bee line for Arkansas" is their only hope.

There is much dissatisfaction among the Unionists of St. Louis on account of the liberation on parole of the prisoners taken with arms in their hands or are known as violent rebels. They argue that so many Union men in the rural districts have been maltreated and driven out by the traitors that leniency to the latter seems hardly justifiable. Their grounds of complaint are very good, and are but the echo of many murmurs of discontent that come to us from the East. I have been present on several occasions when prisoners have been released, and am of the opinion that in nine cases out of ten, these liberated will heed the injunction to "Go and sin no more." In a few instances I judge that a longer detention and a more severe punishment than keeping the traitors under guard for a few hours would have been, to say the least, a healthy precaution. Those who wear a look of honesty of purpose, and appear to have entered into the schemes of Governor Jackson from a sense of right, give their parole with much reluctance and after mature deliberation, while the hardened and apparently unconscionable take the oath with as much alacrity and as little hesitation as they would accept an invitation to drink.

Missouri in the Spotlight

The following is a copy of the parole usually given. It is in all cases sworn to and subscribed to before a notary public, and is as binding as any legal document:

We, whose names are hereunder annexed, fully and unreservedly promise and swear, that we will bear true allegiance to the United States of America in word and deed, in the present political troubles and during our natural lives; and if drafted into the militia of the United States by the proper authorities, we will obey the call immediately and with all our ability. And we hereby give our parole of sacred honor not to serve the faction known as the Southern confederacy during the present rebellion.

The telegraph has reported to you the verdict in the Seventh street shooting affair. The testimony before the jury as to where the firing commenced was very conflicting, but the general belief is that the first shot was from the engine house towards the troops, and the weight of the evidence seems to support this belief.

The melancholy feature of this, as in the Fifth street tragedy, is that innocent persons have been shot down, while the really guilty escaped. It seems to be the rule rather than the exception that bullets are accustomed to hit the wrong man. During a course of travels through Utah, New Mexico, Pike's Peak, and other new countries, I have had the occasion to notice numerous pistol affrays, and that the result of my observation is that the scoundrel generally escapes harm, although often shot at, while your eminently moral and respectable citizen gets a stray bullet of cold lead through his head or heart while innocently passing along the street, perhaps on his way to church or bound on some charitable errand. Of late years I have come to have more fears of a miscellaneous shot than one aimed at me individually.

Government today advertises for a large number of

> mules and horses for the use of the army in the present campaign in Missouri, and wishes them delivered by a week from tomorrow. Four hundred and fifty draught mules, one hundred forty-five draught horses for use of artillery, and one hundred twenty-five saddle horses (for the cavalry) are to be purchased. We have at present but little cavalry in the service in this State – less than one hundred mounted soldiers in the entire force. In Missouri, wild and unsettled as a large portion of it is, mounted men are of far more importance than in the more densely populated East. Had we been provided with three hundred cavalry on the day of the Booneville battle, the capture of Governor Jackson would have been certain.

In 1860, in St. Louis there were twenty-eight different newspapers published as well as nine magazines.[8] Nine of the newspapers were published in German. Newspaper publishing in St. Louis was often an ephemeral task with rapid appearance and disappearance occurring. There were two major German language publications, *Anzeiger des Westens* and the *Westliche Post*.

The major English language papers could easily lead to confusion: the *Missouri Democrat* was Republican in politics, while the *Missouri Republican* espoused the Democratic Party. Both papers reprinted pieces from the German language papers sometimes labeled "The Sense of the German Press."

> The *Republican* appears to be in trouble because some of the Eastern papers will persist in calling it a rebel sheet. It claims to be "sound on the goose" for the Union.[9] Generally speaking, I believe that men and newspapers that are really for the Union have no trouble in making their friends know it. It is a well-known fact that the *Republican* has never opposed secession in Missouri or anywhere else, except on the ground of inexpediency at the present time. Its city reporter has been found to be in correspondence with Gen. Sterling Price, informing him of all that transpired in St. Louis of any

interest to the rebels; and in a letter from a prominent rebel of St. Louis to Governor Jackson, found among the captured documents at Booneville, the writer says of the editor in chief of the *Republican*, "Paschall is with us, but he has not any backbone."[10] The lack of the vertebral column is the only thing that prevents the *Republican* ranking out and out as a rebel sheet.

The railroads running from St. Louis are doing a very light business, their freight transportation being almost entirely cut off and their passenger receipts being much curtailed. The Ohio and Mississippi Railroad has suffered less than the others.

Knox's second letter of July 3 appeared directly after his first of July 1 in the July 8 *Herald*, and included praise for General Lyon and comments on training at the St. Louis Arsenal grounds and battle prospects in Southwest Missouri.

St. Louis, Mo., July 3, 1861.
The principal cause of rejoicing in this city, just at the present, is the promotion of General Lyon to a Major Generalship.[11] All Union men in St. Louis are in high spirits at the recognition at the signal service General Lyon has rendered to their cause, and thus assured they will continue the contest with renewed vigor. They all feel that they owe the safe footing of Unionism in Missouri to the prompt action of General Lyon and Colonel Blair, and are ready and anxious to accord "honor to whom honor is due."[12] Had it not been for the Price and Harney treaty, those two gentlemen would long ere this have had Missouri quite throughout and unreservedly on the side of freedom.

The theatre of war in this State will be, for the immediate future, in the southwestern section. I learn today that active measures were in progress there to resist the efforts of General Lyon. One James McBride,[13] a judge of the Circuit Court of that part of Missouri, and a resident of Houston, Texas County, has raised a force of five hundred rebels in the region over which he holds sway. Captain Lowe, of Doniphan, Ripley county, has a gathering of six hundred men at that point.[14] These two bodies are to march to Pocahontas, Arkansas, landing on the Black river, and about thirty miles from Doniphan, where they will receive arms from their Southern brethren. They expect to be joined at Pocahontas by a force from Memphis or some part of Tennessee, to aid them in subduing the Union troops. The best way to put a stop to their proceedings is to send a regiment down there and capture them before they are quite ready to act; nip the affair in the bud, *à la* Camp Jackson. The principal hope now of the rebels of Missouri for foreign aid is from Tennessee into the southeast corner of the State.

I visited the Arsenal this afternoon, and found matters there less stirring than before the departure of the various expeditions to the interior. Colonel Harding commands in General Lyon's absence, and manages everything in a masterly manner.[15] The Arsenal landing has not a single boat, where three weeks since it had half a dozen. All the members of the Arsenal fleet with the exception of the *J. C. Swon* are up the Missouri river. The latter boat has returned to her first affections, orders having been received today for her rendition to her owners. It is quite likely that they will not again make use of their boat to transport property stolen from one arsenal to a point where it may be used for the capture of another. They will probably consider their late success a salutary lesson, and make a firm determination to "go and sin no more."

On the parade ground a battery of light artillery was drilling for active service – the men "going through the motions" with admirable celerity. The usual "awkward squads" were undergoing the cruelties of the drill sergeants, and a battalion of riflemen was having its daily parade. The two regiments of Illinois troops at Caseyville, nine miles east of here, have orders to break camp tonight and remove to the Arsenal. Their coming will renew the bustle and activity a month since. Colonel Harding is making preparations to dispatch a force to the southeast to take care of the rebels in that locality. He told me that the last authentic information from Colonel Sigel was up to the 27th. On that day Col. Sigel, with his own regiment and the First battalion from Col. Solomon's had left Springfield for Mount Vernon, twenty miles west of that point, with a view of proceeding to Granby and taking possession of the lead mines. A force from Governor Jackson's party had preceded them with the same laudable object in view. He left at Springfield Colonel Solomon, with his Second battalion to guard the place. General Sweeney and Colonel Gratz Brown were within forty miles of Springfield, and have, ere this, joined Sigel's command. Their whole force is upwards of 3,500 men, a battery of six twelve- and six-pound brass pieces. By a telegraphic dispatch from Booneville I learn that General Lyon started from that point this morning, at nine o'clock, *en route* for Springfield.

Hindrances in preparation have delayed his departure till the present time. It is quite likely that Gen. Lyon will not accompany the expedition in person, but give the command to Colonel Andrews or one other of the officers now with him. General Lyon's late promotion to the command of the Western Department would seem to require his presence here or at a similar central point. It will be unfortunate for the expedition to take him from its personal command. Even if an officer just as capable and energetic should be put in highest authority, the prestige of General Lyon's name would be lost, and that prestige weighs heavily against the Missourians. The untaught natives fear him in much the same manner as his Satanic majesty is said to fear holy water.

The force under General Lyon is now not far from 3,500

men. These joined with General Sweeney's command will make an army of 7,000 good fighters – thought to be sufficient to overpower whatever can be raised by Governor Jackson in Missouri and Arkansas.

Ben. McCulloch, the ubiquitous Benjamin, is still in the sacred limits of Arkansas with a considerable force. At latest accounts, he has not crossed the line.

A letter from Cairo and two notes from the Leavenworth *Conservative* about General Rains (Missouri State Guard) and the flight of Governor Jackson continue the tutorial. On the same page is a June 29 piece from the St. Louis *Missouri Republican* about the situation in Springfield. Also, on the same and next page are three columns of biography of twelve Union Generals, Butler, Banks, McClelland, Frémont, Patterson, Cadwallader, Harney, Mansfield, McDowell, Lyon, Keim, and Williams. The *Herald* called them, "the right men in the right places," an appellation that would later be called into question for most of them.

Thus ends the *Herald's* Missouri tutorial. Many questions of future plans in Missouri seemed to be open and fluid. The Union forces in southwest Missouri were out of touch because of the slow communications. The telegraph line running along the "Wire Road" through to Springfield and beyond to Fort Smith, Arkansas, was often cut by marauding bands of southern sympathizers.

With this prospect, St. Louis and the nation anxiously awaited further news. One bit of big news for Missouri came to St. Louis from the East. On July 3, in General Orders No. 30, the Army created the Western Department to include "The State of Illinois and the States and Territories west of the Mississippi River and on this side of the Rocky Mountains, including New Mexico." This new department was placed under the command of Major General John C. Frémont, well-known in St. Louis as the "Pathfinder."[16] After considerable dalliance, Frémont arrived in St. Louis with his wife, Jessie Benton Frémont, and assumed command on June 25.[17]

Chapter 5

Waiting for News

In early July, news from the "front," wherever that might be, was sparse for St. Louisans. Rumors and questions abounded. Where was General Lyon? What was General Sweeny doing? Where was Colonel Sigel? On top of all this, the "Glorious Fourth" was upon them, and St. Louisans were worried about incidents in the city. They were not worried about major attacks by Governor Jackson's pro-session State Guard, as they seemed to be fleeing, from all reports, towards far southwest Missouri or into the Arkansas Ozarks. Rather, the concern was that a hot-headed rebel might start some trouble that could escalate into real problems, something like the attacks that occurred on Union units leaving the Arsenal in previous weeks. On July 5, Knox, in a long letter, described some of the interesting July 4 events and attitudes in St. Louis. In general, the city was quiet with only a few, generally drunken, provocations.[1]

St. Louis, Mo. July 5, 1861.
The Fourth in this city passed off very quietly. The national holiday was probably less observed here than any other loyal city in the Union. The stillness arose partly from the fact that rebels in some quarters had threatened a revolt, and the attention of Union men was occupied with measures to prevent being overpowered in the event of a disturbance. Patriotism does not manifest itself in St. Louis by a great noise and an ignition of a huge lot of fireworks, but is rather of the undemonstrative sort – the true patriots just now holding to the belief that "still waters run deep." In the West the free and easy element of mental organization that distinguishes

us from the eminently respectable East, and permits every man to do as he pleases without consulting his neighbor, in a great measure precludes the possibility of a successful celebration arranged by committee and conducted according to a fixed programme. Yesterday's festivities were enjoyed on the most approved principles of squatter sovereignty; every man arranged his celebration in his own way, and carried out his own plans. At the groves and beer gardens, crowds gathered to imbibe lager and sherry cobblers, and indulge in occasional fights, according to the rules of noble and manly art. A few inebriated individuals shouted in honor of Jeff Davis, but were speedily silenced by their sympathizing but sober friends, who doubted the propriety of such cheering.

The printer who furnished the bills of fare for the Everett House remembered the day by printing the Stars and Stripes in color at the head of the dinner table. Three secession boarders couldn't stand this insult to their dignity, and left the table with its viands untouched. One of them threatened to quit the house, and was requested by the gentlemanly clerk to pay his board, for which he was considerably in arrears after which his absence would afford much gratification to the proprietors of the establishment. The proprietor attempted to pacify other indignant ones by promising to take the printing from that printer and give it to the *Republican* or some other sound secessionist concern, but was at once confronted by a score or more of Union boarders who threatened to "secede" if he fulfilled his promise. It is quite probable that the enraged Southerners will either bottle their indignation or pick some more congenial house. Some two hundred well drilled but unarmed rebels appeared in one of the outer streets at dusk last evening, marching in military order. They made no trouble or noise beyond a few subdued cheers for the South, and were evidently afraid to let themselves out. After parading a short time they dispersed unmolested.

Knox continued with comments on the rebels.² News from the Southwest came next. Knox gave some sketchy reports of Sweeny's command, its location and its prospects and the location Kansas troops. Governor Jackson's location and that of General Sterling Price were subjects of speculation.³

Business matters came next. Missouri bonds were not to be paid – not surprising considering the shambles the State government was in and counterfeit notes were also appearing, although Knox does not say whether they were issues of the State or of local banks. These comments are in the notes.⁴

Knox's next letter to the *Herald*, printed in the same issue as his July 5 letter,⁵ covered mainly political matters and some troop movements and creation of the Union Army's Western Department and of Major General John C. Frémont's appointment to command.⁶ He also noted the recalling of the State Convention to deal with Missouri's strange situation – no government, or two governments depending on one's point of view. Knox report explained the situation by first quoting the call to the convention:

> St. Louis, Mo., July 6, 1861.
>
> We, the undersigned, being a majority of the Committee of the Convention of the State of Missouri, charged with the duty of convening the said Convention, at such time prior to the third Monday of December, 1861, and at such place they think the public exigencies require, do hereby notify the said convention to assemble and meet at Jefferson City, in the State of Missouri, on the 22nd day of July in the year of our Lord 1861.
>
> R. Wilson,
> J. T. Tindall,
> J. W. McClurg,
> Jas. R. Mccormack,
> Thomas T. Gantt,
> Majority of The Committee.⁷

He then explained the purpose of the re-called convention, the establishment of a State Government in the absence of Claiborne Jackson's functionaries.⁸ J. W. Tucker, the editor and publisher of the *Missouri State Journal*, a St. Louis secessionist newspaper had been arrested.⁹

> The trial of J. W. Tucker for treason will probably be concluded next week. Mr. Tucker is the editor of the *State Journal*, as rank a rebel sheet as the Charleston *Mercury* or the Richmond *Whig*, and his trial has reference both to his curse in his paper, and several private acts. Through his attorney, the accused attempts to throw off the responsibility of several articles on the ground that they were not of his production. In the earlier part of last week an article appeared in the *Journal* indirectly instigating a riot on the Fourth, and recommending a mode of celebration on the part of the rebels quite contrary to the usual manner of commemorating the holiday. On being called to account, Mr. Tucker denies the paternity of the paragraphs and a knowledge of the name of the author, and says he cannot be held responsible for the sentiment of his communications. This is a new dodge, and one that only a rebel editor could be capable of inventing. The fertility of tis quill-driver's brain rivals that of the celebrated cranium of Governor Pickens.¹⁰
> The special session of the United States Circuit Court commences tomorrow – Judge Catron presiding.¹¹ The session promises to be one of much interest.

Knox then commented on the military situation and the arrival and the disposition of the arriving troops. Some may have looked at the printing of this information as aiding the secessionists, but, with so many secessionists in St. Louis, the information had already been sent to the rebels. The appointment of General Frémont to Departmental command was viewed favorably.¹²

July 3 was the date chosen for General Lyon to depart with his troops from Boonville and to advance upon the southwest part of the state. He planned to meet General Sweeny and Colonel Sigel in Springfield. Lyon's command had been augmented with the First Iowa Infantry, a ninety-day unit, under the command of Colonel John F. Bates. Unfortunately, Thomas

Knox was not with Lyon on his march to Springfield; he had returned to St. Louis and was chronicling events there. However, a new reporter had arrived with the First Iowa, Franc Wilkie. Wilkie was acting as a reporter for the Dubuque *Herald* and later the *New York Times*.[13] Wilkie's description of the departure in the *Times* written on July 5 was picked up and used in *Harper's Weekly* with the accompanying illustration.

"Departure of General Lyon and His Command from Boonville, Missouri, for the Arkansas Border," Sketched by O. C. Richardson. (*Harper's Weekly*, July 27, 1861).

The time, since the battle at this point, has been spent in preparations for a march to the southwestern portion of the State. Not less than three thousand men will leave from here, and as thirty-seven days' rations are to be taken along, it can easily be imagined that the preparations are neither few nor small. About one hundred and fifty wagons are necessary to transport the requisite materiel, each of which will be drawn by from two to ten horses or mules. Then a large number of saddle horses is required to carry the higher officers, scouts, etc., making in all a drove of some five or six hundred draught and saddle animals necessary to the starting of our expedition. All these materials, together with forage, haversacks, canteens, and many other articles, have been procured at this point. General Lyon gave out word that he needed a certain number of horses and wagons. If they came in peaceably, good – if not, he would have to send for them. A committee, composed of three officers and two citizens, was appointed to appraise the value of the horses and wagons as they came in and when purchased were paid for by draft on St. Louis. It was thought best not to hire the conveyances, but to buy them outright – a determination on the part of the Government that met with the entire approbation of owners irrespective of politics.[14]

The start of the move to Springfield was also described by Eugene Ware, a private in the 1st Iowa Infantry:[15]

We marched out of Boonville in the mud, with drums beating and flags floating. Old men and good-looking girls in long cavalcades escorted us far out of town, riding on the side of the road.

In his July 12 letter to the Herald, Knox noted the suppression of the rebel sheet *Missouri State Journal*.

About 400 men belonging to Col. McNeil's regiment, a reserve corps,[16] visited the *State Journal* office early this morning, removing type, paper, &c., &c. They then read an order from Gen. Lyon, prohibiting the further publication of that sheet. The proprietors of the *Journal* will respect the order, and lay the whole matter before General Frémont on his arrival here.[17]

Colonel McNeil publishes a proclamation to the people of Missouri stating that the suppression of the *State Journal* was in consequence of its giving aid and comfort to those in active rebellion against the authority of the United States Government, encouraging the people to take up arms against that authority, to commit acts of violence and oppression against loyal citizens, and by the fabrication of false reports respecting the United States troops, inciting disaffected citizens to the commission of overt acts of treasons with a view of entirely subverting the federal authority in the State.[18]

The *Journal's* editor, Joseph W. Tucker, had been arrested and posted a $10,000 bond. Tucker apparently decided not to "lay the whole matter before General Frémont," but jumped his $10,000 bond and joined Governor Jackson and General Price.[19]

On July 12, Knox also reported:

> A good deal of excitement has existed in this city today, in consequence of the suppression of the *Journal*, but no disturbance has yet taken place. Two companies, a reserve corps, are stationed at the Custom House tonight, and some 2500 troops are under arms in different parts of the city to preserve the peace.[20]

In his July 7 letter to the *Herald*, a short one, Knox reported on some troop movements.[21] "The Twentieth Illinois regiment, Colonel March, arrived on Saturday and went into quarters at the Arsenal whence they will probably proceed south by the Iron Mountain Railroad."[22] He also noted the departure of the 13th Illinois Regiment for Rolla and that Lyon was thirty-one miles south of Booneville on July 4.[23] Finally, in his short note, he reported a scouting expedition and "a little skirmish" near Valle Forge and the death of one and capture of three secessionists.[24]

Knox's letter of July 10 contained the important news about the battle at Carthage in the southwest corner of the state.[25]

> St. Louis, Mo., July 10, 1861.
> Last evening there was considerable excitement in this city, owing to the reception of the intelligence that the rebel forces had met Colonel Sigel and defeated him, cutting his command to pieces and taking him prisoner. The rebel crowd at the Planter's House exulted over this information, swallowing large quantities of whiskey and similar bibulants, in the exuberance of their joy. Late in the night a messenger from General Sweeney's command, who left Springfield on the 7th, arrived at the Arsenal bringing tidings of a different sort. I

visited the Arsenal this forenoon and learned the following particulars:

On Gen. Sweeney's arrival at Springfield, he at once sent to Cols. Saloman and Siegel, ordering then to move on towards Carthage from their camp at Neosho, and occupy that town. They obeyed the order, and on arriving at Carthage ascertained from their scouts that Gov. Jackson and Gen. Price had formed a junction with Gen. Raines at a point on the Lamar road, eight miles north of Carthage. The precise number of the rebel troops was not known, but is was supposed to be not far from five thousand men. Without waiting for orders from Gen. Sweeney, Cols. Siegel and Saloman, with a force of 2,500 men, left Carthage about one AM on the 5th, marching towards the rebel camp, and coming in sight of the enemy's lines at six AM of that day. With no delay they commenced the attack, throwing in shot and shell from their battery, and following up this movement with their Minié rifles. The rebels replied with artillery and small arms – the latter in as great variety as at the battle of Booneville, and the former not very well served. There appeared to be no skillful gunners among them and the firing from the rebel battery of six-pounders was neither precise nor rapid, doing but little damage. The nature of the ground where the action commenced is not given, but the locality is said to be in a range of wooded hills, interspersed with stretches of prairies. Along the streams the slope from the prairie to the valleys is quite gentle and the water courses are generally through a meadow or "bottom" land, and it was probably one of these streams that the rebels were encamped.

After the formation of the line of battle the firing was general from both sides from cannon and small arms, neither party giving evidence of much haste or desperation in pushing the contest. It thus continued for some two hours, when the rebels commenced a retreat, still keeping up the fight.

"The Battle of Carthage, Missouri. From a Sketch Made on the Spot."
(*Harper's Weekly*, August 3, 1861).

At this point, Knox's report strayed from what was later known. What actually happened? Sigel spotted rebel cavalry beginning to flank to the east and west of his position. Being outnumbered, he conducted a masterful fighting retreat, extricating his outnumbered troops from potential disaster. He retreated through Carthage and ultimately to safety at Mount Vernon.

Governor Jackson's forces continued into farther southwest Missouri. The rest of Knox's column should not be taken as fact. Knox's near contemporaries, Peckham (Union) and Snead (Confederate), got the story straight.[26] Knox's story now continues with these caveats.

Knox tells of Governor Jackson's troops moving to the southeast and reaching towards Cassville hoping to reach the Arkansas border with Sigel doggedly pursuing them and "playing upon them with cannon and continually harassing them in the rear." A body of "rebel recruits had left Forsyth with intention of joining Governor Jackson at Cassville" And General Sweeny was supposed to have "sent out two hundred fifty mounted men to check their advance and prevent their junction with the main body of the rebel army." These "events" did not occur.

Knox continued with more speculation:

> If the rebel forces make a halt north of McDonald,[27] and engage with General Sweeny in their front, and Saloman and Siegel on their rear, we shall have to record the bloodiest fight in the history of Missouri. Too great confidence should not be placed in General Sweeny's checking their southward march, not from any lack of ability of that commander, or want of bravery in his men, but simply from the small numerical strength of his command and the desperate situation of the rebels.

Knox's report of a separate battle "on the prairie near Mount Vernon, on the morning of the 7th between a detachment of five hundred men under Lieutenant Colonel Wolff and fifteen hundred rebel troops" was entirely false, since Wolff was at Carthage with Sigel. Another problem report was that of the capture of Colonel Coffee, "one of the most active and violent rebels of the Southwest." It did not happen. Knox qualified his statements with, "The report in regard to this affair is from good, though not perfectly reliable sources. I give it just as I heard it." Knox's report is an example of reporting rumors and incomplete information gathered at a distance from the action.

He reported on the advance of General Lyon, "at Leesville, Clinton county, about ten miles west of Warsaw" and of Major Sturgis (Clinton, Henry County) and their expected junction at Chalk Level (southwest of Lowry City, St. Clair County). Finally, he mentioned that "The *Democrat* has just issued an extra containing a letter from Dr. Franklin, Surgeon to the Fifth (Saloman's) regiment dated the 6th instant, and containing substantially the same information in regard to the battle …as is contained in this letter. The rebels are not as jubilant as they were last evening."

Knox also commented on Judge John Catron hearing cases for the United States Circuit Court:

> Today the special session of the United States Circuit Court commenced, Judge Catron presiding. There was considerable anxiety among the politicians to know what would be Judge

Catron's charge to the Grand Jury. The Judge is a Tennessean, but does not display any manifest leaning towards the South as it stands at present, though he has heretofore been considered sound on the side of slavery.[28]...His charge to the Grand Jury was one of marked ability, and showed no favor to any one. In his view, treason consists not only in taking up arms against the government, but in every act whatever that can interfere with its working or furnish aid or sympathy to its enemies. Some of the guilty ones among the rebels turned slightly pale on hearing this, especially several who were prominent in the Camp Jackson movement.[29]

On July 4, General Sweeny had issued a proclamation in Springfield castigating the actions of Governor Jackson, "he has already committed treason by levying war against the United States." Sweeny's troops were there by "proper authority" and were pledged to protect "loyal citizens" and their property "including slaves." He called on loyal citizens to help him "prevent the shedding of blood and to restore peace and quiet to this portion of the State," and to "take an oath of loyalty." He warned that the government would "deal leniently, yet firmly, with all its citizens who have been misled."[30]

Beyond the battle at Carthage on July 5, there was little serious action for Thomas Knox to report to his editors. Carthage had been reported and re-reported, the official reports of Sigel and others printed, but there was precious little that could be considered "exciting" to write about. Knox's July 15 letter reflected that situation. He added some further details about the previously reported suppression of the *State Journal*:

> The only incident of interest that has lately happened here is the suppression of the *State Journal*, a rabid rebel organ, which used to abound in the most outrageous lies concerning the position of the Union troops and of the wonderful things Ben McCulloch proposes to do to clean out the Union men of the State. It excited considerable feeling among the rebels, and they threatened the *Democrat* and *Anzeiger*[31] offices with

demolition that very night, to prevent this – the outbreak of a mob – about two hundred men were stationed at the Custom House,[32] within two and a half squares of both offices named, until Saturday morning. On Saturday night, fifty of the Home Guard were stationed in the *Democrat* building to guard the premises. This affair has blown over, however, and all is quiet again.[33]

There were a few troop movements, but Knox commented:

At the Arsenal all hands have been busy fitting out regiments and companies leaving for the interior with extra stores and ammunition. An immense quantity of cartridges for Minié muskets have been sent to the troops already in the field. Evidence accumulates from several sources that the present uprising of the rebels in several sections of the State is the result of concerted action planed either in Richmond or Tennessee."[34]

Two new rebel players now enter Knox's reportage. The first of these is Missouri's elected Lieutenant Governor, Thomas Caute Reynolds.

There are many fugitive Missourians in the Confederacy at this tune, including Lieutenant Governor Reynolds, who recently issued an address inviting his former constituents to assist Jeff. Davis by weakening the Union army in the northwest. [35]

Reynolds had left Jefferson City in May for Richmond, but not daring to go through St. Louis, he went via Springfield, Fort Smith, and Little Rock, Arkansas, to Memphis.[36] By the end of May, he had been in conference with Jefferson Davis. The other new player was Colonel John S. Bowen.[37] About him, Knox wrote:

Colonel John S. Bowen, formerly a Colonel in the Missouri militia, and commander of the Southwest expedition which went in search of Montgomery's Jayhawkers last November.[38]

> Bowen is brave, but unscrupulous, and has given evidence of it by publicly recanting his intention to obey the parole given after the capture at Camp Jackson. Bowen now commands a regiment at Yellville, Arkansas, near the Missouri line, and has a flag inscribed, "Remember Camp Jackson," borne by fugitive Missourians. Bowen has been in correspondence with Governor Jackson, and it is no betrayal of a government treatment to state that some of his letters to sympathizing friends in St. Louis have been intercepted. They develop a plot for the retaking of Jefferson City at an early day, and a general uprising throughout the State.[39]

Knox continued to report business matters in Missouri to his Eastern readers.[40] Finally, he concluded with a condemnation of rebel treatment of the telegraph lines, a major communications source for a journalist:

> One of the meanest acts which has characterized the conduct of the rebels in this State is the continual cutting of the telegraph lines along the Missouri river. After the affair at Booneville, the telegraph company repaired the line at a heavy expense, and, to avoid one particularly bad place named Jimtown, about half the way between Jefferson City and Rocheport, built some ten miles of line around it. The wires were unmolested for nearly two weeks; but within a few days the old spirit of vandalism has cropped out again, and the wires have not only been cut, but large pieces removed, poles burned down, and other means resorted to for the purpose of making the destruction as complete as possible.[41]

Major General Frémont's progression to St. Louis was a slow one. The *New York Herald* reported on some of his movements after his appointment was announced in Washington on July 3: New York to Baltimore (July 6), New York to Washington (July 9), "probably leave" Washington (July 12), arrived at the Astor House, New York (July 13) "and will remain in this city until the arrival of the steamship *North Star*, now about due from California. Mrs. John C. Frémont is a passenger on board the

North Star, and her husband will await her arrival in this city before proceeding to Illinois."[42] It was not until July 25 that General Frémont and his wife Jessie Benton Frémont arrived in St. Louis.[43] The Frémonts took up residence in the Brandt Mansion, which they rented as residence and army headquarters at the rate of $6000 per year.

Knox was getting restless. It was time to move on from St. Louis. Springfield and its pending military action beckoned.

"Frémont's Head-Quarters at St. Louis, Missouri."
Sketched by Alexander Simplot.
(*Harper's Weekly*, August 31, 1861).

Chapter 6

Seeking Action – Forsyth

Finally, Knox decided it was time to move again. General Sweeny's actions around Springfield and General Lyon's approach to Springfield drew him away from St. Louis to the hive of activity in southwest Missouri. On July 11, he boarded the train of the Southwest Branch of the Pacific Railroad bound for Rolla, the end of the rail line and a growing military base.[1] His first letter from Rolla was strictly about the soldiers and the progress of the war.[2]

> Rolla, Mo., July 12, 1861.
>
> Three hundred Union men, who were run out of Arkansas on account of their supposed hostility to the Southern confederacy, arrived here yesterday. They bring information that seven thousand men are encamped at Pocahontas, Arkansas, preparatory to marching upon Southeast Missouri. They intend to form a junction with Captain McBride,[3] who is in Texas County with 1,500 men.
>
> These refugees say there is no discipline in the camp at Pocahontas; that the rebels are short of provisions and ammunition, and are poorly armed and badly equipped. Fights in the camp are of almost daily occurrence. When their visits may be expected, I do not know, but I think you can look out for something from Southeast Missouri before long.
>
> Today, Colonel Wyman,[4] the officer in command at this point, sent out a detachment to capture some rebels who were hastening south to join McBride. After a march of twenty miles, they secured their prizes and returned in high glee.

They captured six men, thirty horses with saddles, twenty-one guns and two loads of provisions. Several men fled to the forest, and were not taken. The captured men acknowledge the corn, and state they were on their way to join McBride and fight for the South. They have been sent to St. Louis.

Colonel Wyman's Thirteenth Illinois regiment, now stationed at this point, is one of the finest in service. The men are from the fields and workshops of the Prairie State, and in stature can be beaten by few if any regiments in the Union. Full of fight, they are at the same time well behaved and are under admirable discipline. The morale is excellent. One half the regiment are Sons of Temperance,[5] and three hundred of the one thousand are members of the church. Such men will come to the mark when on the battlefield, and will show the Southern gentry the play of five to one.

While Knox did not write of his rail journey for the *New York Herald*, he did colorfully describe the train line and its 1861 passengers in his book:[6]

On the morning of the 11th of July, I left St. Louis, to join General Lyon in the Southwest. It was a day's ride by rail to Rolla, the terminus of the Southwest Branch of the Pacific road. I well recollect the strange and motley group that filled the cars on that journey. There were a few officers and soldiers *en route* to join their comrades in the field. Nearly all of them were fresh from civil life.

They wore their uniforms uneasily, as a farmer's boy wears his Sunday suit. Those who carried sabres experienced much inconvenience when walking on account of the propensity of those weapons to get between their legs. In citizen's dress, at my side, sat an officer of the old army, who looked upon these newly-made warriors with much contempt, mingled with an admiration of their earnestness. After an outburst of mild invective, he pronounced a well-merited tribute to their patriotism.

"After all," said he, "they are as good as the material the Rebels have for their army":

> In some respects, they are better. The Northern blood is cold; the Southern is full of life and passion. In the first onset, our enemies will prove more impetuous than we, and will often overpower us. In the beginning of the struggle, they will prove our superiors, and may be able to boast of the first victories. But their physical energy will soon be exhausted, while ours will steadily increase.
>
> Patience, coolness, and determination will be sure to bring us the triumph in the end. These raw recruits, that are at present worthless before trained soldiers, distrusting themselves as we distrust them, will yet become veterans, worthy to rank with the best soldiers of the Old World.

The civilian passengers on a railway in Missouri are essentially different from the same class in the East. There are very few women, and the most of these are not as carefully dressed as their Oriental sisters. Their features lack the fineness that one observes in New York and New England. The "hog and hominy," the general diet of the Southwest, is plainly perceptible in the physique of the women. The male travelers, who are not indigenous to the soil, are more roughly clothed and more careless in manner than the same order of passengers between New York and Boston. Of those who enter and leave at way-stations, the men are clad in that yellow, homespun material known as "butternut." The casual observer inclines to the opinion that there are no good bathing-places where these men reside. They are inquisitive, ignorant, unkempt, but generally civil. The women are the reverse of attractive, and are usually uncivil and ignorant. The majority are addicted to smoking and generally make use of a cob-pipe. Unless objection is made by some passenger, the conductors ordinarily allow the women to indulge in this pastime.

> The region I traversed by the railway is sparsely settled, the ground being generally unfavorable to agriculture. For some time after this portion of the route was opened the natives refused to give it patronage, many of them declaring that the old mode of travel, by horseback, was the best of all. During the first week after opening the Southwest Branch, the company ran a daily freight train each way. All the freight offered in that time was a bear and a keg of honey. Both were placed in the same car. The bear ate the honey, and the company was compelled to pay for the damage.
>
> I have heard a story concerning the origin of the name of Rolla, which is interesting, though I cannot vouch for its truth. In selecting the name for the county seat of Phelps County, a North Carolinian residing there, suggested that it should do honor to the capital of his native State. The person who reduced the request to writing, used the best orthography that occurred to him, so that what should have been "Raleigh" became "Rolla." The request thus written was sent to the Legislature and the name of the town became fixed. The inhabitants generally pronounce it as if the intended spelling had been adopted.

Since at that time the railroad ended at Rolla, Knox next set out by stage to get to Springfield. In his first report to the *Herald*, dated July 20 from Springfield, before tackling military matters, he first described his stagecoach trip from Rolla to Springfield.[7]

> The road from Rolla to this place is one of the worst in the country, bad even for Missouri. I have traveled by stage some thousands of miles, over prairie, plains, and among the Rocky Mountains, but never found a ride of one hundred and twenty miles that furnished as many horrors for the same money as did mine between Rolla and Springfield. The road is like a nutmeg grater, but on a gigantic scale, and the accommodations furnished by the company that runs a tri-weekly (try

weakly?) hack for the transportation of the mail and a few deluded passengers, are meagre in the extreme. If any reader of this ever has occasion to pass between those two points, let him travel in any way other than by stage.

When Knox came to the writing of his book, some of the horrors of his travel in 1861 had passed from his memory, and he added more scenic details of Missouri and recounted the trip somewhat differently:[8]

The journey from Rolla to Springfield was accomplished by stage and required two days of travel. For fifty miles the road led over mountains, to the banks of the Gasconade, one of the prettiest rivers I have ever seen. The mountain streams of Southwest Missouri, having their springs in the limestone rock possess a peculiarity unknown in the Eastern States. In a depth of two feet or less, the water is apparently as clear as that of the purest mountain brook in New England. But when the depth reaches or exceeds, three feet, the water assumes a deep-blue tinge, like that of the sky in a clear day. Viewed from an elevation, the picture is one that cannot he speedily forgotten. The blue water makes a marked contrast with surrounding objects, as the streams wind through the forests and fields on their banks. Though meandering through mountains, these rivers have few sharp falls or foaming rapids. Their current is usually gentle, broken here and there into a ripple over a slightly descending shallow, but observing uniformity in all its windings.

My first night from Rolla was passed on the banks of the Gasconade. Another day's ride, extended far into the second night, found me at Springfield. When I reached my room at the hotel, and examined the bed, I found but one sheet where we usually look for two. Expostulations were of no avail. The porter curtly informed me, "People here use only one sheet. Down in St. Louis you folks want two sheets, but in this part of the country we ain't so nice."

I appreciated my fastidiousness when I afterward saw, at a Tennessee hotel, the following notice:

Gentlemen who wish towels in their rooms must deposit fifty cents at the office, as security for their return.

Travel in the Border and Southern States will acquaint a Northerner with strange customs. To find an entire household occupying a single large room is not an infrequent occurrence. The rules of politeness require that, when bedtime has arrived, the men shall go out of doors to contemplate the stars, while the ladies disrobe and retire. The men then return and proceed to bed. Sometimes the ladies amuse themselves by studying the fire while the men find their way to their couches, where they gallantly turn their faces to the wall, and permit the ladies to don their *robes de nuit*.

Notwithstanding the scarcity of accommodations, the traveler seeking a meal or resting-place will rarely meet a refusal. In New York or New England, one can journey many a mile and find a cold denial at every door. In the West and Southwest "the latch-string hangs out," and the stranger is always welcome. Especially is this the case among the poorer classes.

Knox continued in this, his first report from Springfield, with a summary of the units present at Springfield.[9] And he brings up a problem that was to bedevil General Lyon and other Union generals throughout the early months of the war. Ninety-day units, enlisted in the early enthusiasm for the war in April and May, were seeing their terms of enlistment expire and were expecting to return home. Many of these units, but not all, were convinced to reenlist for a three-year term, but that did not solve the manpower problem for General Lyon:

General Lyon's command reached this place on Saturday last, and camped at a point twelve miles from town, on the road to Molville. It comprises the First regiment of Missouri

Volunteers, under Lieutenant Colonel George L. Andrews; Iowa First, Colonel J. F. Bates; Kansas First and Second regiments, Major Sturgis in command of nine companies regulars (infantry), five companies cavalry and ten pieces of artillery. General Sweeny's command had gathered at Springfield several days previous, and comprised Colonel Sigel's brigade, his own regiment and seven companies of Colonel Saloman's, a battalion of three companies from Colonel McNeil's regiment, Major Backoff's battery of eight pieces and one company of regulars. The whole force now here is not far from 8,000 men. Of these, the Iowa regiment, Sigel's, Salomon's and McNeil's regiments, and Major Backoff's artillerymen are three months' men, the rest being enlisted for three years, or the war. Colonel Sigel will probably reorganize at once with a loss of perhaps three hundred of his present force, including those who gave their parole to McCulloch at Carthage. He sent sometime for three companies of three year recruits, to be raised in St. Louis and forwarded to this point. They arrived yesterday, and will be sufficient, with a few recruits raised here, to keep Colonel Sigel's regiment full. Colonel Salomon will lose two companies,[10] and is now filling their place with country recruits. McNeil's men started for St. Louis this morning and will probably be disbanded there.[11] They are a fine body of men and their loss will be much felt. Colonel Brown's regiment[12] left a few days ago, having accomplished nothing in the field. Their commander formerly figured in St. Louis as an editor, and displayed considerable ability in the quill-driving profession; but his course as an officer proves in his case most emphatically that the pen is mightier than the sword. The other officers, with scarce an exception, have displayed much zeal and efficiency in the campaign, and have been admirably seconded by their men. The Iowa regiment is the only one, besides Brown's that we shall completely lose. Its time expires on the 14th of

August, and both officers and men are determined to go home. They think of reorganizing for three years, but are not certain to do so.

Next, Knox brought up the problem of supplies. Expiring enlistments were bad, but the lack of supplies had become an even more serious problem. Knox railed against the bureaucracy and the "red tape" that was stifling Lyon's plans.[13]

[SUPPLIES]

The departure of these troops, and the absence of others to take their place destroy some of the plans formed for the campaign. Far more annoying than this reduction of force is the neglect of the government to put General Lyon on a proper footing to go ahead. The eternal red tape has encircled him, and he finds himself tied up in Springfield and unable to depart at once, as he would wish. His success in Missouri up to the present time has been owing to a great measure to the celerity of his movements, and though he does not say so, I know that he is greatly annoyed by the dilatoriness of his superiors. We are now in a country having little resources for feeding an army, and when we push forward towards Arkansas shall be in a sparsely settled region, where the scant productions are eaten up by Jackson's forces. It was promised that a supply and ammunition train should be here on his arrival with everything to favor an immediate advance. A small train only has reached here, and the larger portion of what is needed has not yet even left Rolla. Supplies to General Sweeny's command were not properly forwarded, and the men were often on half rations, and at one time had nothing to eat for forty hours. At present the Missouri and Kansas regiments are out of sugar and coffee and have been so for a week. This lack of proper subsistence for the men falls upon somebody, and is chargeable upon the Quartermaster in St.

Louis, and through him upon the great soul-less system at Washington.

[FIGHTING MEN]

In addition to this crippling of General Lyon by withholding supplies, I have it on good authority that an order came yesterday for the cavalry and a portion of the regular infantry to be sent at once to Virginia, and for General Sweeny to go to Washington for service in that vicinity. General Sweeny cannot well be spared from Missouri. His experience and sagacity render him of great importance to General Lyon in the present contemplated movements, and he should by all means be retained. To deprive Gen. Lyon of cavalry, situated as he now is, and with his present enemy before him, would be a most ill-advised act. Half of Jackson's men are mounted, but without discipline, and the fugitive Governor himself takes care on all occasions to bestride a good steed. Had Gen. Lyon been provided with three hundred good cavalry at Booneville, Jackson could, doubtless been taken; and if Col. Sigel, at Carthage, had had the same number, he would have given Jackson and Rains a most disastrous defeat, instead of being himself obliged to fall back upon Sarcoxie.

[TERRAIN AND THE REBELS]

We are fighting in a sparsely settled country, with an enemy that can move more rapidly than we, and, with half the men on horseback can lead us on weary marches, and chose his own distance and ground for battle. When we defeat him, he naturally runs, and if we have nothing but infantry it is impossible to pursue. If we can keep our cavalry we will make not only a defeat, but a perfect rout of all the forces of the *ci-devant* Governor of Missouri. Our infantry and regulars should be retained as they can be relied upon in all emergencies, where there is a possibility that volunteers though their bravery is unquestioned might not always stand fire. The order above mentioned will not, I am told be at once acted upon, and in the meantime all pray most earnestly for its countermanding. Its issuing would seem to indicate that the powers that be are jealous of the rapid progress of affairs in Missouri, and wish to make in Virginia the first movement of magnitude. With the Governor of the State refusing any aid to the cause, throwing obstacles in the way, and eventually coming out in open rebellion, the Union men of the State have nearly succeeded in putting it in order, but at the last moment are held back by the heads of the nation. "Let us alone" and afford us a little assistance, such as you lately promised us, oh ye powerful potentates of the Potomac, and we will make an end of the rebellion out here in the far West.

Knox reported men were arriving from Arkansas, hoping to enlist in the Union army, were often frustrated by the new requirement for three-year, rather than their expected ninety-day enlistments. They brought with them reports on the status of McCulloch's army:[14]

Yesterday forty-nine men came from Northern Arkansas to enter the three-months' service in the Union Army. As none can now be accepted for that time they were refused admission for the short term, but twenty of them at once volunteered for three years; the remainder were heads of families who could not so long stay away.[15] They report that Ben McCulloch is at Camp Walker with 5,000 Arkansas troops, well-armed and fairly disciplined.[16] His men are short of provisions, and are very poorly supplied with shoes, the latter article being hitherto a Northern production is generally "scarce" among the Southerners. The redoubtable Benjamin will not march to attack Springfield, but will wait at Camp Walker until General Lyon goes down there. He is receiving additions to his force daily. Governor Jackson with Generals Price and Rains is near Granby, in Newton County, with about 10,000 Missourians.

> They are in a desperate condition, without proper arms, undisciplined, and unprovided with decent subsistence. For days past they have been living on fresh beef without salt, and with neither bread, sugar, coffee, nor even whiskey, the *sine qua non* of a Missourian. Desertions by dozens occur daily, but the accessions to the force are fully equal to the desertions. Governor Jackson is despairing and is said to meditate a disbanding of his whole army. The most important enemy now before us is the Arkansas army under McCulloch, which will no doubt do vigorous fighting.

Knox continued his long letter with some comments on the Battle of Carthage and the performances of Colonel Sigel and Governor Jackson. Details on the casualties at Carthage remained hazy, while Sigel was lionized and Jackson disparaged. This portion of his letter is to be found in the notes.[17]

Finally, Knox took care of some personnel matters by announcing promotions and arrivals. Many of those named went on to receive general officer status.[18]

> Among the promotions lately are Major Horace A. Conant, formerly of the First Missouri regiment, to the post of Quartermaster-in-Chief of General Lyon's division. Acting Adjutant I. F. Shepard,[19] of General Sweeney's command has been made Lieutenant Colonel in General Lyon's staff. Captain Stanley, formerly in command of Fort Smith, is now with this division, commanding the cavalry.[20]

Springfield was busy, but probably a bit boring for the action-oriented Knox and his fellow Bohemians. When news came of a rebel force assembling in Forsyth, south of Springfield on the White River, Knox, Lucien Barnes of the Missouri *Democrat*, and Franc Wilkie of the Dubuque *Herald* joined the expedition.[21]

> On Saturday morning last [July 20] Brigadier General Sweeny, commanding in Southwestern Missouri, received orders

from Major General Lyon to proceed with a proper force to Forsythe, a small town on the White river, and within twelve miles of the Arkansas line.[22] It had been ascertained that a rebel force of from eight hundred to one thousand men had gathered at that point and were daily expecting reinforcements from Arkansas and Tennessee, Forsythe being at the head of navigation of White river, and accessible by steamboat from the Mississippi at the present stage of water.[23] General Sweeny, on receiving orders, at once made selection of Companies C and D of First cavalry, under the command of Captain D. S. Stanley; one section of Captain Totten's battery, under Lieutenant Sokalski;[24] one company of Kansas mounted men, Captain Wood;[25] five hundred men of the First Iowa regiment, Colonel Merritt,[26] and five hundred of the Kansas Second, Colonel Mitchell.[27] A squad of eighty Home Guards accompanied the mission, joining it some ten miles from its starting point. The whole left Springfield about noon on Saturday and took up its line of march for Forsythe, fifty miles distant.[28]

Knox reported rain and that their march was slowed. His reporter-companion Franc Wilkie, on the other hand, was much more graphic:

> That night it rained as if the Indian Ocean had been upset on us, the thunder roared through the mountain tops as if ten thousand devils were howling from each peak, while the whole skies seemed for hours one incessant blaze of white ghastly flame. I generally enjoy quiet "family" thunder showers, but this was considered too much of what generally may be called a good thing, especially in the country. A hard shell Baptist Church served a majority of the men for protection; a hundred or so got in the covered bridge of the river, and a squad of reporters, enjoyed the hospitalities of the roof and fireside of an ardent secessionist in the vicinity, who rejoiced in the euphonic designation of Abner Dabbs.[29]

Seeking Action – Forsyth

On the approach to Forsyth, General Sweeny sent forward some of the cavalry to scout and, hopefully, roll up unsuspecting rebel pickets. Knox and his companions embedded themselves in the advance force. Knox continued:

> After our noon halt, twelve miles from Forsythe, General Sweeney sent forward the entire force of mounted men to a small hamlet[30] within three miles of the town, where the enemy was said to have a mounted picket of fifty men. These advanced, and having with them your correspondent, but no picket could be found. Captain Wood, with ten men, went along the route to reconnoiter, while an orderly was sent back to General Sweeny for further commands. In a short time he returned, bringing orders for the cavalry force to advance upon Forsythe, and if an enemy were found there, to hold him in check till the artillery and infantry could come up. Captain Stanley gave the word to move forward, and we advanced at a gentle trot, meeting about two miles from town, four of Captain Wood's men, with two pickets of the rebels, captured within a mile of Forsythe. The pace was then quickened to a gallop until we reached a small stream called Swan Creek, which skirts the town on the north and west. Forsythe is situated in a romantic glen upwards of a mile in length and about three fourths of a mile in width. On the south side flows White River. Swan Creek strikes the town lines at the northeast corner and after flowing along the northern and western boundaries falls into the first-mentioned stream. On all sides, bluffs, from one to four hundred feet in height push themselves abruptly from the edge of the town site, some of them precipitous and others with a regular but steep ascent to the summit. The road from Springfield enters from the north side of town, crossing Swan Creek and winding some twenty rods directly under the edge of a high cliff and opening into Forsythe in the rear of the Court House.

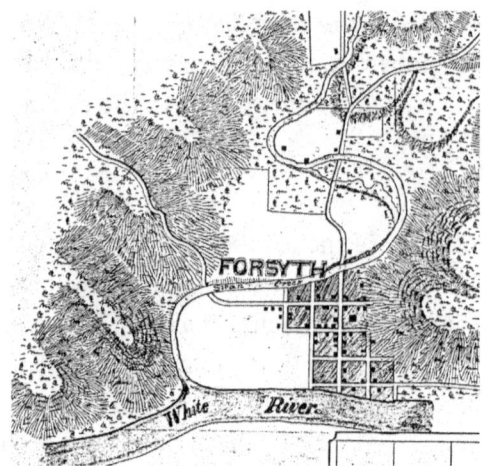

Lyman Bennett Map of April 1862.
(*State Historical Society of Missouri Research Center, Rolla, MO*)

Continuing his narrative, Knox described their approach to the town.

> It was supposed – correctly as the sequel proved – that the rebels had posted men along the cliff who would be able greatly to trouble our troops passing beneath, and be themselves but little exposed. Accordingly, Captain Stanley turned from the road before reaching the cliff, and passed through a small copse of oaks, entering a corn field, where the corn some twelve feet in height, completely screened his men from view. Our distance from the cliff was some thirty rods, too far for the guns of the rebels to have any effect, provided we had been in sight. Passing through this cornfield it was necessary to recross the creek. At the ford, the bank we descended was so steep that our horses did not attempt to reach the waters edge, but planted their feet firmly in position and slid down the moist clayey soil, with all the grace of schoolboy enjoying his winter holiday on his favorite coasting track. On the opposite side was a level ground plat of sufficient width to form the cavalry in line. This was the work of a moment. The advance was sounded, and the whole column of regular

cavalry made a dash into town at full gallop, entering by the Springfield road, while Captain Wood, with his Kansas rangers swept around to the right and joined Captain Stanley near the Court House. The village was completely deserted, all the inhabitants, anticipating trouble, having moved away some days since. Fire was opened upon us from the bluff, on the northeast and from the south bank of the White river, the stream being about a hundred yards in width. The most rapid firing was from across the river, and the cavalry made for the northern shore, dismounting and advancing on foot. A row of bushes skirting either bank concealed both bodies of combatants, but the firing was rapid, and several of the enemy were seen to fall. In about ten minutes the order was given to cease, as the rebel fire had been silenced.[31]

The cavalry and infantry responded to the rebel fire and forced them to flee. Lieutenant Sokalski's battery arrived and mistakenly began to fire on the courthouse. Knox continued:

At the time the shells were fired into the court house several of our men were inside the building. None were injured with the exception of F. B. Wilkie, correspondent of the Dubuque *Herald*, who was hit on the head by a piece of brick, the sharp edge just breaking the skin. The party made a speedy exit from the hall.[32]

Franc Wilkie's report of the courthouse incident again, was considerably more personal and colorful:

The Court House, a fine three story brick, stood in the centre of the town, and leading my horse into a blacksmith shop, I tied it, and walked into the Court House. The lower story was filled with benches and rifles, which the secessionists had abandoned in their hot haste. Accompanied by Captain Callaway of the Home Guards, and a Kansas Sergeant, we proceeded to the upper floor, which was filled with clothing.

> The Sergeant seated himself at a table, the Captain and I entered into a small talk, when – whang! For a second I thought the bluff had tipped over on the Court House – next that the Comet had collided with mother earth, but finally concluded that somebody had sent a shell through the Court House. Through the dim media of flying brick and mortar I perceived the Captain bolting for the door; the Sergeant was getting himself unmixed from the bricks and table, in whose embraces he had rolled on the floor. Another second and I was doing "tall traveling" after Captain Callaway, only pausing the briefest part of a second to notice an immense opening in the wall, through which had broke the shell, passing between the Captain and myself at about the height of our knees, and then tearing on had smashed through the partition beyond. Down stairs forty steps at a leap for all that I know, but not more than half down – myself in the rear – when again another tremendous whang, and something tore through just over my head, tearing things all to splinters, and sending me without further effort on my part, to the bottom of the stairway. I got up and dizzily staggered on and reached the door just as another shell tore through the lower story making kindling wood of a score of benches and burying itself in the south wall without exploding. I found a severe wound on the back of my head, from which the blood ran in streams, and for the moment supposed myself killed, as I felt so weak and unsteady – a mistake, however, as the writing of this letter (with a very sore head though) some thirty-six hours after will abundantly demonstrate.[33]

Knox summarized the achievements of the expedition in a final paragraph:

> Gen. Sweeny has displayed much tact and ability in the management of the expedition thus far. He has been ably assisted by his principal staff officer, Maj. James K. Mills.[34] The march

has been into a rough and partially settled region, where the rebel leaders had prophesied that an army could not be sent. A considerable amount of provisions and ammunition were taken. Twenty-seven guns were received in the court house. Two tons of lead were thrown into a well by the rebels, but it was speedily brought to light.[35]

General Sweeny's report of this "Expedition" appeared, written in the traditional, stiff, military terms.[36] Knox made no mention of the Forsyth adventure in his memoir, *Camp-fire and Cotton-field*.

Thomas W. Sweeny (*Courtesy of Mehdi Schneyders*)

Chapter 7

Dug Springs

After the minor Forsyth skirmish, action cooled down in the Springfield region. Knox described the importance of Springfield in this way:[1]

> Springfield is the largest town in Southwest Missouri, and has a fine situation. Before the war it was a place of considerable importance, as it controlled the trade of a large region around it. East of it the country is quite broken, but on the south and west there are stretches of rolling prairie, bounded by rough wood-land.
>
> Considered in a military light, Springfield was the key to that portion of the State. A large number of public roads centre at that point. Their direction is such that the possession of the town by either army would control any near position of an adversary of equal or inferior strength. General Lyon was prompt in seeing its value and determined to make an early movement for its occupation. When he started from St. Louis for Booneville, he ordered General Sweeney to march from Rolla to Springfield as speedily as possible.

Spies were everywhere in southwest Missouri. There were military scouts and also civilian reports. Both rebels and Unionists were active. Knox reported, "Our scouts were constantly employed bringing us news from the Rebel camp, and it is quite probable the Rebels were equally well informed of our own condition. We were able to learn that their number was on the increase, and that they would soon be largely reinforced."[2]

General Price and his rebels were reported to be on their way to Springfield to engage in battle with Lyon and his men.

General Lyon continued to be vexed by expiring short-term enlistments of his volunteers. About half of his approximately six thousand troops were "three-month men," that is, men who had volunteered to serve for ninety days only. The events in Missouri in early May, Camp Jackson for example, had stimulated enthusiastic enlistments, and expectations had been of a short war with the "enemy" (on both sides) rapidly succumbing to discouragement and defeat. This had not happened. But for Lyon, disaster loomed. Major General John C. Frémont had finally arrived in St. Louis and assumed command of the Department of the West. Lyon had called on St. Louis for men and supplies, but none were forthcoming. Frémont's concern for events near Cairo, IL, dominated his attention. Lyon was on his own. Some of Lyon's regiments marched back to St. Louis to disband, others agreed to stay beyond their term of enlistment, while some others were made to remain in Springfield. At the same time the rebel forces were growing. Price was reinforced by Brigadier General Ben McCullough's Arkansas troops and the Third Louisiana infantry under Colonel Louis Hébert.[3] At this point, spies reported that the rebel army numbered some

Louis Hébert and Ben McCullough (*Wikipedia*)

twelve thousand men. In Springfield, Lyon's forces numbered only six thousand and were beginning to melt away. With his united host of Missourians, Arkansans, and Louisianans, Sterling Price began to move northward.

From the beginning of his service in Missouri, Nathaniel Lyon had always been in favor of aggressive action. Both Camp Jackson and his move up the Missouri River to capture Jefferson City and Boonville proved his propensity for assertive warfare. With the reports of rebels under Sterling Price and Ben McCulloch moving north toward Springfield, Lyon ordered a full-scale offensive action.

Thomas Knox and Franc Wilkie accompanied this movement and both chronicled the results, Wilkie in the *New York Times*[4] and Knox both in the *New York Herald* and later in his book *Camp-fire and Cotton-field:*

> About nine AM of August 1 General Lyon issued orders for the entire command to be ready to march from Springfield by two o'clock PM, but it was not until nearly four in the afternoon that the column was "in motion." It moved forward to a creek, ten miles from town, on the Fayetteville road, and there encamped.[5] At six AM of the 2nd, the command again started on its march. The force consisted of five companies First Missouri regiment, under Col. G. L. Andrews; the Iowa First, Col. Bates; Second Kansas regiment, Colonel Mitchell, two companies the Third Missouri, Colonel Siegel, four hundred men of the Fifth Missouri, Colonel Saloman; three companies First infantry, under Captain Plummer; two companies Second infantry, Captain Steele; and Lieutenant Lothrop, with seventy Fourth artillery recruits. All the regulars, infantry, cavalry and artillery, were under the command of Major S. D. Sturgis. The artillery consisted of eighteen pieces, and was composed of Captains Totten's and Dubois's batteries and six pieces from Colonel Siegel's battery, which did such excellent service at Carthage, commanded by Major Schaffer. In addition to this was a large reserve force, which could be brought up at short notice. The expedition

was undertaken to meet the rebels to battle at some point outside of Springfield, General Lyon having ascertained that the enemy was moving on that town with a large force, under the impression that the federal troops would easily be overcome by superiority of numbers.[6]

This was nearly all of Lyon's forces; only a small garrison, essentially Home Guards, under the command of Major Cronenbold,[7] remained to defend Springfield. Scouts were sent out to reconnoiter and gather information. One scout who was particularly bold caught Knox's attention:

> Just as camp was broken on the morning of the 2d a scout arrived, who was sent out the evening previous, and who had succeeded in entering the enemy's camp and staying some time within the lines. He was not permitted to walk about the camp, but was told they were fifteen hundred strong, under General Rains, and had about five thousand under General McCulloch, some three miles further on.
>
> The rebels informed our scout that they had thirty-two thousand Missouri, Arkansas and Texas troops within the State, with thirty pieces of cannon, and could bring forward still more men if needed. In return for this information the scout told them that General Lyon had evacuated Springfield on hearing of the rebels approach, and was in full retreat towards Rolla. At this welcome intelligence, the rebels gave three cheers, and said they would be to Springfield within twenty-four hours. In the morning, the scout was let out of camp, and headed for General Lyon's command.[8]

Typical of southwest Missouri in August, the heat was stifling, especially for the troops in their wool uniforms. Many suffered from the intense heat. Once again, Knox used great detail to describe the tactical situation for *Herald* readers:

> The distance to be marched to reach the enemy was some ten miles, and the men at first stepped off with vigor. As the

sun rose high in the heavens the heat increased, and by ten in the forenoon became almost unsupportable. Water could be found only at springs and small creeks, and on approaching these the men would almost rush with the greatest eagerness to secure a cooling draught, at times becoming heedless of the commands of their officers until their thirst was quenched. The heat became visible in the atmosphere – the peculiar wavy motion known in some sections as "dry rain" being plainly and painfully perceptible, while the sky assumed a brassy tinge, cheerless as the horizon of an Arabian desert. Many fell from the ranks, but at once came in place whenever it was reported that the enemy was in front.[9]

In his later book, Knox was much more descriptive of the problems of heat and thirst the troops encountered in summertime Missouri than is found in Wilkie's report:

A long ride in that hot atmosphere gave me a thirst of the most terrible character. Making a detour to the left of the road in a vain search for water, I fell behind the column as it marched slowly along. As I moved again to the front, I passed scores of men who had fallen from utter exhaustion. Many were delirious, and begged piteously for water in ever so small a quantity. Several died from excessive heat, and others were for a long time unfit for duty. Reaching the spring which gave its name to the locality [Dug Spring], I was fortunate in finding only the advance of the command. With considerable effort I succeeded in obtaining a pint cupful of water, and thus allayed my immediate thirst.

According to the custom in that region, the spring was covered with a frame building, about eight feet square. There are very few cellars in that part of the country, and the spring-house, as it is called, is used for preserving milk and other articles that require a low temperature. As the main portion of the column came up, the crowd around the spring-house became so dense that those once inside could not get out. The building was lifted and thrown away from the spring, but this only served to increase the confusion. Officers found it impossible to maintain discipline. When the men caught sight of the crowd at the spring, the lines were instantly broken. At the spring, officers and men were mingled without regard to rank, all struggling for the same object. A few of the former, who had been fortunate in commencing the day with full canteens, attempted to bring order out of chaos, but found the effort useless. No command was heeded. The officers of the two regiments of regulars had justly boasted of the superior discipline of their men. On this occasion the superiority was not apparent.

Volunteer and regulars were equally subject to thirst, and made equal endeavour to quench it. Twenty yards below the spring was a shallow pool where cattle and hogs were allowed to run. Directly above it was a trough containing a few gallons of warm water, which had evidently been there several days. This was speedily taken by the men. Then the hot, scum-covered pool was resorted to. In a very few minutes the trampling of the soldiers' feet had stirred this pool till its substance was more like earth than water. Even from this the men would fill their cups and canteens and drink with the utmost eagerness. I saw a private soldier emerge from the crowd with a canteen full of this worse than ditch water. An officer tendered a five-dollar gold piece for the contents of the canteen, and found his offer indignantly refused. To such a frenzy were men driven by thirst that they tore up handfuls of moist earth, and swallowed the few drops of water that could be pressed out.

In subsequent campaigns I witnessed many scenes of hunger and thirst, but none to equal those of that day at Dug Spring.[10]

Just a few miles beyond the spring the Union advance guard met rebel pickets and, in spite of orders from both sides, a fight began. What was called "The Battle of Dug Springs" was not a battle, but rather a small skirmish and was not at Dug Springs but a few miles further south along the Wire Road. The "battle" received a lot of newspaper space simply because there was little war information being generated in other theaters. Knox's report on this particular part of the fight was printed in the *Herald* and reprinted by *Harper's Weekly*, along with a stirring but most likely imaginary illustration.[11]

"Splendid Charge of United States Cavalry at the Battle of Dug Springs, Missouri." (*Harper's Weekly*, August 24, 1861).

About nine in the morning, after a march of seven miles, a picket guard of some fifty mounted men was seen, and a shell was thrown among them as, a gentle reminder that the Union troops were around. They at once made good time toward the main body, some two miles ahead. Near a place called Dug Spring, about nineteen miles from Springfield, our advanced pickets met those of the enemy and exchanged a few shots;

our cavalry formed in line at the right of the road, and Capt. Steele with two companies of infantry, took the left. Capt. Plummer, with three companies of First infantry, supported by Capt. Totten's battery, held the centre. The enemy was posted in a wood crowning a gentle slope, and covering it to the foot, where the road for half a mile ran through a valley between low hills, or rather "swells" of land, covered with a scanty growth of oak bushes, and a few small trees. As the rebels' position and numbers were concealed by the wood, Gen. Lyon did not deem it prudent to advance the column within range, as a masked battery might at any moment open upon it with considerable effect, while at the same time our strength would gain us nothing.

For upwards of an hour nothing was done save the exchanging of a few shots among the pickets, and at length Gen. Lyon gave the order for the column to fall back and; encamp in the vicinity of the spring. This movement was considered by the rebels to be a retreat, and as soon as we were in motion their cavalry made its appearance from the wood and passed to the front of a cornfield which covered their extreme left. Their number was not far from four hundred and they formed in a solid square preparatory to charging. Just as they were at the point of rushing forward, Captain Totten sent a twelve pound shell from his favorite howitzer; but the elevation was too great and the missile passed over its mark. A half minute later another shell followed with better success, bursting directly in the centre of the cavalry and emptying some twenty saddles. The whole body made a retreat for the timber in "precipitous and tumultuous haste." Captain Steele was still on the left, and a body of nearly eight hundred infantry, with a few mounted men, came forward from the enemy's right with the evident intention of engaging and surrounding the Captain's two companies. Company C, of First cavalry, was in the rear (lately front), near Captain Steele and Lieutenant M.

> J. Kelly with twenty men from the company, made a Balaklava charge[12] right in the face of the bullets and bayonets of the whole rebel infantry. Four of the twenty were killed and six were wounded, but they succeeded in breaking the infantry and putting them to flight. Four horses were wounded so badly it was necessary to kill them, one receiving nine, the other eleven, rifle balls.

Knox completed his narrative with some of the small details of the fight, details that added interest and color to his narrative:

> One of the men - Sergeant Sullivan - received three terrible, though not fatal, wounds. As he was falling from his horse he waved his sabre, and shouted, "Hurrah tor the old Stars and Stripes." When brought to camp he seemed to forget his wounds in his joy at having struck a blow for the Union. One of the enemy's wounded inquired of Lieutenant Kelly, with great earnestness –
>
> "Are your cavalry men or demons?" The Lieutenant replied that it was possible they might be a combination of both.
>
> "Well," said the man, "We can't stand such a charge as that. You can whip us all out if you've got a decent army of such soldiers."
>
> One of our wounded, a private named Jacobs was captured by the rebels, was knocked from his horse while a prisoner, by a blow from a musket, and left for dead. He was found on the field the next morning and carefully attended to. He will probably recover.
>
> The enemy did not again appear that day, and the command encamped and passed the night in quiet. The utmost care was taken to prevent a surprise during the night by posting pickets in all directions, and arranging the camp with special reference to a defense in the darkness. Major Sturgis was particularly active at all hours, and if the enemy had made an attack they would have met a warm reception.[13]

The next morning, Lyon's forces began to move out, further towards the rebel positions. Lyon tersely reported his situation in his official report from "McCulla's Farm, 24 miles from Springfield, Fayetteville Road, August 4, 1861."[14]

> Yesterday (3d) I advanced to this point, where General Rains, of Jackson's forces, had their headquarters, and from which he retired without resistance. I cannot say with definiteness how far in advance the main body is, but without supplies [they had taken only four days rations] and the danger of being turned by a force to cut off our communication with Springfield....I determine to fall back upon Springfield.[15]

As an on-the-scene bystander, Knox provided much more information and details on the actions to his readers in his August 6 report printed in the *Herald* on August 12:

> On the morning of the 3rd camp was broken about six o'clock, and the command moved on toward the position of the rebels. Lines of skirmishers were thrown out for upwards of half a mile on each side, and every foot of ground was carefully examined, to prevent possibility of an ambuscade. One of the cavalry men found the wounded private, Jacobs, before referred to, and he was at once carefully attended to. The four wounded rebels left by their companions were closely questioned, but the interrogation failed to elicit anything of importance. They pretended to be ignorant of their force but were confident we should have a severe battle within an hour or two. One stated that there was a Louisiana regiment to McCulloch's command finely disciplined and equipped, and mentioned the Baton Rouge company as particularly excellent. He did not appear to have much confidence in the fighting abilities of the Missourians, but thought the other Rebel troops would give a good account of themselves. We could not ascertain the loss of the rebel force in the affair of the day previous, but observation and estimates place the

killed at not far from twenty-five and the wounded from fifty to one hundred. These wounded men positively asserted that they had no artillery but, it was the opinion of most of our officers that two pieces were shown at the edge of the wood, and Captain Granger, of the regulars, says that he went within a few rods of two small pieces, which were in charge, of three men and had he been supported by half a dozen men. He would have captured both of them. My own observation convinces me that the rebels had artillery and that two six pounder shots were fired at us. The men said their force was not more than four hundred, but I think their number was not less than three thousand, of whom one-half were mounted. Nothing further could be elicited, and we moved on.

Some four miles from our camp we reached the brow of a hill, overlooking a lovely valley, some four miles in length and about three-fourths of a mile in width. The slope on the side where we were was cleared, as also was valley itself, but the opposite was covered with wood from foot to summit. The road passed down the slope, crossed the valley and wound up the side against us and for a mile along this wooded slope the dense cloud of dust rising above the tree-tops, showing the approach of a large force. Line of battle was at once formed with the expectation that the enemy would march from the timber and engage us in the valley. Companies C and D, of First Cavalry with regular infantry, under Major Sturgis supported by the Kansas Second, Colonel Mitchell, took the centre, followed by Captain Totten's battery. The Iowa First, Colonel Bates, with Captain Dubois' battery, went to the right and were soon followed by a portion of Colonel Siegel's infantry. The Missouri First, Colonel Andrews, and the Kansas First, which had just reached the column from Chesapeake Mills, commanded by Colonel Deitzler, took the right. Colonel Siegel's battery, with a portion of his infantry and Colonel Saloman's infantry remained with the baggage train. The line was formed midway between the slopes and on the left extended upon a small hill at the head of the valley. Dubois' battery occupied this elevation, and as soon as the line was formed the captain sent a shell into the centre of the cloud of dust, which marked the position of the advancing enemy, and followed it with a twelve pound shot. The dust cloud soon showed that the rebels were retreating, and in less than an hour afterwards General Lyon occupied the late headquarters of General Rains, the rebel commander. It was at a house, owned by a Mr. McCulloch (no relative to Ben),[16] a prominent Union man of Stone county. Curran Post Office was kept there, but nearly all the traces of an agency of the Postal Department had been removed by the rebels. The family had been driven away from the house and plundered of everything of value.

The command camped here but our lines extended nearly a mile further along the road. A few shots were exchanged by pickets, but nothing further occurred in the fighting order. The utmost precautions were taken to prevent a surprise – but no attack was made.

Soon after the arrival of our force at McCulloch's house some forty mounted rebels rode leisurely past; engaging in conversation with our men. They were supposed to be Home Guards, and the mistake was not discovered until they were out of reach. They did not ascertain anything of importance. Sixteen of the rebels were taken during the day, and some thirty horses were captured. A deserter, who came over from the rebel side, stated that their force, in his judgment, was between six and eight thousand, though they claimed as high as thirty thousand.

They had eight cannon, and were encamped on Crane Creek, about six miles from our position. On the morning of the 4th a council of war, composed of the principal officers, was held at the headquarters of General Lyon to consider the propriety of a further advance. As we had expected to meet the enemy within twenty miles of Springfield, and had taken rations for but four days, it was not deemed prudent to go on. The enemy had a way, no doubt agreeable to them, of retreating before us, and some of the officers contended that we might follow the rebels to the end of Cape Horn without inducing them to make a stand. Accordingly it was decided to return to Springfield, and the enemy was headed in that direction. In the course of the day we ascertained that McCulloch's force started in a westerly direction at about the same time that the Union troops took their line of march for Springfield.

On the evening of the 4th, a deserter from the Louisiana regiment came in, and was at once brought before Gen. Lyon. He corroborated the statement of the deserter of the 3rd. He said that he was pressed into service at the time the regiment was formed, and added that the desertions since they left Louisiana had been upwards of three hundred. There were with McCulloch, in addition to the Louisiana regiment, two regiments from Arkansas and a few companies from Tennessee. The balance of the force was made up of "shot gun Missourians." But two regiments of the whole command made any pretension to discipline.

McCulloch is expecting two more regiments from Texas before long, and a like number from Arkansas. The men have had enough to eat until within a week or ten days, when they ran short of everything but beef. The camp where they had made preparations to receive us on the 3rd was on the top of a wooded hill, where it was difficult of ascent, excepting in the road. In the middle of the road, on the summit of the hill, they had planted four of their eight cannon, and intended to sweep us as we came up within range. The rebels have for some time been designing to attack Springfield, and would have marched upon it ere this had we not gone, in their direction. What their designs may be in the future the deserter could not say.[17]

Oftentimes in the fog of war, the names of the dead and wounded are lost to history. In his *Herald* article, Knox provided an important service by giving the names of the regulars in the Dug Springs charge:

> The killed in the affair of the 2nd were Corporal Kline and Privates Stokes, Givens and Devlin. The wounded were Sergeant Sullivan and privates Jacobs, Fry, Miller, Dougherty and McLivane, all of company C, First cavalry. They were of the twenty who made, under Lieut. Kelly, the brilliant charge against 800 infantry, breaking their ranks and putting them to flight.[18]

Again, Knox provided some of the lesser information about the situation in Springfield, as rumors of the approach of Sterling Price's troops flowered. While of little importance in the greater story, such information is useful in understanding the state of mind of those in Springfield. The allegiance of Springfield residents was divided – some for the Union and others for the Confederacy. Further confusing the situation was the fact that many Unionists were also slaveholders. Unionists realized that the advance of Lyon's little army as far as Springfield was militarily dangerous and possibly unlikely to last:

> A panic occurred in Springfield on the afternoon of the 4th, owing to the reception of intelligence that the rebels were approaching the town in advance of the federal force. About one half the inhabitants fled to the country, and the remainder, with the battalion, left "in charge" of the place, under Major Cronenbold, prepared to make a vigorous defense. The pickets on all the roads leading into town, with one exception, concluding that their position was not an agreeable one, deserted their posts and came in for safety. They were all of them members of the valiant and brave company of Springfield

Home Guards. No attack was made, as the enemy was not within thirty miles of town.[19]

While Knox had extolled the strength and bravery of the Union troops and their fortitude during the trying march to Dug Springs and back to Springfield, he also reported on the darker side of these patriots. Interestingly, he separated the "German soldiers'" behavior from that of the "native American" troops, while castigating both groups and their leadership:

> On the march, the Union troops committed disgraceful outrages along the road. Several houses, some of them the property of Union men, were entered in the absence of their owners, and plundered of everything portable that they contained. Orchards and milk houses were on no account left unvisited but were stripped of everything edible or bibulous. The German soldiers seemed to have a partiality for the house plundering, while the native American troops attended to the outdoor work, gorging themselves with green apples and greener peaches, and lubricating their throats with all the milk and butter in the milk houses upon the way. Many a hen roost suffered in the decimation of its feathered occupants. There is a screw loose somewhere in our management, or this indiscriminate theft would be stopped.[20]

Knox ended his letter with some housekeeping matters, reporting on troops and leadership assignments, and some deaths from *coup de soliel*, sunstroke. He ended his letter with some speculation:

> The command will probably remain in and around Springfield for the present. It is of no use to pursue the rebels for the present, as they can move faster than we. Our hope is that they will entrench themselves, at some near point thus inviting attack, or will make a direct march upon Springfield and meet us in battle on the prairie near here.[21]

He was correct, but the results were not what he expected.

Chapter 8

Wilson's Creek

When Lyon and his men returned to Springfield after the skirmish at Dug Springs, the rebels, particularly General Price, were emboldened. Spies were everywhere. Union spies reported on the approach of Price and McCulloch, while rebel spies reported on the size of Lyon's army in Springfield and on the rapidly expiring 90-day enlistments of some of the Union units. Price and McCulloch planned their move on Springfield, expecting Lyon's small army to retreat before their much larger force. Meanwhile, Lyon pondered what the future had in store for his command. No reinforcements and few supplies had arrived from Frémont in St. Louis and none could be expected in time to affect the outcome of the current situation. This was the culmination of Lyon's advance to Springfield. This was the time for Generals Price and McCulloch to reclaim the territory lost when Price's Missouri rebels were forced to retreat into the southwest corner of the State.

On the afternoon of August 9, Lyon and his army marched southwest out from Springfield to face the enemy encamped along Wilson's Creek. After a short overnight rest, Captain Totten's battery opened the attack, in the early morning of August 10, shelling the rebel camp. The Wilson's Creek battle was historic and bloody for both sides. General Lyon was killed leading a charge. The Union troops withdrew to Springfield, but the rebels were too spent to follow up. This battle was the second major battle of the Civil War (following Bull Run in Virginia on July 21). Casualties were high on both sides, higher than at Bull Run.[1]

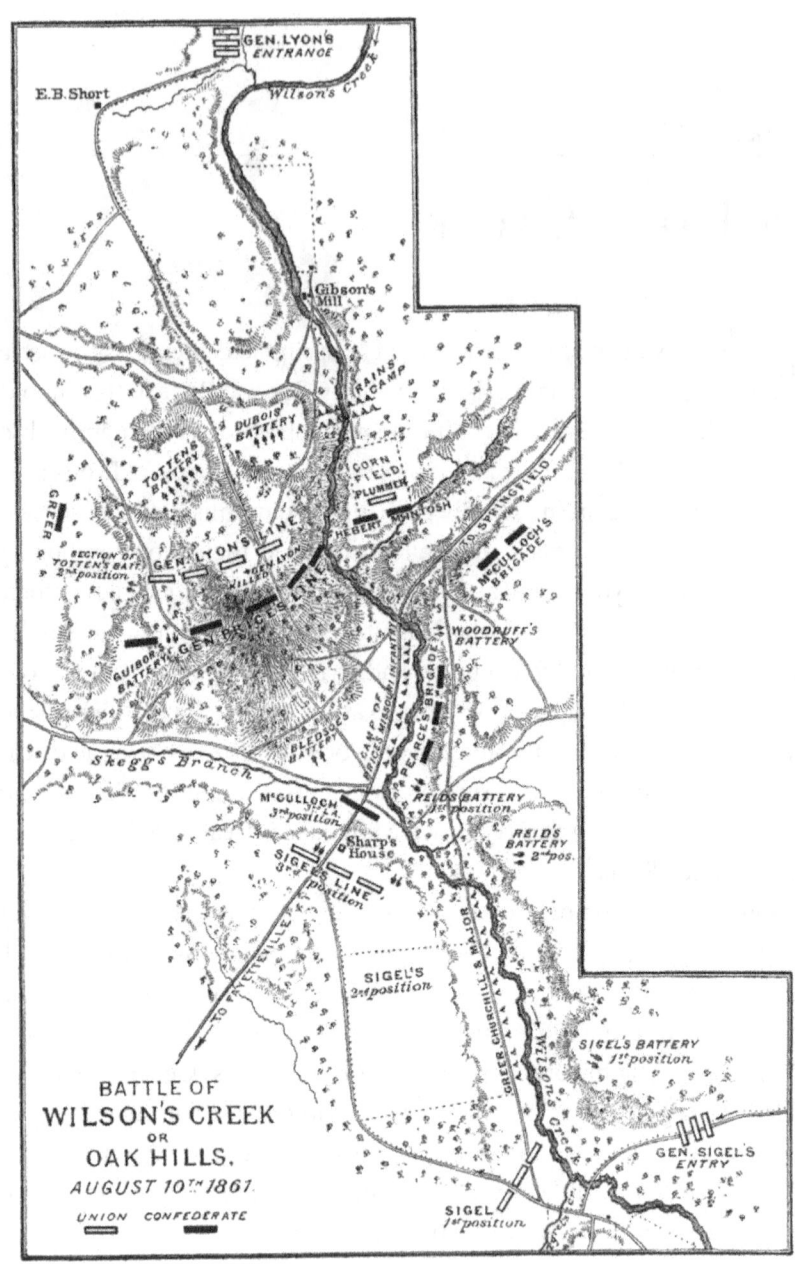

Battles and Leaders of the Civil War, 1:290.

The wildest rumors reached St. Louis, and someone, not Knox, telegraphed them to the *Herald* in New York.[2] Very little of the article was true. One day later, the *Herald* augmented its first report with "additional particulars," datelined Rolla, August 13. The report began, "The following additional of the battle at Springfield is furnished by an eye witness who left Springfield on Sunday morning and came through to this place on horseback." This eye witness probably was Knox and this was his first telegraphed report of the battle appearing in the *Herald* on August 14:[3]

Rolla, August 13, 1861.

The army marched out of Springfield on Friday evening only 5500 strong, the Home Guard remaining at that place. Our forces slept on the prairie a portion of the night, and about sunrise on Saturday morning drove in the outposts of the enemy, and soon after the battle became general.

The attack was made in two columns by Generals Lyon and Sturgis, Gen. Siegel leading a flanking force of about one thousand men and four guns on the south of the enemy's camp.

The fight raged from sunrise until one or two o'clock in the afternoon. The rebels, in overwhelming force charged Capt. Totten's battery three times, but were repulsed with great slaughter.

Gen. Lyon fell early in the day. He had been previously wounded in the leg and had a horse shot from under him.

The Colonel of one of the Kansas regiments having been disabled, the boys cried out, "General, you come and lead us on." He did so, and, at once, putting himself in front and while cheering the men on to the charge, received a bullet in the left breast, and fell from his horse. He was asked if he was hurt, and replied, "No, not much," but in a few minutes he expired without a struggle.

Gen. Siegel had a very severe struggle and lost three of his four guns. His artillery horses were shot in their harnesses and the pieces disabled. He endeavored to haul them off with a number of prisoners, but was finally compelled to abandon them, first however spiking the guns and disabling their carriages.

About one o'clock the enemy order seemed to be in great disorder, retreating and setting fire to their train of baggage wagons. Our forces were too much fatigued and cut up to pursue, so the battle may be considered a drawn one. [Then a partial list of casualties is presented.]

The Missouri First and the Iowa First suffered the most.

General Price was not killed. There were rumors on the field that Ben McCulloch was killed, but the rebels denied it.

On Saturday night Dr. Melcher[4] and others of our army went back with ambulances to the battlefield from Springfield to see about the killed and wounded. They found the enemy on the field and were considerately treated. Gen. Lyon's body had been treated with great respect and was brought back with some of the wounded to Springfield.

Major Sturgis took command on the battlefield after the death of General Lyon. General Siegel took command after the battle. Our losses are variously estimated at from one hundred fifty to three hundred killed and several hundred wounded. The enemy's loss is placed at two thousand killed and wounded. Our boys captured about two hundred horses of the enemy. The enemy carried two flags, the enemy one and the Stars and Stripes.

Gen. Siegel marched back to Springfield in good order after perfecting his arrangements, gathering the baggage and blowing up what powder he could not carry and destroying other property which he did not want to fall into the hands of the enemy.

He left Springfield on Sunday night and encamped thirty miles this side of that place, the rebels not pursuing him.

The only hostility observed during the day was the firing of muskets from a distance at the rear guard.

> General Siegel was confident he could have held Springfield against the force he had but was fearful of reinforcement to the enemy from the southwest and that his line of communication to Rolla would be cut off.
>
> General Lyon began his attack upon receipt of intelligence that the enemy were expecting reinforcements from General Hardee's column, which was approaching from the southeast.
>
> A portion of the artillery of the enemy was admirably served. The fire of the rebel infantry was also very severe. The Springfield Home Guards were not in the fight. They, with a large number of citizens of Springfield, are in General Sigel's camp.
>
> It was thought that General Sigel would fall back no further than Lebanon, where reinforcements would meet him.

This report set the record straight. The only question might be the statement about the enemy's "great disorder." The real source of the fire in the baggage train remained unknown.

The full story of the Wilson's Creek battle is in Knox's second, long report, datelined Springfield, August 10, that appeared in the *New York Herald* on August 19.[5]

These two reports by Knox are particularly important for the historical record for several reasons. First, Knox was close to Lyon, a friend, and one who was perceptive to Lyon's mental and emotional state. Knox had met him shortly after his arrival in St. Louis and had cultivated his friendship, as would any good reporter. Second, Knox was close to Lyon physically during the battle. He saw what Lyon saw and heard the reports Lyon received. Finally, Knox was a good reporter, who not only presented the broad strategy and events at Wilson's Creek but also the small, intimate "human interest" stories that gave a special life to his reports and make them so valuable to a reader today.

> After the occurrences of the 3rd and 4th lasts,[6] and the falling back of the Union troops upon Springfield, the rebels made an advance, and on the evening of the 6th formed their camp

upon Wilson's Creek, about ten miles from Springfield, on the Fayetteville road. Reports of spies, deserters and a few prisoners made it certain they were in force from eight to twenty thousand and were provided with eight to sixteen brass cannon. On the evening of the 7th General Lyon formed a plan of night surprise, but the project was abandoned and nothing of importance occurred until the night of the 9th. On that evening the plan was formed of attacking them simultaneously at either end of the camp, which extended for some three miles along the banks of the creek.[7]

Growing increasingly concerned about Lyon's health and state of mind, Knox reported:

For two or three days before the battle, General Lyon changed much in appearance. Since it became apparent to him that he must abandon the Southwest or have his army cut to pieces, he had lost much of his energy and decision. To one of his staff the evening before the battle, "I am a man believing in presentiments, and ever since this night surprise was planned, I have had a feeling I cannot get rid of that it would result disastrously. Through the refusal of government properly to reinforce me I am obliged to abandon the country. If I leave it without engaging the enemy the public will call me a coward. If I engage him I may be defeated and my command cut to pieces. I am too weak to hold Springfield, and yet the people will demand that I bring about a battle with the very enemy I cannot keep a town against. How can this result otherwise than against us."[8]

According to Knox, General Lyon was a man of honor and patriotism who felt very deeply his responsibility to those around him. He also was aware of the effect of the news of his actions might have on the public as reported by papers of differing political persuasions. He was torn in his decisions by these conflicting passions. Knox, keeping close to him, wrote:

On the way to the field I frequently rode near him. He seemed like one bewildered, and often when addressed failed to give any response, and seemed totally unaware that he was spoken to. On the battle field he gave his orders promptly, and seemed solicitous for the welfare of his men, but utterly regardless of his own safety. While he was standing where bullets flew thickest, just after his favorite horse was shot from under him, some of his officers interposed and begged that he would retire from the spot and seek one less exposed. Scarcely raising his eyes from the enemy, he said, "It is well enough that I stand here. I am satisfied."[9]

Knox then described the advance to the battle in a section titled, "Moving to the Attack":

General Siegel was sent to the extreme left to begin the attack on that side, having with him a force of 1200 men and six pieces of light artillery under command of Major Schaeffer. General Lyon led the main column, which was to open battle on the right, consisting of three companies First Infantry, Captain Plummer; two companies Second infantry, Captain Steele; one company Fourth artillery, recruits, Lieutenant Lathrop; Captains Totten's and Dubois' batteries, six pieces each; Missouri First regiment, Colonel Andrews; Kansas First, Colonel Deitzler; Kansas Second, Colonel Mitchell; Iowa First, Colonel Bates, and one battalion from Second Missouri, under Major Osterhaus. In addition were several companies of Home Guards, a part of whom did good service, but the majority proved an intolerable nuisance, running like frightened deer at the least alarm and getting in the way of others.

The whole force left Springfield about sunset on the 9th. The left column taking the Fayetteville road and the right the road leading to Mount Vernon, having them at proper points for making detours to enclose the rebel camp. Your correspondent joined the right column, under General Lyon, as that promised to be most actively engaged. Midnight found us in a hayfield, four miles from the rebel position, and as it was not deemed prudent to approach nearer before morning, the men were permitted to get what sleep they could extract from the hard ground during the few hours preceding dawn.

At a few minutes before four the whole column was again in motion. It was not long before the camp appeared in sight, located, as we anticipated, along Wilson's Creek. On either side of the stream the valley, averaging some twenty rods in width, was bounded by a range of low and gently sloping hills, covered with a scanty, but occasionally dense growth of scrub oaks of a few feet in height. Portions of these slopes, together with parts of the valley, had been cleared and, turned into corn and wheat fields; the latter had just been visited by the sickle, but the former was still in luxuriant growth, affording complete concealment to either foot or horsemen. The rebels had selected those points which admitted of the best defense as positions for their men and batteries, these being mainly on the north side of the creek. The low oaks, with which the entire camp was surrounded, prevented our seeing many movements until almost at the last moment and the same cause did much to hinder the aim of both artillery and riflemen. At ten minutes past five the rebel pickets were seen and driven in and we rapidly moved forward to take position opposite the rebel battery. This we secured on a gently sloping hill, which had been the extreme of the rebel camp, as several wagons, a few tents numerous cooking utensils, and other et ceteras of a soldiers life plainly indicated.[10]

Knox then continued with a detailed description of "The Battle." In this section of his report, Knox was concerned only with the events under the direct command of General Lyon:

At a distance of eight hundred yards from the rebel battery Captain Totten unlimbered his guns and was speedily joined by Captain Dubois. Captain Totten opened the battle with a twelve pound shell and was promptly answered by the rebels. In a few moments all our pieces were engaged with an equal number of the enemy's cannon, both sides firing with great rapidity.

The First Missouri regiment was placed in position to support the battery, with Major Osterhaus's battalion on the extreme right to act as skirmishers. To the left of our line was a ravine, with precipitous sides; adjoining this ravine was a corn field, and beyond the latter was a wheat stubble field. Captains Plummer and Gilbert, with three companies of regulars, and Captain Wright, with two companies of Home Guards, were sent to occupy these fields and prevent the enemy from making a flank movement on the battery. The rebels did not long allow our forces to wait in line with their rifles unused, but commenced a fire of musketry upon Osterhaus' battalion and those of the First Missouri.

After two or three rounds of Minié balls, the firing became general along the line of this regiment, and an attempt at a charge was broken up and the enemy forced to retire. At about the time of the commencement of the firing by the First Missouri those on our left found themselves heavily engaged in the cornfield with a large body of rebel troops that had been sent out to oppose them. The Home Guards as usual, fell back to a safer locality and the regulars finding skirmishing in the corn more destructive to themselves than to their opponents, the latter knowing well the ground, fell back to the edge of the field and succeeded in there holding position. The fire against the regulars before they fell back was particularly heavy and well directed, as the corn afforded a fine screen behind which to take near and deliberate aim. The regulars gave return shots whenever they obtained sight of an enemy and are confident that they did much towards thinning the rebel ranks.

The First Missouri troops, who were acting to support

the battery in front, stood their ground like veterans and sent many a Minié ball true to its aim. As much of the fire against them was from weapons inferior to theirs, they had the enemy at a slight advantage when placed man to man and though finally much cut up and forced to retire, they were not withdrawn till they had three successive times repulsed the rebels. On each of these occasions the enemy brought fresh troops into the field and it is believed that during the entire day they did not bring the same force twice into action except one or two flank movements. When the Missouri First was withdrawn, after they had been under fire an hour and a half, the Kansas First and Second, and the Iowa First were placed to the front, the latter being to the right of the Iowa troops and further towards the rear thus keeping the Iowa partly in reserve, the rebels again came up in stronger force than ever, but were driven back by the Kansans, the latter, in both instances, bringing their bayonets to the charge and pursuing for some distance down the slope. They would have followed up to the battery had not their officers feared that the retreat might be a ruse to draw them into an ambuscade, the scanty growth of trees and bushes being admirably adapted for forming an ambush. All this time Lieutenant Lathrop's regulars were lying down to the right of Dubois' battery, waiting for an opportunity to come into action. The lieutenant himself sat on his horse in front of his men, displaying the most imperturbable coolness. "Don't dodge," said he to a reporter, who shall be nameless, as that individual turned his head aside to allow a ball to pass, "don't dodge, for you might put your head exactly where a ball was coming and then we should be minus a reporter." About the time the Kansans took the place of the First Missouri, Lieutenant Lathrop's men were ordered to the front of the battery to clear the brush of some rebel attackers known to be lying there. As they advanced and extended their line to the ravine on the left, a brisk fire was opened upon them both from the ravine in front and the bank of the ravine on their left flank, but they succeeded in dislodging the enemy. It was then discovered that the rebel skirmishing in front was partly to draw attention away from a large body of rebel infantry that was advancing about six hundred yards on our left with the evident intention of outflanking us and falling on our rear. There appeared to be one full regiment, six or eight companies and about fifteen hundred men not in ranks. Captain Dubois brought his battery to bear upon them and sent shell, grape and canister in their midst causing a hasty and confused retreat. A large body of them made a rush for an opening in the fence, behind was a clump of timber, and, as they were crowding through, two twelve-pounder spherical case shot were exploded among them, leaving the dead and wounded thick upon the ground. Our rear was not for some time menaced in that direction.

Very soon after this it was seen that the rebel cavalry, some 900 strong, was forming in the rear of our right to make a charge upon the ambulances, which were being brought up for the use of the wounded. Captain Wood's Kansas rangers and two companies of Second Kansas infantry, which happened near the rear at this time, drew up to resist them. As the cavalry came on, the infantry opened with a volley, but did not succeed in checking their advance. When they were within less than two hundred yards of our lines Captain Totten opened upon them two rounds from his entire battery, which had been hastily brought into position unknown to the rebels. The fire was diagonally across the body, and each shot cut a lane entirely through, leaving dead and wounded horses and riders mingled indiscriminately together. The charge was broken and the rebel cavalry made a disorderly retreat to the timber. Some twenty horses were galloping on the field, and were secured by our men. The fight was again renewed with vigor in the front, and the Iowans were brought into the thick of the contest, giving the Kansans a brief respite. They repelled an advance of rebel infantry, which no sooner disappeared than it was succeeded by a fresh force larger than the previous one. The Kansas First was again brought forward and led to the charge by General Sweeny, Colonel Deitzler having been wounded and taken to the rear.

General Nathaniel Lyon had been effectively directing the battle, an unfamiliar task for someone whose previous U. S. Army rank had been captain, but his mood remained gloomy. Then, his mood changed as he assumed a different role, that of an officer of lesser rank, one actively engaged in leading in combat. Knox was standing nearby and related the sequence of events:

> General Lyon was standing by his horse near the Iowans, and several among the latter asked for some one to lead them. Instantly, General Lyon took command of the regiment to lead it forward.
>
> While the line was forming for the charge against the rebels in which he lost his life, General Lyon turned to Major Sturgis, who stood near him, and remarked:
> "I fear the day is lost, if Colonel Sigel had been successful he would have joined us before this. I think I will lead the charge." He had been wounded in the leg, in an early part of the engagement – flesh wound merely – from which the blood flowed profusely. Major Sturgis during the conversation noticed blood on General Lyon's hat, and at first supposed he had been touching it with his hand, which was wet with blood from his leg. A moment after, perceiving that it was fresh, be removed the General's hat and asked the cause of its appearance. "It is nothing, Major, nothing but a wound in the head," said General Lyon, turning away and mounting his horse. Without taking the hat held out to him by Major Sturgis, he addressed the Iowans he was to command with "Forward, men, I will lead you."

Two minutes afterwards he lay dead on the field, killed by a rifle ball through the breast, just above the heart. In death his features wore the same troubled and puzzled expression that had been fixed upon them for the past week. His body was brought to town in the afternoon, and will be forwarded to his friends in Connecticut for interment.

All this transpired in a very few moments, and it was known to but few that General Lyon had fallen. The announcement of his death was not made to the soldiers till after the battle was over. After this but little was done on either side for onward of half an hour, the rebels changing the position of their battery to higher ground in the rear of its former location, and Captain Totten advancing his a few rods, while Captain Dubois remained at his old post.

Captain Granger, of the regular service, detected a flank movement in preparation against our left, and took three companies of the Iowa regiment to the edge of the ravine and caused them to lie down in the grass and await the enemy's approach. Very soon the column approached, Captain Dubois pouring in grape and canister when they got quite near. As soon as they had come up within short range of Captain Granger, the Iowans, taking sight without rising from their position, poured in a most destructive fire of Minié balls with terrific effect. The cannonade and musket fire were too much for the rebels, and they made the best possible use of their pedals back to a place of safety.

Knox continued his tale of the battle with a section entitled, "The Rebel Wagon Train on Fire." His supposition about the rebels causing the fire to destroy supplies to keep them from being captured is unsupported by any facts. The combination of hot cannon balls and combustible material is the more likely cause:

> Immediately after this retreat flames burst forth from the rebel baggage train, which was stationed about a mile

down the creek, and from the extent of the fire and the vast column of smoke, it is supposed that the entire wagon train of the rebel army was destroyed. How the fire originated is not known, but it is supposed that the rebels, fearing defeat and rout, themselves set fire to the wagons rather than have them fall into the hands of the Unionists. They were seen to destroy some twenty wagons near their battery a short time after the fire burst forth in the large train, and it is but reasonable to suppose that the latter was turned to ashes and smoke by the owners themselves. While the conflagration was at its height the rebels made a furious attack on the Union front and right at the same time. The battery in front opened furiously, and several pieces, which had been brought against our right, under cover of the timber, played rigorously from a cleared space some eight hundred yards distant. A very large force of infantry came out in line of battle order from the very place where we had for some time expected Colonel Sigel to appear. No bayonet changes were made by either side, but the roll of musketry and the boom of cannon were more fierce and continuous than at any previous time during the day. For half an hour it was one deep, deafening roar, resounding through the air, and the field became canopied with dense clouds of smoke, the position of cannon could only be made out by the dull, red flash seen through the fog-like atmosphere, and all around was falling a pitiless shower of lead and iron. Too rapid in succession to think of counting came the smooth whistle of the common rifle ball, the shrill buzz of the Minié, the dull hum of the round ball, and above them all the sounds produced by the various descriptions of common munitions. For half an hour it continued, and was ended by the repulse of the rebels, who returned no more to the field. In this last scene of the battle all the Union force on the field was in action, and one half our loss of the day occurred at this time.

Thomas Knox was at the side of Nathaniel Lyon as he died, and Lyon's loss was sorely felt. Major Sturgis assumed command in Lyon's place. But there was another piece to the puzzle that the Battle of Wilson's Creek had become. Where was General Sigel? There was no intelligence of his actions. At the time of Sturgis's order for withdrawal, there still was no news of his fate.

Knox continued his report of the battle with a section entitled, "Operations of General Sigel's Command." In this part of his report, which can be found in the notes, Knox had to rely on second-hand information.[11]

Sigel and his men were beaten and they retreated rapidly to Springfield. Knox made the best of the bad news, but there was no doubt Sigel had failed in his mission. In his *Herald* article, Knox went on to report on conditions, injuries, deaths and some of the small events that give life and color to any story. For the most part he was, as might be expected, not complementary to the actions of the rebels:

> The appearance of the field throughout the day was exceedingly gloomy. The morning was cloudy, and once in the forenoon rain fell. Toward noon the sun shone out but not clearly. The smoke from the cannon and small arms, with that from the burning train, hung over the field, seeming like a pall spread to cover the unfortunate dead. The horrors of Manassas were renewed on this battle field.
>
> Our wounded men were bayoneted or struck over the head with musket butts. An officer, a lieutenant in the First Missouri, was taken prisoner, struck four times with a musket and left for dead. He revived and escaped. A surgeon, who went on the field after the battle, was several times shot at and forced to retire. Later in the afternoon a flag of truce was sent to the rebel commanders, and was received.
>
> Union flags were several times waved to induce our men to go forward. None were taken by this ruse.
>
> At the time the enemy were advancing to outflank our left, and were repulsed by our cannonading, a rebel flag

was borne prominently in their front. The man carrying it was struck by a shell, which exploded at the same moment. Another snatched up the banner, and was carrying it forward when he was killed by a canister shot. The flag was not again seen.

Most of the shot from the rebel cannon passed over our heads. A few horses were killed by round shot and two or three men were badly wounded with pieces of shell. With these exceptions I do not know of their artillery doing damage.

Your correspondent was standing beside his horse under a tree in the rear of Capt. Totten's battery when a six-pound shot passed through the tree top not four feet above his head. Thinking there might be a better place for observation I changed my position some twenty rods, and I was speedily admonished of my insecurity by another ball ploughing up the ground not six feet away, and literally covering me with dirt. Upon the theory that "lightning does not strike twice in the same place," I kept still, and was not troubled by any more of the same sort so near me. A six-pound shot produces a sound anything but melodious.

About the time the action commenced I rode past the First Missouri regiment. One of the soldiers, seeing my citizen's dress, cocked his gun and brought it to bear upon me. I ventured to ask:

"What are you going to shoot me for?"

"I don't know you," was the reply, with the gun still in position. Just then one of the soldiers inquired where I had been since I was with them at Booneville, and my about-to-shoot friend lowered his rifle and disappeared.

Whether the result is a victory, a defeat or a drawn battle, I leave for the reader to decide. Our forces took a position and held it five hours. When they retired the enemy had been several times repulsed, and in the last attack driven from the field. They had burned their baggage train to prevent our getting it, and when we left the field did not attempt to pursue us. Upwards of an hour after our departure they returned and took possession, rendering it necessary that our ambulances should go out under a flag of truce. The rebel troops outnumbered the Unionists at least four to one, and some of our officers estimate their strength as fully six times that of ours. The statements from the prisoners that we took gave them from twelve to thirty thousand.[12]

Among the prisoners was Horace H. Brand, of Booneville, aide-de-camp to General Price. He told me they had twenty-one thousand armed men and twenty pieces of artillery, but thought we could whip them with twelve thousand good troops. Certainly they had force enough to enable them to move always with very large bodies of soldiery, and to bring fresh men into action each time. The Union force, including Colonel Siegel's command, was five thousand, two hundred strong. All our men fought admirably, and it would be unjust to praise any one regiment more than another. Some of the officers of the regular army cherished a supreme contempt for volunteers; but I heard nearly all of them speak in terms of the highest praise of their conduct at this battle. Looking on merely as a civilian, and not qualified to criticize in a military light, I could see no difference between the volunteers and the regulars, save that the latter made their movements in better order and with greater celerity.

The number of killed and wounded it is impossible to state. My estimate would be that the Union loss was two hundred killed and six hundred wounded, and the rebel loss double those figures. Our men never moved denser than in two ranks, and never showed in large bodies, while the rebels nearly always made their movements in strong columns and several times in solid squares, thus revealing a fine mark for our artillerymen, who were not slow to use it. The official report may very much reduce the figures of the loss on both sides. It would not be a matter of surprise should they be doubled. It was one of the bloodiest, if not the bloodiest battle, ever fought in the United States.

No full returns have yet made of the names of killed and wounded. We hear of no officer of importance on the rebel side being killed or wounded. On the Union side Captain Gratz, of Missouri First; Captain Mason of Iowa First, and Captain Brown, of Kansas First, were killed. Colonel Andrews, Missouri First; Colonel Deitzler and Major Hinderman, Kansas First, and Colonel Mitchell, Kansas Second, were wounded – none fatally. Lieutenant Purcell, Company C, Iowa First, was mortally wounded and Lieutenant Brown of Captain Burke's Company, Missouri First, slightly. One of the officers was saved by his watch, a heavy time keeper. A rifle bullet somewhat altered its outward appearance and its running qualities have lost their excellence. It bears the mark of "American Watch Company, Waltham, Mass." The abbreviation "Mass." seems to be the special target for the bullet as all trace of the mark is obliterated.

Captains Cavender, Yates, and Cole of the First Missouri, Captains Gottshalk and Herron of the First Iowa, Captains Plummer and Gilbert, First Infantry, and Lieutenant Wood, of First infantry, were wounded – none fatally. Captain Burke, of Missouri First, had three balls pass through his clothes, but did not receive a scratch. Two hundred and fifty prisoners were made and over four hundred horses captured. Had a company been detailed for the purpose, a thousand good horses could have been secured.

The rebels appeared to be short of cannon munition with the exception of round shot. Towards the close of the battle they used small pieces of inch diameter rod, cut off with a cold chisel. One of these struck General Sweeny's foot, but caused no injury. They fired but little grape and shrapnel. Most of the small arms taken from them were coonskin rifles and shot guns and flint lock muskets. They had a good supply of excellent arms but were careful not to let them fall into Union hands. They have a quantity of Enfield and revolving rifles, and some regiments are armed with the Minis.

Corporal Grant of Company H, Missouri first, received a grape shot through both legs. He sat upon the ground, loaded and fired his musket four times and then fell back faint from loss of blood. His wound is not fatal.

Major Mudd[13] of General Sweeney's staff, was approached by two soldiers armed with rifles. One of these he dropped with his revolver at fifty yards distance and the other he brought in as prisoner. Major Mudd is a famous St. Louis pistol shot, whose friends some times since offered to back to any amount against Travis.

General Sigel takes command of the main force since General Lyon's death. As it is not possible to hold Springfield, keep open communication with the east, and carry out operations against the enemy, he has decided to fall back upon Rolla. The troops will take up their line of march tomorrow. The wagon train is five miles in length. The wounded will remain here under charge of Doctors Franklin, Melcher, Smith and Davis.

Private Grant, of Company C, First Iowa, after the captain, lieutenant and color-bearer were shot down, seized the flag and took command of the Company. Grant is an old soldier, having been in service in Mexico, Oregon and on the upper Missouri.[14]

There is much excitement in town in reference to the departure of the Union troops. Many families are preparing to leave with them, thinking it unsafe to remain. Twelve overland coaches left for Rolla in the afternoon, as soon as it was rumored that General Lyon was killed, filled with women and children. All who can get away are busy with preparations.

The following are some of the killed and wounded.

[There follows a long list of names.]

The above names are all that could be obtained up to the time of the departure of the mail. For the list I am indebted to Dr. Franklin, in charge of the hospital.

Knox also described the battle in much less detail in his book, *Camp-fire and Cotton-field*.[15] There he repeated some of his newspaper accounts and provided a more accurate account of the casualties. He then summed up his impressions of General Lyon and the merits of the Union fighting men:

It was my fortune to be acquainted with General Lyon. During the progress of the war I met no one who impressed me more than he, in his devotion to the interests of the country. If he possessed ambition for personal glory, I was unable to discover it. He declared that reputation was a bubble, which no good soldier should follow. Wealth was a shadow which no man in the country's service should heed. His pay as an officer was sufficient for all his wants, and he desired nothing more. He gave to the Nation, as the friend he loved the dearest, a fortune which he had inherited. If his death could aid in the success of the cause for which he was fighting, he stood ready to die. The gloom that spread throughout the North when the news of his loss was received, showed a just appreciation of his character.

> *How sleep the brave who sink to rest*
> *by all their country's wishes blest!*[16]

At that battle there was the usual complement of officers for five thousand men. Two years later there were seven major-generals and thirteen brigadier generals who had risen from the Wilson Creek Army. There were colonels, lieutenant-colonels, and majors, by the score, who fought in the line or in the ranks on that memorable 10th of August. In 1863, thirty-two commissioned officers were in the service from one company of the First Iowa Infantry. Out of one company of the First Missouri Infantry, twenty-eight men received commissions. To the majority of the officers from that army promotion was rapid, though a few cases occurred in which the services they rendered were tardily acknowledged.

The death of General Lyon echoed throughout the United States. It was commemorated in pictures and in song. Illustrations varied widely, on horseback (a favorite) or on foot. White horses were an integral part of many of the images. The image chosen here is from Knox's own 1865 book, *Camp-fire and Cotton field*.

Knox, *Camp-fire and Cotton-field*, facing 80.

A broadside, "The Death of General Lyon," was published by J. H. Johnson Co. of Philadelphia without date or author listed. A song was made from the broadside and set to the tune of "John Anderson, my Jo."[17]

Chapter 9

Retreat and Repercussions

The Wilson's Creek battle was over. Lyon was dead. The Union troops were back in Springfield with most of their wounded. General Sigel made the decision to retreat to Rolla. For many of the units, their ninety-day enlistments were over; soldiers returned home to demobilize. Many, but not all, would turn around and reenlist for three-year service.

The newspaper correspondents, Knox, Wilkie, and the others, were on their own. They were not in the army, but were only attached to the army and thereby vulnerable to rebels seeking revenge. Knox wrote nothing of his retreat to Rolla, in the company of other correspondents, for the *New York Herald*, but in 1865, he described his trip from Springfield to Rolla in Chapter 7, "The Retreat from Springfield," of his book *Camp-fire and Cotton-field*:[1]

> On the night after the battle, the army was quartered at Springfield. The Rebels had returned to the battle-ground, and were holding it in possession. The court-house and a large hotel were taken for hospitals, and received such of our wounded as were brought in. At a council of war, it was decided to fall back to Rolla, a hundred and twenty miles distant, and orders were given to move at daylight.
>
> The journalists held a council of war, and decided to commence their retreat at half-past two o'clock in the morning, in order to be in advance of the army. The probabilities were in favor of the enemy's cavalry being at the junction of certain roads, five miles east of the town. We, therefore, divested ourselves of everything of a compromising character.

In my own saddle-bags I took only such toilet articles as I had long carried, and which were not of a warlike nature. We destroyed papers that might give information to the enemy, and kept only our note-books, from which all reference to the strength of our army was carefully stricken out. We determined, in case of capture, to announce ourselves as journalists, and display our credentials.

One of our party was a telegraph operator as well as a journalist. He did not wish to appear in the former character, as the Missouri Rebels were then declaring they would show no quarter to telegraphers. Accordingly, he took special care to divest himself of all that pertained to the transmission of intelligence over the wires. A pocket "instrument," which he had hitherto carried, he concealed in Springfield, after carefully disabling the office, and leaving the establishment unfit for immediate use.

We passed the dangerous point five miles from town, just as day was breaking. No Rebel cavalry confronted us in the highway, nor shouted an unwelcome "halt!" from a roadside thicket. All was still, though we fancied we could hear a sound of troops in motion far in the distance toward Wilson Creek. The Rebels were doubtless astir, though they did not choose to interfere with the retreat of our army.

As day broke and the sun rose, we found the people of both complexions thronging to the road, and seeking, anxiously, the latest intelligence. At first we bore their questions patiently, and briefly told them what had occurred. Finding that we lost much time, we began, early in the day, to give the shortest answers possible. As fast as we proceeded the people became more earnest, and would insist upon delaying us. Soon after mid-day we commenced denying we had been at the battle, or even in Springfield. This was our only course if we would avoid detention. Several residents of Springfield, and with them a runaway captain from a Kansas regiment, had preceded us a few hours and told much more than the truth. Some of them had advised the people to abandon their homes and go to Rolla or St. Louis, assuring them they would all be murdered if they remained at home.

In pursuance of this advice many were loading a portion of their household goods upon wagons and preparing to precede or follow the army in its retreat. We quieted their alarm as much as possible, advising them to stay at home and trust to fortune. We could not imagine that the Rebels would deal severely with the inhabitants, except in cases where they had been conspicuous in the Union cause. Some of the people took our advice, unloaded their wagons, and waited for further developments. Others persisted in their determination to leave. They knew the Rebels better than we, and hesitated to trust their tender mercies. A year later we learned more of "the barbarism of Slavery."

Southwest Missouri is a region of magnificent distances. A mile in that locality is like two miles in the New England or Middle States. The people have an easy way of computing distance by the survey lines. Thus, if it is the width of a township from one point to another, they call the distance six miles, even though the road may follow the tortuosity's of a creek or of the crest of a ridge, and be ten or twelve miles by actual measurement.

From Springfield to Lebanon it is called fifty miles, as indicated by the survey lines. A large part of the way the route is quite direct, but there are places where it winds considerably among the hills, and adds several miles to the length of the road. No account is taken of this, but all is thrown into the general reckoning.

There is a popular saying on the frontier, that they measure the roads with a fox-skin, and make no allowance for the tail. Frequently I have been told it was five miles to a certain point, and, after an hour's riding, on inquiry, found that the place I sought was still five, and sometimes six, miles distant. Once, when I essayed a "short cut" of two miles, that was to save me twice that distance, I rode at a good pace for an hour and a half to accomplish it, and travelled, as I thought, at least eight miles.

On the route from Springfield to Lebanon we were much amused at the estimates of distance. Once I asked a rough-looking farmer, "How far is it to Sand Springs?" "Five miles, stranger," was the reply. "May be you won't find it so much."

After riding three miles, and again inquiring, I was informed it was "risin' six miles to Sand Springs." Who could believe in the existence of a reliable countryman, after that?

Thirty miles from Springfield, we stopped at a farm-house for dinner. While our meal was being prepared, we lay upon the grass in front of the house, and were at once surrounded by a half-dozen anxious natives. We answered their questions to the best of our abilities, but nearly all of us fell asleep five minutes after lying down. When aroused for dinner, I was told I had paused in the middle of a word of two syllables, leaving my hearers to exercise their imaginations on what I was about to say.

Dinner was the usual "hog and hominy" of the Southwest, varied with the smallest possible loaf of wheaten bread. Outside the house, before dinner, the men were inquisitive. Inside the house, when we were seated for dinner, the women were unceasing in their inquiries. Who can resist the questions of a woman, even though she be an uneducated and unkempt Missourian? The dinner and the questions kept us awake, and we attended faithfully to both.

The people of this household were not enthusiastic friends of the Union. Like many other persons, they were anxious to preserve the good opinion of both sides, by doing nothing in behalf of either. Thus neutral, they feared they would be less kindly treated by the Rebels than by the National forces.

Though they had no particular love for our army, I think they were sorry to see it departing. A few of the Secessionists were not slow to express the fear that their own army would not be able to pay in full for all it wanted, as our army had done.

Horses and riders refreshed, our journey was resumed. The scenes of the afternoon were like those of the morning: the same alarm among the people, the same exaggerated reports, and the same advice from ourselves, when we chose to give it. The road stretched out in the same way it had hitherto done, and the information derived from the inhabitants was as unreliable as ever. It was late in the evening, in the midst of a heavy shower, that we reached Lebanon, where we halted for the night.

I have somewhere read of a Persian king who beheaded his subjects for the most trivial or imaginary offences. The officers of his cabinet, when awaking in the morning, were accustomed to place their hands to their necks to ascertain if their heads still remained. The individuals comprising our party had every reason to make a similar examination on the morning after our stay in this town, and to express many thanks at the gratifying result.

On reaching the only hotel at Lebanon, long after dark, we found the public room occupied by a miscellaneous assemblage.[2] It was easy to see that they were more happy than otherwise at the defeat which our arms had sustained. While our supper was being prepared we made ready for it all the time keeping our eyes on the company. We were watched as we went to supper, and, on reaching the table, found two persons sitting so near our allotted places that we could not converse freely.

After supper several individuals wished to talk with us concerning the recent events. We made the battle appear much better than it had really been, and assured them that a company of cavalry was following close behind us, and would speedily arrive. This information was unwelcome, as the countenances of the listeners plainly indicated.

One of our party was called aside by a Union citizen, and informed of a plan to rob and probably kill, us before morning. This was not pleasing. It did not add to the comfort of the situation to know that a collision between the Home Guards and a company of Secessionists was momentarily expected. At either end of the town the opposing parties were reported preparing for a fight. As the hotel was about half-way between the two points, our position became interesting.

Next came a report from an unreliable contraband that our horses had been stolen. We went to the stable, as a man looks in a wallet he knows to be empty, and happily found our animals still there. We found, however, that the stable had been invaded and robbed of two horses in stalls adjacent to those of our own. The old story of the theft of a saw-mill, followed by that of the dam, was brought to our minds, with the exception, that the return of the thief was not likely to secure his capture. The stable-keeper offered to lock the door and resign the key to our care. His offer was probably well intended, but we could see little advantage in accepting it, as there were several irregular openings in the side of the building, each of them ample for the egress of a horse.

In assigning us quarters for the night, the landlord suggested that two should occupy a room at one end of the house, while the rest were located elsewhere. We objected to this, and sustained our objection. With a little delay, a room sufficient for all of us was obtained. We made arrangements for the best possible defense in case of attack, and then lay down to sleep. Our Union friend called upon us before we were fairly settled to rest, bringing us intelligence that the room, where the guns of the Home Guard were temporarily stored, had been invaded while the sentinels were at supper. The locks had been removed from some of the muskets, but there were arms enough to make some resistance if necessary. Telling him we would come out when the firing began, and requesting the landlord to send the cavalry commander to our room as soon as he arrived, we fell asleep.

No one of our party carried his fears beyond the waking hours. In five minutes after dismissing our friend, all were enjoying a sleep as refreshing and undisturbed as if we had been in the most secure and luxurious dwelling of New York or Chicago. During several years of travel under circumstances of greater or less danger, I have never found my sleep disturbed, in the slightest degree, by the nature of my surroundings. Apprehensions of danger may be felt while one is awake, but they generally vanish when slumber begins.

In the morning we found ourselves safe, and were gratified to discover that our horses had been let alone. The landlord declared everything was perfectly quiet, and had been so through the night, with the exception of a little fight at one end of the town. The Home Guards were in possession, and the Secessionists had dispersed. The latter deliberated upon the policy of attacking us, and decided that their town might be destroyed by our retreating army in case we were disturbed. They left us our horses, that we might get away from the place as speedily as possible. So we bade adieu to Lebanon with much delight. That we came unmolested out of that nest of disloyalty was a matter of much surprise. Subsequent events, there and elsewhere, have greatly increased that surprise.

After a ride of thirteen miles we reached the Gasconade River, which we found considerably swollen by recent rains. The proprietor of the hotel where we breakfasted was a country doctor, who passed in that region as a man of great wisdom. He was intensely disloyal, and did not relish the prospect of having, as he called it, "an Abolition army" moving anywhere in his vicinity. He was preparing to leave for the South, with his entire household, as soon as his affairs could be satisfactorily arranged. He had taken the oath of allegiance to protect himself from harm at the hands of our soldiers, but his negroes informed us that he belonged to a company of "Independent Guards," which had been organized with the design of joining the Rebel army.

This gentleman was searching for his rights. I passed his place six months afterward.[3] The doctor's negroes had run away to the North and the doctor had vanished with his family in the opposite direction. His house had been burned, his stables stripped of everything of value, and the whole surroundings formed a picture of desolation. The doctor had found a reward for his vigilant search. There was no doubt he had obtained his rights.

Having ended our breakfast, we decided to remain at that place until late in the afternoon, for the purpose of writing up our accounts. With a small table, and other accommodations of the worst character, we busied ourselves for several hours. To the persona of the household we were a curiosity. They had never before seen men who could write with a journalist's ordinary rapidity and were greatly surprised at the large number of pages we succeeded in passing over. We were repeatedly interrupted, until forced to make a request to be let alone. The negroes took every opportunity to look at us, and, when none but ourselves could see them, they favored us with choice bits of local information. When we departed, late in the afternoon, four stout negroes ferried us across the river.

A hotel known as the California House was our stopping-place, ten miles from the Gasconade.[4] As an evidence of our approaching return to civilization, we found each bed of this house supplied with two clean sheets, a luxury that Springfield was unable to furnish. I regretted to find, several months later, that the California House had been burned by the Rebels. At the time of our retreat, the landlord was unable to determine on which side of the question he belonged, and

> settled the matter, in conversation with me, by saying he was a hotel-keeper, and could not interfere in the great issue of the day. I inclined to the belief that he was a Union man, but feared to declare himself on account of the dubious character of his surroundings.

Knox made some observations on the secessionists' methods of communication and some pungent comments on their veracity:

> The rapidity with which the Secessionists carried and received news was a matter of astonishment to our people. While on that ride through the Southwest, I had an opportunity of learning their modus operandi. Several times we saw horsemen ride to houses or stables, and, after a few moments' parley, exchange their wearied horses for fresh ones. The parties with whom they effected their exchanges would be found pretty well informed concerning the latest news. By this irregular system of couriers, the Secessionists maintained a complete communication with each other. All along the route, I found they knew pretty well what had transpired, though their news was generally mixed up with much falsehood.
>
> Even in those early days, there was a magnificence in the Rebel capacity for lying. Before the war, the Northern States produced by far the greatest number of inventions, as the records of the Patent Office will show. During the late Rebellion, the brains of the Southern States were wonderfully fertile in the manufacture of falsehood. The inhabitants of Dixie invent neither cotton-gins, caloric engines, nor sewing-machines, but when they apply their faculties to downright lying, the mudsill head is forced to bow in reverence.[5]
>
> In the last day of this ride, we passed over a plateau twelve miles across, also over a mountain of considerable height. Near the summit of this mountain, we struck a small brook, whose growth was an interesting study. At first, barely perceptible as it issued from a spring by the roadside, it grew, mile by

mile, until, at the foot of the mountain, it formed a respectable stream. The road crossed it every few hundred yards, and at each crossing we watched its increase. At the base of the mountain it united with another and larger stream, which we followed on our way to Rolla.

Late in the afternoon we reached the end of our journey. Weary, dusty, hungry, and sore, we alighted from our tired horses, and sought the office of the commandant of the post. All were eager to gather the latest intelligence, and we were called upon to answer a thousand questions.

With our story ended, ourselves refreshed from the fatigue of our long ride, a hope for the safety of our gallant but outnumbered army, we bade adieu to Rolla, and were soon whirling over the rail to St. Louis.

Thus ends Knox's tale of the correspondents' trek to Rolla. He does not specify the names of any of his "companions," but one can infer that there were at least three or four traveling together. One of them must have been Franc Wilkie of Iowa.

Knox wasted little time in filing his next report, from St. Louis, and dated August 14.[6] He wrote a summary of Lyon's achievements and reported on recent events in St. Louis, especially on the repercussions of the declaration of martial law:

> General Lyon is dead. Such was the announcement that cast a gloom over the glorious victory of Saturday, and sent a pang to the heart of every Union man in the city. Although his loss is the country's, the sorrow for his death must be felt more keenly by the loyal men of Missouri, to them it seems but yesterday that with three hundred men be held the Arsenal against a State ripening for rebellion, and ready at any moment to break out into open revolt.
>
> A little later, when treason, becoming bolder, rushed to arms, he, without hesitation and embracing the responsibility, struck the first powerful blow, and made prisoners the gang

of rebels assembled at Camp Jackson. Since then his conduct in Missouri, his noble bravery and the acts and measures that displayed the workings of a mighty intellect, endeared him not only to the soldiers whom be always led to victory, but to the loyal men of Missouri, who looked to him for the salvation of their State and its rescue from the eager graspings of an unprincipled Confederacy, and at last, in the very moment of his proudest victory, he was struck to the earth and lay dead upon the field which he had won.

The Union men of Missouri feel that they could ask no prouder or more glorious death for their beloved leader than that of falling while cheering his little band of five thousand on to a pursuit of four times their number. To them the spot where he fell, on the western slope of the Ozark range will hereafter be honored ground. The effects of the victory are yet uncertain, and the city is plunged into wild excitement – thousands of rumors being abroad of General Sigel being pursued and his reinforcements cut off. This, however, to not believed, and it confidently expected that he will be able to conduct his retreat with safety.

Knox then turned to affairs in the city. Martial law was declared in St. Louis City and County by General Frémont on August 14.[7] The appointment of Major (later Brigadier General) Justus McKinstry as Provost Marshall was one that Frémont would later come to regret:[8]

> Here in the city the changes which two days have brought forth have been wonderful indeed. Martial Law was this morning proclaimed, and all day the Home Guard have been busy arresting prominent rebels. Houses have been searched, and in several instances successfully.
>
> The residence of Dr. McKellog's was a few hours ago surrounded, but the inmates, seeing the soldiers coming, had made an undignified escape through a back window. On searching the house twenty-eight muskets were found

secreted, being part of the ones known to be secreted, which I mentioned in my last letter. McKellog is a notorious rebel and meetings of rebel leaders have taken place nightly at his house.[9] As many as twenty others of the same proclivities as the fleeing M.D. have to-day made acquaintance with the inside of the Arsenal. Before the week is ended, rebel plotting will be effectually removed from St. Louis.

Major J. McKinstry has been appointed Provost Marshal of the town, and a fitter man for the office could not have been selected. Brave, energetic and thoroughly understanding the task before him, he has already taken measures that will speedily restore quiet to the city. With him there is no hesitation; red tape cannot prevent him from doing his duty, and Union men may rely upon it that there is hereafter safety for them in this city.

No more rebels will be released as soon as arrested, and suffered immediately to resume their guilty conduct. In my letter of the 11th I mentioned that one of the most notorious instruments of secession in the city is Mr. Brownlee, President of the Police Commissioners, and that he would speedily be arrested.[10] To-day he consequently found himself at the Arsenal. It was at first thought that the present police would be removed and others substituted in their places by General Frémont. It has been considered sufficient, however, to arrest the guilty President of the Commissioners, and the men will, at least for the present, go on with their usual duties, subject at any time, under the rule of martial law, to be superseded by the military. It is highly probable that the hundreds of arms known to be secreted by rebels will come forth from their hiding places in the next few days.

To-night the body of Gen. Lyon is expected to arrive on the Pacific Railroad, and will, if possible, lay in state for a day. Circumstances, however, may prevent this honor, so dearly wished for by the loyal men for whose principles he so bravely fought. It is impossible to describe the deep, earnest sorrow that exists in the city over the sad affair, although the feeling is felt less keenly from the circumstances under which he met his death. Large numbers of troops are constantly arriving. Today three fine looking regiments came in from Illinois.

Large reinforcements have been sent out on the Pacific road to Siegel. The battle at Springfield confirmed the belief expressed in my last, that even with their immensely superior forces, the rebels would have to be attacked by Gen. Lyon, if a battle was fought.

Four days later, on August 18, Knox filed another report from St. Louis.[11] Among the arrivals in St. Louis was Colonel Geo. L. Andrews who had taken command of the First Regiment of Missouri Volunteers after Frank Blair left the regiment to attend the special session of Congress.[12] Knox reported on the first official regimental casualties of the First Iowa and First Missouri Regiments, both 90-day units and also gave some second-hand reports of goings on in Springfield after the rebel troops occupied the town. Finally and importantly, he touched on the feelings of the public on the lack of reinforcements for the late General Lyon and added some personal comments to set rumors straight:

The army of the Southwest, under Major Sturgis, reached Rolla two days since, and several officers of the command are now In St Louis. Among them is Colonel Geo. L. Andrews, of the Missouri First regiment, who was wounded in the leg on the day of the battle. The Missouri First regiment was badly cut up. They went into battle seven hundred and twenty-five strong, and their casualty list foots up as follows:[13]

Killed: 77
Dangerously wounded: 93
Otherwise wounded: 126
Captured: 2
Missing: 15

Retreat and Repercussions

The First Iowa regiment went into battle 825 strong, and came out in the following manner.[14]

Killed: 12
Mortally wounded: 6
Otherwise wounded: 137
Missing: 4

The loss of the other regiments has not yet been reported.

It has been several times stated and contradicted that General Lyon's body was left at Springfield. As late as midnight on the 10th, only three hours before the column started for Rolla, I saw the body at the headquarters, and was told it was to be taken with the command. Later that the night, it was decided to bury it in Springfield and it was accordingly interred on Col. Phelps's farm.

The interment had not yet taken place when the rebels reached the town, but their officers showed every courtesy to Mrs. Phelps and others who attended to the burial. Several of General Lyon's friends have arrived here and are to proceed to Springfield with a military escort, under a flag of truce, to disinter the body and take it East for permanent burial. They leave tomorrow morning by way of Rolla.

After the arrival of the rebel forces in Springfield there was an active run upon all the stores in town, especially those where boots and shoes were to be found, as one half of their soldiers were almost barefoot. No resistance was shown to any price demanded, but payment was invariably made in Confederate scrip. The rebel flag was, of course, hoisted in the most conspicuous place, and saluted with deafening cheers. Our wounded were kindly treated and the surgeons with them were not molested. A man named McIntosh – whether an officer or a private I have not been able to ascertain – was borne about the streets on the shoulders of his comrades and otherwise treated with distinguished honor on account of his claim of having killed General Lyon. The rebels found on the field the carcass of General Lyon's favorite horse and cutting off the mane and tail, divided the long glossy hairs among them, and wore it as decoration to their hats. General Price issued a proclamation promising security to the citizens who were and had been neutral, but seems particularly bitter towards the Home Guards, and says that they may expect no quarter from the rebels. The whole army had not taken possession of the town at last accounts, but were principally occupied in the viewing the battlefield.

In the battle of the 10th, General McCulloch was not killed. The only officer in high authority known to have been injured is General Price, who was wounded by a piece of shell, but not seriously. A rebel surgeon stated to Dr. Melcher of Salomon's regiment, that the rebel loss in killed and wounded would nearly equal in number the entire command of General Lyon. Many of their colonels and captains are among the dead, and some of their regiments were almost annihilated.

To sum it all up, General Lyon's army of five thousand two hundred attacked an army of almost twenty five thousand on their own ground, fought them for five hours, repeatedly repulsed and drove them from the field, caused them to burn their baggage train and then retired in good order, first to Springfield and afterward to Rolla, unharmed and unmolested. Though the whole result, when the evacuation of the country is considered must be ranked as a defeat, the battle itself is nothing less than a victory for the Union forces.

There is much excitement among the Union men of St. Louis in reference to the non-reinforcement of General Lyon. General Frémont states that he considered General Lyon strong enough to hold out successfully against the enemy, and added that all the forces at his command were needed to strengthen Bird's Point and Cape Girardeau and Ironton. Where the fault lies is not well known, but it is evident to all that there is a loose screw somewhere in the government machinery, and that some person or persons must bear the responsibility of General Lyon's sacrifice and the retreat of his little army.

Colonel Stevenson's regiment (Seventh Missouri), now at Rolla, was ordered to march to Lyon's support ten days before the battle, but could not move on account of a lack of transportation. Want of transportation has been the excuse for allowing the half starvation of the soldiers of the southwest for weeks past. Someone is responsible for this lack of wagons and motive power and it is hoped that the matter will soon be investigated.

A complete listing of the killed, wounded and missing in the battle has not yet been obtained. The figures given above were principally obtained from the surgeons of the Missouri and Iowa regiments. The Medical staff was particularly active during the engagement, none more so than Dr. Wm. White of the First Iowa. Dr. White was the last to leave, and did not depart until he had attended to the needs of all in his regiment, and assisted Dr. Cornyn in relieving the sufferings of the unfortunate maimed in the First Missouri.[15]

General Frémont is busy night and day pushing forward matters for a vigorous campaign. The government fleet of boats is kept constantly employed in transportation of troops and nearly all the railways find their rolling stock in constant use. The failure of the expedition to the southwest will cause more careful movements in the future. Daily and almost hourly, troops are pouring into St. Louis from Ohio, Indiana, and Illinois, and being sent to the various threatened points. Not less than thirty thousand men are in service of government in the State of Missouri, and the cry is, "Still they come."

The remnant of the Iowa First regiment came here from Rolla yesterday. They are to disband in St. Louis and go home, where some of them expect to reenlist. Their term of service expired on the 14th.

Knox wrote another letter from St. Louis on August 26 using some colorful speech to vent his opinions.[16]

St. Louis, Mo., August 26, 1861.
The city is at present, and has been for two or three days past, one of the most quiet in the Union. The prompt action of the Provost Marshal, McKinstry, in dealing in with the sympathizers of the rebellion, has produced this calm, and to-day one may walk the streets without hearing secessionism proclaimed at each corner, or seeing a revolver protruding from the pockets of many of the persons he meets. Two gentlemen were sent yesterday to enjoy themselves by working on the entrenchments of Cairo, in the lovely temperature for which city is famous at this season of the year. The offence of which they were guilty is the oft-repeated and publicly proclaimed wish that our soldiers might all be killed and avowing allegiance to Jeff. Davis and the Southern Confederacy. Since their arrest street secessionism has become a matter of history, and the advocates of the Southern cause nurse their pent-up wrath, in the hope of soon being in the ascendancy and wreaking their vengeance upon those they call their oppressors.

The *St Louis Christian Advocate*, a sheet that has only by its excessive piety been preserved from seizure, last evening received a gentle reminder. For some weeks, in its advocacy of the interests of the Methodist Church South, it has attended assiduously to the movements in the political arena, and favored emphatically the Southern cause, to the extent of exceeding bitterness towards everything of a Union nature. Yesterday its editor received a letter from headquarters advising him either to close his business or attend to the legitimate occupation of furnishing spiritual pabulum to the benighted Missourians. Whether the advice will be heeded remains to be seen.[17]

The line of circumvallation around the city, or rather around the land side of it, is progressing rapidly. It will not be long before the defenses are in a state of sufficient strength to protect St. Louis against any force now in the State. Camps of instruction and rendezvous are fast being formed, and the troops which arrive daily from the North and East are at once put into drill and discipline. All the laborers, of whatever class, in the employ of the government, are kept, constantly active, and it is hoped that Missouri will soon be on as good a Union footing as she was three months ago.

It is time for the government to wake from its apparent lethargy, and discover that it is fighting with an active and enterprising enemy. One half the area of the State is now in undisputed possession of the rebels, and they are making the most active demonstrations towards getting still more of it under their control. A fight may be looked for at Ironton or in that vicinity within a week and a collision is imminent at Jefferson City. In Lexington the secessionists are particularly exultant, declaring that the town will be in their hands within ten days, and threatening to drive out all Union men. It is quite certain that a force under General Price is advancing in the direction of the Missouri river to attack Jefferson City, and a detachment will probably visit Lexington. One of the papers a few days since astonished us by announcing that "Ben McCulloch is advancing in three divisions in the direction of Rolla." It turns out that the romantic Ben is still in Springfield, and is not likely to appear in "three divisions." The Police Commissioner Brownlee does not seem to like it he being ordered to leave the city and take up his residence in some free State until the end of the war.

It is astonishing what an amount of arrogance prevails among the Missouri secessionists. The most highhanded enforcements of their decrees in regions where they have the power are considered by them mild and forbearing, and they cannot understand why the Union should complain. But the instant the tables are turned every movement against them is denounced in the most bitter terms. In May last Brownlee notified Gen. Lyon that officers and soldiers would be liable to arrest if found outside the arsenal, and wrote a letter to Gen. Frost recommending that he seize the city and capture the arsenal the latter before it was reinforced. It is refreshing to perceive that he takes to heart the late order of the Provost Marshal, that he "leave his country for his country's good."

A late arrival from Springfield brings some particulars of the rebel loss in the battle of the 10th. Col. J. H. McBride reports that out of six hundred and five men he lost seventy two killed, sixty seven badly wounded, ten mortally wounded and many others slightly. Gen. Rains reports that he lost fifty-six killed, one hundred and eighty-six wounded and sixty missing, but does not state the strength of his division. Gen. John B. Clark, who, was himself wounded, out of a force of two hundred and ninety men lost seventeen killed and seventy-two wounded. Col. Hughes, from six hundred and fifty men, lost thirty six killed seventy-seven wounded and thirty missing. The above are only among the State forces – none of the Louisiana, Mississippi or Arkansas regiments having yet reported.[18]

Among the killed was General Richard H. Weightman of the First Brigade, Second Division, Missouri State Guard.[19] Weightman has been quite notorious on the frontier for several years past. A few years ago in a drinking house in Santa Fe he stabbed F. X. Aubrey, the famous express rider, who once accomplished the distance from Santa Fe to Independence (800 miles) in five and a half days. The affair originated in a remark of Aubrey's concerning a slanderous article published by Weightman in reference to Aubrey's celebrated ride. After killing the latter, Weightman was compelled to leave Santa Fe, and since then has been on the border figuring in numerous difficulties, and becoming somewhat noted during the late troubles in Kansas. He was killed at an early hour in the Springfield battle.[20] Not far from two thousand rebel wounded are now in the town, and about four hundred of the Union troops. The rebel physicians seized all the medicines on hand at the time of their entrance, and our wounded are without medicines or bandages. The ladies of the town are assiduous is their attention to the wounded of both sides. Springfield is one grand hospital.

The Army of the West is in a very good state of efficiency, but there are some bad features about it. There is a very bad feeling among the various regiments engaged in the late battle, the officers of each desiring to receive more credit than any or all the others, with this laudable object in view, many officers of the above mentioned regiments, knowing me to be a *Herald* correspondent, have told me lies enough to cause a believer in the damning nature of falsehoods to give the epauletted gentlemen over as hopeless. The difficulty is to decide between the merits of two radically different stories, when each is supported by an abundance of testimony, and when, as is often the case, the narrators firmly believe they are telling the truth.

The real fact, that cannot be questioned, is, that all the regiments did nobly, and fought like veterans, as the records – the lists of killed and wounded – abundantly testify. As I stated is my report of the battle, no one regiment can be praised above another. One of the regular officers remarked to me to – day: "I think that was the best fighting I ever saw, and I have seen considerable in my lifetime. Those volunteers fight like old regulars. I saw more of the Kansas regiments on that day than of any others, and it is my opinion that if they were ordered to charge upon hell they would storm and carry it."

There is complaint that large quantities of intoxicating beverages are allowed about camp, and that two or three of the officers set bad examples to their men in the matter of orderly conduct. This, if true – and my observation leads me to believe the charge – should be at once looked into by the proper authorities.

General Prentiss, a teetotaller himself, has initiated the example in the Western army of interdicting spirituous liquor as a beverage, and his command now holds the foremost rank for efficiency and good conduct. The order of General McClellan compelling officers to stay with their commands, instead of spending their time at hotels, would be well to apply here.

One day later, Knox was in Rolla. He reported not only on the conditions there, but also about events in Springfield.[21]

Rolla, Mo., August 27, 1861.
The post as lately been strengthened by the arrival of two regiments of Illinois volunteers (the Fourteenth and Fifteenth) and others are being sent along as fast as they can be sent to St. Louis from the States where they were enlisted. Several thirty – two pounders look grim and threatening, and would be likely to cause much havoc among an attacking enemy. On most of the slopes around the oaks and underbrush have been removed, so as to give a full view of anything that approaches, and afford a fair sweep to death – dealing missiles, whether from cannon or small arms. Colonels Wyman and Stevenson have their camps where they can command the village, and the other troops are within easy call. If General Hardee contemplates an attack upon Rolla, in order to possess the terminus of the railroad, and should put his design into execution, he will be sure to meet with a warm reception.

Colonel Wyman's regiment is under drill for seven hours daily, and the other volunteer regiments are fast becoming perfect in military evolutions. Major Sturgis today abandoned Camp "Carey Gratz"[22] for one where the natural defenses are much better, and where his command can be easier supplied with water. The Missouri First regiment at present remains with Major Sturgis, but has been ordered to St. Louis, where it will be reorganized and formed into an artillery and infantry regiment. The loss to the various regiments and companies on the occasion of the battle will be at once made up by filling the vacancies with recruits. General Sweeney's company of recruits has been divided for this purpose, and the men scattered among the various companies of regular infantry.

Recruiting offices have been opened in St. Louis for the Missouri regiments and in Leavenworth for the Kansas regiments. It will not be many days before the muster rolls will again be full, quite a number of the wounded have recovered and taken their places in the ranks, and many of the missing after the battle have straggled into camp.

Captain McDonald, who came from McCulloch's camp to treat for an exchange of prisoners, has returned to his bosom friends.[23] He admits that their loss was quite severe, and says that nearly all their baggage train was destroyed by fire. It is hastily believed that our officers learned as much from him concerning the condition of the rebel forces as he obtained from them. He was on very intimate terms with several of them during the time of his visit, and left evidently much wiser than when he came. We hear occasionally from Springfield that our wounded who were left are generally doing well, and that they are kindly treated by the rebels. In the morning after we departed from the town forty-two of those who were not severely wounded determined to follow and overtake the command, as they had great fears of ill treatment on the arrival of the rebels.

Though weak from loss of blood, they traveled that day twenty-seven miles, coming into camp about midnight, and falling exhausted upon the ground. Several have come in since, three yesterday morning, having travelled the entire distance from Springfield to Rolla (130 miles) in five days.

It is not yet known or even guessed, when the Southwest will be reoccupied, but probably not for some time. The command here is in readiness to move at any time, but it must be doubled or trebled in numbers before it will be sufficiently strong to hold the country and carry on offensive operations at the same time. It is suggested by many that the government would do well to complete the railroad as far as the Gasconade – a distance of some twenty miles on the direct road to Springfield. The track is graded thus far, and all the stone work for the bridge is completed; and it is proposed that the Home Guard amuse themselves by building the bridges and laying the track, the ties being already on the ground and the rails in St. Louis in the storehouses of the company. Certain it is that a completion of this unfinished portion of railway would cut off twenty miles of the worst part of the road between the two posts.

The regimental flag of the Second Kansas Volunteers has thirteen bullet holes through it, and the staff is embellished with a deep gash from a Minié ball. Two standard bearers were successively shot down, and more were killed and wounded within twenty feet of it than on any other similar area during the entire day. The members of the regiment take particular pride in exhibiting the battle scars on their favorite flag, and we may feel confident that after such a gallant defense of their colors they will never desert them. At the time General Lyon fell their flag was not far behind him, and it is barely possible that the ball which gave him his death wound was one of many that were aimed at the banner.

On September 5, Knox again provided more information on the battle at Wilson's Creek.[24]

A gentleman, who requests me not to give his name, arrived here yesterday morning, direct from Springfield. He was impressed into the rebel army some time before the battle of the 10th ult., and was on the ground on that memorable day. He corroborates what we have before learned, that the rebels were ready to march upon Springfield the evening before the battle. They were to advance in four divisions, entering by the four main roads at the same time, but did not move from camp on account of the rain. While he was at breakfast on the morning of the 10th a cannon ball from Totten's battery passed through the tree under which his tent was pitched, and was speedily followed by others. This was the first warning that he received of our proximity, and the surprise was just as complete at the other end of the camp where Sigel made his attack. At the time our retreat was ordered they were uncertain as to the fate of the day, and did not suppose they were victorious. As soon as they ascertained that we had left the field, they returned and took possession. A portion, but not all their train was burned, but he is not certain as to the cause of the conflagration. They being so badly crippled, and Gen. McCulloch wishing to move with caution are given as reasons for not making any pursuit. He thinks that not less than six hundred of their men were killed and a proportionate number wounded. After remaining for a time in Springfield, the forces were divided and moved off in different directions. On the day of the battle they had 28,000 men and sixteen pieces of artillery, and for several days after the battle these were all in and around the town.

Ten days ago General Price with 13,000 men, moved towards the north, and on Wednesday of last week, were at Bolivar, probably bound for Jefferson City, though his exact destination was not known. Rains went with 1,000 men to whip out Montgomery in the vicinity of Fort Scott, but sent back for reinforcements and was furnished with 660 additional men. Like the bad boy of the story, nothing has since been heard from him. Five hundred men were left in charge of Springfield, and McCulloch, with a large portion of the men under his command, moved back towards Arkansas, taking with them all of his wounded that could be moved. It is thought that he may remain a while at Camp Walker, as he is marching in that direction; and it is also supposed that he will go to Fort Smith.

I heard a rumor on the streets to-day that all the Arkansas, Louisiana and Texas troops, with a portion of those from Tennessee and Mississippi, are to rendezvous at some point on the Arkansas river, and are to be reviewed and inspected by General Johnston – the General whom Patterson didn't intercept.[25] This may or may not be true. There is certainly some cause for the withdrawal of those troops from the State further than has yet been given. The quarrel between Price and McCulloch in reference to the behavior of the troops on the field and the propriety of a pursuit after the battle, could hardly have been sufficient to induce the latter to quit the rebel cause in the southwest of Missouri. We shall know the whole story when the proper time comes.

At the time my informant left Springfield there were 750 wounded men in town, of whom 250 belonged to the Union forces. They were well cared for by the physicians of both sides, and the ladies of Springfield were unremitting in their attentions to all. There was a scarcity of medicines, and especially of alcohol and brandy for the use of the sick, the rebel officers having drunk nearly the whole supply. He was not molested while on the way from the rebel lines to Rolla, as he wore the rebel badge – a piece of red cloth around the arm – until he got almost within sight of our camp, at the railway terminus. When within sixteen miles of Rolla, he passed General McBride with one thousand men, who said they were on their way to that place to drive out the Union troops. No tidings have been received here of an attack by this rebel band, and it is quite probable that they have thought better of the matter and concluded not to make trouble.[26]

There would be more information coming out about the Wilson's Creek battle, but for now, Knox shifted to other areas, both geographic and political.

Chapter 10

Knox Afield

Thomas Knox was restless. Looking about for action, or potential action, he decided to travel down the Iron Mountain Railroad to Pilot Knob. There were three railroads emanating out of St. Louis: the North Missouri which connected with the Hannibal and St. Joseph at Hudson; the Pacific Railroad which went west, splitting at Franklin into the Southwest Branch to Rolla and the main line through Jefferson City to Sedalia; and the St. Louis and Iron Mountain Railroad that ran south to Pilot Knob in Iron County.

The Iron Mountain Railroad was built to tap the iron ore resources in the region. This ore had previously been smelted and carried overland through Farmington to Ste. Genevieve on the Mississippi River. With the new railroad to Pilot Knob, completed in April 1858, the overland route to Ste. Genevieve slowly died away. Knox had already traveled both branches of the Pacific Railroad, and things seemed to be quiet in North Missouri. This may have been the reason he chose to visit Pilot Knob. There were the beginnings of fortifications and a troop buildup was occurring. On August 18 he wrote from Ironton, the Iron County seat, sharing, as usual, his assessment of the troops at hand as well as the lay of the land.[1]

> Ironton, Mo., August 18. 1861.
>
> Yesterday morning I left St. Louis by the St. Louis and Iron Mountain Railroad for a visit to the war district of Southeast Missouri. I found each one of the numerous, bridges along the line strongly guarded by United States troops, and nearly every station house was also in possession of the Union forces. General B. M. Prentiss,[2] late the commander at Cairo, has

been appointed by General Frémont commander at this post, and arrived here by special train day before yesterday. The force at his command is quite large, but consists entirely of raw troops. One regiment is from Nebraska, and has seen a little border service; with that exception, none of them have ever been under fire.[3]

The valley in which Ironton is situated at the foot of Pilot Knob is completely shut in by hills. All the approaches to this valley are defended by batteries, and there are suitable earthworks, behind which our troops can do some vigorous and effective fighting if driven into them by a superior force. The design of the defenses is merely for a place of security to retire to in case of repulse below by the rebel troops. The location is but a mile from the terminus of the railroad, thus affording an easy means of reinforcement or supply.

On Friday morning last Colonel Hecker's regiment started in the direction, of Fredericktown, in search of some rebels who were encamped in that vicinity.[4] Yesterday he came upon them just as their dinner was prepared. Before Colonel Hecker arrived in sight of them the rebels fled, leaving prandial repast hot and smoking, for the use of our men, who lost no time in partaking of it. It was not considered of any use to pursue them and Col. Hecker is now on his return.

Colonel Alexander went in the direction of Greenville but as yet has met with no adventure. Another detachment is advancing upon Centreville, a small town some twenty-five miles in the south west direction, and is of but little importance. Fredericktown is about the same distance, but lies to the southeast, and Greenville is nearly to the southward, about forty-five miles away.

Colonel Hardee is at or near Greenville preparing to advance upon Ironton. He has with him not far from ten thousand Arkansas and Tennessee troops, three thousand of them under command of Jeff. Thompson, and expects reinforcements of from three to five thousand in a few days.[5] I have just seen a gentleman who was ten days a prisoner in Hardee's camp, and was liberated by order of the commanding officer. When he left there, some two weeks ago, they were near Pocahontas, awaiting the arrival of a Tennessee regiment of cavalry. He says that Colonel Hardee was perfecting his troops in military evolutions and drill, and for six or eight hours daily had them under drill. They then had not far from six thousand soldiers in camp, all of them well-armed and equipped. They had twelve pieces of brass cannon, but did not appear expert in working them. There was a plentiful supply of provisions, but their transportation train was very small, and they were pressing into service all the teams that could be found in the vicinity. It is probable that we shall hear from them at this point within a week.

General Prentiss is active in putting Ironton and vicinity on a war footing. His videttes[6] are kept out constantly for twenty miles in all directions, and he has sentinels posted from dawn till sunset on the summit of Pilot Knob, which commands a view of the country to a considerable extent. Yesterday the sentinel observed a party of horsemen heading to the southward, apparently with the intention of joining the rebel forces. The big guns are so mounted that they command in several directions, and their position is masked by bushes, so that few can tell where they may be found. Look out for something interesting from this region before long.

Knox penned another letter from Pilot Knob on August 24. This time he expanded upon the threats from the south, but reassured his readers that General Prentiss would be able to handle things.[7]

Ironton, Mo., August 24, 1861.

General Hardee, with a portion of his force, has left Greenville for some point further South. With two of his staff officers be has gone to Pocahontas, Arkansas, to arrange for reinforcements and supplies, matters there being in such a condition as to require his immediate presence. Greenville is occupied by Solon Borland – the noted and notorious Borland – with two to three thousand troops.[8] The soldiers in his command are generally well armed and have been under severe drill for some weeks. At Benton is a rebel force variously estimated at from two to four thousand, and said not to be very well-armed and disciplined. It is thought they intend to make an attack upon Bird's Point simultaneously with one upon Ironton by Borland's force. Pillow is supposed to be still at New Madrid. An attack by the latter on Ironton from New Madrid would be far more difficult than is usually supposed.

By looking at a map of Missouri it will be noticed that the regular outline of the State is broken by an area of some fifty miles square added at the southeast corner. The cause of the addition was as follows: – Along the Little and Great Francis rivers stretches an interminable swamp, which is passable at a point between Buffington[9] and Bloomfield, and at no place below until the junction of the two streams is reached. The people living between this swamp and the Mississippi, to the region that would have been in Arkansas had the northern boundary of that State been made a straight line to the Big river, petitioned to be joined to Missouri, as they had to go up into that State to do their trading and milling, and did not wish when doing so to enter another sovereignty. So that little spot of land became a part of the "Puke State,"[10] and the same cause that produced that effect prevents General Pillow from marching with a small force in the direction of Ironton, as he must pass through Buffington, which is easily accessible from Cairo and Bird's Point by the Fulton and Cairo Railroad.[11]

The nature of the country is such that a large force cannot well march through it, and General Pillow, in going with a few thousand, would run a brilliant chance of being cut to pieces by Union troops from Bird's Point. It is therefore concluded that he will remain at New Madrid in a condition of inactivity, and keep up just enough show of alertness as will necessitate keeping a force at the mouth or the Ohio.

Every day adds to the effectiveness of the troops here. General Prentiss is a thorough disciplinarian and has his brigade, so lately brought together, in as nearly as good a state of military perfection as was that he formerly commanded at Cairo. His artillery is in very fine condition, and his cavalry will do its duty in the field. He has the town well defended and has taken every precaution to insure success to the Union flag in case of a battle. By the end of the coming week, should the rebels not make an attack before that time, we shall probably be on the move towards the location they occupy, and try our hands at giving them battle.

During a return visit to St. Louis, Knox reported some local news and gossip as well as the quiet status of Rolla and Ironton.[12]

St. Louis, Mo., August 21, 1861.

A little excitement was caused today by the arrest of an agent of the Confederate States, with $20,000 in his possession, with which to pay McCulloch's troops. The arrest was made by the Provost Marshal of the city, who somehow found out the rebel paymaster was in our midst and the captured gentleman is now in durance vile charge of United States soldiers. How the information concerning him was obtained or what name the prisoner answers to, has not yet transpired. Some disposition of his case will be made in a day or two.

There is quite the howl being made by the rebels of St. Louis in regard to a military despotism in the shape of martial law. The honest upright citizens of the metropolis have not yet been able to perceive any differences in the rule over them. Martial law has been proclaimed simply to touch some cases and to bring to justice some offenders who could not be handled by civil law. The plan works admirably and it is only by the rebels that are printing treason that make any complaint. The arrest today was one that could not have been accomplished under the civil courts but the cases under the new regime will all be as impartially adjudicated as they would be in a New York court with several head bandaged goddesses holding view.

I paid a visit today to the rooms where the manufacture of clothing, haversacks, &c. for government is carried on. It is in three large halls on Fourth Street in the most capacious of which four hundred women are employed and some fifty sewing machines are housed. The quartermaster has hit upon the plan of having the government make its own goods for soldiers wear instead of letting out the business to contractors. By the present system, a thousand pairs of pants or other garments in production are turned out daily of better quality than by contract and at little more than half the cost. Almost one thousand women are employed and were it not for the difficulty of procuring material for manufacture, the number would be doubled or trebled. The plan delivers a large amount daily to the department and furnishes employment to many of the honest poor of St. Louis and it would be well to adopt it at the East.

A large force left St. Louis this morning for Jefferson City, to protect it from an apprehended attack by the rebels. The latter are moving in that direction and already have several towns of the interior in their possession. The most of those they now have were secesh in the beginning but their occupation by rebel forces of course mean something, it is the avowed intention of the rebels to have sufficient hold of the state at the time of the autumn election to control the popular vote and put Claiborne F. Jackson once more in the Gubernatorial chair.

Unless the government at once takes offensive steps towards them and drives them from the State, there is a strong probability that they will succeed. Should the present rebel army of the southwest remain within our limits, and vote as they have been accustomed to in Virginia, they show a heavy strength in the election returns against the Union men, especially when we consider the large number of ballots their presence will influence. A determination to have the state in their power before the election is probably the cause of the vigor with which they have prosecuted their campaign in the Southwest, and also the impelling reason of the approach at this time towards Ironton and Cape Girardeau

From Ironton, to-night's train brings us little of importance. General Hardee is entrenching himself at Greenville and we hear of works being thrown up at one or two other points where they expect an attack. General Prentiss is accumulating his forces at Pilot Knob, Ironton, and Arcadia, and is about ready to make a good fight.[13] The Quartermaster of his command, Captain Hatch, is busy getting his wagons and supplies ready for moving and in case the column should move on Hardee, it will be far better than was the late unfortunate army of the southwest.

General Prentiss has the troops each day under severe drill and when they do move it will not be easy to fatigue them. A finer body of men it would be difficult to find. Two or three skirmishes have taken place in the southeast between small bodies of rebel and Union troops and in every instance the result has been in favor of the latter. These battles have all been reported by telegraph in the East.

From Rolla, the news is pacific. The camp there has been unmolested, though it is rumored that McCulloch is marching thither with nearly the full strength of his army. The camp has been strengthened by several regiments of Iowa and Illinois troops, and would probably make a victory for themselves if attacked. Batteries of artillery and regiments of cavalry seem to be in the *desideratum* at present, and General Frémont is determined to perfect these two arms of the service. If the powers that be were compelled to make a journey through the length and breadth of Missouri they would at once appreciate the invaluable nature of cavalry in the present war. In the reinforcements sent to Jefferson City this morning were a large cavalry force and some efficient batteries of light artillery. They will do more to keep the rebels from town than treble their strength of infantry. The merchants of various parts of the State are sending their goods to St. Louis for storage, rather than to trust them to the tender mercies of the Confederate army. Many storehouses in this city are being filled with goods put in safe keeping.

Since the declaration of martial law and the suppression of the incendiary sheets published here, the rebels have caused the New York *Daily News* to be peddled about the city by the newsboys. This pleasant little arrangement will soon be ended by an edict from headquarters. At the time of the suppression the editor of the St. Louis *Morning Herald* called upon the Provost Marshall and asked to be permitted to continue his publication. The Provost Marshall replied,

"If you will give a written obligation not to publish anything, directly or indirectly, treasonable, you may go on with your paper."

"As an independent citizen, I cannot make such a promise," was the editor's answer.

"I am obeying orders of my superior officer," said the Provost Marshall, "and cannot let you continue your paper."

The editor became excited at this, and asked, "What would you do if your superior officer ordered you to hang me?" The man in authority gave a cool glance at his visitor and replied, "I should most certainly obey orders," whereupon the editor withdrew.

For a time, actual battle news from Missouri abated. Even as this was true, there remained much for Knox to report from St. Louis. Frémont was stirring up hornet's nests not only from his inaction on helping Lyon at Springfield but also from political actions in St. Louis that had national implications.

Camp Blood at Pilot Knob. (*Harper's Weekly*, Sept. 21, 1861).

Chapter 11

Frémont's Troubles

On the evening of August 31, 1861, Major General Frémont, Commander of the Department of the West, released a bombshell: a proclamation of martial law within the state of Missouri.

The "lines of the Army of occupation in this State are for the present declared to extend from Leavenworth, by way of the posts of Jefferson City, Rolla, and Ironton, to Cape Girardeau, on the Mississippi River":

> All persons who shall be taken with arms in their hands, within these lines, shall be tried by Court Martial, and, if found guilty, will be shot.
>
> The property, real and personal, of all persons in the State of Missouri, who shall take up arms against the United States, or who shall be directly proven to have taken active part with their enemies in the field, is declared to be confiscated to the public use, and their slaves, if any they have, are hereby declared freemen.[1]

The "fire-eaters" and radical abolitionists approved of this proclamation, but Abraham Lincoln had considerable doubts. On September 2, he expressed them in a letter to a friend.[2] Lincoln then wrote directly to Frémont:

> Should you shoot a man, according to the proclamation, the Confederates would certainly shoot our best men in their hands in retaliation; and so, man for man, indefinitely. It is, therefore, my order that you allow no man to be shot

under the proclamation without first having my approbation or consent.³

He also warned that abolition would alienate slave-holding Unionists in states such as Maryland and Kentucky as well as Missouri. Kentucky was a particular problem. Lincoln asked Frémont to modify that part of the proclamation of his own will.⁴

For most of September, Knox remained in St. Louis. He did report on events outside the city, but these were second-handed ones. In his September 5 letter (see Chapter 9 for Wilson's Creek matters), he noted problems in North Missouri but then turned to St. Louis matters.⁵

> St. Louis, Mo., September 5, 1861.
> Reports reached here this morning of difficulty on the line of the Hannibal and St. Joseph Railroad. The statement was that the Second Kansas regiment, on its way home to re-form, was attacked at Shelbina, a station on the Hannibal and St. Joseph Railroad, and was badly cut up. The attack is said to have been made by Martin Green, with 2,500 men. The telegraph wire was cut at the time the fight commenced, and nothing definite is known of the result. The secessionists here claim that the Kansas men were annihilated, and that Green lost but few men. If the Second Kansas regiment was whipped, I will venture the prediction that somebody was hurt on the other side. I saw that regiment in action at Springfield, and know many in it that were prominent in the border warfare, and there is not a more plucky and indomitable set of fellows in the whole country.⁶
>
> A steamboat plying between this point and Cairo was detained here two days by the Provost Marshal, McKinstry, because its owners would not make certain promises with regard to loyalty to the Union. The men finally "came to time," and the boat was this morning released. Prisoners are daily sent to Cairo to work on fortifications, and quite a number are now in durance vile in this city, awaiting their sentence.

One of the prisons is an old slave pen on the corner of Fifth and Myrtle streets, formerly kept by an old slave dealer named Lynch, a relative, doubtless, of the famous Judge of that name who is so conspicuous in Dixie's land. In this prison are some fifteen convicts, or rather about-to-be convicts, most of them men who have been prominent as traitors. Among them is one McDonald,[7] a sculptor of considerable note, who is said to have been particularly active in furnishing information and material aid to the rebels, and it too quite probable his punishment will be of grave nature. In May last he was in favor of driving out everybody who did not hurrah for treason, and it is quite refreshing to perceive the effect of a change of rule.

[PRINCE NAPOLEON]

The great event of yesterday was the arrival of Prince Napoleon[8] and suite, last from Chicago. A body of cavalry and artillery had been drawn up on the levee to meet him on his landing from the ferry boat, but he managed to evade these attentions and proceed at once to the Planter's House, and was nearly through the enjoyment of his supper before the crowd at the water became aware that he had slipped away. Today he made an excursion to the mouth of the Missouri, on the steamer *D. A. January*, under the auspices of Commodore Able. In the afternoon he made a call on General Frémont, and will probably remain at the headquarters of Commander-in-Chief of the Western Department, during his stay here.

On September 10, the concerns over General Frémont's Proclamation, predicted by President Lincoln, came to pass as Knox reported:

St. Louis, Mo., Sept. 11, 1861.

A flag of truce, borne by Capt. W. H. Kidd,[9] of the rebel army, reached here last night. On Saturday last Dr. E. C. Franklin,[10] Surgeon to Gen. Sweeny's brigade, and who remained at Springfield to take care of the wounded, prepared ambulances for one hundred and fifty of the men to come in to Rolla and thence to St. Louis. Just as they were about starting they were stopped by the rebels, who stated that they had just received General Frémont's proclamation, and if the intention expressed in a paragraph stating that all rebels found in arms within our line of posts should be shot was carried out, they would shoot man for man our prisoners. They furthermore stated that they would hold the two hundred and fifty wounded men, and would shoot or hang them all if the intent of the proclamation was carried out. Captain Kidd made preparations to leave for St. Louis on the following morning, in order to confer with General Frémont on the matter, and if possible have the obnoxious clause of the proclamation stricken out. He arrived, and was at once put under guard and allowed to communicate with no one. The result of his endeavors has not yet transpired.

Dr. Franklin came with him, and on reaching the telegraph station forty miles out telegraphed to General Frémont that he was on his way to St. Louis, in company with Captain Kidd, bearer of a flag of truce, and would report at headquarters on his arrival. On reaching the depot he was met by a file of soldiers, and at once put under arrest and conveyed to Barnum's Hotel, along with Captain Kidd. No explanation of the cause of his arrest has yet been given and unless there is something more is known to those most intimate with Dr. Franklin, his arrest is entirely unwarrantable. Dr. Franklin has been most indefatigable in his efforts for the wounded, and the statements of all who have come in from Springfield are very highly in his favor. The arrest was made by the Captain of General Frémont's bodyguard and not the slightest explanations were given.

The Missouri *Republican* noted the arrival of the flag of truce in its September 12 edition. However, no further information was reported.

Knox commented on the increasing secrecy of Union troop movements and actions taken by Commanding General Frémont:

> The famous Eleventh Indiana Zouaves, Col, Lew Wallace, left St. Louis two days since for Paducah and have probably arrived there by this time. They were accompanied by several other Indiana regiments, and will probably do as good service in Kentucky when the battle opens there on the "dark and bloody ground," as they did in western Virginia.[11] The arrivals and departures of troops are now generally made in the night and but few, except those in high office, know anything about the military condition of St. Louis and of Missouri. Troops go in and come out, prisoners are sent to Cairo, military commissions are held and a dozen other things transacted, without the public knowing of anything, or at least but little about them.
>
> At the office of Provost Marshal McKinstry I spent an hour yesterday and with pleasure noticed the rapid manner of conducting business. Twenty individuals, with documents in their hands, would find their cases attended to, and themselves referred, to the proper clerks and bureaus, almost as fast as one could count their number. When an answer was once given, there was no opportunity for further questioning; the next case was taken up and speedily disposed of. When I was there, a clerk from the Passport Office entered, and stated to General McKinstry that a gentleman was in there who declined signing the obligation on the back of the document requiring him to be loyal to the government. Without looking up from the papers he was examining, the General asked, "Does he positively refuse to sign the obligation?"
>
> "Yes Sir."
>
> "Give him thirty days' wheelbarrow work at Cairo," was the reply and the clerk departed.

[COMMUNICATIONS AND RUMORS]

The telegraph corps of the army has been completely organized, and is under the command of Captain Geo. H. Smith,[12] a gentleman of long experience in telegraph matters. It consists of a battalion of line builders, repairers, and operators, each furnished with a light carbine, and furnished with the instrument most useful in his particular branch of the business. They are intended to be taken along wherever the army moves and will keep open communication with St. Louis or some other central point.

There are still numerous rumors in reference to a battle between Montgomery and the rebel forces near Fort Scott. It is highly probable that something of the kind has occurred, but with what result it is impossible to say, though most of the rumors are favorable to the Union cause.[13] Reports of small skirmishes between squads of Home Guard (Union) and rebels are daily received, but excite bit little comment. Attention is turned to the northern part of the State, and all are daily looking for news of importance from that section, though nothing of interest has yet been heard.

The relationship between Colonel Frank Blair and General Frémont was becoming increasingly troubled and Washington – primarily President Lincoln – was becoming concerned. Both Blair and Frémont had influential friends in Washington. In view of Frémont's recalcitrance and arbitrariness, envoys, including Postmaster General Montgomery Blair, Frank Blair's brother, were sent to St. Louis at about the same time Jessie Benton Frémont went to Washington to plead her husband's case with Lincoln. A piece entitled, "The Reported Trouble with Major General Frémont," appeared in the September 14 *Herald*, but with a New York byline, it probably was not written by Knox. It is found in the endnotes.[14]

Problems were brewing for the Frémonts. Jessie Benton Frémont carried a letter from her husband to the president in which the general justified his actions against traitors and the freeing of slaves. In it, he asked

Lincoln to "openly direct me to make the correction....I acted with full deliberation, and upon the certain conviction that it was a measure right and necessary, and I think so still."[15] The meeting was a stormy one, and Mrs. Frémont's anger boiled over. She wrote of the meeting later in a manuscript, which she called "Great Events,"[16] Frémont's request for a direct order was fulfilled on September 11 in a letter from the president:

> It is therefore ordered that said clause of said proclamation be so modified, held, and construed so as not to transcend the provisions on the same subject contained in the act of Congress entitled "An act to confiscate property used for insurrectionary purposes," approved August 6, 1861, and that said act be published at length with this order.[17]

Jessie wrote to her husband warning him of the dispatch of the president's men, General Meigs and Montgomery Blair, to St. Louis. In that letter she also warned him that "things evidently prejudged" and to "guard originals and have copies ready."[18] Jessie Frémont was waiting to hand-carry Lincoln's response. On Sept. 12, she sent two copies of a letter to Lincoln asking for a prompt response and also for a copy of the letter sending Montgomery Blair to St. Louis. Lincoln replied that his response had been sent by mail and declined to provide a copy of the letter sent to Blair.[19] After less than six weeks on post, problems were mounting for General Frémont.

On September 15, Knox wrote another letter, fast on the heels of the two previous ones that appeared in the *Herald* of September 18. He was not complementary to General Frémont and his accomplishments, reflecting the growing unpopularity of the man who had been welcomed by Missouri Unionists and leaders like Frank Blair.[20]

St. Louis, Mo., Sept. 15, 1861.

It is related in some historical anecdote that a negro doing business in Chicago did once, while on a visit to the East, telegraph to his partner, "How Is things doing?" and received the answer, "Things is workin." Should you ask me the question propounded by that African, I should reply as did his business associate.

During the past three days I have visited the camp of instruction, the fortifications of St. Louis, the Arsenal, the dockyard, where the gunboats are being built, and the several government warehouses in and around the city, and am fully convinced that "things is workin." It would not be judicious for me to describe minutely all that I saw, and I can only speak in general terms. The camp of instruction contains accommodation for twenty-five thousand men, and its capacity will soon be increased to thirty thousand. The barracks, if placed in a continuous line, would extend upwards of three miles, and the parade ground is sufficiently large for the evolutions of five thousand troops. As fast as soldiers arrive they are sent to this camp and kept in drill until the time comes to take the field, and whenever there is a deficiency in the force it is made up by a draft from the reserve corps. The camp will be kept up during the war, and will become an important feature of St. Louis. Within a day or two it will be inaugurated and receive its permanent title of "Benton Barracks," in honor of the father of Mrs. Frémont.[21]

The fortifications are approaching completion, the work being conducted by night as well as by day. When finished they will make a line of circumvallation in the form of a semi-circle, extending from the river above the city to the same stream below the Arsenal. At the latter place the utmost activity prevails in the preparation of arms and ammunition for the soldiers in the field. At the boat yards in Carondelet the contractor for the gunboats – James B. Eads, Esq. – of long experience with river craft, is pushing forward the work as rapidly as possible, and expects to have the boats ready for the government at the appointed time, the 10th of October. Their armament is now at the Arsenal.

The ostensible purpose for the visit of these two men, Lincoln cabinet member Postmaster General Montgomery Blair (Frank Blair's brother) for resolution of postal route problems, and the quartermaster situation relating to supplies for Quartermaster General Meigs, was seen in a different light by many. Public dissatisfaction was rising in St. Louis and President Lincoln had sent two trusted advisors to find out why.[22]

> The arrival of the Hon. Montgomery Blair and Quartermaster General Meigs, on Thursday evening last, caused considerable speculation. It is given out by the friends of the former that he came for the purpose of looking after the overland mail, which cannot reach St. Joseph regularly in consequence of the troubles on the Hannibal and St. Joseph Railroad. I learn that orders have been issued to send it by way of Council Bluffs, Iowa, and Omaha, Nebraska, for the present, and that a contract has been made with the Western Stage Company to carry it from the latter point to Fort Kearny, where it will reach the route of the Overland Company. Any other business on which the Postmaster General may have visited St. Louis is quite as likely to become public in Washington as in this city.
>
> The knowing ones make numerous surmises, most of them to the effect that the department is not pleased with the way General Frémont has expended money and made proclamations, while at the same time he has done nothing in the way of getting the State into federal possession. It is a lamentable fact that the rebels have undisputed possession of nearly half the area of Missouri, while in half the remainder they are exceedingly troublesome. When General Frémont came here, two months ago, there were but few counties where the rebels were in power, and their army at that time was by no means a formidable force far down in the southwestern corner. Governor Gamble's visit to Washington to procure government aid for the equipment of the State troops was successful, but the organization of the State forces does not appear to progress very rapidly. One regiment only has been

raised, but we are promised others very soon. The fear that the State will not be very prompt to pay, as she is already is debt to the amount of twenty-three millions of dollars, operates to some extent against the enlistment of troops. The Governor and other State officers are now in St. Louis, looking after the organization.

Col. Frank P. Blair has been tendered the Major Generalship of the State forces, but will not probably accept until there is a strong prospect of the number called for being raised and equipped.[23]

Knox assessed the military situation in the west, particularly that at Lexington, Missouri. For clarity, part of the map from Chapter 4 is included below.

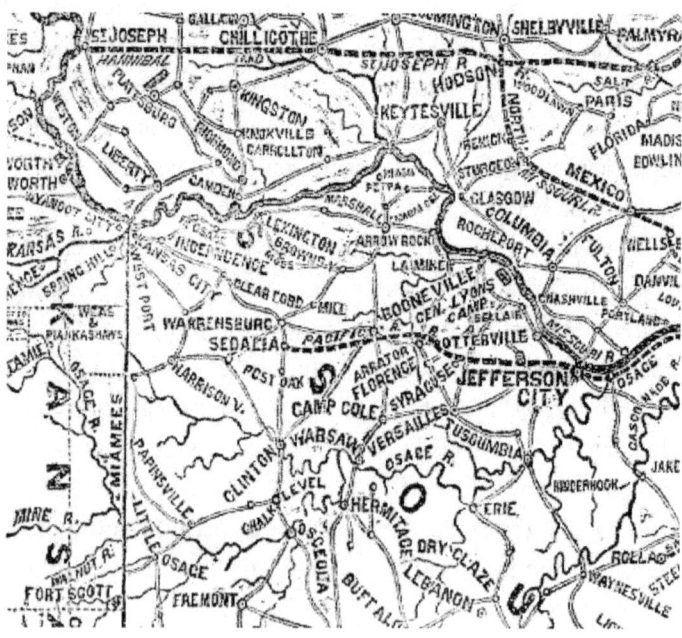

In the interior the rebels are active, conducting affairs in their own way in most cases, but occasionally meeting with a slight reverse. Up to the time of writing we have no news from Lexington, but it is highly probable that place has fallen into rebel hands, as on Tuesday last Gen. Price was at Warrensburg, with sixteen thousand men and fifteen pieces of cannon.

The Union force at Lexington consisted of three thousand men, with entrenchments strong enough to resist anything except artillery, but likely to fall before that possessed by the rebels. Gen. Lane is supposed to be in the rear of Price, with about three thousand men. The skirmish between Lane and Price in the vicinity of Fort Scott, and the retreat of the former, was an attempt to draw the rebels into an ambuscade. Failing in that, the Kansas troops are following closely behind their enemies, in the hope of being sufficiently reinforced to offer battle. The position of Martin Green[24] on the Missouri, near Glasgow, blockades that stream, and will keep it closed until the Union troops remove the obstruction. Two government steamers, the *Sunshine*[25] and another one, name not given, have fallen into rebel hands, and will probably be destroyed.

Knox then detailed some information he had gathered about affairs in other parts of Missouri:

St. Joseph was several days under martial law, by order of a rebel officer, but I learn this morning that General Sturgis has arrived there and hoisted the Stars and Stripes. The manner in which the rebels took possession was rather amusing. Colonel Peabody's Home Guards were rather troublesome to the inhabitants, and a deputation of the oldest and most honored citizens requested their removal. Their request was complied with by the obliging Colonel, and the next day the rebels entered and took possession. The forces at Rolla and Jefferson City have lately been strengthened, in anticipation of a demonstration against those points. An attack upon Ironton has been threatened, but so many threats have lately been made without a fulfilment that a battle there is not looked upon as imminent. The rebels were at Sikeston a few days since, but are this morning, reported as withdrawing to the southward. Several prisoners from Hardee's camp, who were brought here on Saturday, report that there is much disaffection in the rebel army, and that a Louisiana and a Mississippi regiment are on their way home, with a determination to fight only in case of actual invasion of their own States.

Then Knox reported on some personnel and political matters, including opinion on the effect of Frémont's proclamation:

General McKinstry until yesterday expected to take the field during the present week, but an order which came last night will keep him longer in St. Louis, as most of the troops called for will be taken from his brigade.[26] Operations here have been somewhat restricted, owing to the demand at Washington for most of the available material of war. General Frémont's proclamation, though satisfactory to the Union men, is not looked upon as very judicious. The men of the rebel army are not generally rich in slaves and other of this world's goods and the portion of the proclamation which frees their slaves will not affect them seriously. The fact that the rebels have more than half the State in their possession and can at once lay hands on many Union men, does not create favorable comment upon the portion condemning to death all rebels found in arms within certain lines. At present the rebels are holding our wounded at Springfield, with a threat to shoot them upon the first attempt to carry out the conditions of the proclamation. Had General Frémont followed up the proclamation by a vigorous aggressive movement, as was expected, it would have been everywhere hailed with delight. The regulars that were in the battle of Springfield came in from Rolla two days since. On their arrival they were received with considerable military display, and a splendid flag, with "Springfield" embroidered in huge letters across its centre, was presented to Captain Totten. The friends of the First Kansas and First Missouri, who fought equally well with the regulars with earnestness wonder why the volunteers were not received with similar demonstrations. There was no turnout even of a single company, when the volunteer regiments came in. Captain Totten takes the position of Lieutenant Colonel of the First Missouri, lately formed into an artillery regiment.

Finally, Knox added a bit of levity:

> A few days since two prominent rebels were riding through the German portion of St. Louis, and being somewhat inebriated allowed their impulses to get the better of their discretion. They protruded their heads from the carriage and cheered for "Jeff. Davis and the Confederacy." Instantly their carriage was surrounded by the enraged Teutons, who drew them gently forth, and after rubbing their noses together until the skin was completely abraded, replaced them in the vehicle and allowed them to continue their ride. Yesterday a friend of mine met one of the seceshers, and after the compliments of the day asked: "What's the matter with your nose?"
> "I was run away with on horseback yesterday and got scratched in the bushes." "Didn't the Dutch have something to do with it?" The lover of the Southern Confederacy disappears around the corner, filling the air with curses upon the d——d Hessians.

There was little news of military importance coming into St. Louis. General Price was moving north, but his destination, perhaps, Lexington, was uncertain. Telegraph wires had been cut to the west of Jefferson City. Other small rebel movements were reported, but nothing of consequence. Five days later, on September 20, the day that Lexington fell to Sterling Price and the Missouri State Guard, Knox wrote another letter to the *Herald*. By the time it was published, on September 25, the news of Lexington's fall was known, and an additional piece, "A Short Description of Lexington," also appeared. The final paragraph expresses the paper's assessment.[27]

The surrender of the city, with its beautiful residences, to the wanton deviltry of the rebels, is a serious calamity. It is a prize which has doubtless stimulated the rebels to their most desperate efforts to obtain.[28]

Knox's letter also included comments on the situation in North Missouri and details of tests on gunboat armor:

St. Louis. Sept. 20, 1861.
General John Pope arrived here yesterday from North Missouri, and is expected to go in the direction of Jefferson City, in command of a brigade. He represents the portion of the State north of the river as free from rebels in any force, and thinks there will be no more trouble in that direction. He ascribes his failure to overtake Martin Green to the neglect of General Hurlbut and Colonel Williams to send the men he needed at the time appointed, thus causing a delay in his movements and giving the enemy time to learn of his intentions. Green, having now crossed the river and made a junction with Price, leaves Northeast Missouri comparatively free from rebels.[29]

Yesterday there was a trial of the iron plates designed to cover the gunboats for service on the Mississippi. Major Thos. Merritt, Engineer in Chief of Western Department, superintended the experiment and found it in every degree satisfactory. A six pounder rifled cannon was used, throwing a twelve and a half pound shot. The plate experimented upon was of boiler iron, two and a half inches in thickness and four feet square, placed upon a target of timber thirteen inches in depth. The first shot, at 800 yards, made a slight indentation upon the iron, and the second and third, at 500 and 300 yards respectively penetrated 3 sixteenths of an inch. At the final shot, at a distance of 160 yards, the projectile was shattered, some of the pieces flying back to the gun, but in no case was the iron plate broken. The boats are to be clad with this iron, which is thought to be sufficiently strong to resist a thirty-two pound shot. Major Merritt is displaying commendable zeal and efficiency in the management of his department, and the gunboats when completed will be a formidable arm for service on the great river of the West.[30]

Another question arose from Frémont's Proclamation – what would be status of foreign nationals, non-U.S. citizens, and the declaration of martial law? The passes required under martial law to leave the city of St. Louis carried an oath of loyalty that many, especially British nationals, questioned.[31]

> At the Provost's Marshal's office trouble arises occasionally with reference to British subjects. As the obligation on the back of each pass to leave the city requires that the person receiving it shall bear allegiance to the United States, and never in any way afford aid to her enemies, some of Her Majesty's subjects object to signing it. When satisfactory proof, is given that the applicant is not a citizen of the United States, he is furnished with a pass without being required to sign the obligation.
>
> About two hundred men of foreign birth, employed on the fortifications, refused work one morning on being required to take oath to their loyalty. One of them addressed a letter to the English Consul at Chicago, asking advice as to the best course to pursue, and received in return a document full of the most abstruse English, but in no way answering the interrogatory. What the British subjects will do in the matter is not known. It is contemplated to administer to them an oath which shall be exactly similar to the one now in use, with a proviso that it shall not affect their relations to any foreign Power.
>
> General Frémont is engaged in pushing matters at a rapid rate, and it will not be long before he will be dealing aggressive blows at the enemy. About the time you receive this letter you will hear of a move that will astonish you. The difficulty

between the Blair's and the General continues unremoved, and the matter, though still the subject of much conversation, it not as engrossing as it was a few days since. While each party has its adherents, with the preponderance in favor of General Frémont, all regret the occurrence of the unfortunate quarrel between those hitherto warm friends, and especially that it should occur at this particular juncture. When Colonel Blair's trial will take place is not known, though it is evident that it will not be long postponed.[32]

General Price, whether he has or has not taken Lexington, is evidently in a position where only the most powerful anti-laxatives will save him.[33] With General Sturgis on the north, Lane on the southwest, Hunter (at Rolla) to intercept a retreat towards Springfield, and a strong force at Jefferson City, with the railroad to Sedalia in federal possession, General Price is in a far tighter condition than he was at Booneville or Carthage. Preparations for an immediate forward movement in some direction, probably towards Price's rear, are being pushed with the utmost rapidity. Brigadier General McKinstry informed me to day that he would very soon be in active service in the field, but was uncommunicative as to the precise time or place. He will be succeeded temporarily in the Quartermaster's Department by Captain Turnlee, an officer of known ability and integrity.[34] The office of Provost Marshal will be filled by Captain D. B Greene, a gentleman of New York origin, who was attached to the Iowa First, and became particularly distinguished at the battle of Springfield. General McKinstry's brigade is promised the of honor of first position in whatever expedition may be first made, and will contain in part of the regular and the First Missouri. Adjutant General J. Kelton was today appointed Colonel of the Ninth Missouri, and takes his position immediately.

At the passport office, a few days since, a gentleman called to procure a pass for Springfield, stating the purpose of his visit to be the recovery of the body of his brother reported killed on the 10th ultimo. A clerk told him that a wounded man belonging to the same regiment (the First Iowa) arrived in town the evening previous, was to call at the office in the afternoon, and perhaps could afford some information concerning the missing man. The stranger returned at the designated hour and was overjoyed to find the brother who was supposed to be dead on the battlefield.

The rafts intended for mortar service on the river are nearly complete. The number and the size of their armament you may find out for yourself. One thing is certain, no amount of shot can sink them.

With the fall of Lexington, the controversy over the fitness of General Frémont for command in the Western Department was coming under much more scrutiny. Newspapers all over the North were beginning to take sides. Blame for the fall of Lexington was being laid at his feet. Knox's letter of September 22 was still unable to provide concrete evidence on the fate of Lexington. He did, however make comments on Frémont's old friends, contractors who were getting some contracts. He began, however, with news of the situation in Springfield under rebel rule.[35]

St. Louis, Mo., Sept. 22.1861.
A lady arrived from Springfield last evening, to join her husband who came from that town on the 11th of August with the Union army, and who has since been stopping in St. Louis. She states that it was reported there that McCulloch's army was beyond Bentonville, Ark., on its way to Fort Smith, and would not return to Missouri unless its presence became absolutely necessary. She says the rebels took all their wounded that could be moved at the time of their departure, and also forced nearly all the negroes in the vicinity to go with them, declaring it their intention to make the nigger pay as much as possible of the expense of the war now waged on his behalf. Nearly all the Union men who owned slaves were

deprived of them, as they were of nearly all other kind of property. Many secessionists were also made niggerless, the Confederate officers and soldiers not being very discriminating. Much delight was manifested by the rebel troops when they ascertained that the five cannon captured on the day of the battle were the same that were taken from the Missouri traitors at Camp Jackson. They left about a thousand men to hold Springfield and keep possession of our wounded soldiers there. This force has dwindled to less than five hundred heroes, who amuse themselves by drinking Missouri whiskey and making loud threats to kill all the Union soldiers that fall into their hands. Their dead (those who have died since the battle) have been buried in the fields around the town, and are estimated at not less than five hundred. The mortality among their wounded is very large, and bears strong testimony to the assertion that a wound from a Minié ball, however slight, will in a few days or weeks prove fatal.

[DEFECTIONS]

A young man who entered the rebel army in June last, receiving a captain's commission, has become disgusted with life among the rebels, and, through the United States District Attorney, applied to Gen. Frémont for permission to come home, and make war no more. As several prominent Union men of St. Louis are convinced of his sincerity, and are ready to vouch for his good faith in the matter, Gen. Frémont has granted him a pardon on condition of his taking the oath of allegiance on his arrival here, and holding no communication whatever with the rebels. Much care will be exercised in the matter, as it is well known that several reformed traitors have returned, with the most earnest protestations of repentance, who have gained all the information possible respecting our strength and movements, and then disappeared, to tell to the enemy all that they knew.

Questions were beginning to be raised about the contracts being issued by the Frémont administration. Some former friends from California appeared on the scene implying that their "help" was necessary to obtain these lucrative contracts.[36]

> Individuals anxious to secure contracts continue to arrive here daily from the Eastern cities, with now and then a wanderer from the Pacific shore. Several Californians, to whom reference has before been made, still continue to make themselves as prominent as ever, conducting their operations with the accustomed modesty of San Francisco money makers. One of them claims to be on the most intimate and confidential terms with Gen. Frémont, and is said to assure everyone seeking a contract that it cannot be brought about unless this "intimate and confidant" of the Major General has a respectable interest in the matter. I am assured from reliable authority that this individual has no influence whatever with Gen. Frémont, and is not often in his presence. It may be said of most of the other Californians here that they have little to do with the General or with the Department of the West, making most of their money by outside operations. A complete history of the California speculators, now in St. Louis, is promised me by a gentleman who was for several years a resident of San Francisco, and within a few days I shall be able to give the life and exploits of each member of the El Dorado delegation.
>
> Since the date of my last nothing save a few telegraphic Items has been received from Lexington. The last rumor is to the effect that Sturgis crossed the river on rafts, and had put the rebels to flight.
>
> Some thirty prisoners taken in arms below Ironton were brought here yesterday, and set to work upon the entrenchments. They all stoutly refused to take the oath of allegiance until they found that they were really to be put to hard labor. When this was ascertained fourteen of them at once expressed

a desire to subscribe to the obligation but were not let off so easily.

Government continues to neglect to furnish a sufficient supply of arms for this department. A regiment of cavalry goes into the field tomorrow, armed with nothing but carbines, and those were not procured until last evening. Another cavalry regiment is waiting for arms, with but little prospect of getting them, and should they not be forthcoming within a few days, General Frémont expresses his determination to set the blacksmiths at St. Louis at work to furnish the regiment with lances, after the manner of the knights of old.

Two days later, on September 24, Knox wrote again from St. Louis. The news that Lexington had fallen, though expected, caused serious repercussions in the city. Murmurs against Frémont were increasingly heard throughout the city. The suppression of the *St. Louis Evening News* for its editorial on the loss of Lexington was especially vigorously criticized. The suppression was reported not only by Knox for the *New York Herald*, but also noted by the *New York Times,* which reprinted the offending editorial in its entirety commenting, "It seems that military authorities are willing enough to be praised, but cannot endure to be criticized by the newspapers. The *Evening News* is, and has always been, a staunch Union paper, and its statements in regard to the loss of Lexington are moderate compared with the utterances of the Press generally on that shameful affair."[37] Knox in his letter called the *Evening News* editorial "improper and injudicious," because of the tense situation in St. Louis between Frémont and Frank Blair and between loyalists and secessionists. Knox wrote:[38]

St. Louis, Mo., Sept. 24, 1861.
The fall of Lexington created great excitement in St. Louis, notwithstanding its fall had been expected for some days. Yesterday the St. Louis *Evening News* appeared with an article, "The Fall of Lexington," in which there were some severe reflections upon the Western Department for allowing a little army of twenty five hundred to be overcome by a force of

fifteen to twenty thousand when there were forty thousand soldiers within a few days' march, and when the department had on hand hundreds and thousands of tons of shot and shell and was plentifully supplied with all the means and appliances of war.

The article was an improper and injudicious one to be issued at the present time in Missouri, though all its comments on our defeat were exactly similar to those which had been made by hundreds of loyal citizens hours before the paper appeared. The *News* is a sheet of not much importance in the city or out of it, but has been throughout most emphatic and unquestionable in its loyalty. It supported Bell and Everett in the campaign of 1860, and, though it hesitated slightly when the doctrine of "coercion" was promulgated, promptly overcame its scruples and hoisted the Stars and Stripes at the head of its columns in advance of the *Missouri Democrat*.

About an hour after the paper of last evening made its appearance, the office was visited by a file of men, in obedience to an order of Major General Frémont, the delivery and sale of the *News* was stopped, the publisher and all the *attachés* of the paper were put in arrest, all the business of the establishment closed up.

The article entitled "The Fall of Lexington," had offended the commander of the Western Department, and particularly so because the official had been told the article had been either written or dictated by Col. Frank Blair. Mr. Grissom, editor of the *News*, states emphatically that the obnoxious editorial was penned by himself, and was not even in any way suggested by anyone else. He has not for weeks conversed with Col. Blair on any political subject, and the latter individual has no influence, control or interest in the St. Louis *Evening News*. The *attachés* of the concern, with the exception of Mr. Grissom and the publisher, Mr. Ramsey, were released last evening, but these two gentlemen are still under arrest in the military prison, but are allowed to see all their friends who call to pay their respects and are allowed servants at the expense of the Government of the United States. Throughout today, the office has remained closed, and can only be reopened by consent of the commanding general.

The affair has created much excitement in the city and the suppression of the paper is spoken of in severe terms by nearly all the loyal citizens of St. Louis. Had the *Republican*, 'til lately a secession sheet, and even now almost daily giving important information to the enemy, met with the fate of the *News*, would have elicited favorable comment from a majority of citizens, but for a paper hitherto loyal to be suppressed because it ventured to criticize acts of the department arouses public indignation to no small extent.[39]

General Frémont was expected to take the field Monday, but has not yet gone to the war. He is intending to leave St. Louis tomorrow noon, but may be still further delayed. The army is making its rendezvous at Jefferson City, and is expected to march upon Lexington and whip out the redoubtable General Price. You must wait in order to see results.

Knox then described some of the contracting procedures in St. Louis and contrasted them with those found in the East. The problems caused by McKinstry and his friends had not yet come to light:

> The quality of the clothing furnished to the Army of the West is an improvement upon that which almost completely failed to cover the nakedness of the soldiers at the East. Much of it is purchased direct from the dealers and is not furnished by contract. One firm, that of Tichnor & Co., for years transacting the most extensive clothing business in the West, has its establishment on the corner of Washington avenue and Fourth street directly opposite the headquarters of the Quartermaster, and keeps its large force of employees constantly at work on army clothing, and is daily in receipt of immense

quantities of ready-made uniforms from the East. These goods are purchased by the government according to their actual value, and are not passed through the hands of a contractor. The advantage of this system over that of Pennsylvania and other swindling States will at once be obvious.

Government has now in its employ upwards of twenty steamboats. The most of them at present are in use as transports between St. Louis and Jefferson City. A ferry boat, long in use between this city and the Illinois shore, has been purchased by Uncle Sam, and is being fitted up as a gunboat. The gunboat building at Carondelet are progressing nicely, though none of them have yet been launched.

The editors of the *St. Louis Evening News*, Grissom and Ramsey, were released and the paper reopened after they agreed to no longer publish anything "injurious to the government."[40]

How far Frémont had fallen in both public and political esteem! When he arrived in St. Louis at the end of July, he was hailed by almost everyone as the right choice for the job. But then came blame for not helping General Lyon in Springfield and abandoning the Union commander at Lexington, Colonel James A. Mulligan. His proclamations of martial law, first in the city and then in the state received mixed receptions. The manumission of slaves from masters aiding the Confederacy caused more problems in Washington. His lavish lifestyle (renting the Brant mansion in St. Louis for his headquarters for $6,000 a month and other over-spending) and the presence of a large "body guard" made up of many different foreign nationals further alienated the populace. And finally, his self-imposed isolation, surrounding himself with layers of functionaries, made it nearly impossible for officials to meet with him.[41] His popularity in St. Louis was fading rapidly.

Finally, Frémont began to move. Knox wrote:

St. Louis, Sept. 27, 1861.

General Frémont and part of his staff left for Jefferson City this afternoon. Reports reached here to-night that General

Price has dismounted all his horsemen except four regiments, and is organizing his army for a determined stand against General Frémont.[42]

Rumors abounded that General Frémont had been ordered to Washington to stand court martial based on charges from Frank Blair. But –

St. Louis, Oct. 3, 1861.
The following dispatch was received here to-day:
Washington, D. C., October 2, 1861.
General Frémont is not ordered to Washington, nor from the field, nor is any court martial ordered concerning him.
Wm. H. Seward.[43]

Now, it was time for Frémont to act. He had left St. Louis for Jefferson City. But much more was expected of him if he were to have any chance of redeeming others' opinions and retaining his command.

"Major General Frémont, U. S. A., and Staff Inaugurating Camp Benton, at St. Louis, Missouri, Before Starting For Lexington. From a photograph."
(*Harper's Weekly*, October 12, 1861).

Chapter 12

Jefferson City

Frémont was on the move! Finally! But this time there was something different. Many more newspaper correspondents and even some staff artists assembled to cover the events. Eastern newspapers (except the *Herald* and the *Times*) had missed covering the battle at Wilson's Creek, but that was not to happen again. Their assembly point was Jefferson City. Junius Henri Browne of the New York *Tribune* was there; Albert D. Richardson, also of the *Tribune*, was there; Franc B. Wilkie of the *New York Times* was there; as were representatives of the main St. Louis papers, the *Democrat* and the *Republican* as well as other reporters. Thomas W. Knox had plenty of company. In Jefferson City, while waiting for some action, this "Bohemian Brigade" grew bored. Several of them described the raucous situation and shared their impressions in books they wrote after the war. None of these reports appeared in contemporary newspapers.

First, Thomas W. Knox shared his view of the war correspondents:

> As the army lay at Jefferson City, preparing for the field, some twelve or fifteen journalists, representing the prominent papers of the country, assembled there to chronicle its achievements. They waited nearly two weeks for the movement to begin. Some became sick, others left in disgust, but the most of them remained firm. The devices of the journalists to kill time were of an amusing nature. The town had no attractions whatever, and the gentlemen of the press devoted themselves to fast riding on the best horses they could obtain. Their horseback excursions usually

terminated in lively races, in which both riders and steeds were sufferers. The representatives of two widely-circulated dailies narrowly escaped being sent home with broken necks.

Evenings at the hotels were passed in reviving the "sky-larking" of school-boy days. These scenes were amusing to participants and spectators. Sober, dignified men, the majority of them heads of families, occupied themselves in devising plans for the general amusement.

One mode of enjoyment was to assemble in a certain large room, and throw at each other every portable article at hand, until exhaustion ensued. Everything that could be thrown or tossed was made use of: pillows, overcoats, blankets, valises, saddle-bags, bridles, satchels, towels, books, stove-wood, bed-clothing, chairs, window-curtains, and, ultimately, the fragments of the bedsteads, were transformed into missiles. I doubt if that house ever before, or since, knew so much noise in the same time. Everybody enjoyed it except those who occupied adjoining rooms, and possessed a desire for sleep. Some of these persons were inclined to excuse our hilarity, on the ground that the boys ought to enjoy themselves. "The boys!" Most of them were on the shady side of twenty-five, and some had seen forty years.

About nine o'clock in the forenoon of the day following Price's evacuation of Lexington, we obtained news of the movement. The mail at noon, and the telegraph before that time, carried all we had to say of the affair, and in a few hours we ceased to talk of it. On the evening of that day, a good-natured "contractor" visited our room, and, after indulging in our varied amusements until past eleven, bade us good-night and departed.

Many army contractors had grown fat in the country's service, but this man had a large accumulation of adipose matter before the war broke out. A rapid ascent of a long flight of stairs was, therefore, a serious matter with him.

Five minutes after leaving us, he dashed rapidly up the stairs and entered our room. As soon as he could speak, he asked, breathing between, the words –

"Have you heard the news?" "No," we responded, "what is it?" "Why" (with more efforts to recover his breath), "Price has evacuated Lexington!"

"Is it possible?"

"Yes," he gasped, and then sank exhausted into a large (very large) arm-chair.

We gave him a glass of water and a fan, and urged him to proceed with the story. He told all he had just heard in the bar-room below, and we listened with the greatest apparent interest.

When he had ended, we told him our story. The quality and quantity of the wine which he immediately ordered, was only excelled by his hearty appreciation of the joke he had played upon himself.

Every army correspondent has often been furnished with "important intelligence" already in his possession, and sometimes in print before his well- meaning informant obtains it.[1]

Junius Henri Browne was somewhat more circumspect in his report of the journalistic escapades.[2]

"The Bohemian Brigade" was the name the little corps of army correspondents and artists that soon assembled at Jefferson City had received. They were only seven or eight in number: Albert D. Richardson, of the New York *Tribune*, Thomas W. Knox, of the *Herald*, Franc B. Wilkie, of the *Times*, Richard T. Colburn, of the *World*, Joseph B. McCullagh, of the Cincinnati *Commercial*, Geo. W. Beaman,[3] of the St. Louis *Democrat*, Henri Lovie, artist for Frank Leslie, and Alex. A. Simplot, for *Harper's Weekly*; with several other scribblers and sketchers, who were there for a few days, but grew tired or disgusted, and did not accompany our expedition to the South-West.

Of course, we had considerable leisure, and amused ourselves as best we could, in the absence of books which were very scarce. We smoked pipes, played whist, discussed Poetry, Metaphysics, Art, the Opera, Women, the World, the War and its future, and various themes on which [we] could merely speculate.

Most of our Brigade were bachelors – unless Michelet's idea of bachelordom, as expressed in "L'Amour," be correct – and enthusiastic members of the anti- matrimonial school of philosophy.[4]

The unwedded bore camp-life resignedly and cheerfully; but the Benedicks seemed delighted with it, because, as most confirmed celibates declared, they then had an excuse for absenting themselves from their domestic hearths, and, to use that exquisitely satirical phrase, the "blessings of connubial life."

On the other hand, Albert D. Richardson expanded the correspondents' story.[5]

The war correspondents "smelled the battle from afar off." More than twenty collected two or three weeks before the army started. Some of them were very grave and decorous at home, but here they were like boys let out of school.

They styled themselves the Bohemian Brigade, and exhibited that touch of the vagabond which Irving charitably attributes to all poetic temperaments. They were quartered in a wretched little tavern eminently First Class in its prices. It was very southern in style. A broad balcony in front, over a cool brick pavement; no two rooms upon the same level; no way of getting up stairs except by going out of doors; long, low wings, shooting off in all directions; a gallery in the rear, deeper than the house itself; heavy furniture, from the last generation, with a single modern link in the shape of a piano in the ladies' parlor; leisurely negro waiters, including little boys and girls, standing behind guests at dinner, and waving long wands over the table to disconcert the omnipresent flies; and corn bread, hot biscuits, ham, and excellent coffee. The host and hostess were slaveholders, who said "thar" and "whar," but held that Secessionists were traitors, and that traitors ought to be hung....

The Bohemians took their ease in their inn, and held high carnival, to the astonishment of all its *attachés*, from the aged proprietor down to the half-fledged negro cherubs. Each seemed to regard as his personal property the half-dozen rooms which all occupied. The one who dressed earliest in the morning would appropriate the first hat, coat, and boots he found, remarking that the owner was probably dead.

One huge, good-natured brother they called "the Elephant."[6] He was greatly addicted to sleeping in the daytime; and when other resources failed, some reckless quill-driver would say: "Now, let's all go and sleep with the Elephant." Eight or ten would pile themselves upon his bed, beside him and upon him, until his good-nature became exhausted, when the giant would toss them out of the room like so many pebbles, and lock his door.

There was little work to be done; so they discussed politics, art, society, and metaphysics; and would soon kindle into singing, reciting, "sky-larking," wrestling, flinging saddles, valises, and pillows. In some recent theatrical spectacle, two had heard a "chorus of fiends," which tickled their fancy. As the small hours approached, it was their unceasing delight to roar imitations of it, declaring, with each repetition, that it was now to be given positively for the last time, and by the very special request of the audience. How they sent that demoniac "Ha! ha! ha!" shrieking through the midnight air! The following account of their diversions was given by "J. G." in *The Cincinnati Gazette*. The scenes he witnessed suggested, very naturally, the nomenclature of the prize-ring:

> Happening to drop in the other night, I found the representatives of *The Missouri Republican*, *The Cincinnati Commercial*, *The New York World*, and *The Tribune*, engaged in a hot discussion upon matrimony, which finally ran into metaphysics. *The Republican* having plumply disputed an abstruse proposition of *The Tribune*, the latter seized an immense bolster, and brought it down with emphasis upon the glossy pate of his antagonist. This instantly broke up the debate, and a general *mêlée* commenced. *The Republican* grabbed a damp towel and aimed a stunning blow at his assailant, which missed him and brought up against the nasal protuberance of *Frank Leslie*. The exasperated Frank dealt back a pillow, followed by a well-packed knapsack. Then *The Missouri Democrat* sent a coverlet, which lit upon and enveloped the knowledge-box of *The Herald*. The latter disengaged himself after several frantic efforts, and hurled a ponderous pair of saddle-bags, which passed so close to *The Gazette's* head, that in dodging it he bumped his phrenology against the bed-post, and raised a respectable organ where none existed before. Simultaneously *The Commercial* threw a haversack, which hit *Harper* in the bread-basket, and doubled him into a folio – knocking him against *The World*; who, toppling from his center of gravity, was poising a plethoric bed-tick with dire intent, when the upturned legs of a chair caught and tore it open, scattering the feathers through the surging atmosphere. In falling, he capsized the table, spilling the ink, wrecking several literary barks, extinguishing the "brief candle" that had

faintly revealed the sanguinary fray, thus abruptly terminating hostilities, but leaving the panting heroes still defiant and undismayed. A light was at last struck; the combatants adjusted their toilets, and, having lit the calumets of peace, gently resigned themselves to the soothing influence of the weed.

They did not learn, for several days, that a meek chaplain, with his wife and three children, inhabited an adjacent apartment. He was at once sent for, and a fitting apology tendered. He replied that he had actually enjoyed the novel entertainment. He must have been the most polite man in the whole world. He is worthy a niche in biography, beside the lady who was showered with gravy by Sidney Smith, and who, while it was still dripping from her chin, blandly replied to his apologies, that not a single drop had touched her!

When in-door diversions failed, the correspondents amused themselves by racing their horses, which were all fresh and excitable. That region, abounding in hills, ravines, and woods, is peculiarly seductive to reckless equestrians desiring dislocated limbs or broken necks.

One evening, the "Elephant" was thrown heavily from his horse, and severely lamed. The next night, nothing daunted, he repeated the race, and was hurled upon the ground with a force which destroyed his consciousness for three or four hours. A comrade, in attempting to stop the riderless horse, was dragged under the heels of his own animal. His mild, protesting look, as he lay flat upon his back, holding in both hands the uplifted, threatening foot of his fiery Pegasus, was quite beyond description. One correspondent dislocated his shoulder, and went home from the field before he heard a gun.

All the above reports were for the post-war future. Knox and the others wrote serious reports on the state of affairs in Missouri. Knox wrote from Jefferson City on October 2[7] and again on October 3.[8]

Jefferson City, Mo., Oct. 2, 1861.

General Frémont continues actively occupied, and the various division commanders have had interviews with him today. His programme is said by those in his confidence to be excellent in every particular, and to have met the approval of all the military authorities to whom he has disclosed it. Since his arrival here, confidence in the Union cause has greatly increased, and is now believed that before the end of the month, Missouri will be purged of her rebel foes.

The steamer *Emma* left for Lexington this evening, to convey our wounded to the hospitals in St. Louis.[9]

Colonel Philip St. George Cooke, of the Second United States Dragoons, arrived here this evening, and had a lengthy private interview with General Frémont. His force of regulars from Utah will no doubt be ordered to this vicinity for service. It is said that a Brigadier Generalship will be conferred upon him.[10]

Jefferson City, Mo., Oct. 3, 1861.

"The busy note of preparation"[11] is the only sound to be heard around this city. Troops are constantly arriving from below [east] by boat and by rail, and after a detention of a day or two are sent above [west] to Sedalia or Georgetown. A force of about 15,000 is in and about Jefferson, but is daily diminished by the numbers sent forward to a point neared the scene of active operations. There is a good proportion of cavalry and artillery, and the whole army is fast taking shape. General Frémont is confident that he can successfully engage the whole rebel force in Missouri, and only desires a few days' further preparation.

It is thought that General Price will make a stand at

"General Frémont's Camp Near Jefferson City, Missouri."
Sketched by Alexander Simplot. (*Harper's Weekly*, October 26, 1861).

Lexington, and will engage the force of General Frémont when it moves forward. The latter will convey his troops and munitions of war by rail to Sedalia, whence the distance to Lexington is fifty-five miles, which will require a march of three days. It will be five or six days from the present date before the army will move from Jefferson, and you can safely put aside all anxious expectation of startling news from Missouri until the 12th or 15th instant. General Hunter will not take the field with the main army, but is to operate on the Osage River, keeping a watch over the ferries of that stream, to prevent the crossing of any reinforcements from the southwest. General McKinstry will lead the foremost brigade whenever the battle occurs.

General Frémont has his camp about half a mile west of the town, on an elevation that commands the capital, and holds the approaches from the direction of Springfield and

Tuscumbia. Since his arrival he has attended closely to the perfection of his army and the completion of preparations for a forward movement.[12]

The Missouri river is now very low – not more than three feet of water in the channel between Lexington and Jefferson City. The gunboat *New Era*,[13] which was fitted up to aid in the attack on Lexington, was unable to come up the Missouri, and has returned to St. Louis.

On the same day, October 8, the *New York Herald* carried an editorial, not written by Knox, but certainly influenced by him, that expressed high hopes but also considerable doubts about Frémont's movements.[14]

He [Frémont] has leisure to perfect his arrangements without much danger of their being interrupted by the enemy, and nothing but the grossest mismanagement and imbecility can prevent his striking a death blow at treason within the next few weeks. With Generals Hunter, Siegel, Totten, Dubois, Sturgis and McKinstry, together with the gallant Sweeney to support him, it would require almost miraculous incompetency for Frémont to prove inadequate to the task he is called upon by the country to perform as this juncture of affairs in Missouri.

Most valuable time has been lost, already, by the slothful and feeble manner in which Western matters have been hitherto conducted. The gloom that was created by the loss of Lyon, and the defeat of Mulligan will not easily be dispelled; but success will come better late than never; and it is sincerely to be hoped that past errors may be repaired, and that the immense advantages which the Union army in Missouri possesses over their opponents may not be thrown away.

Thus high achievements were expected of Frémont, but at the same time, his controversy with Frank Blair, the powerful Missouri political leader, and his allies remained to dog him. On October 9, the *Herald*

Jefferson City

published the letter from Chauncey McKeever, Assistant Adjutant General in St. Louis at the behest of General Frémont to Frank Blair. In it, Blair was released from arrest, but at the same time accusing Blair of using his "family position" to lay private letters "before the President, disturbing the President's confidence in the commanding General."[15] In the same piece, Blair's letter to General Thomas appeared denying and refuting the charges made by McKeever.[16] On October 10, the *New York Herald* published the exchange of charges and countercharges between Blair and Frémont. They had originally been published in the St. Louis *Democrat*. Frémont, always thin-skinned, reacted angrily at their publication.[17]

> Captain C. McKeever, Assistant Adjutant General at St. Louis, received a dispatch from General Frémont on the 6th inst., to the following effect:
>
> Headquarters Western Department,
> Camp near Jefferson City, Oct. 6, 1861.
> The publication of the charges and specifications, with accompanying papers, in the case of Colonel F. P. Blair, Jr., as in the St. Louis *Democrat* of yesterday, has shocked and vexed me. You will immediately proceed to investigate this violation of my confidence; and inform forthwith that the perpetrators may be proceeded against and punished accordingly. I have telegraphed the President and General Scott that it has been done wholly without my knowledge or sanction, and meets with my unqualified disapprobation and regret.
>
> John C. Frémont, Major General Commanding.

On the same day, the *New York Herald* printed a stinging editorial criticizing its competitor, the *Tribune* as well as General Frémont.[18]

THE OFFICIAL CHARGES AGAINST FRÉMONT BY COLONEL BLAIR.

The New York *Tribune* accuses us of changing our opinion about General Frémont, and quotes largely from the columns of the *Herald* to prove it. We could have saved our contemporary all this trouble by admitting that we have changed our opinion. We do not profess to be infallible. When we find we are in error we always hasten to correct it. Unlike party organ grinders, who can play only one tune as it is fixed for them, we make our own music, and give utterance to the truth, from day to day, as far as we can discover it. We want to be always right, and therefore change when we see we have been wrong. In common with the whole community, we entertained high expectations of General Frémont as to his campaign in the West. We confess our disappointment. The reasons of our change of opinion may be found in the charges of Colonel Blair, printed in another page.

These charges are of the gravest nature; and, on the ground of some of them, notoriously true; we have changed our opinion of General Frémont, as we believe the majority of the people have done. To the Blairs he owed his nomination for the Presidency, and to them he owes his present appointment in Missouri.[19] The fact of his incapacity has compelled them to throw him overboard. For the sake of General Frémont himself, as well as for the interest of the country and the government they ought to be investigated immediately. If half of them are proved to be true, then the government ought not to have a moment's hesitation in removing General Frémont; if they are all disproved, then General Frémont will be enabled to carry on the war in the West free from that load of popular odium which now presses him down and necessarily impairs his efficiency. But, till this is done, it would appear to us that it is too great a risk to entrust him with the command of a campaign, the loss of which would involve the most serious consequences we cannot afford any more disasters.

This editorial was the product of the *Herald's* editorial staff. But one has to wonder if some informal, "not for publication" communications had been received from Thomas Knox. A few days later another tirade appeared in the *Herald*. Again, this unsigned editorial bore Knox's imprint, even though he was in Jefferson City or beyond at the time of its publication.[20]

CLIPPING THE FEATHERS OF FRÉMONT.

The Secretary of War has found that his visit to Missouri to look into the affairs of that military department was a good idea, if we may judge from his consequent instructions. It appears that he has ordered General Frémont to suspend his fortification of St. Louis, to suspend the work on the barracks he was building near his residence for his bodyguard (The Great Mogul) of three hundred cavalry; and that his military debts, accumulated to the extent of $4,500,000, must remain unpaid until they can be investigated; and that some two hundred of his officers, appointed without the President's authority, need not expect to be paid for their services as officers; and that all said Frémont's contracts must be made hereafter by the regular disbursing officer of the army, &c, &c. The reader will agree with us that in these instructions, Secretary Cameron has done good service to the Treasury. We dare say, too, that unless Frémont, with the abundant army and facilities at his command, shall soon clean the rebels out of Missouri, there will soon be an end to the splendid and costly military arrangements of Frémont, and very much to the satisfaction of the country. As an emancipation philanthropist, upon his own responsibility, General Frémont went pretty far; but when he assumes the airs, graces, and grandeur of the Great Mogul, General Cameron serves him right in clipping off his peacock feathers. So fine a bird, left to his own discretion, would be too expensive for any country [to] sustain except the empire of the Indies. No wonder Frémont has failed to become rich, with all the gold mines of Mariposa in his hands, when his ambition is to eclipse the barbaric splendor of the Great Mogul.

Politically, Frémont obviously was in very serious trouble as the press and the politicians were turning against him. Even a victory in his campaign in the West might not be able to sustain him in command.

"Head-Quarters of Major-General Frémont's Body-guard, at St. Louis, Missouri." From a Sketch by a Correspondent. (*Harper's Weekly*, September 21, 1861).

Chapter 13

On to Springfield

All was ready; the various divisions of Frémont's army began to move. The leaders of these divisions were called "generals," but two of them had not been officially confirmed.

- Major General John Charles Frémont led the Army of the West after his appointment as a major general in the Regular Army on May 14, 1861.
- Brigadier General David Hunter was the senior member of Frémont's staff, (although not his chief of staff – that role belonged to Asboth) having been appointed by Lincoln on March 17, 1861.
- Brigadier General John Pope was appointed June 14, to rank from May 17
- Brigadier General Franz Sigel was appointed August 7, also to rank from May 17.
- Brigadier General Justus McKinstry, appointed by Frémont on Sept. 2, was never confirmed by the Senate and his appointment lapsed.
- Brigadier General Alexander Asboth was appointed by Frémont. However, Asboth's official appointment was only made by Lincoln on December 23, to rank from September 3, and confirmed by the Senate on March 24, 1862 to rank from March 22, the formal date of the proposal.

This then, was the leadership of Frémont's move on Springfield and General Price. Back in St. Louis, Brigadier General Samuel R. Curtis assumed local command.[1] Albert D. Richardson of the *Tribune* described this group of leaders:[2]

Sigel is slender, pale, wears spectacles, and looks more like a student than a soldier. He was professor in a university when the war broke out.³

Hunter, at sixty, and agile as a boy, is erect and grim, with a bald head and a Hungarian mustache.⁴

Pope is heavy, full-faced, grown-haired, and looks like a man of brains.⁵

Asboth is tall, daring-eyed, elastic, a mad rider, and profoundly polite, bowing so low that his long gray hair almost sweeps the ground.⁶

McKinstry is six foot two, sinewy-framed, deep-chested, firm-faced, wavy-haired, and black mustached. He looks like the hero of a melodrama, and the Bohemians term him "the heavy tragedian."⁷

Other forces were also moving toward southwest Missouri seeking Price. "General" Samuel D. Sturgis led troops coming from Kansas to join Frémont's army. Sturgis's regular army rank was major, and he was appointed brigadier general in March 1862, to date from August 10, 1861.

Then there was Frémont's "staff." Franc Wilkie, who was also a member of the "Bohemian Brigade," gave a description of Frémont's staff. The staff, he wrote:

"General Frémont's Army On The March Through Southwestern Missouri." Sketched by Mr. Alexander Simplot. (*Harper's Weekly*, November 16; 1861).

was a mixed polyglot, characterized by infinite variety. It was suggestive of the would-be builders of the Tower of Babel, after their speech had become confounded. The language least spoken was English. The hoarse and guttural German, the nasal French, jaw-breaking Magyar from the vicinity of the Ural regions, broken English, Spanish, Italian, Russian, and in fact more tongues than were spoken at the pentecostal gathering, were heard in and about the staff of the commander.

There was almost as much variety in the dress of the various attachés and in their equipment. There were the regulation cavalry, with an extra supply of yellow trimmings, armed with sabres, pistols, and carbines, and a company of Lancers with hussar hats and legs bandaged to the knees in white cloth, and long poles with lance-heads and pennons, like the Uhlens of the Germans. There were still other forms of uniforms and equipment, all of which gave to the headquarters, when in motion, the appearance of a procession of a brilliant flower-garden.[8]

A more complete listing of Frémont's staff is found in the Appendix. This was the group that set out from St. Louis to lead Frémont's scattered garrisons to assemble and attack General Sterling Price who was reputed to be near Springfield.

Knox began his next letter from Syracuse with remembrance of the past summer.[9]

Syracuse Mo., Oct. 13, 1861.

In June last, a few days subsequent to the battle of Booneville, I entered this town with the command of Capt. Totten, who had been sent thither from Booneville by General Lyon. We came into the village only four hours subsequent to the departure of Governor Jackson with his rebel forces, and a few of us, who were mounted and in advance, had an exciting chase after a rebel scout who remained behind to give notice of our arrival, and who tarried a moment too late.

Since then I have wandered over a large portion of Missouri, following the varying fortunes of the Union arms. When we came here in June we had a small force of five hundred infantry and four pieces of artillery. The present force gathered here is much more imposing in point of numbers and efficiency, and forms, with the strength at Tipton, Georgetown, and Sedalia, an army sufficiently large to make a successful advance into the territory of the rebels.

Hon. Simon Cameron, Secretary of War, was today present at a review of General McKinstry's division, on the prairie a mile east of the town. He expressed himself highly delighted with the appearance of the army of the West, as far as he had inspected it, and stated he had the utmost confidence in its efficiency. His stay was only of an hours' duration, and at its close he took the train for St. Louis, accompanied as far as Tipton by General Frémont. It is thought that the hampering of this department by the administration will cease on the return of Mr. Cameron, and that henceforth General Frémont will receive proper aid in men and material for the war.[10]

[SUPPLY PROBLEMS]

The long looked for departure of the army towards Dixie's land has not yet transpired, and the delay is in part is the result of the negligence of the administration. General McKinstry's and General Siegel's divisions are under orders for marching toward the Osage this morning, but are utterly unable to move. Neither of them has half the wagons necessary for transporting the various camp *impedimenta* needed on the expedition, and from present indications there is no prospect of their being immediately supplied. So many days have been set for a forward movement and so many postponements have been made that we are all incredulous whenever we hear it announced that the day of departure is at hand, and no one, except the commanding General, has any but the most nebulous ideas as to the time of leaving.

On to Springfield

Knox, *Camp-fire and Cotton-field,* facing 98

The formation of the army into divisions and brigades is not yet completed, but is sufficiently advanced to afford an idea of the arrangement. General McKinstry will have all the regulars, the Nebraska regiments, and regiments from Missouri and Iowa. General Siegel will have the regiments containing the strongest German element. General Pope's division will consist mainly of Missouri troops and Generals Hunter and Asboth will have their divisions formed from Illinois, Indiana and Ohio Volunteers.

The bitter feeling among the officers of American birth towards the foreign officers and soldiers who have volunteered to fight under the Stars and Stripes still continues as strong as ever. What makes it worse is the fact that the abuse indulged in by the Americans is not reciprocated by the Germans, who bear the insults heaped upon them, generally without offering complaint. A day or two since the provost marshal at Tipton, Col. E. B. Brown,[11] shot a German soldier for refusing to obey an order. Two stories are in circulation in regard to the affair – one to the effect that the soldier struck and kicked the officer, at the same time using abusive language toward him. The other version is that the soldier could not understand a word of English, and consequently did not comprehend the order given him. The circumstances attending the affair have been given by telegraph, so that it is not necessary to repeat them. A court of inquiry was held, and is adjourned until to-morrow, but the understanding is that the officer is to be fully acquitted. Not only among the regular army officers, but with our volunteer commanders, does this feeling exist. It was but a few moments since that I heard a volunteer "'political Colonel," who cannot possibly manœuvre a regiment or even a company on the field speak of one of the ablest officers in the country as a "damned Dutch son of a bitch," and express a most earnest hope that he might be killed at an early day. The jealousy of officers toward others of decided military ability is the cause of this bitterness against the Teutonic element. Every citizen, officer and soldier, who has really at heart the interests of the Union, should do his best to have this ill feeling removed.

General Frémont and staff are still at Tipton, but are daily expected to take up abode in Syracuse until the army is ready to move. From Tipton to Syracuse, the distance is about seven miles, and on reaching the former point, Mr. Cameron decided to come hither on horseback. He led the staff on a breakneck pace, and on arriving here several of them, who are but little accustomed to the saddle and are at best very bad riders, appeared desirous of throwing the principal portion of their weight upon their stirrups than upon the saddle seat. A pair of tongs thrown across the saddle would convey a fair idea of the appearance presented by some of these staff officers, especially if the tongs are liberally applied with buttons and epaulettes. General Frémont returned to Tipton by the train which took Mr. Cameron, while the staff went "overland."

[NEWS OF STERLING PRICE]

The last heard from General Price, he was on his way South with his rebel army, intending to cross the Osage at Poffinsville. He had a force of twenty thousand men, a train of two thousand wagons and not far from sixteen thousand horses. He was intending to make a junction with McCulloch, somewhere between the Osage and Springfield, and would then make a stand to encounter General Frémont.

Gov. Jackson was with him, and indulged in sundry lamentations at his ill success in getting Missouri out of the Union. The farce of calling the Legislature together at Lexington was enacted during the brief time the rebel army remained there, though with rather ill success, as but few members were present. The fugitive Governor now intends calling another session in the neighborhood of Springfield or Sarcoxie, and while under protection of rebel bayonets pass a secession ordinance.[12]

Horses and mules had a dual value to the Union. Every animal that could be obtained in any manner was of value for transportation and denied that animal to rebel foragers. Knox told of some Union ingenuity in one instance:

A few days since a captain of the First Nebraska heard of a quantity of mules and horses that had been gathered at a point a few miles from here for use of Price's army. Taking his company to a wood within half a mile of the residence of the rebel agent, he approached the house alone, representing himself as a captain from the rebel force, he was very gladly received, and after partaking of a fine dinner that had been prepared in expectation of a visit from some ambassador from the rebel lines, he was shown the *caballada*,[13] and informed that he could have the animals upon his own terms. His offer was at once made to pay in Confederate scrip at the customary prices for mules and horses in the rebel army. This offer was most gladly accepted, and under some pretense the captain disappeared for a short time and returned with his company, displaying to the astonished rebels the Union uniform and a small edition of the Stars and Stripes. Forty mules and twenty-four horses were taken in the name of Uncle Sam and are now in training for the service of the Federal Government.

Orders have been issued to press into government service all the horse and mule teams within twenty miles of Syracuse. Two companies of cavalry will start to-morrow morning for that purpose. The teams will be receipted for by the officers who take possession of them and will be paid for in due time. It is not likely that much transportation can be procured in this way. The most of the farmers in this part of Missouri keep for draught animals a pair of mares as uncertain in age as a maiden who has passed her teens, and with them generally a rickety wagon that can hardly be depended upon for a hundred mile trip. In June last General Lyon took all the spare teams in this portion of the State, at the time he was preparing for his march to Springfield, and it is doubtful if many teams can now be raised.

Secretary of War Simon Cameron's visit to the "front" for inspections (and evaluation of General Frémont's capability) also led to an amusing incident:

A good story is told of Secretary Cameron while on his way hither. At a station this side [west] of Jefferson City, while the engine was wooding up, the honorable Secretary engaged in conversation with a ragged boy upon the platform. Asking the youngster how many brothers he had, and whether they were good looking, the urchin replied:

"I've got five brothers – I'm the homeliest of the lot I but, I reckon I'm good looking by the side of you."

Of course the crowd laughed at the response. Mr. Cameron

On to Springfield

joined in the applause, and rewarded the modest youth with a quarter.

Yesterday an individual was caught selling whiskey to the soldiers on guard. General McKinstry ordered the whiskey poured out, the man put on the first down train, and five hundred lashes applied to him if he returned here during the stay of the army.

In the same issue of the *Herald*, Knox filed two later telegraphic reports under the heading, "Impending Decisive Battle in Missouri."[14]

Headquarters at Warsaw Mo., Oct. 16, 1861. We are here with part of Generals Sigel's and Asboth's divisions.

General Siegel's advance is already across the Osage. His cavalry today had a skirmish with one of the enemy's mounted parties, and took three prisoners. He is in possession of the bridge over the Pomme de Terre River, with infantry and artillery.

The main body of the enemy is reported forty-five miles distant.

Camp McKinstry, Near Syracuse, Mo., Oct. 17, 1861 General Frémont has sent a dispatch here, stating that he has reason to believe that Sterling Price has retraced, or will retrace his steps to the Osage, and there make a stand and give our forces battle.

Adjutant Smith informs me that he has raised over 10,000 men for the Missouri State Militia, and thinks he will be enabled, in due season, to obtain the remainder of the 42,000.

A large supply of transportation is now on its way here from St. Louis.

On October 22, the *Herald* printed a telegraphic dispatch from Knox at Syracuse. Impending battles were often reported by members of Frémont's command, but seldom came to pass.[15]

> Syracuse, Mo., Oct. 21, 1861.
> Major Scott, of General Sigel's staff, from Warsaw yesterday, says that definite and satisfactory information has been received at General Sigel's camp that General Price has broken up his camp in Cedar County (where he arrived last Sunday week, and where it was said he would stand and give battle), and continued his retreat towards the Arkansas line.

Thomas Knox, however, had a problem as a reporter. News about Frémont's advance on Springfield was coming into St. Louis from the sources – from Rolla and Jefferson City, for example – while he was with the moving troops and forced to rely on a mail service that certainly was not a top priority with officers concerned with arriving food and armaments.

By the time his October 23 letter from Warsaw reached New York and was printed on November 1, the public already knew of Frémont's arrival in Springfield and of Zagonyi's heroic charge into the city. His only advantage was the small, human interest stories and details that he could provide that anyone not directly on the scene could not. He provided examples of bridge building and of civilian life in the little town of Warsaw, the County Seat of Benton County in his October 23 letter.[16]

> Camp Columbia, Warsaw, Mo., Oct. 23, 1861.
> Late last evening reports arrived here that Price had broken his camp at Stockton, and was on the march to the South, moving as rapidly as possible, in order to keep out of the reach of Gen. Frémont's advance. The scout bringing the intelligence said that Price was at Lamar, in Barton County, and was designing to move still further towards Dixie. About midnight another scout came in, stating that Price's rebel army was at Sarcoxie, in Jasper county, and had there been joined by McCulloch, with fifteen thousand fighting men and two thousand camp followers, and that they had commenced fortifying Sarcoxie, with the intention of making a final stand.

If this be true an action is not far distant, as our army will move forward as speedily as possible.

General Lane's advanced guard was at Osceola on Monday evening, the 21st.[17] Lane has fallen in with a portion of the rebel army, which was fleeing to escape from Frémont's advance, and after a short skirmish near the town of Butler, Bates County, captured a captain and a lieutenant of the rebel army, together with men, arms, baggage wagons, with clothing and commissary stores. At Rose Hill, in Johnston County, Lane found the sick of the rebel army, who had been left behind in the haste of their flight. General Sturgis is also at Osceola, and will join General Frémont's division as soon as practicable.

The bridge over the Osage is completed, and the army is now crossing. All parts of the bridge, with the exception of the flooring, are made of green timber, fresh from the forest. The flooring is principally formed of logs and heavy plank, and is amply sufficient for the army purposes. Unless the river should rise ten or more feet above its present stage of water there is no danger of the structure being carried away. Material for the flooring was procured by tearing down log houses throughout the town, and using the timber from the sides and ends. Though not an elegant structure, it is a strong and well-built bridge, and reflects great credit upon Captain Pike, under whose superintendence it has been constructed.

The army is on its move southward.

[WARSAW, MISSOURI]

On Sunday last, learning that a bearer of dispatches, accompanied by an escort, was to leave Syracuse for Warsaw, I made arrangements to become one of the party. The distance between the two points is forty-seven miles, and as the country was full of rebels just returned from Price's army, it was not considered safe for single individuals to pass through. Just after leaving

Syracuse the road enters a belt of timber, some fifteen miles in width. Beyond this timbered land is a stretch of fertile, rolling prairie of about the same extent, crossing which the timber is again reached.

This alternation of prairie and wooded country extends through the western portion of Missouri in a southwesterly direction, passes into the Indian nation and terminates at the Red River on the Texas border. It is well watered throughout, and at the present season of the year is a fine country for an army to march through. Were it north of the line of demarcation between the slave and the free states, it would doubtless be densely populated and tested to the fullest extent of its agricultural resources. Just now it is the battling ground between treason and loyalty.

From Syracuse to Warsaw the journey which was accomplished in eight hours, was devoid of special interest. At one time a body of horsemen made their appearance from a thicket and drew up, as if intending to dispute the way. Our escort at once brought their carbines to the "ready," and the cavalcade of Missourians made no attempt to interfere with us. At Cole Camp, the scene of the massacre in June last, we made a halt of two hours, and during that time I made some inquiries concerning that bloody affair. A party of four hundred rebels from Warsaw made an attack upon a body of Union men while the latter were sleeping in a barn, where they had formed a temporary camp. The attack was a complete surprise, and resulted in the death of some thirty of the Union men and a loss of nine or ten of the rebels.

Cole Camp is settled almost entirely by Germans, many of whom have enlisted under the Union flag for the war. The few Americans, or rather Missourians, residing there, are of rebel sympathies, and manifest a deep and malignant hatred of their Teutonic neighbors.

Arrived at Warsaw, I found a village of scattered frame

houses, eminently Southern in appearance, and containing a population of from fifteen hundred to two thousand inhabitants. It is the county seat of Benton County, and is situated on the left bank of the Osage River. The State road from Booneville to Springfield, which is also the route lately followed by the Butterfield Overland Mail, passes through Warsaw and crosses the Osage at this point. The telegraph from Syracuse to Fort Smith, which was designed to continue to San Francisco by way of El Paso and Los Angeles, passed through here and was in working order in May last, but since then has been torn down by the rebels, and every foot of the wire carried away or concealed.

Warsaw possesses the strongest secession majority of any town in Missouri, there being scarcely a dozen Union men living within its limits, and none of them showing any energy or activity. General Frémont, on his arrival, gave orders for the staff and field officers to be quartered throughout the town.

One of the charms of Knox's reporting was his ability to capture some small, colorful events that gave personalized substance to otherwise grim war news. They were often humorous or sardonic in tone. His descriptions of events in Warsaw ably fit this description. In Warsaw, Knox saw and reported on the impact of rebel propaganda that sought to demonize the German-Americans ("damned Dutch, Hessians") and the Americans ("Black Republicans") who were coming to destroy everything and everybody:

> The inhabitants evidently had the greatest fears of the Federal army, as the most exaggerated accounts of the ferocity of the Union troops had been spread among them by the rebel leaders. Many of the most bitter secessionists had left with their families, and at least half the male population was away from home, in the ranks of the rebel army. From two to ten officers were quartered in each house, and their forbearance from at once slaughtering the occupants has been a matter

of agreeable surprise to the latter, and it is hoped that the acquaintance with officers in federal uniform will have a good effect. A strict prohibition was made against plundering of any kind whatever, and any violation of the order has been speedily punished.

As an instance of the terror of the natives may be mentioned the experience of a member of the staff in search of a comfortable dwelling. Conceiving that the schoolhouse would be suited to his purpose, he ascertained where the key was kept, and called upon its custodian. Upon stating the object of his mission the old lady who had the key in charge, at once broke into tears, and after much persuasion reluctantly consented to accompany the officer to the building, and took with her a basket to bring away some books that had been left. On her way thither she wept violently, and was several times interrogated by the neighbors as to the cause. Her only reply was: "The abolitionists are determined to have our schoolhouse, and I don't know what they will do with it."

Today she has become pacified, and thinks the abolitionists are not so bad after all. I find that the prevailing idea throughout Missouri with reference to the federal army, is that it is composed entirely of abolitionists, who are making the expressly to steal all the negroes in the State. Till lately there was a general belief among the lower classes that Lincoln's army was, in many cases, officered by negroes, the idea being obtained from the natives beholding the officers' colored servants wearing the cast-off apparel of their masters.

[WARSAW AND THE HARDSHIPS OF WAR]

The effect of secession in Missouri is perhaps as patent to the eye in Warsaw as in any town of the State, with the exception, perhaps, of Springfield. The market is entirely drained of the necessaries of life, as no merchant has for months dared to bring any kind of merchandise to the town for fear of its being seized. I breakfasted yesterday at the house of a well-to-do family, residing near the edge of the village, and all that could be placed upon the table was corn bread, beef and butter. The matron of the house felt so annoyed at the meagre appearance of her table that she deserted the room before we entered it, and left her husband to do the festive honors. He stated that for weeks they had been unable to procure tea, coffee, sugar or flour, and that their only reliance was upon beef and corn meal.

He inquired eagerly for a newspaper saying, as an excuse for his earnestness, that the mails had ceased since the stock of the company was seized by Gov. Jackson in June, and that their only dependence since that time had been upon the generosity of travelers who might happen to have a spare paper.

All kinds of business had been entirely prostrated, and those who were dependent upon their daily labor were suffering for the commonest necessaries of life. Already there has been much inconvenience felt among the better portion of the population, and this will be much increased as winter comes on. The corn which has lately been harvested is being devoured by the immense *caballada* of horses and mules belonging to the army, and the stock owned by the natives must depend upon other sources for sustenance till the grass grows again. Missouri, which has twice given an overwhelming majority for the Union, seems to be suffering more than her sisters in this treasonous war. Could those towns in which the traitor element is as universal as in Warsaw be the only sufferers it would seem far more just.

Warsaw boasts of several hotels, a court house, a bank and a printing office. The hotels, the court house and the churches are occupied as hospitals and storehouses; the bank has been seized by Gen. Frémont in the name of the government, and is now surrounded by sentinels. The printing office is the one from which the *Southwest Democrat*, a rabid secession sheet, made its hebdomadal appearance. Its editor, a Mr. Leach, was killed in the attack upon Cole Camp, and since his death, no paper has been issued. Two years since Mr. Leach was a member of the Legislature from Benton County, and was particularly anxious to affect the expulsion of a reporter of the *Missouri Democrat*. The gentleman who then acted as reporter for that paper now holds a position in the army, and has taken possession of the office of the late Mr. Leach, and is busily superintending a squad of printers engaged in striking off army orders, requisitions, and whatever other jobs are called for.

The inside of the last issue of the *Southwest Democrat* is still in type, and contains a furious and urgent appeal to the people of Benton County to rise in their might and aid in expelling the abolition fanatics of Lincoln's army from the soil of Missouri.

The Osage River is crossed at this point by means of a rope ferry, capable of taking but two wagons at a time. Immediately

"Building General Frémont's Bridge Across The Osage." Sketched by Mr. Alexander Simplot. (*Harper's Weekly*, November 16, 1861).

on arriving here General Sigel, who reached Warsaw in advance of General Frémont, gave orders for the construction of a bridge, as a long time would be required for crossing by the ferry. After a day's delay General Sigel, having found a point where the water was but four feet deep, forded the stream, with the infantry and cavalry of his division, and took the artillery and baggage over by the ferry. The bridge, a strong trestle work, will be completed to-night, and will afford facilities for crossing the whole army without delay.

The engineers found much difficulty in the preliminary work of construction, owing to the strong current of the Osage. This river, which is formed by the junction of the Marias des Cygnes and Grand Rivers, has a current as rapid as that of the Missouri and is free from ice for most of the winter. During an ordinary stage of the water the Osage is navigable to Linn Creek, and sometimes to this point, and even to Papinsville. The color of the water in this river is of a deep blue, a marked and agreeable contrast to the dirty yellow of the Missouri.

Considerable material and merchandise designed for the rebel army has been seized in and around Warsaw. The second day after the arrival of the army, seventy-six mule wagon loads of shoes, salt, clothing, whiskey, &c., were discovered in some caves in the rocks about a mile from town, and were at once taken in charge by the federal officers. Every day something is unearthed and turned over to the federal authorities and it was only this morning that a large quantity of clothing was seized at a farmhouse near the village.

Information of whereabouts of these rebel deposits is usually derived from "contrabands," whose masters are away with the rebel army, or are actively engaged in furnishing aid and comfort to the traitors. Search is constantly being made for rebel supplies, and it is quite likely that much more will be obtained. Foraging parties are busy securing feed for the horses and mules of the army, and the owners of the seized property are properly remunerated.

At the latest intelligence (Friday last) from the rebel army, Price was at Stockton, in Cedar County, with twenty-four thousand armed and four thousand unarmed men. His army, though not destitute, was badly off for provisions and clothing, and was experiencing considerable difficulty in procuring supplies for both men and horses. The scouts are not certain as to whether he intends to make a stand at that point or push on; but from his tarrying several days it is thought he will remain to encounter the Union army. McCulloch was on his way northward from Camp Walker, evidently with the design of joining Price. The strength of his division is not known, but is supposed to be about ten thousand. When the army will move South from this point is not known, but it will probably be before many days.

Most of Knox's reporting to the *Herald* was about military matters and movements. However, in his book *Camp-fire and Cotton-field*, written after the war, he added many "human interest" touches. In Chapter 8, "General Frémont's Pursuit of Price," he recounted some incidents in the field and he poked fun at some of the eastern "dandies":[18]

One after another, the divisions of Frémont's army moved in chase of the Rebels; a pursuit in which the pursued had a start of seventy-five miles, and a clear road before them. Frémont and his staff left Tipton, when three divisions had gone, and overtook the main column at Warsaw. A few days later, Mr. Richardson of *The Tribune*, and myself started from Syracuse at one o'clock one pleasant afternoon, and with a single halt of an hour's duration, reached Warsaw, forty-seven miles distant, at ten o'clock at night. In the morning, we found the general's staff comfortably quartered in the village. On the staff, there were several gentlemen from New York and other Eastern cities, who were totally unaccustomed to horseback exercise.

One of these recounted the story of their "dreadful" journey of fifty miles from Tipton.

"Only think of it!" said he; "we came through all that distance in less than three days. One day the general made us come twenty-four miles."

"That was very severe, indeed. I wonder how you endured it."

"It was severe, and nearly broke some of us down. By-the-way, Mr. K———, how did you come over?"

"Oh," said I, carelessly, "Richardson and I left Syracuse at noon yesterday, and arrived here at ten last night."

Before that campaign was ended, General Frémont's staff acquired some knowledge of horsemanship.

Delays were encountered at Warsaw. The bridge over the Osage had to be replaced after it was destroyed by rebels to delay pursuit. The Bohemian Brigade settled in for a few days, boarding with a widow. Knox continued the story in his book:

At Warsaw the party of journalists passed several waiting days, and domiciled themselves in the house of a widow who

Bohemians as housekeepers, from Browne, *Four Years in Secessia*, 43. Knox may the one holding the frying pan.

had one pretty daughter. Our natural bashfulness was our great hindrance, so that it was a day or two before we made the acquaintance of the younger of the women. One evening she invited a young lady friend to visit her, and obliged us with introductions. The ladies persistently turned the conversation upon the Rebellion, and gave us the benefit of their views. Our young hostess, desiring to say something complimentary, declared she did not dislike the Yankees, but despised the Dutch and the Black Republicans.

"Do you dislike the Black Republicans very much?" said *The Tribune* correspondent.

"Oh! yes; I hate them. I wish they were all dead."

"Well," was the quiet response, "we are Black Republicans. I am the blackest of them all."

The fair Secessionist was much confused, and for fully a minute remained silent. Then she said,

"I must confess I did not fully understand what Black Republicans were. I never saw any before."

During the evening she was quite courteous, though persistent in declaring her sentiments. Her companion launched the most bitter invective at everything identified with the Union cause, and made some horrid wishes about General Frémont and his army. A more vituperative female Rebel I have never seen. She was as pretty as she was disloyal, and was, evidently, fully aware of it.

A few months later, I learned that both these young ladies had become the wives of United States officers, and were complimenting, in high terms, the bravery and patriotism of the soldiers they had so recently despised.[19]

The autumn march toward Springfield was slow. Some of the divisions moved faster than others, and were forced to pause and wait for the arrival of the laggards. The Osage River constituted an impediment to the march as did several other streams. There were no bridges, only rope ferries in that part of southwest Missouri. Autumn tended to be a dry season so that while the streams were not fast-flowing and full, the steep banks themselves could prove to be a problem. Knox complemented the autumn weather in Missouri, but he still preferred that found in New England. He wrote from Hickory County on October 25:[20]

> Camp Morrissey, Yost's Station, Hickory County, Mo., Oct. 25, 1861.
> About noon on the 23rd the bridge over the Osage was finished, and the army at once commenced its march. As the hour of starting was so late the troops on the road made but twelve miles by nightfall, camping on the edge of a prairie on the main road to Springfield and Fort Smith. The night was cold, and the ground in the morning was snow white with frost; but, so far as I could ascertain, the troops did not suffer from the cold. Your correspondent slept in a tent with seven others, most of them reporters, and found no inconvenience from the low temperature. Weather like the present is far better for a campaign in Missouri than the hot months of July and August. The days are warm, but on no occasions uncomfortably so; there is usually a very gentle breeze stirring, but not often a high wind, and the haziness of the atmosphere, joined with the stillness that reigns in the natural elements, denotes that we are in the midst of the Indian summer, though that delightful season does not in Missouri attain such perfection as in New England.
> On the morning of the 24th camp was broken at eight AM, and a march of twelve miles was made by eleven AM
> As we were waiting for several regiments that had been detained at Syracuse and other points, we could not make long marches, and accordingly went into camp before noon. The camp was named Camp Haskell, in honor of Captain Haskell, of General Frémont's staff, a gentleman who holds the position of Director of Police, but whose duties appear to embrace nearly all the management of the camp and the march. From daybreak until late at night he is in the saddle,

riding at full speed from regiment to regiment, or he can be seen on foot among the tents and wagons or the camp, carefully noting the condition of everything around.

On the morning after our departure from Warsaw a telegram was received announcing the engagement near Fredericktown between Col. Plummer and Jeff. Thompson, and the defeat of the latter with a loss of four guns. Capt. Haskell rode throughout the entire command, and read the dispatch at the head of each regiment. The policy of such a measure was at once apparent when we heard the loud cheering at the termination of each reading, and afterwards saw the elasticity of the step of the men on the march. The four successes that have lately obtained to the Union arms, the taking of Lexington by Major White, the capture of a rebel baggage train by Gen. Lane, the defeat of the rebels at Wet Glaze and the battle of Fredericktown, appear to indicate that the tables are turning, and that the Union arms are again destined to be successful.

On our march on the 24th we passed through a small town in the northern part of Hickory County, exulting in the name of Quincy. The village, a row of about twenty frame and log houses, had been partially deserted, many of the men residing there having joined the rebel army. A small hotel, with a modest sign proclaiming it to be the Quincy House, which was formerly kept as a station of the Overland Mail Company, bore evidences of having been visited by the rebels during some of their pilgrimages. The proprietor was a gentleman from New York, and was robbed by Jackson of his own and the stage company's horses, and had his house pillaged when the army marched through there in June last. In several other respects, the town seemed to have suffered from the visits of marauders and the prostrate fences and unreaped fields gave evidence of the blighting effect of the rebellion in Missouri.

During the day, we noticed the prairie on fire a mile more

from the road, and a few of us determined to visit the spot. The dense growth of vegetation with which the prairie was covered, and which had become dead with the advance of the season was burning to the ground over a tract of a quarter of a mile in width, and sending out an enormous mass of smoke, that rose in a cloud to the height of several hundred feet. The fire advanced slowly, threatening to burn some houses that lay in its track, but was stopped by the efforts of the soldiers before it reached the buildings. The flame was not by any means terrifically hot, and but for the smoke one would suffer but little inconvenience in riding through it.

Camp Haskell was made within a mile of General Sigel's camp, where he had been for two days waiting for us and for the remainder of the army. General Sigel has shown much energy in pushing forward his command ever since he started from Jefferson City. Everything about his camp and around his division goes to prove that he is one of the best officers in the service, and if he has anything like a fair chance at the enemy he will retrieve his ill-fortune of Springfield. From Camp Haskell a scouting party of 250 mounted men, under Major Zaconyi, [sic] was sent out in the direction of Springfield and before this is written, they, doubtless, have that town in their possession.

The position of the enemy at latest accounts was in Jasper County, in the vicinity of Carthage. The report of Price having from twenty-five to thirty thousand men still continues. General Sturgis, whose command is at Osceola, designing to move on a road parallel to General Frémont, reached here in person to-night. General Lane is within twelve miles of this place, and will join us in a day or two.

Knox sent a short note on October 28. It almost seems that he was trying to whip up a patriotic fervor from its tone:[21]

Fifth Division, Army of the West
Pomme de Terre River, Oct. 28, 1861.

We arrived here from Syracuse the day before yesterday with part of our division, in order to secure the bridge at this place so as to command the passage of the river. We are now waiting the arrival of our supply train from Syracuse, escorted by our cavalry, before moving forward. Our advance guard is supposed to have entered Springfield yesterday and will probably move on as far as Sarcoxie before halting. Every indication goes to show that the enemy intends making a stand in the southwestern corner of this State. It is believed here that General Johnston, of Salt Lake notoriety,[22] has been ordered here, with heavy reinforcements, to take command of the rebel army, and if such is the case, we shall have some hard fighting within the next two weeks. I believe from my knowledge of the southern part of this State and the previous movement of the enemy, that they are concentrating at Cowskin Prairie, in McDonald County, within a few miles of the Arkansas line, where it is more than probable they have an intrenched camp, as in all probability they will outnumber us two to one, and their army will be composed of some of their best troops, we shall have a pretty tough time in whipping them; but whip them we must, as we are too far from our supplies to suffer a defeat. When you have news of the coming battle, look out for the "Fighting Fifth division," which, if I do not mistake will make its mark.

An incident characteristic of our fellows occurred three days ago. Frémont's body guard, consisting of one hundred and fifty mounted men, dashed forward in advance of their division and rode into Springfield. The town was garrisoned by two thousand men, who scattered in every direction, and before they discovered it, they were stampeded by a few men, and before they could collect in sufficient force to offer any resistance our fellows had released all our prisoners, and fell back on the main body.

On to Springfield

All the divisions of Frémont's grand army were finally approaching Springfield. The dash into the town by Frémont's bodyguard, led by Major Charles Zagonyi, was a thrilling, if foolhardy, exploit. This gaudily-dressed group of mounted men had often been derided at Frémont's pets, full of foreigners and also young men of the "best families." In this grand charge into Springfield they proved their bravery, but at a heavy cost. At a combined strength of about 325 men, which included Major Frank White's Prairie Scouts, losses were heavy, with a total of 18 killed, 37 wounded and 30 missing.

Now that all the divisions of Frémont's army were nearly in place, planning was beginning for the expected grand battle of Springfield. Rumors were rife that General Johnston was in command of reinforcements pouring in to strengthen Price. Confidence and morale was high in expectation of the honors to be gained in the upcoming battle, seen as revenge for the loss at Wilson's Creek. However, Zagonyi's Charge would be the only battle fought around Springfield. Messengers arrived from St. Louis carrying information from Washington. Frémont had been sacked.[23]

"Brilliant Charge of General Frémont's Body-Guard through Springfield, Missouri on October 24, 1861". Sketched by Mr. Alexander Simplot. (*Harper's Weekly*, November 16, 1861).

Chapter 14

Farewell to Springfield

So Frémont was gone, superseded by General David Hunter.[1] Frémont's "Hundred Days" in Missouri produced controversy instead of military action and corruption instead of patriotism. His staff was a mixture of dedicated Union men, "foreigners," some with limited English, and boodlers, old friends from California more interested in profits than soldiers' welfare. Chief among the latter were Justus McKinstry and Leonidas Haskell. McKinstry, in the Quartermaster Service had previously been court-martialed in Mexico City (1848) and in California (1853).[2] Haskell had served on Frémont's staff and, at the same time, acted as a contractor for mules for the army.[3]

David Hunter
(Harper's Weekly, March 14, 1863)

While trouble had been brewing for some time, the proximate cause of Frémont's removal was the stinging report by Adjutant General Lorenzo Thomas to Secretary of War Simon Cameron dated Oct. 21, 1861.[4] While in Tipton, Missouri, both Cameron and Thomas talked with many of the men serving under Frémont and reached the conclusion that Frémont had to go. In that report, Adjutant General Thomas wrote:

> General Hunter expressed to the Secretary of War his decided opinion that General Frémont was incompetent and unfit for

his extensive and important command. This opinion he gave reluctantly, owing to his position as second in command.

The opinion entertained by gentlemen who have approached and observed him is, that he is more fond of the pomp than the stern realties of war; that his mind is incapable of fixed attention or strong concentration; that by his mismanagement of affairs since his arrival in Missouri the State has almost been lost, and that, if he is continued in command, the worst results may be anticipated.

This is the concurrent testimony of a very large number of the most intelligent men in Missouri.[5]

Thomas Knox wrote three pieces from Springfield, two short and one longer, describing the events and army reactions after the news of Frémont's removal. All appeared in the November 7 Herald.[6]

Springfield, Mo., Nov. 3, 1861.
General Frémont has been induced to delay his departure until the arrival of General Hunter, who is expected this evening.

General Pope arrived this morning.

Efforts are making by the friends of General Frémont to induce him to remain in the army, even in a subordinate capacity. Many of his staff officers are anxious to stay until after a battle, and Colonels Lovejoy, of Illinois, and Starks and Hudson, of Indiana, will do so whether the General does or not.

The enemy are reported moving north from Cassville, and General McKinstry is just about to start, with a considerable body of cavalry and artillery, to make a reconnaissance in force.

The next day, Knox gave more details including the details of a "scout" that reported that the enemy were heading out from Cassville toward Springfield. Asboth's departure was hardly surprising considering he had been chosen by Frémont while both were friends in New York.[7]

Springfield, Nov. 4, 1861.
The efforts to induce General Frémont to remain with the army, to act in the coming battle in subordinate capacity to General Hunter, have failed.

General Hunter arrived during last night, and General Frémont and most of his staff departed today.

General Hunter had an interview of an hour and a half duration with General Frémont this morning, in which the latter gave the former all his intelligence in reference to the position of the enemy, and laid before him the plan of battle decided upon by himself and the commanders of divisions at their councils of war held last evening.

The reconnaissance determined on yesterday was postponed just on the eve of its departure by order of General Frémont.

A scout who arrived last night reports the enemy moving slowly in this direction. McCulloch has the advance post, and on Friday was ten miles this side of Cassville, so that by to-day they must be very near us. A battle is imminent at any moment. The enemy greatly exceeds our force, but no fears are felt for the result. Our army is all here now, expecting General Hunter's division.

The body guard and Holman's sharpshooters were the only troops that left with General Frémont. General Asboth accompanied the General, and acting Brigadier General Carr has taken command of his division.

Colonels Lovejoy, Starks and Hudson, late of General Frémont's staff, who remain here to participate in any battle which may take place, have received appointments on General Hunter's staff.

Knox's letter, also dated November 4, repeated some of the details from his short notes expanded on the effect on the troops of Frémont's removal, and covered some other matters.[8]

Farewell to Springfield

Springfield, Nov. 4, 1861.

On the morning of the 2nd inst., information was received at these headquarters that the enemy was advancing in force upon Springfield, with the evident intention of giving us battle, either at the place where our army were, encamped, or to meet us, could we march out. Preparations were at once made to meet the rebel army, and in a few hours everything was in complete order for battle.

About noon on the same day an officer from Gen. Hunter's division arrived bringing the unconditional order from Washington to Gen. Frémont to be superseded by the first mentioned commander. Immediately Gen. Frémont announced to the army that he was about to leave, and desired that the obedience and devotion be shown to his successor that had been shown to him. The camp, on it being communicated to them that their General was about to depart, were at once in a semi-mutinous condition, and only the timely exertions of General Frémont prevented the most fearful consequences. As it was, several regiments threw down their arms and refused to serve under any other commander, and deputation after deputation of field officers and line officers came to the headquarters and protested in the most earnest manner against the change of commanders. Particularly among the Germans was this feeling noticeable, and nothing but the earnest request of General Frémont, that no insubordination should be shown, saved the army from utter demoralization. Had the enemy made an attack at any time within twelve hours after the order of removal became known, we should have been, without doubt, utterly routed and driven from the ground.

The soldiers had come to love Frémont; he was bringing them to fight to "get even" for Lyon's death at the hands of the rebels at Wilson's Creek. But their untrained eyes did not see their lack of supplies and preparation for battle.

It was General Frémont's determination to leave for St. Louis at daylight on the next morning subsequently to the reception of the order, as that document was peremptory and admitted of no delay. General Hunter was not here, and General Frémont decided to turn the command over to General Pope, the ranking officer under General Hunter.

On the reception of this information, all the commanders of divisions and brigades united in a remonstrance against General Frémont's relinquishing the command until General Hunter came up. Answer was returned that their request should be complied with, and that the command should not be given up to any one save the proper officer. In the afternoon of the 3rd Gen. Hunter not having arrived, and no intelligence being received from him, another request was made that the army should be led to battle on the following morning, as it was stated that the enemy were in force in the old battle ground on Wilson's Creek. After duly considering the request, Gen. Frémont replied that he would accede to it in case Gen. Hunter should be heard from, and at once issued an order to all the commanders of divisions and brigades for a full and exact statement of the size and condition of their respective force, and on the reception of that information, proceeded to perfect his plan of battle.

The question must be asked, what was Frémont doing before the remonstrance to lead his troops in battle? He should already have known the "size and condition" of his troop units. Even Knox's subsequent statement about a dozen bands serenading the commanding general indicated the lax situation prevailing in Frémont's army camp.

> The intelligence of this determination of the Commanding General was at once communicated from camp to camp; and the wildest enthusiasm prevailed. Every five minutes during the succeeding two and a half hours, the wildest cheering could be heard from some portion of the army

as the information was conveyed to the various regiments. A dozen bands at once proceeded to the headquarters and serenaded the General. Crowds of officers gathered in front of his quarters and greeted him by loud and prolonged cheering, and had the battle transpired according to arrangements the troops would have fought in the most determined manner; but the arrival of General Hunter, about ten o'clock in the evening, made a complete change in the matter, and the battle has been delayed.

Generals Frémont and Hunter had an interview of two hours, in which the former stated his entire plan of battle, and turned over to the latter all the official documents pertaining to the headquarters of this department. The interview was entirely official in its character, and at its close the Generals retired to their headquarters for the night.

Frémont and most of his staff left quietly, heading north to the railroad at Tipton. Knox expressed his own feelings about Frémont's removal. Yet he thought victory was possible and the enemy was near, wondering what action the new commander, Major General David Hunter, would decide upon.

General Frémont and staff, with the exception of Colonels Lovejoy, Hudson and Schenck, left for Tipton today, at six AM The camps were not generally made aware of the departure, as it was not deemed prudent for the soldiers to receive the information until the General should be some distance on the way.

The faces of all who were around headquarters at the time of the departure wore an expression of sadness, and evinced that a sore blow had been struck at the enthusiasm of the Western army. Only the immediate presence of the enemy, and the prospects of battle in a few days, kept our camp in order and the army from demoralization.

Whatever may have been the information that furnished

grounds for the removal of our commanding General, it is certain that the administration is in error in taking him away on the eve of a great and decisive battle with the rebels of the Southwest. The soldiers of this command had implicit faith in General Frémont, and would have followed him to victory over a foe of treble their number. At present they are much dispirited, and though they would behave well and gallantly in action, their great enthusiasm in serving under Frémont is lost.

Many of the regiments were raised with the special view of being placed in the command of the man whom such a feeling of admiration has been raised throughout the West, and these in particular regret his loss.

Gen. Hunter will make his headquarters at the Chambers House on the public square of the town, the same building occupied by the Confederate commander at the time the rebels occupied Springfield. A portion of his staff is here, and the remainder will soon arrive or be appointed at once. What his plans will be against the enemy I am not aware, but it is quite probable that he will in a great measure carry out the designs of General Frémont.

The latest intelligence from the enemy was from a scout who arrived this morning. He reports that the Legislature, under the control of Governor Jackson, is in session at Cassville, and that a portion of the army remains there as a guard.

Wilson's Creek, the battle ground, is held by a portion of the rebel army, who are engaged in throwing up earthworks, and the remainder of the force, with the exception of the body at Cassville, is within ten or fifteen miles of the creek, some of them being at Curran, and others at Crane Creek and Dug Springs.

Four days ago General McCulloch issued ten days rations to his men, and informed them that they would fight before those rations were exhausted. McCulloch is very anxious for battle and his troops share his enthusiasm.

The whole force of the rebels is said to be about 60,000, but of these some 10,000 or 15,000 are not in fighting condition.

My opinion is that we shall meet not far from 45,000 men in battle, many of them finely armed, and having from thirty to fifty pieces of artillery. It is possible that the battle may occur before this letter reaches you, and, at best, it cannot be much delayed.

The families of Union men in the vicinity of Wilson's Creek and below there are coming in very rapidly to escape the violence of the rebels with their approaching army. Yesterday the public square was half-filled with wagons containing the household goods of these refugees.

On November 6, Knox wrote again from Springfield.[9] General Hunter seemed to be well thought of, but what moves he would make were still unclear. The camp was rife with speculation. Scouts were sent out to probe the enemy, but no significant enemy was found anywhere near Springfield. Reports of previous scouts were in error.

General Hunter has now fairly entered upon the duties of the chief command of the army of the West. All who know of his previous services speak very highly of his abilities as an officer, and the utmost confidence is expressed that he will manage the campaign successfully. What course he will take for the conduct of army movements is not yet known – whether he will make an advance towards and into Arkansas or march towards the Mississippi river striking that stream at or below Columbus, is yet uncertain.

There are several rumors in camp relative to our plan of future operations, most of which indicate that no advance will be made from this point – one of them hinting that the administration does not think it proper to have too long a line of road to keep open between the army and the railway termini. Another rumor is that when we march hence we shall go to the Mississippi and act in conjunction with the fleet now being fitted out at St. Louis. Still another rumor hath it that we shall retreat and make our winter quarters at St. Louis; while this last story of all is that we are to keep on our way toward the Gulf, visiting Little Rock as we proceed. The reader can believe any or all the above reports at pleasure. General Hunter yesterday made a reconnaissance of the ground around Springfield, so as to be able to move in the best manner in case of battle. Yesterday and the day previous he sent three large trains to Syracuse and Rolla to procure supplies, thus indicating that we will remain here ten or twelve days at least, and it is barely possible that the enemy may attack us in the meantime.

Today General Hunter, with a large escort, and accompanied by many field and staff officers, pays a visit to the old battle ground on Wilson's Creek. Two days ago Colonel Merrill visited that vicinity with a regiment of cavalry and a section of artillery, to ascertain if the enemy was there in force, as reported, He found that a considerable body had camped there for three days, but left on the morning that General Frémont was expected to attack them. Twenty-five of their number came within half a mile of our lines to a house occupied by a rebel family, the head of which is a captain in the rebel army. What information they gained is not known, but it is quite probable that they heard of the arrival of our reinforcements, as a retreat from the position on Wilson's Creek was ordered the following morning.

The rebels are now nearly all this side of Cassville and reported as slowly advancing in this direction. They have left a small force at Cassville to protect the rebel Legislature that Claib. Jackson has in session. We have not yet learned what the body of lawmakers is engaged upon, but it is supposed that the legislators are busy in voting Missouri out of the

Union and making provisions for her reception into the rebel confederacy.

Knox was correct in in his suppositions. A secession ordinance was adopted on October 30 and signed by Governor Jackson the next day. However, the "rebel Legislature" was meeting in Neosho, not Cassville. The Confederacy officially admitted Missouri on November 28, 1861.

John B. Wyman
(*Library of Congress*)

> The Arkansans have very strong objections to the visit of the Union troops to their State, and Gen. McCulloch consequently desires to fight them in Missouri. It is also rumored that Jeff. Davis has given orders to Gen. Price to give battle north of the Arkansas line, and not on any condition allow the latter State to be invaded. Those orders, if such have been given, may cause an attack to be made upon this town before many days.

The departure of General Frémont and his staff created vacancies and vacuums. The newly appointed Provost Marshall, John B. Wyman, began to crack down on the laxness that had grown under the previous administration.

> Major James H. Phinney, Paymaster, who was here with General Frémont and departed at the time the staff of that commander left for St. Louis, is much needed in Springfield at this time. Orders were yesterday given for his arrest wherever found, and his return to these headquarters. Of course the order for his arrest is nothing more than a measure to insure his speedy return.[10]

> Acting Brigadier General John B. Wyman was yesterday appointed Provost Marshal of Springfield, by order of General Hunter. General Wyman is well known throughout New England and the West as a railroad man of large experience and great ability. For several years he held a high position in the State military of Massachusetts and Illinois, and was everywhere eminently successful.[11]

Knox reported on the proclamation that Wyman issued in Springfield in the attempt to tighten discipline in the ranks, noting that some orders had been issued but disregarded by both officers and men. Knox decided to leave Springfield for St. Louis by the same route he had taken after the battle at Wilson's Creek. By November 13, he was in Rolla and he filed a long report in which he commented on his own view of future plans in Missouri and on General Price and his army.[12]

> Rolla. Phelps Co., Mo., Nov. 13, 1861.
> Long before you receive this, the telegraph will have informed you that on Saturday last three divisions of the Army of the West marched north from Springfield, in the direction of Sedalia and Tipton, and that Sigel and Asboth's divisions took position near the old battle ground on Wilson's Creek, leaving the command of Acting Brigadier General Wyman in occupation of the town itself.
>
> The orders of the portion that marched to the north gave them directions to proceed to Warsaw, on the Osage, and there await further commands, General Hunter not revealing any of his plans for the future.
>
> The supposition was general that we were to fall back to the line of railway and go thence to St. Louis, with a view to operations down the river. General Hunter received orders from Washington in regard to the conduct of affairs in the Western department, and among those orders was one for the withdrawal of our troops from Southwest Missouri and their concentration at some central and available points.

Farewell to Springfield

> It will be a week or more from the time of starting before the advance of the army reaches the railway, and by the time that shall arrive the division left at Springfield will be on its way, giving up the country to the Confederates. General Wyman's orders were to remain there until the sick were able to be moved, when he was to take them in charge and march either to Rolla or Sedalia, at his option, leaving Sigel and Asboth's divisions to bring up the rear. The physicians at the hospital reported that the patients could be moved by Thursday or Friday of the present week, and unless General Hunter has issued new orders, or the rebels have made a hostile demonstration requiring an earlier departure, you may consider Springfield abandoned by the 16th of the present month.

Knox reported that "reliable sources" had provided information on the movements and intentions of General Price and his rebels. Fall was the time for harvesting and preparing for the approaching winter, but he found crops unharvested and devastation upon the land. Union families were molested, but rebel families also suffered by their men being away in the rebel army. He also speculated, accurately, on future Union actions.[13]

> It has been ascertained through reliable sources that the orders from Richmond to General Price are to amuse and dally with our army as much as possible, and to draw it well into the interior, where it could only be supported at immense expense, but not to engage it in battle unless certain of success. It can readily be seen that the policy is to keep as many as possible of our troops away from the scene of operations on the Mississippi and at points where they could not be readily withdrawn for use elsewhere. That General Price did not intend to fight was shown by his falling back whenever our forces advanced. Two days before the main body of the army left Springfield the rebels fell back from Cassville, a distance of eight miles, to near the Arkansas line and for several days

they had been engaged in devastating Stone County along the Fayetteville road, to prevent our army from following them with rapidity.

Hay, corn and other fodder belonging to Union men was burned in the stack or in the field, and in some instances houses, and all they contained, were destroyed. In one township the property of rebels was burned to prevent it being used by our troops, but the owners were reimbursed for their losses. Of course it would be utterly impossible to prevent the army from marching, by reason of such devastations; but it could be much impeded, so that it would never be able to overtake the fleeing rebels unless the latter were willing.

The policy to be pursued will doubtless be the concentration of the army at St. Louis, and the occupancy of Rolla, Jefferson City and Pilot Knob, as permanent garrisons, each of which can suddenly be strengthened whenever threatened, and will not require an enormous outlay for transportation over the fearfully bad wagon roads of Missouri.

The voluntary relinquishment of the Southwest is of little consequence in a strategic point of view, as it will hardly be occupied by a large rebel force when demonstrations are made upon Memphis and other points on the Mississippi. The principal thing to deplore is the annoyances to which our Union friends in that section will again be subjected to at the hands of the rebels, greater, perhaps, than during our abandonment of the country after the battle of August 10. With the main body of our army at St. Louis, instead of the interior of the State, we can strike at short notice down the river whenever deemed proper, and as each of the posts I have named to be garrisoned are accessible by railway, reinforcements and supplies cannot be long in reaching them in case of a threatened attack.

The Southwest part of Missouri was again to be abandoned to the care of Sterling Price and his Missouri State Guard. Thomas Knox understood that

Unionists were being abandoned and he understood the military rational for withdrawal but he deplored the abandonment. To Knox, the "optics" of the withdrawal were a disaster. He left Springfield on November 9 and made his way to Rolla, again complaining about the quality of the road.[14]

> About noon of the 9th, learning that there was no prospect whatever of a battle with the rebels, I left Springfield for a horseback ride to this point, [Rolla] over one hundred and twenty-one miles of the worst road in the world. I accomplished the distance in two and a half days, reaching Rolla day before yesterday, in an extremely "used up" condition. The army had commenced moving to the North but three hours before I took my departure; yet the people along the road knew of its march, and from nearly every house I was eagerly interrogated as to the prospective and actual condition of things in the Southwest. It needed but a word or two with a man to determine for myself on which side he was to be found, unless particular care was taken to assume a disguise. In most instances the inhabitants favorable to the rebellion showed no fear of the Union troops, contending that, beyond stealing a few pigs and chickens, they did not take anything that was not paid for, and never molested individuals for entertaining the most radical Southern sympathies. The Union people, on the contrary, manifested the greatest consternation lest our army should abandon the country, and most of them declared they should be forced to leave should the Southwest again go into the hands of the rebels.
>
> It is a common remark of the rebels of Missouri that they are safe in any event; that their own army spares them, while it plunders from Union men, and that the Union army is too mindful of law and order to interfere with the most active traitors. On General Frémont's march from Tipton to Springfield he took whatever rebel property was required by the army, and General Hunter had announced the same policy

the day before I left. What the new commander, Gen. Halleck, will do, is not known.[15]

On the road to Rolla from Springfield, Knox saw the results of the conflict in Missouri and provided his readers with unusual detail. Missing husbands, gone to fight with the rebels, unharvested crops, and depredations by both sides confronted him. He also confronted misinformation, prejudice, and malice.[16]

> On the road from Springfield to Rolla at least half the houses are deserted, the families having fled through fear of molestation; from half the remainder the men were absent in the two contending armies, leaving their farms to run to waste. At one house where I dined I found a pleasant lady, with an interesting family of six children, and everything about the premises indicating prosperity. On my asking if her husband was at home, she replied in the negative, with that peculiar intonation that closes all further questioning. I subsequently ascertained that he had been the entire summer in the ranks of the rebel army, and aspired to no higher position than that of a private soldier.
>
> The lady was bitter in her animosity towards "the Dutch," who, as she averred, stole everything they could lay their hands upon, even taking from women and children everything needed for their sustenance or clothing. Interrogating her closely, I found they had appropriated several of her chickens at the time of the retreat from Springfield. She said of Gen. Sigel that he could hardly speak a word of English, and was utterly unable to give a military command except in Dutch. My assertion that he spoke our language as well as the best of us astonished, but failed to convince her.
>
> Hers was only a specimen of the ignorance prevalent among the better class of women in Missouri. It was not long since that I heard a young and apparently intelligent rebel female speak of Mr. Lincoln as a negro, and in such a manner that it admitted no doubt of the sincerity of her statement.

Knox arrived at Rolla and found the post to be in good hands. Fortifications were completed and included cleared fields of fire for the fort's cannon. The fort had become an important strong point at the railhead of the Southwest branch of the Pacific Railway with storage for arms and supplies.[17]

> The post of Rolla is at present in the command of Col. G. M. Dodge, of the Fourth Iowa, an able and efficient officer.[18] Col. Dodge is busily engaged in putting Fort Wyman, which commands the town and the country around within range of its guns, in a finished condition. The force here is adequate for the protection of the post, and is in an admirable condition. Col. S. H. Boyd's regiment, which was raised from the refugees from Springfield and the country around, marched hence yesterday for the last mentioned town. Some of the men live on the line of road between here and Springfield, and on my way in I met several who had been granted the privilege of taking their own time on the way and reporting themselves on a certain day in Springfield.[19] A large lot of rebel property, unfit for government use, has accumulated here, and Colonel Dodge advertises to sell it at public auction to-morrow, and devote the proceeds to Union purposes.

Knox was stung by the *New York World* report that the correspondents had been under the control of Frémont and his friends, implying that "bogus dispatches" had been sent from Springfield.

Grenville M. Dodge
(Stuart, *Iowa Colonels and Regiments*)

The special to the *World* of the 11th, stating that Frémont's friends controlled the army correspondents in camp, and that the *attaché* of the St. Louis *Republican* was the author of bogus dispatches relative to the feeling in the army concerning Frémont, is a stupendous falsehood. There was never any attempt whatever, within my knowledge, to influence a member of the press in General Frémont's camp, and as for the correspondent of the *Republican* riding and living at public expense, he only received the same courtesies extended to all.

The "Bohemian Brigade," consisting of eight or ten correspondents and artists, was furnished with a tent and horses, for which each man gave his receipt, and no distinction or partiality was shown in the courtesies extended, though some of the reporters were strong opponents of the Pathfinder. The *Republican* correspondent was in no way treated differently from the other members of the Bohemian Brigade, and, for the last ten days of the stay of the army in Springfield, rode a horse loaned to him by your correspondent.

All the dispatches of the *Republican* correspondent are supported by facts, and can be abundantly proved if the "religious daily" desires it. The *World* had better pick up another handful of mud and try again.[20]

Knox returned to St. Louis and filed a short report from there on November 16.[21]

St. Louis, Nov. 16, 1861.
General Hunter and staff arrived here tonight.

Sedalia and Rolla will be strongly garrisoned, and sufficient provisions, stores and munitions be sent to each point for an army of 15,000 men, should necessity at any time require the presence of such a force.

The bulk of the army will come to St. Louis, and be held in readiness for movements in Kentucky, Southeast Missouri, or down the Mississippi river.

General Hunter had assumed command on November 3 upon his arrival in Springfield, but actively served only sixteen days.[22] He was replaced by General Halleck and given command of the Department of Kansas.

Chapter 15

Halleck in Charge

Thomas Knox returned to St. Louis by November 15, 1861 and began the task of sorting out all the changes that had occurred. Hunter had arrived one day later, but the news of his replacement was already known.[1]

St. Louis, Nov. 18, 1861.

Generals Halleck and Hamilton arrived here this morning.[2]

Generals Sturgis and Wyman arrived here last night.

The divisions of Generals Hunter, Sturgis and Pope have reached different points on the Pacific Railroad, where they will await orders from General Halleck.

General Wyman's Brigade reached Rolla on Saturday, and the divisions of Generals Siegel and Asboth will arrive here to-day or to-morrow.

General Wyman brought a number of rebel prisoners, among them Colonel Price and several other officers.[3]

One day later, Knox wrote a further, longer report and gave some of his first impressions of General Halleck. And they were favorable.[4]

St. Louis, Mo., Nov. 19, 1862.

General Halleck arrived her yesterday morning in the Cincinnati train, and without parade or ostentation made his way to the quarters that had been provided for him. During the day and until late last night he was busy in acquainting himself with the position of affairs in St. Louis and in Missouri generally, and only received a few visitors whose business could not be delayed. This morning he made a brief and formal call on General Frémont, the *ci-devant* commander of the Western Department, with whom he had a slight acquaintance in California.

To-day has been spent in business matters, of which, I am told the campaign of the Mississippi Valley has been a prominent portion.

On questions that have been asked him relative to the immediate future he has maintained a judicious silence, but is, I think, fully aware that a condition of war exists, and will conduct affairs accordingly. The army lately in the southwest is being rapidly drawn to St. Louis, as if with a view to a blow in some other direction.

Henry W. Halleck
(*Harper's Weekly,* November 30, 1861)

Knox, of course, was unaware of the instructions that General McClellan had given Halleck before his departure for St. Louis, but these covered several points. They were both specific and general concerning his far-ranging duties in St. Louis and the Department of Missouri. In part these instructions said:

You have not merely the ordinary duties of a military commander to perform, but the far more difficult task of reducing chaos to order, of changing probably the majority of the personnel of the staff of the department, and of reducing to a point of economy, consistent with the interests and necessities of the State, a system of reckless expenditure and fraud, perhaps unheard-of before in the history of the world....

With respect to military operations, it is probable, from the best information in my possession, that the interests of the Government will be best served by fortifying and holding in

> considerable strength Rolla, Sedalia, and other interior points, keeping strong patrols constantly moving from the terminal stations, and concentrating the mass of troops on or near the Mississippi, prepared for such ulterior operations as the public interests may demand.[5]

Knox's assessment was correct about the army's plans. He continued his letter giving the text of Halleck's first order as commander and commenting of General Hunter's departure.

> Gen. Halleck to-day issued his first general order, which was as follows:
>
> General Orders-No. 1.
> Headquarters Department of Missouri,
> St. Louis, Nov. 19, 1861.
>
> I. In compliance with general orders No. 97, headquarters of the army, Washington, November 9, 1861, the undersigned hereby takes command of the Department of Missouri, including the States of Missouri, Iowa, Minnesota, Wisconsin, Illinois, Arkansas, and that part of Kentucky west of the Cumberland river.
>
> II. All reports and returns required by army regulations will be made to the headquarters in the city of St. Louis.
>
> H. W. Halleck, Major General, U. S. A.

Knox commented on the leadership changes:

> General Hunter leaves in a day or two for Leavenworth, to assume command of the Department of Kansas. His command here has been exceedingly brief, briefer even than that any one of his three predecessors. General Halleck is the fifth commander of the Department of the West,[6] and the hope is sincerely cherished that he may have some degree of permanence. The expression from Kansas through the press and from residents of that state now in St. Louis, is quite favorable to General Hunter; though there is considerable

disappointment manifested by the friends of Jim Lane[7] at the refusal of the administration to place the border General in command of the frontier.[8]

Knox did not comment beyond noting the disappointment of the friends of Jim Lane, but he must have known the general disfavor felt in Washington over Lane and the behavior of his Kansas Jayhawkers. His sacking of Osceola, Missouri on September 23, 1861 was probably on everyone's mind. Knox's letter continued,

> The Claims Committee still pursues its investigations into the disbursements of moneys in this department, and I am credibly informed that it has yet found no proof of anything like fraud in the giving out of contracts or orders. The work of adjusting the accounts of those who have claims against this department is very great, and it is possible that the committee may be employed for two or three weeks to come, At present there are not many new orders given out, save those requests for the subsistence of the army now in the field.[9]

In the matter of fraud, Knox was totally incorrect. General McKinstry was later arrested and incarcerated for the criminal behavior. He was the only general officer cashiered and dismissed from the army during the war.[10] Knox's wide-ranging letter then turned to personnel matters:

> Major J. M. Schofield,[11] who acquitted himself creditably at Wilson's Creek and latterly at Fredericktown, has been made a Brigadier General of volunteers. In the former action he was grazed several times by the enemy's bullets, but escaped unhurt. At one time, while in conversation with General Lyon, a rifle ball passed through his beard, just escaping his chin, and buried itself deep in a tree by his side.
>
> Captain James Totten,[12] who has borne a gallant and prominent part in nearly every action in Missouri since the outbreak of the rebellion, has been made an Inspector General, with the rank of Major in the regular army. Major

Frank J. White, who commanded a battalion of Prairie Scouts under General Frémont, and made himself famous for the capture of Lexington, is now engaged in the reorganization of his corps. Major White is a resident of New York, and was prominent at the Bull Run battle. Captain Mulligan (better known as Billy Mulligan) is still here with his men, and has not been assigned to any particular portion of the army.[13]

Next, Knox turned to river matters. The Missouri River was an unsafe riverway, especially in the fall when water was often low. There were multiple shifting sandbars and river snags. On top of the natural hazards, both banks of the Missouri could harbor Confederate forces and guerrillas. Combining these hazards, attacks on the boats could easily occur when, due to shifting currents and sandbars, a boat could be forced to sail close to the shore. He noted:

The navigation of the Missouri is not entirely free. A few days since the steamer *Sunshine*, which was proceeding to Kansas City and Leavenworth with a cargo of wagons and flour for private parties, was overhauled by a party of rebels, who took off some two hundred sacks of the latter article, and then allowed the boat to proceed.[14] The rebels along the Missouri do not appear to be in large numbers, but only in roving bands. The presence of Jennison, with his Kansas cavalry, in the country east of Kansas City and Independence, may tend to restore quiet.[15] It is reported here tonight that the steamer *Platte Valley*,[16] on her way from Cairo to this city, was stopped at Price's Landing,[17] a short distance below Cape Girardeau, by a considerable force under Jeff Thompson. The story is, that Thompson heard that General Grant was on the boat, on his way to St. Louis, accompanied by several officers of importance, and thought it would be a good opportunity to "bag" somebody. General Grant was not on the *Platte Valley*, and so Thompson, in his disappointment, administered the oath to the passengers, and then allowed them to proceed.[18]

In the first part of his letter, Knox speculated on the possibility of a move downriver. Newspapers from the Confederacy, especially from Memphis were available; troop lines were indistinct and information flowed in both directions and appeared widely in print. In the last section of his letter, Knox reported on Confederate attitudes about a Union push south:

> From Columbus and Memphis I learn that formidable preparations are being made to receive the Union army whenever it chooses to make an attack. For several miles the banks of the river are guarded by batteries that are daily being made stronger, and steps have been taken to make formidable resistance to an approach from the rear. It is the general belief that our severest battle will be at or near Columbus, though strong defenses have been prepared near Memphis. Memphis papers of late date call attention to the danger of an expedition from St. Louis, and urge the utmost diligence in preparation to repulse the enemy. In a long leader the *Appeal* gives thanks to General Price for drawing our army into the interior, and thus saving Memphis from capture. This accords with the belief I expressed a few weeks since, that it was the design of the rebels in Missouri to amuse and dally with the Union army rather than engage it in battle, there is a bitter feeling among the rebels of the Mississippi Valley because General Grant refuses to recognize them as belligerents, and it is to be feared that our prisoners may receive bad treatment in consequence.[19]

General Halleck dug into the mass of problems facing his command after the departure of Frémont. One of these problems was "leakage" of information into the hands of rebels and rebel sympathizers. General Halleck responded with General Order No. 3 (below). On November 21 Knox reported on the order and his letter interpretation was printed the next day.[20]

General Orders, No. 3
Hdqrs. Dept. of the Missouri,
Saint Louis, November 20, 1861.

I. It has been represented that important information respecting the numbers and condition of our forces is conveyed to the enemy by means of fugitive slaves who are admitted within our lines. In order to remedy this evil, it is directed that no such persons be hereafter permitted to enter the lines of any camp or of any forces on the march, and that any now within such lines be immediately excluded therefrom.

II. The general commanding wishes to impress upon all officers in command of posts and troops in the field the importance of preventing unauthorized persons of every description from entering and leaving our lines, and of observing the greatest precaution in the employment of agents and clerks in confidential positions.

By order of Major-General Halleck:
William McMichael,
Assistant Adjutant-General.[21]

ORDERS OF GENERAL HALLECK RESPECTING FUGITIVE SLAVES, ETC.

St. Louis, Nov. 21, 1861.

General Halleck has issued orders that in consequence of important information respecting the number and condition of our forces being conveyed to the enemy by fugitive slaves, no such person shall be hereafter be permitted to enter the lines of any camp, nor any forces on the march, and any now within such lines to be immediately excluded therefrom.

The General also calls the particular attention of all officers commanding posts or troops in the field to the importance of preventing unauthorized persons of every description from entering or leaving our lines, and of observing the greatest

Halleck in Charge 271

precaution in the employment of agents and clerks in confidential positions.

The General also directs all staff officers of this department, whose staff duties have ceased under the recent special orders from Washington, but who still hold commissions in the regular army, or volunteers mustered into the service of the United States, to immediately report in person, if in St. Louis, or by letter, if elsewhere, to these headquarters.

The latest accounts from Gen. Price place him in Barry County, making preparations to advance to Springfield.[22]

Halleck's order provoked a firestorm. Abolitionists read the first paragraph and erupted. Senator Charles Sumner called this Order No. 3 "irrational and inhuman on its face." Radical Republican George Washington Julian thundered for, "a more vigorous prosecution of the war and less tenderness toward slavery."[23] Halleck stood his ground and the affair blew over. He also allowed ex-slaves who had been employed as, for example, cooks or officers' servants to remain in camps. Halleck had many more important things to contend with in St. Louis.

On Nov. 27, Halleck wrote to McClellan on the state of affairs in St. Louis:

> Headquarters,
> Saint Louis, Mo., November 27, 1861.
>
> Maj. Gen. George B. McClellan:
>
> Affairs here in complete chaos. Troops unpaid; without clothing or arms. Many never properly mustered into service and some utterly demoralized. Hospitals overflowing with sick. One division of 7,500 has over 2,000 on sick list. Five divisions still in the field two at Rolla and three near Sedalia. Price and McCulloch said to be moving north, crossing the Osage on Sunday near Osceola, and intended to attack either Lexington or Jefferson City. Have sent out strong reconnoitering parties from Sedalia and Rolla. Some skirmishing with enemy's advance guard and flankers, but nothing certain as

to position of main body. Telegraph wires all work well, and I am in hourly communication with headquarters of divisions. All troops ordered to be in readiness to move. Price's forces estimated at from 15,000 to 23,000. Local rebels have risen in arms in Ray County and are fortifying themselves in Albany. General Prentiss ordered to move against them from Chillicothe with all the available troops of his command.

H. W. Halleck,
Major- General.[24]

Knox did not comment on the deplorable situation in Missouri, largely due to the mismanagement of Frémont, thinking, possibly, to keep things quiet to give Halleck a chance to succeed. He wrote another letter on November 29. There was little real news from the front; it appeared, despite rumors, that large scale fighting was over for 1861.[25]

> A gentleman just arrived from Sedalia states that there is much excitement in that town relative to the rumored approach of Price's army. All sorts of stories are in circulation, most of them averring that the whole rebel army of the Southwest is at Warsaw, on the north bank of the Osage, and making ready to fall upon our forces at Sedalia. All the government stores at the railway terminus are being forwarded to Tipton for safety, and in accordance with a design of abandoning Sedalia, in case we are hard pressed, and concentrating all our strength at Tipton. It is not yet ascertained beyond doubt that any considerable force of the rebels is at Warsaw, and in the minds of the majority of our officers along the railway line an attack is exceedingly problematical. At Rolla, considerable activity is being shown by the Union forces in making preparations to resist Ben McCulloch's redoubtable Texans, who are reported at Lebanon, making demonstrations of aggressive hostility. Ironton and Cape Girardeau are enjoying a condition of calm and serene inaction, with nothing to

disturb their garrisons save the order for general mounting or the calls for dress parade.

In St. Louis the army has undergone but little change. Arrivals and departures of regiments are but little noticed, and attract scarcely more than a passing glance from the sidewalk throngs. The officers having charge of the organization of the State forces of Missouri are displaying considerable activity in putting their portion of the army into shape. General Scofield, the newly appointed Brigadier, has been placed in command of all the troops raised under proclamation of Governor Gamble, and is pushing forward his work with commendable zeal.

Adjutant Hezcock, of First Missouri artillery, has been assigned by Gen. Halleck as chief aid to the commander of the State forces.[26] Adjutant General G. R. Smith, of the Missouri State troops, an ancient and siliceous fossil, whom I lately heard giving profound advice to General Halleck, and stating that if he were in command the war would be speedily ended, has resigned and retired from the service.[27] Governor Gamble has chosen for General Smith's successor Colonel Chester Harding, Jr., who has been in service since the war commenced, and bears an excellent reputation for soldierly qualities. In a few weeks a fair proportion of the forty thousand troops called for by Governor Gamble will be in the field armed and equipped for actual service.[28]

The *Republican*, for two days past, has the following advertisement, under the head of "special notices."

> Camp Jackson – Generals Grant and Polk having made an arrangement by which the Camp Jackson prisoners, now at Columbus, can receive their camp equipage, side arms and personal property taken at Camp Jackson, and the undersigned having been appointed to receive and forward the same, will start the last of this week, or early next, for Cairo. Friends and relatives of the parties above

named will, therefore, please send to No. 41 Chestnut Street any camp equipage, side arms or personal property they may have belonging to the Camp Jackson prisoners now at Columbus, and the same will be safely forwarded to them, under the agreement between Generals Grant and Polk. I expect to leave either Saturday or early next week.

Henry B. Belt.

General Halleck has signified his intention of vetoing the propositions of the above announcement, and General Grant has already given orders to prevent the carrying out of the rebel designs.[29]

Knox, as always, was interested in reporting the wartime attitudes of both civilians and the military. Many secessionists seemed to be growing bolder:

Within the past week the secessionists of St. Louis have grown suddenly bold, and are as yet unchecked in their treasonable proceedings. One of their generals has been here for ten days under a flag of truce and has the largest liberty imaginable. He is perfectly unrestricted in all his movements, and yesterday I beheld him arm in arm with one of our Brigadier Generals, and arranging to dine with him that afternoon. Recruiting for the rebel army is going on within a stone's throw of the Headquarters of the commanding General, and traitors on the street and elsewhere make no attempt to disguise their sentiments.

Last evening at a fair held ostensibly for the benefit of the orphans of the city, but said by knowing ones to be designed to raise funds to equip the newly enlisted Southern recruits, secession badges and flags were worn and displayed by many of the ladies and gentlemen present. While General Sweeny was promenading the hall with a fair and fascinating female, the latter pinned a rebel flag to the coat collar of the old soldier, and permitted it to remain there until discovered. The indignation of the General can be easily imagined. Tonight the fair is to be held again, and the Provost Marshal, who has been informed of the proceedings, promises to look in.

Finally, Knox mentioned Frémont's colorful bodyguard. As a unit unapproved by Washington, they were abolished. Knox said they were "paid off" but other sources claim that no pay was forthcoming.

> The Frémont body guard, which did such gallant fighting in that charge upon Springfield, has been paid off and discharged from the service. They have nearly all reenlisted in a cavalry regiment now forming, having made the discovery that General Frémont is not the only man able to lead an army or a battalion, as the *Tribune* would fain have us believe.[30] The condition of their original enlistment was that they were to serve solely as a body guard to the late commanding General, and on this ground their discharge was claimed and granted.

The mood of the business community in St. Louis also attracted Knox's attention. The improvement seen in business was almost wholly due to the military establishment.

> Business in St. Louis has latterly shown much improvement. Drays rattle along the streets, and the levee begins to assume its wonted bustle and confusion. River and interior traffic has received a sudden impulse owing to the prospective closing of navigation by the cold weather. Barnum's and all the principal hotels are crowded from roof to basement as they have never before been filled since the flush times of 1856–57. Army officers constitute a large portion of their guests.[31]

On December 10, the *New York Herald* printed three letters from Knox. The first, written on December 1, was concerned mainly with military matters in Western Missouri; the second, on December 5, was about General Halleck and his actions; the third on December 6 was on Missouri politics. He began on December 1 with the rebel situation and Price's plans.

> St. Louis, Dec. 1, 1861.
> A lady who arrived last evening direct from Warsaw – having left that town on Thursday morning – states that at the time of her departure there were about six hundred rebels in possession of the place. They were from Price's army, which they represented to be at Osceola, on its way to Lexington and other towns along the Missouri river, though they did not all agree upon the same story. A part of the gang asserted that Price had not left Springfield, and would come no further north until the return of warm weather; while still others assured their listeners that the rebel army was at Stockton. All agreed that McCulloch had not treated them properly, having deserted them as soon as the Union army was withdrawn; and taken up his line of march for Fort Smith, where he expected to winter. These returned rebels say they have come home to spend the winter in their own houses, where they can get well clothed and shod, and prepared to return to the field again, in the spring. They claimed protection from federal soldiers or office holders, and asserted, with much vehemence, that they could not be troubled after they had voluntarily left the rebel army.

Knox reported on Prices' army from the comments made by his men who had returned home in Western Missouri for the winter season:

> Frémont's treaty with General Price is the shelter under which they attempted to hide, and great was their surprise and chagrin when they learned that it had been annulled by Frémont's successor.[32] It is, however, quite likely that they will not be molested while at their homes, unless some of their loyal neighbors choose to interfere. These returned rebels are thinly clad, and some are badly off for shoes, but the most of them appear in good health and confident of ultimate success. They evince a deep seated hatred and fear of General Sigel, and would doubtless march against him with much reluctance

and many misgivings. General Sturgis was the least obnoxious to them of all our division and brigade commanders.

On the other hand, there was the plight of the refugees and the Union soldiers from the lack of supplies and the efforts being made to meet the need:

"Union Refugees From Western Missouri Coming into St. Louis."
(*Harper's Weekly*, Dec. 28, 1861).

In contrast with our kind treatment and non-molestation of rebels in our lines is the abuse and outrage heaped upon loyal citizens of Missouri wherever the traitor army is now in power. Yesterday I saw a line of some thirty wagons just arrived from the Southwest and containing the families and household goods of Union men who had been driven out in consequence of their loyalty. Those I saw were but a small fraction of the number that has already passed through St. Louis to seek an asylum in some of the Northern states, and they told me that there are full ten thousand now on the way hither.

They are entirely destitute, the rebels having plundered them of nearly everything of value before driving them away. I have known repeated instances of families depending upon the charity of the people here to aid them in crossing the river and getting again on their way. The ladies of Barnum's Hotel are this morning busy in making collections of all the cast-off clothing about the premises, with the view of distributing it among the more needy and thinly clad refugees. They have gathered quite an array of coats, pants, dresses, and many numerous and nameless etceteras of male and female apparel, and will make glad the heart of many a poor, shivering outcast. A ton of such old clothing could be easily distributed where it would do much good among most worthy recipients. Despoiled of everything, and driven destitute upon the world at the approach of winter, for no other crime than that of loving the Union, the refugees of the Southwest seem particularly deserving of sympathy.

Knox returned to military matters, gunboats on the Mississippi, and the coming of the winter season. Winter meant that all river commerce would effectively cease. Autumn usually was a dry season with low water. Ice formation and floes from the north would be a continuing problem even if the Mississippi were not frozen at the St. Louis riverfront. The worst possible scenario for St. Louis would be to have the river frozen so ferries could not be operated, but not so solidly frozen as to allow wagons to cross.

The gunboat *Benton*, which is to be the flagboat of the fleet, will be in a condition to receive her armament in three or four days.[33] She will not take her guns on board here, but will proceed to Cairo for that purpose, as all the other gunboats have done as fast as completed. The most of her sheathing has been put on, rendering her almost completely shot and shell proof. At a little distance one would hardly dare say what kind of craft she should be called. Long, low, black with sloping sides, a convex roof, completely iron-clad, and with no wheelhouse or pilot box visible, one could easily imagine her to be the hull of some mammoth canal boat turned bottom upwards by mistake. Of course a specific detailed description of the flagboat of the fleet would not at this time be judicious.

Up to the hour of my writing there is no news of any battle having occurred in the Southwest, and since the return of McCulloch to Arkansas, and the rumored detour of Price in the direction of Kansas, the chances of an engagement between the rebel and the Union armies in Missouri have grown exceedingly small. The troops at Rolla are engaged in building winter quarters, and I learn that orders have been issued for the forces at Tipton and vicinity to do likewise. The soldiers now under instruction at Benton Barracks have lately been furnished with stoves, and are getting along quite comfortably. There are several regiments in our Western army that have not yet been supplied with overcoats, and large numbers of the soldiers sleep and shiver nightly under blankets of the flimsiest fabric. General Halleck is putting matters in order as fast as possible, and promises to attend in due time to the personal wants of the men.

John A. Thompson, Esq., of Granby, Newton County, Missouri, has lately received a commission as Captain in the Eighteenth United States infantry, and is ordered to report at the headquarters of his regiment at Columbus, Ohio. Captain Thompson was formerly City Attorney of Chicago, and the author of the "Municipal Laws" of that thriving lakeopolis. Three years ago he removed to Southwest Missouri, and was extensively engaged in lead mining at the time the rebellion opened. Early in the summer he was compelled to flee to escape the fury of the rebel bands then organized in the lead regions, and came to St. Louis, leaving his worldly possessions at the mercy of the traitors. A good lawyer and an enterprising lead miner has thus been metamorphosed into an officer of the regular army. Considering his relations with Missouri, it would seem proper that Captain Thompson should be in the service within the limits of the State rather than outside her borders.

The river is steadily falling, and within three days there will be less than five feet in the channel between this city and Cairo. Ice is already running past St. Joseph and Dunleith,[34] though none is apparent in front of this city. Old steamboat men are less fearful of a close of navigation by cold weather than they were a few days since.[35]

In his letter of Dec. 5, General Halleck was complemented by Knox for his decision regarding the relief treatment of refugees at the expense of local secessionists.[36]

St. Louis, Dec. 5, 1861.

General Halleck gives evidence of a vigorous policy towards the rebel traitors of this State. For some days past the unfortunate sufferers of the southwest portion of the State, who have been driven out on account of their Union sentiments have lined our thoroughfares and presented many of the most painful scenes of poverty and affliction ever witnessed in this city. Only a small portion arrived in proportion to the thousands who left Springfield and vicinity in company with General Sigel's division. Their appearance half naked, benumbed with cold, and hardly able to stand, has excited the liveliest sympathy and it is evident that something must be done for these destitute people or they will die outright of starvation.

Yesterday General Halleck issued an order on the subject, which has struck consternation into the hearts of the secessionists and at the same time provides an effective remedy. It is as follows:

The law of military retaliation has fixed and well

established rules. While it allows no cruel or barbarous acts on our part in retaliation for like acts of the enemy, it permits any retaliatory measures within the prescribed limits of military usage. If the enemy murders and robs Union men we are not justified in murdering and robbing other persons who are, in a legal sense, enemies to our government but we may enforce on them the severest penalties justified by the laws or war for the crimes of their follow rebels.

The rebel forces in the southwestern counties of this State have robbed and plundered the peaceful non-combatant inhabitants, taking from them their clothing and means of subsistence. Men, women and children have alike been stripped and plundered. Thousands of such persons are finding their way to this city barefooted, half-clad and in a destitute and starving condition. Humanity and justice requires that these sufferings should be relieved, and that the outrages committed upon them should be retaliated upon the enemy.

The individuals who have directly caused these sufferings are at present beyond our reach but there are in this city, and in other places within our lines, numerous wealthy secessionists who render aid, assistance and encouragement to those who commit these outrages. They do not themselves rob and plunder, but they abet and countenance these acts in others. Although less bold they are equally guilty.

It is, therefore ordered and directed that the Provost Marshals immediately enquire into the condition of the persons so driven from their homes, and that measures be taken to quarter them in the houses, and to feed them and clothe them at the expense of avowed secessionists, and of those who are found guilty of giving aid, assistance and encouragement to the enemy.[37]

The above order is the tenth section of General Order No. 13, the balance of which comports with the extract. The other section provides that all spies shall be arrested and if condemned as spies, shall be shot without regard to sex. The vigorous tone employed to give expression to General Halleck's determination to deal with the rebels with an iron hand, is what causes the latter the greatest uneasiness.

Upon inquiry at headquarters this morning, I learn that the above order will be strictly enforced. The disposition of the matter has been handed over to the Sanitary Committee, composed of Messrs. Yeatman, Elliot, Partridge, Greely, and Johnson, who have been invested with full power by General Halleck to use any building owned by a rebel in the city that may be needed for the shelter of the refugees from the Southwest, to seize blankets, stores, bed furniture, and, in short, everything needed to make the exiles comfortable without regard to cost or consequence.[38]

The Provost Marshal has already turned over to the committee several hundred dollars worth of property, consisting of blankets, clothing, medicines, etc. taken from the baggage of the Camp Jackson captives lately sent south as exchange prisoners.

It was remarked as a curious fact that, if General Halleck wished to use a "secesh" building for sheltering the exiles, he could commence upon the one occupied as his own headquarters, the building being owned by a rampant secessionist. The enforcement of the order is an easy matter. There are plenty of empty buildings owned by secessionists within reach, and other articles to make the sufferers comfortable will not be long forthcoming.

Knox then reported on the prisoner situation. Most of these men were on parole, that is, free to walk about the city, but unable to return to either Price's Missouri State Guard or the Confederate army until officially exchanged. The transfer of Union command from General Frémont to General Hunter and then General Halleck had undoubtedly slowed the process:

> The departure of the Camp Jackson prisoners for Cairo by steamboat was to them an unexpected alteration of destination. Their programme was to pass the Federal lines at Sedalia and forage through the country until they reached Price's lines. The sudden change in their route was a severe damper upon that interesting programme.
>
> It is a good thing for the city that these men have left. For more than two weeks they traveled around the streets dressed in the recognized uniform of rebel soldiers, and flaunting treason in the faces of loyal people in the most objectionable manner. They tried all sorts of dodges to obtain advantages not laid down in the law for the exchange of' prisoners. One of their schemes was to appeal very vigorously to the military courtesy of the obliging Provost Marshal.
>
> Last Tuesday General Frost, the kingpin of the Camp Jackson gang, and Mayor Henry W. Williams,[39] who, in part arranged the terms of exchange, cornered the Provost Marshal in his office and endeavored to persuade him that courtesy required him to permit them to carry various contraband packages to their friends in the south. They urged that some day hereafter the Confederates might be in possession of St. Louis, and that he, Capt. Leighton, might be in their fix and requiring favors at the hands of the victors. But they could not convince the gallant Captain, and he told them plainly that they would be restricted to their personal effects, recognized by military usages; so the rebels will have to wait awhile for their packages.
>
> It appears that Kansas City, and, in fact, all the country west of Sedalia, from the Missouri river to the Arkansas line, is to be given up entirely to the rebels. Gen. Hunter has ordered Col. Jennison and his band of Jayhawkers to return to Kansas. Jennison evacuated Kansas City day before yesterday,

and by this time is safe in Leavenworth. It is generally believed so I am informed by a gentleman just arrived here from Leavenworth that a portion of Price's army intends to attack that point, and extensive preparations are being made to give them a warm reception. Kansas City will soon be depopulated by the Union men and their families. Merchants are moving their goods by steamboats and by wagons to Leavenworth as rapidly as possible. Families are emigrating to safer quarters, and a general alarm prevails. The telegraph wires between Kansas City and Independence have already been cut in several places, and it is designed by the telegraph company to immediately close the office in Kansas City. There will doubtless be many outrages on the property of Union men which cannot be removed, and a little further retaliation in St. Louis will be necessary to make good the loss of Union property in that vicinity.

President Lincoln's Message was received here with pretty general satisfaction.[40] The radicals on the slavery question of course wish for a more decided policy on the emancipation question, but nine-tenths of the people, excluding the secesh, think Lincoln is right in defining the principal object of the war to be the restoration of the authority of the Union. The secesh take particular delight in comparing the late Message of Jeff. Davis, as a literary effort, with that of Honest Abe.

Jeff. Thompson's men are returning as well as Price's, to their homes for the winter, in squads of five or six at a time. An officer who came in from Pilot Knob last night says that the Union scouts report the return of many of the rebels who were in the Fredericktown fight. They are in a destitute condition generally.

The Lieutenant Colonel, Chappelle, who was Jeff. Thompson's aid, and who lately arrived at Cairo with a flag of truce, asking permission to go after Jeff. Thompson's wife, was formerly an employee on the Pacific Railroad of this State, and lived at Allenton. He only left here last summer.⁴¹

Knox's December 6 letter contained some amazing political speculations about rumored changes in office-holders. While the "fog of war" surely existed, and Knox and other correspondents were obsessed in reporting and "scooping" others, their reports sometimes were untrue. So it was with a game of musical chairs in a Knox letter in early December about Frank Blair's future.⁴²

St., Louis, Dec., 6, 1861.

A rare piece of political gossip is in circulation here and is told with such strong asservations of truth as to warrant its publication in the *Herald*. It is well known that our plucky young Congressman, Hon. Frank P. Blair, Jr., has Senatorial aspirations, and the gossip all turns upon his elevation to that high office. The way the story runs is this: The present Attorney General, Hon. Edward Bates, is to be persuaded to resign his office, upon which a series of changes will take place in the political world. Governor Gamble who was formerly Chief Justice of the Missouri Supreme Court, is to be appointed upon the Supreme bench in place of Daniels, deceased.⁴³ As Judge Gamble is a native of Virginia, there is no manifest impropriety in such an appointment. Hon. Samuel T. Glover, one of the ranking lawyers of St. Louis, an old resident of the State, and at present, counsel for the government in the prosecution of claims before the Holt-Davis-Campbell commission, now in session, is to succeed Judge Bates as Attorney General. Hon. T. Polk, who is an avowed secessionist, is to be forced to resign or expelled from the United States Senate, and Governor Gamble promises to appoint Frank P. Blair, Jr., to the place. By this means Lieutenant Governor Hall, who has hitherto been a very prominent candidate for the Senate, will be out of the way and will use his influence, on the assembling of the next Legislature, to have Bates's appointment confirmed by the

Legislature. Waldo P. Johnson, the remaining United States Senator, will be got out of the way by a similar manœuvre, and the office left vacant, so that when the Legislature meets the contestants for the second Senatorship will be called on to play into the hands of Blair's friends to assure his election to succeed Polk's full term.

The first thing necessary to be done is to oust Mr. Polk from the Senate. Now watch how this is to be accomplished. Your Washington correspondent can give you the particulars of the movements of the parties; but let me show you how St. Louis is to be brought into the game. Today a building owned by Mr. Polk, situated on Fifth Street, near Elm, opposite the unfinished Southern Hotel, was seized by the Provost Marshal for the use of the Sanitary Commission, to be devoted to sheltering the exiles from the Southwest arrived and arriving in this city, by General Halleck's order. I mentioned yesterday the test of loyalty applied in these cases. It is an oath of allegiance to the United States, and a declaration that any aid or encouragement to the enemies of the United States shall be punished with death. Mr. Polk is one of the richest men in St. Louis. He has numerous houses, and probably others will be seized. If he objects, the oath of allegiance will be tendered to him. If he takes it a plantation in Arkansas and property in New Orleans will be in danger; if he refuses to take it, his Senatorial head will be cut off, and then the first part of the programme will be accomplished. It is not improbable that Polk will quietly submit to having his houses used to serve the Southwesters. His wisest course will be to say nothing. In this case some other plan will be devised to hoist him from the Senate. His secession sympathy is undoubted. His daughter was sometime ago engaged in making lint and sending shirts to the South for secesh soldiers, and his sentiments on the start-at the time of the Camp Jackson capture-were outrageously disloyal.

Perhaps the execution of this scheme may be deferred

for weeks. The probable reorganization of the United States Supreme Court at the present session of Congress may delay the appointment of Governor Gamble to the Supreme Bench, and perhaps Judge Bates may be obstinate and decline to resign. He is a relative of Governor Gamble by marriage, however, and as it is all in the family, why the inducement may overcome his repugnance. There is another motive for his resignation. When the Chicago Convention assembled, the strongest friends of Edward Bates for the Republican nomination were the Blairs. Their political skill and cunning were exercised in a large degree to secure the Presidential nomination for Bates. It was Frank P. Blair, Jr., also, who first presented the name of Edward Bates to the President, at Springfield, as a member of his Cabinet. These considerations will have a strong influence in persuading the present Attorney General to resign. The development of this interesting political scheme will bear the closest watching-and many votes will be given In Congress this winter bearing upon the proposed trade. It is assumed that President Lincoln will acquiesce, as a matter of course, in the whole arrangement. That is the most ticklish difficulty to be overcome in the whole transaction.

None of these speculations, except for the removal of Senator Trusten Polk happened in the time frame Knox proposed. Frank Blair ultimately became a major general serving under Sherman. After the war, he served briefly as senator from Missouri. Governor Gamble died in office in January, 1864. Edward Bates continued to serve as Lincoln's attorney general until resigning in November, 1864.

By late in 1861, financing the war had raised problems. National loans were promoted, but money in St. Louis preferred the interest rates to be found in the east rather than the local rates.[44]

> The newspapers here have been ashamed to publish the list of subscriptions to the national loan at the Sub-Treasury of this city. It is meager enough, and their qualms of conscience

are quite natural. It is but just to say that many savings institutions and private capitalists are interested largely in subscriptions in Eastern cities, preferring to have the bonds and coupons paid there so as to gain the difference in exchange. The list of subscriptions in this city, for which I am indebted to the kindness of the Assistant Treasurer, Benjamin Farrar, is as follows. [Continued in the endnotes] [45]

The admission of this State into the Southern Confederacy, so far as the acts of the rebels can accomplish it, will lead to several complications.[46] Heretofore General Price has levied war on the United States exclusively in the name of the State of Missouri, and his sympathizers have claimed that they were still citizens of the Union. But now the aspect of affairs is changed, and Missouri presents the anomalous picture of a State under four different governing powers, being governed according to the occupation of the military authorities, by Jeff. Davis and Claib. Jackson where the rebels are in power, and by President Lincoln and Governor Gamble where the Unionists have the upper hand.

After severe snow storms and a cold snap, we have settled down into very mild spring-like weather.

During its October Session, the State Convention had prescribed a "test oath" to be taken by all civil officers.[47] Knox reported that, on Dec. 7, General Halleck issued General Orders No. 19 that this test oath be administered:[48]

St. Louis, Dec. 9, 1861.

General Halleck has issued orders stating that the Mayor of St. Louis will require all municipal officers immediately to subscribe to the oath of allegiance prescribed by the State Convention in October last, and directs the Provost Marshall to arrest all State officers who have failed to subscribe to such oath within the time fixed by the Convention, and attempt to exercise civil authority in violation of the ordinance.[49]

Knox followed up with another long letter on December 8 (found in the endnotes) mainly covering local, St. Louis matters and concentrating once again on what might be called "the mood of the city."[50]

Knox then turned to the refugee problem. The primary source of these refugees was Southwest Missouri and Northwest Arkansas. Both had a considerable Union population. The land was not suitable for plantation agriculture; yeoman farmers predominated. In Arkansas delegates from the region had originally voted against secession. Vengeful pro-Confederates cruelly drove many from their homes giving them little time or consideration. Knox reported on the situation with a certain gleefulness at the situation of local secessionists.[51]

> Trusten Polk's house on Fifth Street, near Elm, is now occupied by about thirty Union refugees from the Southwest, and they have been made comfortable by the energy of the sanitary commission at a very trifling expense. One effect of the order of General Halleck to quarter the refugees on the wealthy secessionists of St. Louis is noticeable. The individuals constituting the latter class are coming forward voluntarily and offering their contributions to support the exiles. Many of the largest contributors are notorious secessionists, and some of them noted for their obstinacy and bitterness in holding fast to their money and means heretofore. One of them is especially marked for his forced liberality, and when his name appeared in print as contributor of fifty dollars for the refugee fund, the whole city, rebel and Union alike, indulged in a general guffaw.
>
> The rigor of General Halleck's order and the readiness of the Provost Marshall to execute it to the letter are somewhat impaired by the hesitation and reluctance manifested by the sanitary commission to put it into practice. There are at least a couple of old fogies on that commission whose hearts are so tender that they are afraid apparently of hurting the feelings of avowed secessionists in case their houses and goods are used for the comfort of the Union men who have been driven from

their homes in the Southwest by the rebel friends of the rebel secessionists of this city.

Knox did not neglect "culture." There were many printing houses in St. Louis, some of them with strong, if not overt, rebel sympathies.[52] Surreptitious printing of tracts, poems and notices occurred and the products were distributed quietly to southern sympathizers. Knox reported some for his Eastern readers:

> A rebel printing office was broke up a few days ago by the Provost Marshall, and a large number of rebel songs and odes and poems generally found. Many of them are doggerel of the shallowest kind, ornamented at the top with Confederate flags in colors, with twelve stars, the twelfth being added for Missouri. One of these interesting songs is headed as follows:
>
> SECESSION FOREVER
>
> (Confederate flag.)
> Composed and sung by,
> Florence Montessori
> Air – "Ever Be Happy."[53]
>
> The following verse is a specimen of the whole:
>
> *Go in, Jeff, we will support you*
> *In your good and glorious cause*
> *We know you can defeat the Union*
> *With your brave and glorious boys.*

There is, however, a rebel song in private circulation, one which as a literary composition, is a very fair production. It is far above the average of such things, and the readers of the *Herald* will, I am sure, thank the young lady that gave it to your correspondent for its appearance in print. Nearly every rebel family in St. Louis has a copy of the song. It is as follows:[54]

REBELS.

Rebels! 'tis a holy name!
The name our fathers bore
When battling in the cause of Right,
Against the tyrant in his might,
In the dark days of yore.

Rebels! 'tis our family name!
Our father, Washington,
Was the arch-rebel in the fight,
And gave the name to us—a right
Of father unto son.

Rebels! 'tis our given name!
Our mother, Liberty,
Received the title with her fame,
In days of grief, of fear, and shame,
When at her breast were we.

Rebels! 'tis our sealèd name!
A baptism of blood!
The war—ay, and the din of strife –
The fearful contest, life for life –
The mingled crimson flood.

Rebels! 'tis a patriot's name!
In struggles it was given;
We bore it then when tyrants raved,
And through their curses 'twas engraved
On the doomsday-book of heaven.

Rebels! 'tis our fighting name!
For peace rules o'er the land
Until they speak of craven woe,
Until our rights receive a blow
From foe's or brother's hand.

> *Rebels! 'tis our dying name!*
> *For although life is dear,*
> *Yet, freemen born and freemen bred,*
> *We'd rather live as freemen dead,*
> *Than live in slavish fear.*
>
> *Then call us rebels, if you will –*
> *We glory in the name;*
> *For bending under unjust laws,*
> *And swearing faith to an unjust cause,*
> *We count a greater shame.*
>
> *November 25, 1861.*

Knox then added additional information on other events in Missouri, including an opinion of General Prentiss, the mortar boats built in St. Louis, and claims filed against Frémont's administration.[55]

> Mr. Joseph L. Bittinger, Postmaster of St. Joseph, arrived in town yesterday, and reports that on Thursday an expedition left St. Joseph to break up a rebel nest in Platte County, under the infamous S. Gordon.[56] This expedition consisted of the Sixteenth Illinois, Colonel R. F. Smith and the Fiftieth Illinois, Colonel Wm. Bane,[57] and a battalion of State troops under Major Josephs, and a section of artillery manned by regulars from Fort Leavenworth, name of commander not stated.
>
> There will soon be a warm time in the vicinity of St. Joseph. General Prentiss has declared in a public speech that he means to make every rebel in town take the oath of allegiance or work on the fortifications; and, as he is a man of action as well as promises, nobody questions his earnestness. It was General Prentiss who first suggested the policy in Missouri of arresting every prominent rebel in the State and holding them as hostages for the good behavior of their friends. General Halleck is understood to favor it.
>
> The army at Syracuse is hard at work constructing winter

Halleck in Charge

quarters, and General Pope has been placed in command of the entire force between the Osage and Missouri rivers, west of Jefferson City. From the vigorous administration of affairs while in command along the North Missouri and Hannibal and St. Joseph railroads, some excellent results are expected from General Pope's appointment.

The thirty-eight mortar boats ordered to be built by Quartermaster General Meigs, to accompany the expedition down the Mississippi, are finished, and will all be safely at Cairo in a few days. Each boat carries a mortar capable of throwing a ten-inch shell three miles, and they are especially adapted to shelling high bluffs on river banks, such as will be encountered on the way to Columbus, Ky.

Twenty-six hundred and thirty-four claims have been filed with the commission consisting of Messrs. Joseph Holt of Kentucky, David Davis, of Illinois, and Hugh Campbell, of Missouri. None of the claims have been paid. They come from every loyal city in the Union, and an immense number are from New York.

One month had gone by since General Henry W. Halleck assumed command in St. Louis. In naming General Halleck, General McClellan had given him a two-fold charge: to bring order to the military command structure in the Western Department and to clean out the Augean Stables of corruption in contracting that St. Louis had become. Progress had been made on both challenges, but more needed to be done.

Chapter 16

Winter Quarters

Traditional military thinking before the Civil War was that, during the winter months, armies went into winter quarters and warfare was suspended, at least in European and North American climates. There are many examples of use of winter quarters – Washington's Valley Forge of the American Continental Army is one. There are examples of failure when the doctrine of winter quarters was ignored. A prime example is Napoleon's Russia campaign in 1812.

Advances in technology called these ideas into question. Railroads, for example, eased the transportation problems of winter roads. Additionally, it appeared that the Civil War would be fought in the Southern states, less affected by winter weather. However, mounting winter campaigns in the Ozark or the Appalachian mountains still posed many problems.

During the campaign lull, on December 10, Knox wrote again about events occurring in the city. He turned his attention to foreigners, their residency, and the responsibilities of citizens of England, Canada, and Ireland.[1]

St. Louis, Dec. 10, 1861.

Since the arrival of J. Edward Wilkins, Esq., her Britannic Majesty's Consul, in this city, from Chicago, where he was recently stationed, the tone of British subjects, including native born Englishmen, Irishmen and Canadians has visibly improved. Before the restraints imposed upon them by the presence of a British consular agent there were no more blatant secessionists in the State than certain subjects of Queen Victoria. Mr. Wilkins is a thorough neutral, and has made many enemies among his own countrymen by strict perseverance in a neutral course. If anything his sympathies lean in favor of the triumph of the government, and his efforts have been mainly directed to restricting his countrymen from aiding and encouraging the rebellion. There is no fear that those who live in this neighborhood will do anything to assist the United States in its present struggle, and hence the restraint upon their conduct amounts to a positive benefit to the Union cause, by preventing aid and comfort to the enemy.

The British Consul has held several protracted interviews with General Halleck and General Curtis and the Provost Marshal, and it is probable that a correspondence will soon be published upon the rights and duties of neutrals. The most pleasant relations subsist between our military authorities and the representative of the Queen. An arrangement has been perfected by which British subjects may procure Provost Marshal's passes, direct from the Consul, without any tedious circumlocution. The passes differ from those issued to our own citizens by the omission of the oath of allegiance and read as follows:

```
                OFFICE OF PROVOST MARSHAL,
            ST. LOUIS, MO., ———, 1861.
       Permission is granted to ———, a subject
   of ———, to pass beyond the limits of the
   city and county of St. Louis, to go to ———.
       Issued by ———.
            GEO. E. LEIGHTON, Provost Marshal,
                  Capt. Nineteenth Mo. Vols.
       [Turn over.]
```

(Carry this with you. Good while the bearer complies with the conditions herein expressed.)

Upon the reverse the description of the party and the following certificate, signed in the presence of the Consul:

```
   The subscriber, a subject of ———, accepts this
   passport upon a full understanding of his duties as a
   neutral person during the present rebellion:
```

A gentleman who happened to undergo the process of procuring a pass from the British Consul lately says Mr. Wilkins exacts the following oath:

"You do solemnly swear that you are a subject of Queen Victoria, and have never, at any time foresworn allegiance to Great Britain, so help you God."

The strictness of the Consul may be inferred from the following conversation:

Consul: Do you know what you have signed? (Alluding to the pass above mentioned.)

Britisher: Yes, Sir.

Consul: Well, what is it?

Britisher: Why, I have sworn not to take up arms on either side of the war.

Consul: Yes, and if you are caught as a spy, by either the secessionist or Union army, you may be shot as a spy, without one bit of sympathy from England; remember that, now.

A case developed that called upon all the tact needed by a consular office working in an area undergoing wartime conditions. The issue was slaves traveling through the Underground Railroad to Canada. Claiming Canadian birth, one was captured and re-enslaved in Missouri. When he was found, his case referred to the Consul. As Knox reported:

Already a case has arisen calling for the intervention of the British Consul. Several days ago, Captain Wood, of the Kansas Rangers, while on a scouting expedition from Rolla, found a negro chained to an ox wagon, to prevent his escape. His master was *non est*. The darkey was released and taken to Rolla. The next day a man named Wheelan, a pretended Englishman, came into the Union camp and claimed the negro as his property. He said he was on his way to Dent County, and showed a pass endorsed by T. W. Souper, English commercial agent at St. Louis, certifying to his British citizenship.[2] It appears that Souper had no authority whatever to sign such a document, and moreover Capt. Wood, of the Kansas Rangers, obtained abundant testimony to prove that Wheelan had been a rank secessionist and violated a neutral position by directly giving aid and comfort to the enemy since the rebellion commenced, thereby forfeiting English protection. An investigation was ordered by the commander of the post, Colonel Dodge, of the Fifth [4th] Iowa regiment, pending which the negro himself claimed protection as a British subject, and stated that he was born in Canada.

On this representation, the British Consul of this city took the matter in hand, and procured a special order on Saturday from General Halleck to have the colored individual in question brought to St. Louis, where the question of British birthright will be investigated. To get all the information possible on the subject the consul has sent a special messenger to Canada, where the negro says he was born, to hunt up evidence, and also to the interior of the State, where the darkey says there are parties who know all the facts of his captivity.

Thus, we have the consular representative of Great Britain stretching forth his hand to save a poor, ignorant negro from captivity. The case is likely to become famous. The claimant, the man Wheelan, insists that the negro has been owned by him a great number or years, and says he was born on a farm within two and a half miles of St. Louis. Judge Goode, the owner of the farm, who owned the slave at the time of his birth, endorses the testimony of Wheelan.[3] The secretary of Consul Wilkins left for Rolla yesterday morning, armed with the necessary papers to bring the darkey to this city, and the case will be regularly tried before the consul on the return of the messengers from Canada. In any event, it is doubtful whether Wheelan ever recovers his negro.

Knox then turned to naval news. The Eads gunboats (or "Pook's Turtles") were under construction in shipyards at Carondelet, south of St.

Louis, and at Mound City, near Cairo.[4] In addition to these, gunboats were being constructed. They were simple, lightly armored, reinforced, unpowered rafts, designed to hold a thirteen-inch mortar and be towed into firing position.

"General Halleck's Fleet of Mortar-Boats for Service on the Mississippi." Sketched by Mr. Alexander Simplot. (*Harper's Weekly*, Dec. 27. 1861).

> Twelve of the mortar boats destined to co-operate with the fleet of gunboats in the expedition down the Mississippi left here early this morning for Cairo in tow of the steamer *Sam Gates*.[5] The Illinois River Packet Company have taken the contract to tow these boats to Cairo at eighty dollars each. As there are thirty-eight of them, the aggregate cost will be only three thousand and forty dollars. This is the smallest sum ever paid for similar service on Western waters. The rest or the mortar fleet will depart in a day or two.

Knox closed his letter with comments on one of the local firms under investigation as part of the questionable procurement dealings with General McKinstry, the refugees from southwest Missouri, and the low river stage.

The reported seizure of the books of Child, Pratt & Fox, the extensive hardware dealers, whose transactions in government contracts have been so severely commented upon, causes something of a sensation. The testimony taken before the Congressional Committee will show this noted hardware firm dealing in all kinds of contracts, some of them as foreign to their trade as the crater of Vesuvius is distant from the moon.[6]

The exiles from the Southwest arrive slowly. Many of them find a shelter on the road between this city and Rolla, and as they are broken down in spirits and fatigued from exposure, any rest is desirable. The provision made for their reception is ample to insure their comfort during a temporary sojourn in this city. The people of Illinois have thrown open their houses and farms to these unfortunate men, and deserve great credit for their benevolence.

The river is remarkably low at this point, and the ferry boat, to get straight across the river, is forced to describe a half circle, in order to avoid an ugly sand bar. The weather is unusually warm for the season.

Thomas Knox often "followed the money" in his reporting. In one of these, he took up the military order affecting the pocketbooks of wealthy secessionists who had to either prove their loyalty or pay a heavy assessment. He wrote from St. Louis on December 12:[7]

The following order will be issued tomorrow morning:

> Headquarters Department of Missouri, Dec. 12, 1861. The suffering families driven by the rebels from Southwest Missouri, which have already arrived here, have been supplied by voluntary contributions made by Union men.
> Others are on their way, to arrive in a few days. These must be supplied by charity from men known to be hostile to the Union. A list will be prepared of the terms. All persons of this class who do not voluntarily furnish their quota contribution will be levied on them of $10,000 in clothing, provisions and

quarters, or money in lieu thereof. This levy will be made upon the following classes of persons in proportion to their guilt and property of each individual.

First – Those in arms with the enemy who have property in this city.

Second – Those who have furnished pecuniary and other aid to the enemy or to persons in the enemy's service.

Third – Those who have verbally, in writing or by publication given encouragement to the insurgents and rebels.

Brigadier General Curtis, B. G. Farrar, Provost Marshall, and Charles Borg, Assessor of St. Louis County, will constitute the Board of Assessors for levying the aforementioned contributions.

As soon as any part of this contribution has been assessed, the Provost Marshal General will notify the parties assessed, their agents or representatives, stating the amount, provisions, clothing or quarters, and the money value thereof required of each, and if not furnished within the time specified in such notice, he will issue an execution, and sufficient property will be taken and sold at public auction to satisfy the assessment with the cost; and as there will be a penalty of twenty-five per cent additional if any person on whom the assessment shall be made, shall file with the Provost Marshal General affidavit that he is a loyal citizen and has been true to his allegiance to the United States, he will be allowed one week to furnish evidence to the Board to vindicate his character, and if, at the end of that time, he shall not be able to satisfy the Board of his loyalty, the assessment shall be increased ten per cent and the levy immediately made.

Supplies so collected will be expended for the object designated under the direction of the Provost Marshall General and by the State Sanitary Commission, where money will be received instead of supplies. It will be expended for them as required, and any money not so expended will be turned over to the Sanitary Commission for the benefit of sick soldiers, and anyone who shall resist or attempt to resist the execution of these orders will be immediately arrested and imprisoned and will be tried by the military commissioner.

John C. Kelton
Major General Halleck.[8]

General Halleck began to tighten the screws on the rebellion in additional ways. Even though the river levels were low and navigation was also beginning to be impeded by ice, the Provost Marshal announced further operational restrictions.[9]

St. Louis, Dec. 13, 1861.

In order to suppress entirely and prevent any aid, assistance to, or communication with any person or persons directly or indirectly, disloyal or in arms against the, Union government, the commerce of the Mississippi and Missouri rivers has been placed under military control and surveillance, and no boat will be permitted to take freight or passengers, or be allowed a clearance, except those authorized and commissioned by proper military authority. All owners, officers and employees of boats will be required to take a strong oath of allegiance, and any owners or officers committing any act contrary to the above expressed object of this order, will cause the immediate forfeiture of their boat and cargo to the Union government, and such owners or officers will be subject to all the penalties prescribed by the articles of war for giving aid to the enemy.

Knox penned another letter from St. Louis on December 13 about the "disappearance" of Senator Polk.[10]

The secesh friends of Senator Trusten Polk are laughing heartily at what they call the smartness of that individual, and the stupidity of the correspondents who have never noticed the fact that he has not been in Washington this winter at all. In truth, Polk is such a dull, unimportant person that he never was noticed when he was in Washington, and there is nothing extraordinary in the failure to miss from the Senate now. The current gossip relating to this obscure Senator places him where he belongs by inclination in the land of Dixie somewhere in the South. It seems that he left home in a buggy, with a pair of horses and a small valise containing only a few necessary articles of wearing apparel. It is ascertained that he drew about ten thousand dollars in gold from a bank a few days before he started, and it is supposed he took the principal part of that money with him. His family is yet here, residing in a palatial mansion on Lucas Place, the Fifth Avenue of St. Louis. Polk evidently intended to avoid any unpleasant proceedings in the Senate during the present session, and in hurrying off to the Southern Confederacy was perfectly consistent with his disloyal sentiments and of moral treason while here. His expulsion from the United States Senate can no longer be postponed.[11] The papers here are ventilating a letter written by the absconded Senator last spring, approving the course of Governor Jackson plunging the State into revolution, and advising his correspondent that Missouri ought not to hesitate to go with the South. Another of the traitorous gang has thus disposed of himself by flight.

Knox returned again to the strange case of a young black man who was enslaved in the countryside, but claimed that he was a free black, born in Canada. His "owner," Judge Goode claimed otherwise. The English consul was also involved. Knox presented the case at length, (to be found in the endnotes) presenting his unique insights into wartime Missouri, but gave no hint of its resolution.[12]

General Halleck, in Knox's view, was making necessary changes in the military position in Missouri, from taking care of the last prisoners taken at Camp Jackson in May to moving units to various positions along the rail line, hoping to stymie any forward movements of General Price. Correspondent Knox was also not above making some armchair military proposals that showed a good understanding of the military situation in Missouri.

Eight of the Camp Jackson boys were brought in from Sedalia last night, by the Pacific Railroad, under arrest and are safely lodged in the military prison. Those eight persons were duly exchanged in pursuance of the agreement made between Price and Frémont; but they failed, to report themselves at the time their companions were sent down the river to Cairo by the steamboat *Liaten*[13] ten days ago. Together with about twelve others, who had been picked up since the previous departure of the Camp Jackson boys, they will be sent down to Cairo tomorrow to be transferred, under a flag of truce, to Columbus.

It is whispered around military headquarters that as soon as all the prisoners now on hand are duly exchanged or otherwise provided for, that General Halleck will issue the most important general order that has ever emanated from this military department. What it will be, nobody – high or low – seems able to state; but members of the staff, and those whose positions bring them into close personal contact with General Halleck give knowing winks, as much as if to say, "just wait." They have certainly succeeded in rousing public curiosity to a high pitch, whether or not there is anything in it. *Quien sabe?*

Military movements, though quiet in this vicinity, are not of the idle sort. The soldiers at Tipton, Syracuse and Sedalia are building winter quarters. Those at Rolla are already well provided for. From Sedalia, almost every day scouting expeditions are sent out, which generally result in the capture of a few prisoners and the receipt of valuable information.

To an unmilitary eye there seems to be no obstacle whatever to moving a half dozen regiments and a couple of sections of light artillery and a proportionate force of cavalry to some point in Johnson County, where the supply trains constantly sent to Price's disorganized army at Osceola could be easily intercepted and cut off. It is life and death now with Price's rabble to hold together during the next sixty days, and the rebels in Saline, Pettis and Lafayette counties are using extraordinary efforts to supply them with food and raiment. It is highly important, that these supplies should be cut off, and it is incomprehensible to unpracticed civilians why no exertion is made in that direction.

The continual sending of fresh troops to the interior does not indicate any intention to abandon Missouri to the enemy this winter; but, on the contrary, linked with other facts, foreshadows the prospect of early activity. Price, with his usual sagacity (and it must be admitted that rebel general has shown uncommon tact in overcoming obstacles and holding his own against the Union forces), does not dare to advance to the Missouri river for fear of being cut off by a forward movement from Rolla.

In brief, "the situation" in Missouri may be summed up as follows: The rebels and Unionists are watching each other, ready to spring upon the first sight of advantage, with all the advantage of location and ability to concentrate upon the Union side. The Thirteenth Iowa Regiment left this city to-day for Jefferson City. They number 927 men, rank and file, and are armed with smooth bore muskets, the flanking companies having French Minié rifles of late importation.

Investigation of the accounts from the Frémont administration continued. This probe threatened to dig deeper and there was rising concern among those who had dealt with Frémont's minions. The Christmas season encouraged charitable giving and at least some attempts to raise the holiday spirit even as more fighting loomed, as Knox reported:

> The seizure of the books of Child, Pratt & Fox,[14] was followed by the seizure or the books of the Oak Hall clothing establishment.[15] These seizures were by the special order of General

Halleck, at the request of the Commission, of which Judge Joseph Holt, of Kentucky, is chairman. The books are now in the possession of Messrs. Holt, Davis and Campbell for examination. These seizures create a considerable excitement among all those who have furnished government supplies.

Fairs, festivals, tableaux, concerts and all kind of exhibitions are the great rage of this city just now. Troops of children flood the stores and streets daily begging everybody to buy a ticket for one affair or another. The Ladies' Union Aid Society have realized $1,000 from one entertainment.

Both Union and rebel armies had gone into winter quarters, but that did not mean that troubles ceased. The destruction of bridges and culverts on the North Missouri Railroad by rebel sympathizers near the rail line was the theme of Knox's next report written from Warrenton, about thirty-five miles west of St. Charles.[16]

COMPLETE DESTRUCTION OF THE NORTH MISSOURI RAILROAD.

Warrentown [sic], Mo., Dec. 23, 1861. The destruction of the North Missouri Railroad is complete, as was at first stated. At short distances all the way from here to Hudson the track is torn up, ties burned, rails broken or bent so as to be useless. Wellsburg station was burned, with all its contents.

The large bridge over Davis's fork, on the Salt River, west of Mexico, and the bridge crossing Quiver [sic] river were burnt, and all the culverts either burnt or torn down, and cars or all kinds destroyed. Who the parties were engaged in this work of wholesale destruction is not yet known, but it is stated that the inhabitants along the road say no repairs can be made except where the road is guarded by Union troops.

An extra from the *Army Argus* office has been in circulation for two days, which says that the day of retribution is at hand, that nine thousand men who have been under Price's command, are now north of the Missouri river, and that more are coming.

Halleck responded strongly to the destruction.[17]

St. Louis, Dec. 23, 1861.
General Halleck has issued an order in which he says that any one caught in the act of burning bridges and destroying railroads and telegraphs will be immediately shot, and that any one accused of the crime will be tried by a military commission, and, if found guilty, suffer death. Where injuries are done to railroads and telegraph lines the commanding officer nearest the post will immediately press into service, for repairing damages, the slaves of all secessionists in the vicinity, and, if necessary, the secessionists themselves and their property. Any pretended Union men having information of intended attempts to destroy such roads and lines, or other guilty parties, who do not communicate such intention to the proper authorities, and give aid and assistance in punishing, will be regarded as *particeps criminis,* and tried accordingly.

Hereafter, towns and counties in which such destruction of properly takes place will be made to pay the expenses of all repairs, unless it shall be shown that the people of such towns and counties could not have prevented it on account of the superior force of the enemy.

Knox then filed another report which again made clear that the war in Missouri was indeed "cruel" and not limited to regular armies.[18]

THE DAMAGE TO THE NORTH MISSOURI RAILROAD.

Warrenton, Mo., Dec. 24, 1861.
The damage to the North Missouri Railroad may be summoned up as follows:

Bridges at Sturgeon, Centralia, Mexico, Jeffstown and Warrentown [sic], burned; also one station and perhaps twenty cars, from fifty to sixty culverts large and small; three or four water stations, 10,000 ties, from 250 to 300 telegraph poles and five miles of iron destroyed and ten miles of wire rendered useless.

Two trains, one having eight car loads of hogs and several car loads of hemp, and two cars of merchandise are in the possession of the rebels. Four engines are lying where they can be seized by them.

Some of the men who belonged to the trains have arrived here from whom I learn that the persons who did the damage are yet encamped along the road, about five hundred being at High Hill, and other bodies at or near Martinsburg, Mexico, Centralia, Sturgeon, and Allan. At Centralia they went within half a mile of the Berge Sharpshooters and destroyed a bridge and water station. Two freight trains were captured within four miles of the camp of a detachment of the same force.

At Renick the work was directed by practical railroad men, and the right course was always taken to make the destruction complete. Where the track was taken up, the rails were removed, the ties gathered in piles and set on fire and the rails thrown across the pile so that when the centre of the rails became heated the weight of the cold ends bent them so as to render them useless.

In destroying the bridges the fires were kindled around the corners, where they would soon throw the bridge down, and the trestle guides which spanned the open culverts were burned as were also the frames on which the water barrels stood usually.

The houses of railroad men and of all Union men in the vicinity of the road were surrounded, and the inhabitants assured that no harm was intended them while they remained indoors.

We hear of scarcely any pillage, or any other outrage beyond the destruction of the road and telegraph line.

The damage to the road cannot fall short or $300,000 and at least one month will be required to repair it so that trains can pass.[19]

General Pope achieved some amazing results in a skirmish in Johnson County. A series of maneuvers allowed Pope and Colonel Jefferson Davis to surround a regiment-size gathering of recruits led by Missouri State Guard Colonel Franklin Selden Robertson on December 19.[20] This action occurred at the hamlet of Milford at the juncture of the Whitewater River and Clear Creek. At the time, there was significant coverage of the event in the eastern newspapers, including the *Herald*, but the event has faded from Missouri memory. For the Union, the toll of this skirmish was light, 2 killed and 10 wounded. For the Missouri State Guard, the toll of killed and wounded is unknown, but the key result was the capture of 684 guardsmen plus several civilians.[21] While Knox did not report directly on the battle, he did report on the prisoners arriving on the Pacific Railroad and their prison situation, not often reported in the press.[22]

St. Louis, Dec. 24, 1861.

The first installment of prisoners recently captured by Colonel Jeff. C. Davis, of the Twenty-fifth Indiana regiment, at Milford, and by the various expeditions sent out by General Halleck from Sedalia and Otterville, arrived here about eleven o'clock last night. Owing to the possibility of escape if taken from the cars and marched to McDowell's College, prepared for their reception, the Second Iowa Regiment, Lieutenant Colonel Baker commanding, was ordered to surround the train and guard the prisoners during the night. The train was composed of thirty- four cars; mainly closed stock cars, provided with plain board seats and plenty or clean straw for the occasion. Many of the prisoners never before rode on a railroad, and their sensation under the circumstances must have been peculiar indeed.

The Twenty-fifth Indiana, who escorted the prisoners, from Sedalia, also remained on guard all night, and at nine o'clock this morning the transfer from the depot to the college building commenced. The prisoners were marched in fours between two files of the Twenty-fifth Indiana and Second Iowa, and, on reaching the building, led in single file to three immense rooms on the first, second and third floors of the building. Here they still remain and will continue until bunks can be erected and separate wards are arranged.

The passage to this city from Sedalia occupied nearly twenty-four hours from the time the men first entered the cars. It was intended that they should arrive in this city at seven PM on Sunday; but an unavoidable accident on the railroad prevented the accomplishment of such a design and even when the loading of the cars was finished a long delay occurred before the train started. The prisoners were regularly fed, however, and maintained good spirits. The train was four hours coming from Sedalia to Tipton, owing to the snow and frost on the track.

Excepting the delay, the trip to this city was marked by one incident of note. At Tipton, a portion of the men were allowed to leave the cars for wood, each prisoner being guarded by two privates of the Indiana Twenty-fifth. One prisoner attempted to escape, and was shot by both his guards and instantly killed. His name was Magree from Saline County. Out of this, large stories of insubordination grew, and were circulated through the city yesterday. I am assured, however, by Major Harris, of the Indiana Twenty-fifth regiment, that this is the only instance of shooting since the regiment started from Sedalia.

The *Herald* correspondent having concluded to pay a visit to the prisoners this morning after their arrival from the cars, applied to Captain Leighton, the Provost Marshal, for a permit, and was politely informed that, until the prisoners were registered at the new government hotel, no visitors would be admitted. An application to Captain Kelton,

Adjutant of General Halleck, met with a similar refusal. Nothing daunted, it was resolved to try to run the blue coat and bayonet blockade, and get all the information possible.

On proceeding to Eighth Street, at the corner of Gratiot, the first thing that met the eye was the Second Iowa Regiment taking possession of the row of dwellings opposite McDowell College, and converting them as rapidly as possible into quarters for themselves. Men were lugging their baggage upstairs, others were carrying huge lumps of Illinois coal to the grates and stoves, and all sorts or expedients for comfort were being improvised for the occasion. A line of sentinels patrolled across the street, at each end of the block and curious lookers-on gazed at the busy scenes in front or the building where the prisoners were confined. It required neither a permit nor password to get by the sentinel, and we were soon in front of the main entrance of the building itself. Several carpenters' laborers were carrying boards up stairs, and mortar and bricks were each going in the same direction as fast as a gang of men could carry them.

A word about the building itself where the rebels are confined. It is known as McDowell's College, from the fact that it was formerly used by a medical association of which Dr. Joseph N. McDowell was the President. McDowell himself is now a surgeon in Jeff. Thompson's army at New Madrid. He was notorious here for blackguardism towards the Dutch and Irish during the Know Nothing excitement a few years ago.[23]

Lately in New Orleans he came near being mobbed for some impudent expression of the same sort. The college is properly divided into three buildings – the centre one being circular in form, tapering off above the roof in an ill-shaped apology for a dome. The wings, or large buildings on each side, are each three stories high. The northern wing was used for medical lectures, and the second story was thrown into a single apartment, about one hundred feet long, fifty wide, and ceiling sixteen feet in the clear. A large room even with the ground and a low but large room on the third floor complete the description. The southern wing is divided into lodging rooms, offices, dissecting and experimenting rooms for the use of the faculty and students. It is built of brick, and, with a few improvements, will make an excellent prison house for the rebels-far better than any of the Richmond tobacco warehouses, where our prisoners are confined.

McDowell's Medical College
(Holland, *Scribner's Monthly*)

Having obtained an introduction to several of the officers, no further difficulty was met with in gaining access to the building and the prisoners. In company with several of the officers of the Twenty-forth Indiana Regiment we made a tour of the premises. Every passageway and outlet is closely guarded by sentinels. The prisoners are on the third floor of the north wing at present.

A motley sight, truly, they presented.

As a general thing, we were surprised to find them so well-dressed. They were none of your ordinary butternut-jean-suited rebels, but many of them had first rate overcoats, good thick shirts, first rate shoes, and looked well and hearty.

Defiance was seated on every face, and they laughed and chatted over their misfortunes in the gayest manner. Now and then, when we conversed with one more intelligent than the rest of the crowd, a shade or frown would come over his face when talking of his situation, but there were very few regrets, and a unanimous wish to try it over again. Some of the fellows told huge stories, as the following conversation will show:

Reporter: Well, my friend, what did you leave home to fight for?

Rebel: Why, for principle, of course. We don't fight for money, sir.

Reporter: Wouldn't you take pay if it was offered you?

Rebel: Just to pay expenses; that's all.

Reporter: Were you not better off at home before Governor Jackson precipitated the State into war, than since?

Rebel: Damn Governor Jackson! We don't go a cent on him, but you took our property and we were bound to fight.

Reporter: But how many of you (by this time a crowd of rebels had gathered around, listening to the conversation) had any property? Had one in ten property worth fifty cents above his clothes a year ago?

Rebel: Yes, indeed. I had a farm, and paid taxes on $1,000.

Another Rebel: I say Mister, this 'ere crowd'll average $4,000 apiece on the tax books, all around.

The *Herald* correspondent expressed his doubts, and retired.

Many of the men were returning to Price's army, having been with him since spring. One of them discovered Captain Edgar of the first Missouri Regiment, and asked if he was not at Springfield. The captain said he was, and the rebel said he recognized him as one or the bearers of a flag of truce for General Lyon's body.

They crowed considerable over that, and talked of every battle and skirmish that had been fought since the commencement of the war, as a rebel victory commencing with Bull Run and including Hatteras and Port Royal – professing to have lost all respect for the Stars and Stripes. They persistently asked where our flag had been victorious.

Among these prisoners is the notorious Bill Magoffin,[24] brother of Governor Beriah Magoffin, of Kentucky. Magoffin's adventures are liable to be brought to a close as soon as a military court can adjudge his case. Magoffin was one of the cowards who fired into Colonel Marshall's Illinois cavalry on its passage through Georgetown, *en route* to Lexington last August.[25] He was arrested, carried to Lexington, and released on Colonel Mulligan's surrender. A few weeks ago he asked permission to return within our lines to see his wife, who was then dying, and gave his parole to Dr. Hughes, of Pettis County, to surrender himself a prisoner as soon as his wife was buried. General Steele, at Sedalia, consented to the arrangement, and Magoffin remained in Georgetown unmolested for nearly three weeks. After his wife died Magoffin started for the camp at Milford, and when well on his way sent back a messenger to Hughes recalling his parole. This proceeding was irregular, and would nowhere be recognized. Magoffin was found in arms at Milford, and is now under arrest. His career will probably be brought to an end, and a rope's end, at that.

The plunder brought to this city along with the prisoners fills several cars. The most interesting portion is embraced in a lot of splendid shot guns, some four hundred in all. The Indiana boys are of the opinion that it would be impossible in any section of the country to collect such an assortment of first class shot guns. Many of the weapons are recognized as worth from fifty to seventy-five dollars apiece.

The style of provisions found in the Milford camp is eminently suggestive of New England. There is in fact everything that a well-to-do farmer would think of putting in a wagon for a long and tedious journey – pots of honey, jars of preserves, barrels of hard biscuit, papers of sugar, tubs of butter and various other articles. As the camp was composed of recruits on their way to join Price, no artillery and only a small amount of ammunition was found on the ground.

The contrabands taken with the prisoners numbered sixty in all, and are highly delighted with their present condition. They have been set to work on the new prison, and are exceedingly useful. The fifteen contrabands lately confined in the county jail have been taken out to assist doing the hard work at the McDowell College. Most of these contrabands came to St. Louis with General Frémont's staff as servants, having run away from their rebel masters in Southwest Missouri.

The damage on the North Missouri Railroad has not been exaggerated, and there is no longer the slightest doubt that it was a preconcerted movement to tear up the road and inflict as much damage as possible on the Union cause in North Missouri. The promptness of Gen. Halleck in issuing order No. 32, impressing the slaves of rebels, and, if necessary, the rebels themselves, into the work of repairing the damage, is another proof that we have a man of nerve at the head of the Department of Missouri. Ten of the bridge burners are reported killed, and seventeen taken prisoners. Two regiments have gone up the river since yesterday, and we shall soon have more reliable accounts of the state of affairs in that locality.

The "secesh" are given till Thursday (Christmas not being counted) to pay up their assessments on account of the $10,000 tax levied by General Halleck. I learn this morning from the Provost Marshal's general office that three of the assessed have paid under protest. Some of the strongest secessionists of a few weeks ago are now trying to convince the military authorities of their *bona fide* loyalty. Such stuff won't go down any longer.

Another load of prisoners, eight hundred strong is expected to-morrow morning.

Winter Quarters 315

Knox wrote a short, interesting summary of recent events. Knox invokes a "reliable source." The military summaries in the first three paragraphs are correct. The railroad was being repaired and many of the bridge burners were in jail awaiting trial. Price was indeed in retreat, but to Springfield, not Arkansas.[26]

St. Louis, Mo., Dec. 27, 1861.

The following *resume* of the recent military operations in Missouri is obtained from a reliable source:

Within the last two weeks the Union army has captured 2,500 rebels; including about seventy commissioned officers, 1,200 horses and mules; 1,100 stand of arms, two tons of powder, 100 wagons; and an immense amount of commission stores and camp equipage. A large foundry at Lexington, used by the rebels for casting cannon, shot and shells, most of the rebel craft on the Missouri, including ferry boats, have been destroyed or captured. A pretty clean sweep has been made of the whole country between the Missouri and Osage rivers, and General Price, cut off from all supplies and recruits from North Missouri, is in full retreat for Arkansas, with his whole army, having passed through Springfield on Monday last.[27]

Our loss in accomplishing these important results did not exceed one hundred killed and wounded. These are the fruits of brilliant strategical combinations of General Halleck, which have been so ably executed by Generals Pope, Prentiss and McKean,[28] and Colonels Jeff. C. Davis, of Fort Sumter fame,[29] and Frederick Steele of the Eleventh Regular Infantry, and the brave officers and soldiers or our army, regulars and volunteers.

Gen. Price's designs to stir up rebellion in North Missouri, and simultaneously burn all railroad bridges, stations and rolling stock on the twentieth of this month, in accordance with a plan promulgated from the rebel camp, have been foiled to a great extent in their plans by the energy of General

Halleck and activity of our forces, which are kept in constant motion, notwithstanding the severity of the weather.

The damage done to the North Missouri and Hannibal and St. Joseph Railroad has been greatly exaggerated. Repairs are being rapidly made, and both the North Missouri Railroad and telegraph wire will be in working order to Wellsville to-night.

Ten bridge burners have already been shot, and fifty are in close confinement to be summarily dealt with under General Halleck's stringent orders.

It is confidently expected that our moving columns will as effectually in a few days break up bridge burning in North Missouri as the rebellion has been crushed south of the river. No mercy will be shown the scoundrels.

General Halleck's emphatic orders with reference to all bridge burners are to shoot down every one making the attempt.

Major Glover has just returned from a scout in Camden County with ten wagon loads of subsistence, a rebel captain and thirteen men, who left Price's army since his retreat commenced.

General Pope's official report of his expedition in Central Missouri has been received, but contains nothing important which has not previously been reported.[30]

On the same day, Knox wrote a much longer chronicle of some noteworthy events. Knox called them "rumors" but then proceeded to look into each one, finding the kernel of truth in all of them. Even though the armies were supposedly in "winter quarters," General (not Colonel as Knox wrote) Curtis's move to Rolla boded some action, and bridge burning continued.[31]

St. Louis, Dec. 27, 1861.

The city has been filled with various rumors relating to military movements in this department, and I have taken the trouble to chase a few or them to headquarters. Yesterday it was given out on the street, and generally believed, that Major General Halleck and staff had suddenly left the city, by the Pacific Railroad, for Rolla. Everybody was on the *qui vive* at once for news. On going to headquarters I saw General Halleck very quietly giving audience to callers, as if nothing had happened. The story arose from the departure of General Samuel R. Curtis, to take command of the post at Rolla, the late commandant, Colonel Dodge, of the Fourth Iowa, having asked to be relieved from that duty.

Another rumor was that two regiments had started to Sedalia during the night, and that Price had attacked our camp at that point. The origin of this story was the return of the thirty-seven empty cars in which the eleven hundred rebel prisoners and their escort, the Twenty-fifth Indiana, came to the city on Monday night. The balance of the story was mere bosh; yet, strange to say, it was so thoroughly believed by some as to occasion quite a scare, which was heightened by the audacious offers of the secesh to bet upon the truth of the report.

Samuel R. Curtis
(Oshkosh Public Museum, Oshkosh, WI)

The departure of Colonel Curtis for Rolla, coupled with the fact that General Sigel has been appointed to command all the troops at that point, including his own and the division recently commanded by Col. Asboth, does necessarily imply a forward movement, although the troops are in a condition to march at two hours' notice. General Halleck evidently designs some movement this winter to quiet the rebels in this State. It is all important that Price should be cut off from receiving supplies from his friends in North Missouri, and that reinforcements should be prevented from reaching him. But it is far from certain that the Rolla forces are available for that purpose. The active movement from Sedalia or Otterville may be supported by an advance from Rolla; but that is all. It is improper to speak of the developments of military preparations; but a few interesting facts linked together indicate another swoop at the rebels, which will be more important in its results, if successful; than the last.

Yesterday advices were received from the Big River Bridge, which was burned by some of Jeff. Thompson's marauders a few weeks ago, that another visit was expected, and that reinforcements were required. An extra train was got ready in half an hour and sent to Sulphur Springs, where the Eighth and Eleventh Wisconsin Regiments were encamped. Five companies of the Eighth Regiment were put on board and sent to the bridge. It is believed they are sufficient to protect it from any marauding force the rebels can bring against them. Last night a battalion of cavalry, with horses and equipments complete, left for Sulphur Springs by steamboat, and doubtless arrived early this morning. The audacity of the threats against the Big River Bridge may be inferred from the fact that it is only forty-six miles from this city. The road is well guarded now, and is believed to be safe.

The news this morning that two spans of the Chariton River Bridge, on the Hannibal and St. Joseph Railroad, have been burned by the rebels, is another evidence of the preconcerted character of the late uprising. The mischief has been incited and perpetrated by the returning troops lately belonging to Price's army.

The plot failed to accomplish any great damage, excepting upon the North Missouri Railroad and was not carried out half as effectively, as rebel designs upon railroad bridges are usually. The North Missouri trains will be running the entire length of the road in a few days, excepting at the crossing of the Davis Fork of Salt River, where a temporary structure will be put into operation for transferring passengers and freight from train to train on each side. Luckily there was enough railroad iron on hand to replace the rails, and ties were borrowed from the Pacific Railroad Company sufficient to put the track in order promptly. Trains are already running to Montgomery City, and the telegraph is working above Warrenton. There is a gap of twenty miles to be covered yet, and at the present rate of repairs the work will be done less than a week.

Brigadier General Schofield, who has been placed in command of the State troops, is now on the line of the North Missouri road in person. Several regiments have been sent up since the first news of the bridge burning, and State troops at Palmyra, and the brigade of General John B. Henderson, lately quartered in the Insane Asylum building at Fulton, the county seat of Callaway County, have been ordered to join General Schofield.[32] These are State troops, raised in Pike, Boone and adjoining counties. Birge's sharpshooters, at Renick, were reported in a tight place a few days ago, and considerable anxiety was felt for their safety. In the absence of any contrary news, it is safe to say that, in view of the recent movements of troops in that vicinity, the sharpshooters are safe.

The prisoners housed in the converted McDowell Medical College again gained Knox's attention. He like many others sought their names, but identification was going slowly. Knox had previously circumvented orders to obtain interviews, but rules had tightened very considerably:

> Admission to the new government hotel (late McDowell College), where eleven hundred rebel prisoners are confined, is strictly prohibited. The rule is so stringent that yesterday

Major Farrar, Provost Marshal General, was unable to pass the sentries until the officer of the guard was, summoned. The troops in charge are the Second Iowa Volunteers, Lieut. Colonel Baker commanding. The secesh females in town have made so many applications to the Provost Marshal General for permission to visit the prisoners and carry them dainties and comforts that the following notice is posted on the door of that officer's headquarters:

NOTICE

No person, under any circumstances, will receive permission to visit the prisoners confined in the McDowell College, and no application for such permission will be entertained. Ladies and others who wish to send parcels to the prisoners are informed that until arrangements are made for that purpose no parcels will be received. Due notice will be given publicly of any relaxation in this order.

I learn that the work of registering the names of the prisoners is going on as rapidly as circumstances will admit. There is reason to believe that in many instances false names have been given, and the authorities have resolved that in case of detection of this fraud the guilty parties shall be put upon bread and water for two weeks, as a punishment. It is noticeable that thus far the prisoners are very tractable, and not the slightest sign of insubordination has been manifested. They express now, as on the first day of their arrival the most perfect satisfaction with their treatment. Those who have money (and they are very few), are allowed to purchase the morning papers.

The mechanical pursuits of this motley crew may be judged from the fact that, yesterday an officer ranged the prisoners on each floor on one side of the large rooms and stated that, as the making of the sleeping bunks and other carpenter work necessary to ensure their comfort was going on slowly, they would facilitate their own comfort and hasten the work by assisting. At a call for all the carpenters to step forward only five persons in eleven hundred responded; and it was so manifestly so much to their own interest to assist in the work that there is no room for supposing that any considerable deception was practiced. Take the same number of Northern troops and ask for carpenters and fifty at least would step forward.

[ASSESSMENTS]

The secesh individuals who have been assessed by Gen. Halleck's order to the tune of $10,000 for the benefit of Union refugees have drawn up a protest against the legality and justice or that proceeding. This is rather rich – the idea of secessionists, who justify the stealing of forts and mints, harping on the "legality" of a military proceeding, rather excites the risibles, but it is true. General Halleck has taken the order, and if he does not increase the amount to punish the protestants for their impudence, it won't be because they do not deserve it.

There is one point in the protest worthy of notice: the parties say that the courts are open here, and if they are disloyal their property may be confiscated according to the act of Congress. Distant readers will be surprised to learn that the idea of obtaining a decree of confiscation of property owned by rebels, in the United States District Court here, is considered perfectly impossible. Jeff. Davis himself would go scot free if his conviction was contingent on the co-operation of the federal courts in this city. No wonder the signers of the secession protest wished to have their cases tried in the courts.

A new secret secession organization, confined to this State, has been discovered, and at the proper time full particulars will be given to the public. The oaths and obligations are of the most diabolical description and bind the members "to do anything" to overthrow the present government of the United States.

The weather here has alternated from warm to cold and *vice versa*. The river is now and has been free from ice for several days, but the present cold snap will bring an avalanche of ice down upon us from the upper country.

Thus ended the year 1861 in St. Louis. In the months since his arrival in May, Knox had been in two battles, Boonville and Wilson's Creek, and often had lived a life of hardship. He also had lived comfortably in St. Louis and had met important men. Two year-end actions, the dispatch of Colonel Eugene A. Carr and his cavalry towards Lebanon and the move of General Curtis to Rolla boded well for Union action in the future.[33]

Eugene A. Carr
(*Library of Congress*)

> St. Louis, Dec. 30, 1861.
>
> Twenty-four hundred and sixty cavalry, under Colonel Carr, with fifteen days rations, left Rolla yesterday, destined, it is supposed, for Springfield by a circuitous route.[34]

General Curtis's intent was emphasized by part of his orders to Col. Carr to:

> March tomorrow at 8 o'clock. All extra baggage, bands of music and surplus equipment will be left in charge of proper officers.[35]

Chapter 17

A New Year

Weather in St. Louis in January could be a series of contrasts. Snow was possible. The Mississippi River could be frozen solid enough to allow wagons to be driven across it. Or the river could be open to navigation. Temperatures could range from well below zero to the 70s Fahrenheit.

Similarly, the political, economic, and military situation fluctuated in St. Louis. The New Year began on a hopeful note for local Unionists. There was a new prison in St. Louis, the converted McDowell Medical College, and it was rapidly filling with rebel prisoners. There had been movement at Rolla, a new commander, General Samuel R. Curtis, and an in-force cavalry scout to the southwest led by Colonel Carr. Thomas Knox in his months in St. Louis reported on numerous rumors. He labeled them as such, investigated them, and often debunked them with humor. Now as winter deepened and military action slowed, rumors abounded in St. Louis, a divided city. For secessionists, rumors provided hope. For Unionists, rumors were a way to harass the local rebels. In his early January letters, Knox reported and clarified more rumors. He wrote a series of letters from St. Louis, dated January 1, 2, 3, 5, 7, 9 & 10, which appeared in print in the *Herald* in out of date sequence. They were published between January 3 and 12 and are presented here in the order in which Knox wrote them. As might be expected, a significant number of rumors are refuted.

St. Louis, Jan. 1, 1862.

The city has been filled with idle rumors for several days last in relation to the reported escape of the rebel prisoner, Magoffin, and seven others. Upon inquiring at the McDowell College, I learn that the report is entirely unfounded. The prisoners are guarded in the most secure manner by the Second Iowa regiment.

Sentries patrol the block upon which the prison is located, and the rear of the dwellings opposite the college buildings is likewise guarded. The building itself is protected in every passageway, and upon staircase by vigilant sentinels.

Accommodations are being fitted up for two thousand prisoners. The number now confined in the building is 1,020. Of these 788 are the fruits of the Milford capture. The others have been sent from North Missouri direct and several small squads have come in from Jefferson City, Rolla, and Pilot Knob.

Yesterday the registration of the prisoners was completed, under the supervision of Lieutenant Butterworth. The list was turned over to the Provost Marshal General. The city reporters applied for a copy, but were refused, and told that the list would be withheld from the press for the present. Notwithstanding this statement, I am enabled, through the kindness of Lieutenant Butterworth, to send a copy to the *Herald* for publication.

News of the departure of twenty-five hundred cavalry from Rolla promises interesting intelligence at an early day.[1]

In a short dispatch on January 2, Knox took note of the capture of some of the men involved in the attacks on the North Missouri Railroad, and several other matters:[2]

St. Louis, Jan. 2, 1862.

Dispatches received at headquarters announce the capture of the notorious Jeff. Owens, Colonel Jones and fifty of their bridge burning gang, near Martinsburg, Adrian[3] County, by General Schofield, commander of the State militia, and the various guerrilla bands along the North Missouri Railroad have been pretty thoroughly scattered.

A New Year 325

The report this morning that six regiments of Union troops had started on a Western expedition is a mistake.

Recent developments disclose embezzlements in the County Collectors office, amounting to $30,000 dollars. These frauds were committed by Stephen D. Axtell, Chief Clerk, and extend back for a series of years.[4]

Also on January 2, Knox composed a long letter covering various topics including Generals Schofield, McKinstry, and Sigel. Knox was quite harsh in his calls for punishment of those attacking the railroads:[5]

> St. Louis, Mo., Jan. 2, 1862.
> A rumor was current in this city yesterday morning that General Schofield had captured a thousand rebels near the line of the North Missouri Railroad, and would shortly send his prize to St. Louis. The story grew out of the fact that General Schofield went several days since to the vicinity of the late railway destruction, in pursuit of a rebel force a thousand strong. Last evening information reached headquarters that he had succeeded in capturing, near Martinsburg, fifty or more who were engaged in the recent outrages, and among them were two notorious ringleaders – Colonel Jones and Colonel Jeff Owens.
>
> Full particulars of the capture have not yet reached the city; but it is known that it was accomplished without loss on our side, the rebels having been surprised and induced to make a prompt surrender. They are to be sent here to undergo an examination, with reference to their connection with the railroad destruction.
>
> Much anxiety is shown, both among Union men and rebels, to know what will be the fate of those convicted of the above mentioned crime. Some time ago, three men, convicted in burning the Big River Bridge on the Iron Mountain Railroad, were arrested, tried and found guilty. The ring leader of the party was put under the sentence of death, but before the

time appointed he died of black measles, and thus thwarted the ends of justice.[6] His two companions, though found to be guilty, were permitted, through some legal prestidigitations, to go at large after taking the oath of allegiance. The administering of the oath to traitors is looked upon by the intelligent loyalists as a great farce, and especially so when bridge burners are allowed to participate in its benefits. We have been waiting patiently for a few summary examples to be made, and when these are given outrages will be checked. If the fifty outlaws now in the hands of General Schofield are convicted and meet the fate promised them by General Halleck, a new era will dawn upon us.

Knox then turned his ire upon General Price at Springfield. In calling Price "his laxative highness" he is referring to Price's apparent indisposition at the battle of Booneville and predicted that upon the approach of Union troops to Springfield, Price would flee to Arkansas. He also mentioned the case of the jailed General McKinstry and his situation:

It is quite certain that measures have been taken by this department to rid Missouri of the presence of the rebels in any considerable bodies. General Price's army now numbers some ten thousand men, and is at Springfield, halting on its way to Arkansas.[7] I am revealing no secret when I state that the cavalry force sent out from Rolla a few days since is designed to operate on this rebel army, in conjunction with the force of infantry which marched recently from Sedalia and Tipton. Very soon after this reaches New York, you will hear of a battle with General Price or his rapid and precipitate retreat into Arkansas, probably the latter, as his laxative highness is too shrewd to be drawn into an engagement when he does not desire it. In either event we shall see the practical working of the sound policy that has controlled the Department of Missouri since the removal of General Frémont.

The papers of this morning announced that a peremptory

A New Year

order had been received for the release of General McKinstry who has been for weeks confined in the St. Louis Arsenal. His counsel, Judge Krum and Reverdy Johnson, have lately laid the matter before the President, who promised that it should be attended to, and the order in question is probably the result of their labors.[8] General McKinstry's arrest was made on the 13th of November last, by order of General McClellan, and though he has since been in close confinement, no official information has been given him of the cause of his arrest. The committee which was lately after Alexander Cummings with a sharp stick was instrumental in the arrest of McKinstry, though they do not evince a willingness to show their attentions to the latter as readily as to the former individual.[9] Whatever may be the charges against General McKinstry, it is but proper that he and the public should know about them.

Comments on the recently-arrived prisoners captured by General Pope followed in Knox's letter. He indulged in a bit of irony at the expense of the secessionists and their prisoner friends:

> Since the list of prisoners sent here by General Pope has been made out, their friends are allowed to send in various articles for their comfort. The secessionists of St. Louis have opened their hearts to a wonderful extent, and those who claim that General Halleck's orders (13 and 24) are unconstitutional, and who contribute with great reluctance for the support of the refugees from the Southwest, are found sending gifts in abundance to the traitors recently caught in arms against the government. One secessionist sent a wagon load of provisions and wines for the use of the prisoners, and many families and associations of ladies evinced their sympathies by donations of cake, jellies and numerous delicacies that are not supposed to be included in ordinary army rations. Yesterday a roast turkey was offered, neatly stuffed and ready for the table. Its weight excited suspicion, and on examination the innocent remains

of the once proud bird were found to contain a select assortment of small dirk knives. The maritime principle that contraband goods taint the vessel in which they were carried was applied in this case, and its application resulted in furnishing a good supper to a portion of the guard. A few loaves of bread presented on Thursday last contained a fine array of burglar's tools, which possibly by accident had become mingled with the dough while it was in preparation for baking. These little attempts at contraband supply render the guard exceedingly vigilant, and it is not likely that any escape will be made. So far the prisoners have shown no sign of insubordination, but, on the contrary, are orderly and cheerful.

Thomas Knox next turned to the situation evolving around General Franz Sigel. The general was popular, especially with the German-American units and was seen as a man of action and willing to fight. His successor at Rolla, General Curtis, was an unknown quantity:

> General Sigel is expected to reach this city tomorrow, he having been relieved of his command by General Curtis. There are rumors that he will resign, and should he do so, some of the best field and line officers in the West will follow his example. His friends complain that he has not been properly treated in being superseded in command of the army at Rolla just at the moment when he was about to make a decisive movement. Since the war commenced, General Sigel has shown as much military talent as any officer in the army, and it will be most deeply lamented if anything should occur to deprive us of his services. Some of our officers – particularly those of the regular army – manifest a deep seated hatred of General Sigel and all other German commanders, based solely on the ground that they are of foreign birth.[10]
>
> The river at this point is full of floating ice, and navigation above St. Louis has almost entirely ceased. Boats leave daily for Cairo and way points.

Knox sent an additional letter on January 3 with the news of General Sigel's resignation. This news caused quite a stir in St. Louis and other areas with large German populations. General Sigel was notorious for his sensitivity to any possible slight. Curtis had arrived at Rolla, shown Sigel his orders, and then they together determined that Curtis's date of commission as brigadier general preceded Sigel's.[11] He also reported on a rumor that Halleck was to be transferred to the East and the dissatisfaction in St. Louis over the rumor. The rumor was untrue. This part of his letter is found in the notes.[12] Other information appeared in his letter. There were signs that preparations were being made for an advance down the Mississippi River, a movement that would be a fulfillment of the "Anaconda" plan proposed by General Winfield Scott at the beginning of the war:[13]

> Recent advertisements calling for boats for the transport service indicate that the expedition for the Mississippi is taking shape. Some of the boats are intended for transporting troops, while others are to be filled throughout with freight, even to the cabin and office. The finest boats for this service are on the lower Mississippi in the hands of the rebels, quite a number of the large packets have gone below just before the blockade went into operation. St. Louis and Cincinnati can, at the present time, furnish transportation for the whole army of the West, so that the want of boats now in Dixie will not be felt.

Secession sentiment was being suppressed, Knox reported, but below the surface it was bubbling up in a number of ways. Such sentiment was often expressed more openly by women and girls than by men, possibly due to the fact that men were treated with greater severity than women:[14]

> There is much chagrin among the rebels of St. Louis at the recent capture of rebels by General Pope. The boast had been made that St. Louis would be in the hands of the traitors by the 1st of January, and the dispelling of that illusion is not at all satisfactory to them.
>
> Treason in this city is only slumbering and waiting for

opportunity to assert its power. To a casual observer, everything is as quiet as in New York or Philadelphia; but to one who day by day walks these streets, the secession feeling is most patent. Secession badges are occasionally seen on the coats of men on the public sidewalks, and it is a frequent occurrence to meet ladies of the upper circles wearing in their bonnet trimmings one white and two red roses, the symbol of treason. It requires considerable Christian forbearance to put up with the insults sometime flung in someone's face by would-be ladies whose sex alone prevents them from receiving a proper return.

Money is constantly being raised for the benefit of soldiers in the rebel army, and at several houses in this city uniforms are being manufactured to be sent, at the earliest opportunity, to certain parties following the flag of Jeff. Davis. Eternal vigilance is the price of liberty, and nothing but the most constant watchfulness on the part of the federal authorities will keep the traitorous element of St. Louis in proper subjugation.

A short time since, Capt. Sweeny, at the head of a band of rebels, was captured near Glasgow, Mo., with his entire gang.[15] The whole party is now in confinement at the St. Louis military prison. Yesterday, Captain Sweeny, of the regular army, who last summer commanded a brigade of three months volunteers, and who lost an arm during the Mexican war, made a call upon his captive namesake. On confronting the rebel officer he found that he too was minus an arm, and on comparing ancestry a relationship was discovered. Their names differed only in the Christian appellative, the initial letter (W) of the "middle" name of each standing for the same word. Deeply regretting that anyone hearing the Sweeny should be found a traitor, the federal officer left the cell of the prisoner, pondering upon what Sam Weller would style "a werry remarkable coincidence."[16]

A New Year

Knox wrote again on January 5. He began with detailed news of General Schofield's pursuits of guerrillas along the North Missouri Railroad:[17]

> St. Louis, Mo., Jan. 5, 1862.
> General Schofield returned last night from the line of the North Missouri Railroad, where he has been doing most effective service in dispersing the rebel marauders of that section. At noon on the 25th ultimo, General Schofield received orders from General Halleck to leave St. Louis immediately for the purpose of attacking the rebels, who had been committing outrages north of the Missouri river. Three hours later he was on his way thither, and arrived the following day at High Hill station, on the North Missouri Railroad, with a command consisting of the Third Iowa, Eighty-first Ohio and Tenth Missouri regiments. He at once started in pursuit of a rebel band, two hundred and fifty strong, that was known to be in Callaway County on its way to join General Price's rebel force beyond Osceola.
>
> General Prentiss at the same time moved south from Sturgeon, and on the 28th encountered the rebels, nine hundred strong, at Mount Sion [Zion] in Boone County, and after a short engagement dispersed them.[18] This force of nine hundred men was made up of the two hundred and fifty pursued by General Schofield, and another body of between six and seven hundred, principally recruits, that were bound southward. Gen. Prentiss having effectually dispersed these rebels, or rather caused them to separate into small bands for the purpose of eluding the Federal troops, General Schofield immediately divided his command into several parts, and commenced a rapid pursuit. He was unencumbered with large baggage trains, and was thus able to make rapid marches. For five days he subsisted his troops on such provisions as the country afforded, and through the aid of his scouts and such information as he could glean from the loyal citizens and the negroes along his route he captured several roving

parties. The counties of Montgomery, Callaway, Boone and Audrain have been completely scoured, and nowhere within their limits does General Schofield think any rebel force remains. Nearly every road through these counties has been traversed, and nearly every post town and village visited and the traitors put to flight. The most of his force has returned to Martinsburg and Mexico, but some portions of it are still on the march.

Eighty-four prisoners that were captured singly or in small squads, are now in the General's possession, and will shortly be brought thither. Five or six of them are known to have been engaged in the railway destruction, and will have their examination before a military commission that has been ordered at Hudson, by Major General Halleck. Among those captured was Colonel Jeff. Owens, a prominent rebel of that region, who has lately been engaged in recruiting for the rebel ranks.[19] He had gathered a company of seventy strong in Monroe and Audrain counties, and had just completed his organization when General Price issued orders for the destruction of the railroads. Colonel Owens – who is more properly spoken of as Captain Owens – says that the plan was laid and the time appointed by General Price. The order was transmitted verbally, and the scheme successfully carried out. Capt. Owens looked upon it merely as an act of war, and asked for a parole, assuring his captor that he should observe it faithfully. When informed that bridge burners could not be released on parole, he manifested great astonishment and was unable to understand the propriety of such an arrangement.[20]

Knox was complementary to the actions of General Schofield in northern Missouri and again commented on the prisoner situation and what to do with them. The Gratiot Street Prison was surely inadequate to house the number of prisoners placed in it and often served as a transfer point for shipment to other northern prisoners. Despite its inadequacies, it served throughout the war. Late in 1861, it was decided to use the closed

Illinois State Prison in Alton, Illinois, as a prison for captured Confederates and Confederate sympathizers. The first prisoners arrived at the Alton Federal Military Prison on February 9, 1862.[21] Then he told the story of a discouraged secessionist taking the oath and who reported on Price's situation in Southwest Missouri:[22]

> A soldier who has been a member of Gov. Jackson's body guard since that officer first started upon his wanderings, returned to this city on Friday last, and has taken the oath not to bear arms against the Federal government hereafter. He was in all the battles that have been fought in Missouri since the war commenced. He says that the rebel loss at the battle of Wilson's Creek was 520 killed and a proportionate number wounded, which is very near the estimate I made at the time. At Lexington, their loss was higher than ours. The entire rebel army has a deep-seated antipathy against the German troops fighting under the Federal flag, and the soldiers have a more earnest dread of Sigel than of any other officer in the country. He represented Price's force now in the field as 8,000 strong and says the rebel General has been much disappointed in the reluctance of the people to arm in response to his recent proclamation.

Knox finished his letter with a comment on the supposed Sigel resignation and the unhappiness of the Germans about it:

> There is still much excitement concerning General Sigel's resignation. It has been forbidden to transmit any announcement of it over the wires, and the local press is silent of it, with the exception of a statement of such a vague rumor from Rolla. The Germans are particularly agitated.

Knox wrote another letter on January 7 that also appeared in the January 12 *Herald*. Again, he discussed the cases of the prisoners accused in the recent railroad destruction:[23]

St. Louis, Mo., Jan. 7, 1862.
The military commission that was convened at Palmyra, Mo., by order of Major General Halleck, commenced its labors on Monday, the 30th ult. The object of the commission was to examine the cases of several parties accused of participating in the recent railroad destruction in North Missouri. Colonel Groenbeck [Groesbeck], of the Thirty-ninth Ohio infantry, acts as President.

There are about thirty persons now held at Palmyra against whom charges have been made, ranging from sixteen to sixty years of age. Among them are two captains and two lieutenants of Price's army. Like all military commissions, the sessions are entirely private, and the questions and answers have to be submitted in writing. Some of the prisoners deny having any part in the railroad outrages, while others put in the plea that they acted under orders from General Price, and can only be held responsible as prisoners of war. Whether the destruction of a railroad can be considered an act of war remains to be seen. The results of the examination will be known in a few days, as soon as the labor is ended.[24]

Knox then turned to the rebel prisoners being held at the McDowell College, and the question of their subsequent and ultimate care and housing:

It has not yet been decided to remove the prisoners from McDowell College to the Alton Penitentiary. The latter building would be much more comfortable for the prisoners than their present quarters, and the labor of guarding them would be far easier. There is an enclosed space of ten acres in extent where the prisoners can be allowed to take air and exercise.

Our authorities are hesitating to remove them, and may possibly decide to have them remain where they are. Their ground of hesitation is that the prisoners will consider it a severe measure to confine prisoners of war in a penitentiary, the same as if they had been convicted of serious crimes, and may retaliate upon our men now in their hands. To an outsider it would seem as if the prisoners of war at present in possession of the rebel army had received sufficient bad treatment at the hands of their captors to remove all squeamishness on our part. The decision of those who have the matter in charge will be known in a few days.

On Saturday last all the prisoners were drawn out in line and searched. The result of this operation was the finding of several bowie knives and a few pistols that escaped the previous examinations or have been smuggled in since the prisoners' removal here. No one is allowed to enter the prison save those having it in charge, the large number of applications rendering such an order necessary.

Two or three reporters have, however, managed to pass the sentinels and spend an hour among the inmates of the building. The result of their morning call has already been before the world.[25]

When Halleck arrived on the scene in St. Louis in November, "chaos and confusion" reigned. He worked hard on several fronts to bring reason and order and to systemize the workings of his Western Department. In Knox's opinion, as reported in January, some of Halleck's work became evident in his rules for officers.[26]

Apparently, old scores were, in some cases being settled in the assessments being levied on secessionists in St. Louis. The Board of Assessors was reconstituted with new members and was instructed to be just in their assessments:[27]

St. Louis, Jan. 7, 1862.

In consequence of disproportionate assessments having been made on rebels in this city under order No. 24, General Halleck has appointed a new Board of Assessors to revise the old list, and make such changes as they deem proper. All other proceedings will be in accordance with the original order, and the board is enjoined to assess no individual unjustly, as there will be no further appeal from their decision.[28]

In the same *Herald*, a second note from Knox appeared giving further notice of the Union control in the State of Missouri. All newspapers were required to submit copies of each edition to the authorities in St. Louis. This was not official censorship, but it was clear that suppression would follow if secession sentiments were too strongly expressed. The St. Louis newspapers were already under similar scrutiny:[29]

> The Provost Marshal has issued an order requiring all publishers of newspapers in the State of Missouri, St. Louis city papers excepted, to furnish him a copy of each issue for inspection, and failure with which order will render the paper liable to suppression.

And, in addition to the newspapers order, the St. Louis Chamber of Commerce also provided some news. The Chamber, organized in 1843, refused to admit a number of Unionists to membership:[30]

> St. Louis, Jan. 9, 1862.
> Great excitement occurred in the Chamber of Commerce this afternoon, on the occasion of the election of officers which resulted in the disruption of the Chamber by the withdrawal of the Union members, who subsequently established a Union Chamber of Commerce, which will be immediately carried out. The trouble occurred in consequence of the secession members refusing by their vote to admit a number of Union applicants for membership.

General Sigel's resignation was the subject of a letter that Knox sent along to the *Herald*. The author of the letter is not identified, but it is obvious that he was a strong Sigel partisan. Sigel surely was temperamental and quick to take offense, but Curtis managed to calm him and named him as second in command, so he did not resign. However, the controversy seemed to have a life of its own; it just would not go away. At Rolla, Sigel claimed "illness," but in a report to General Halleck, General Curtis said, "General Sigel complains of ill health, but seems able for duty."[31]

The following extract from a private letter, dated St. Louis, January 6, explains the cause which led to the resignation of the veteran General Sigel, and will be read with interest:

And so Sigel has been so shamefully neglected that native Americans have grown impatient. His last stay here was more for the benefit of his men than his health. They have never allowed his division to be complete. He has organized regiment after regiment only to be deprived of the effects of his energies; and to his memorial to General Halleck on this subject he has never received an answer. His staff, despite all his efforts has received no pay, and little attention has been paid to his requisitions for his troops. Notwithstanding the cold, his men have been compelled to sleep in torn tents, without fires, while it is notorious that other commands were freely supplied.

Immediately before his last return to Rolla, a conversation took place between General Sigel and General Halleck and Sigel seemed satisfied that the command of the troops at Rolla had been given to him. On the evening of his arrival at Rolla he received news to the effect that the people of Southwest Missouri had petitioned President Lincoln for protection and had recommended Sigel as a fit man to deliver them from the thralldom of Jeff. Davis. Everything indicated that he would see some active service, when, to his astonishment, after being only four days at Rolla, he was ordered to transfer his command over to General Curtis. There was no alternative for Sigel to resign, and resign he did.

During the whole campaign, General Sigel has been subjected to a series of disappointments. Frémont, who knew Sigel's abilities well, would not grant him sufficient troops when there was a splendid opportunity of defeating Price at the passage of the Osage. Frémont was removed and General

Hunter was appointed in his place. A council of war was held and Sigel was sent out to meet the enemy. The main body of the army, however, suddenly retreated, and Sigel was left alone; and had it not been for a mere accident, he might have lost his entire division. He remained forty-eight hours in Springfield for the purpose of procuring means of transportation for the families of those who were serving in the Union army, and gave his carriages, his horses and his all, to save these poor women and children from freezing and starving.

Immediately after Hunter's retreat, Sigel had resolved upon retiring, but the hope of being able to do something for unhappy Missouri changed his mind. General Halleck's last order has dissipated Sigel's last hope, and he has acted only as a man of honor ought to have acted.[32]

Meanwhile, something was stirring in Rolla. Knox felt he had to go and see for himself. On January 9 he wrote a long letter with his observations from Rolla about an army preparing to move:[33]

Rolla, Phelps County, Mo., Jan. 9, 1862.
If I were asked "What is the general appearance of Rolla?" I should answer, "Mud." When you alight from the cars at the depot, you step into mud; when you leave the depot and enter the street you behold mud; when you reach your hotel you find yourself covered with mud; when you get under the hospitable roof of your Boniface you behold his floors coated with the same plastic material. If you betake yourself to the eating department of the caravansary, which in Missouri does not afford an extensive and elaborate bill of fare, the table cloth and crockery arouse suspicions that some infant genius has been amusing itself with pies and cakes fabricated from the mud so prevalent in Rolla. Burying your thoughts in your coffee, you discover that, too, is of the nature of all things around; and as you muse upon the prospect before you from

the open window, you conclude that you have literally "put your foot in it" in making a visit to this out of the way town.

The troops here, numbering some twelve thousand, are under orders for marching at a moment's warning. In the present condition of the roads such a movement would be next to an impossibility. This morning I rode out to the camps, two miles west of the town, and found the highways thither, as well as those leading in other directions, little else save continuous lines of mud, varying from two to six inches in depth. It is of that sticky nature peculiar to the mud of the Great West, and would be a most serious impediment to the march of infantry or the movement of transportation trains. Cavalry alone could get through it without breaking down on the first day's march, and even to that arm of the service it would be very fatiguing. The following is the order for preparation:

SPECIAL ORDER NO. 15.
HEADQUARTERS SOUTHWESTERN DISTRICT OF MISSOURI
ROLLA, JAN. 4, 1862.

The Commanding General of the district is ordered to have this command ready to march at a moment's warning.

It contemplates and requires immediate and vigorous preparation for a winter campaign in a rough and rather desolate country. Such a movement will demand all the energy, courage and sagacity that officers and men can exert.

Officers and privates must so arrange their baggage as to be ready to have all surplusage without the least delay.

Boxes will be provided by the Quartermasters for this purpose, on proper requisitions or orders of officers, and they should be plainly marked and ready to turn over.

Two pairs of shoes, socks, drawers, undershirts and pantaloons, one coat and one overcoat, will be allowed.

Bed ticks and extra blankets may also be carried at the discretion of company officers.

The requisite number of tents should be retained, but no more than necessary.

Field and staff officers are expected to reduce their equipments in proportion to that required for companies, and company officers will be arranged for close quarters similar, but not so narrow, as that of the privates.

For non-commissioned officers and privates the maximum will be:

Eighteen to a Frémont tent.

Fifteen to a Sibley.

Ten to a Wall.

Six to a common.

No stoves but those of sheet iron will be transported. No more cooking utensils than appear absolutely necessary will be allowed, and the company officers will see that the mess is arranged so as to require as little as possible.

Articles such as chairs, mats, stools and luxuries of every kind, will be prepared to be turned over at a moment's warning.

Hands, sutlers and extra servants will be left behind, and extra horses, public or private, turned over to the post quartermaster the moment an order to this effect is issued.

The proper officers will forthwith see to the early execution of this order, having inspections of regiments, companies and files from day to day, until every extra article is in condition to be readily and safely deposited in a few hours after a final order to move may be given.

Quartermasters, commissaries and surgeons are expected to study the utmost economy, without neglecting all necessary provisions for their departments. No extra or useless arms will be taken, but all commanders will see that ample and proper ammunition is provided.

Each man must have a haversack and knapsack, and company officers will immediately inspect and see to the procuring of all the little necessaries for field duty; and every man must see to the preservation of his personal effects, as his life may depend upon it.

This order will be published to regiments and companies, if possible, in the hearing of every soldier, and translated to our comrades of different languages. A prompt response to a call for duty, and a readiness to move with celerity, and a brave exhibition of endurance, will command the admiration of our comrades in other fields, and will receive the cordial commendation of the commanding General.

By order of
Brigadier General Curtis.
N. P. Chipman, Major and A. A. A. General.

These orders indicate a major change in the thinking and planning of operations in Missouri. No longer were there to be the slow massive supply trains and imperial progressions like those seen with Frémont. Now the emphasis was to be on preparation, speed, and mobility for an attack on Springfield. How much of this change was due to Halleck's orders or to Curtis's own planning could not be fathomed at the time. However, when later 1862 actions are compared – Halleck's glacial move on Corinth, Mississippi, and Curtis's march to Batesville and Helena, Arkansas – the details set forth and the thrust of the present operations, credit should be given to Curtis. Knox then continued with his report on military movements and information about Sterling Price's encampments and situation:

It was announced some time since that Colonel Carr, with two thousand cavalry, had left Rolla for Springfield or some point in that direction. Two days ago he was camped on the Gasconade River, fifty miles west of this place. An additional force of three hundred men, under Majors Wright and Bowen, held Lebanon, thirteen miles further on the road to Springfield. Colonel Carr's orders have not yet been made public, but it is supposed he was directed to move upon Springfield with his whole force if he deemed it proper to do so, or hold an advanced position until the main body of the army should come up. To attack Springfield with two thousand men would be running too great a risk, as Rolla – one hundred and twenty miles away – would be too far distant to furnish speedy support, and he has properly made his camp upon the Gasconade.[34]

We have positive information from General Price's army up to the 3rd inst. It evacuated Springfield on New Year's Day, and encamped on Wilson's Creek, near the old battle ground, also taking position at Pond Spring, twelve miles west of Springfield, where General Lyon's army halted for several days on its arrival from Booneville. A picket and foraging party held possession of Marshfield on the 5th, but a force of our troops had gone from Major Wright's command, and will probably succeed in driving them out. A party less than 200 strong were at Bolivar on the road from Springfield to Warsaw engaged in procuring flour and other supplies for the rebel army. The secessionists from Springfield and vicinity have nearly all gone South taking with them their negroes and all their moveable property. A portion of Fort Smith is reported destroyed by fire about a month since. A few refugees have lately come in who state that the rebels are greatly enraged at the outrages committed by Jennison and his men, and will retaliate severely at the earliest opportunity.[35]

I have what I consider reliable information from spies just arrived, and who saw and talked with Price five days since, that the rebels intend to return to some point on the Osage, above Warsaw, as soon as their forces are properly organized. General Price now has in his camp some eight or ten thousand men, but has no drill and but little discipline. He says that if he lives till April, he will be in Jefferson City. About ten days ago a train arrived from the South bringing him supplies and several pieces of artillery. He now has in all sixty-three pieces of artillery, most of them of light caliber, but a large proportion being rifled. All accounts agree that the rebels received a terrible scare when they learned Pope was moving upon Osceola.

Knox then moved on to the topic of General Sigel, still of great interest to readers. Did he resign or did he not resign? Did he submit a resignation to Washington? He recognized that General Curtis's commission as brigadier general predated his own and submitted to Curtis's leadership.[36] In organizing his forces at Rolla, Curtis placed Sigel as second in command. The question of Sigel's status remained in the public's eye and was the subject of intense speculation. Finally on January 14, was it announced that Sigel was still a brigadier general, still serving in Rolla, and with no intention of resigning.[37] In his January 9 letter from Rolla, Knox was still uncertain of the situation and expressed some of the dissatisfaction raised by Sigel's friends:

> The rumors that were current in St. Louis relative to the resignation of Sigel are found to be correct. He has tendered his resignation, and by this time the matter is under advisement in Washington. General Sigel felt that he could not retain the command with honor to himself, and hence his withdrawal. His friends claim that he was urged to take command of the district of the Southwest, and on reaching here he was allowed to retain it but three days.
>
> At various times since the war commenced six regiments have been raised, with the understanding that they were to serve under General Sigel, the officers making that promise to the men at the time of enlistment, and the government acquiescing in the agreement when it accepted their services. Of these six regiments, there is only the skeleton of one,

numbering four hundred men, the remaining five being in other commands. It is hoped that the matter can be settled without our losing this energetic officer, whose services the country at the present time can hardly spare. He stands as the representative man of the loyal Germans, who constitute a large portion of our fighting element in the West, and who will be sadly disaffected should Gen. Sigel leave the service.

Knox then turned to another matter of public concern especially at Rolla, lack of hospital facilities. He also noted some "expeditions" undertaken from Franklin.[38]

> The hospitals at this point are in a horrible condition. Suitable buildings for the accommodation of the sick have not been erected, and the men are obliged to lie upon the wet grounds. Several deaths occur daily. The attention of the proper authorities in St. Louis has been called to the matter, but as yet no response has been given.
> At Franklin, the junction of the main line and southwestern branch of the Pacific Railroad is a force of three thousand troops in command of Lieutenant-Colonel Herron of the Ninth Iowa. A few days since Colonel Herron learned of a rebel depot of arms ten miles distant and, sending out an expedition found nearly a hundred guns and a supply of flour and bacon. Several individuals were taken at the same time. This is the third haul he has made within four weeks.
> The sun has not been visible here since the opening of the new year.

Thomas Knox returned to St. Louis from Rolla and on January 11 reported on conditions in St. Louis. There seemed to be little interest in military movements to the west, possibly because of the fiasco just a few months previous with Frémont's "grand march." While the situation in St. Louis was quiet, Knox gleefully pounced on the rumors displaying the hopes of the secessionists:[39]

> St. Louis, Mo., Jan. 11, 1862.
> The excitement with reference to the contemplated movement of troops from Rolla and Sedalia has passed away, and St. Louis assumed its wonted calmness, as far as matters to the westward is concerned. Yesterday and today the most ridiculous stories are afloat in regard to the movements from Cairo and Paducah. Whenever the operation of the wires is suspended for an hour or more, the secessionists of the city amuse themselves by putting the most absurd statements in circulation, all of them averring that some terrible calamity has fallen upon the Union troops. Day before yesterday Col. Carr's force was reported defeated with the loss of 1,000 killed and wounded, and the balance made prisoners. Col. Carr, with his 2,000 cavalry, was by last accounts encamped on the Gasconade River, fifty miles west of Rolla, and was in no danger of attack. Yesterday rumor had it that a battle was going on at Columbus, our troops having been twice repulsed, with great loss, and three of our gunboats sunk. Today Buell has been attacked and defeated, with terrible loss. So it goes on "rosy morn till dewy eve."[40]

On January 9, Knox reported on attitudes in St. Louis, concentrating on dissention in the St. Louis Chamber of Commerce. In his letter of January 11, he expanded on the Chamber's doings. This part of his report, of little military interest, but indicative of St. Louis events, is found in the notes.[41]

The weather and politics were the subjects covered in Knox's short note of January 17.[42] Senatorial politics had become a tangled mess. Trusten Polk had been elected as a Democrat in the November 1856 election and took office March 4, 1857. He was expelled from the Senate for disloyalty on January 10, 1862, and on January 17, John B. Henderson, Republican, was appointed to fill out his term (and elected to a full term in the November 1862 election). The other senatorial seat was held by James S. Green to the end of his term, March 4, 1861, but the Missouri Senate was unable to elect his replacement until March 17, when it chose Waldo P. Johnson. Johnson was expelled for disloyalty less than one year later on January 10, 1862 and on January 17, Robert Wilson, a Republican, was appointed to continue Johnson's term until a successor could be elected.[43] B. Gratz Brown was elected on November 13, 1863 to complete Johnson's term:

> St. Louis, Mo., Jan. 17, 1862.
> Navigation is entirely suspended here in consequence of the gorging of the ice twenty miles below the city, extending to a point some distance from town.
> Troops are now being sent to Cairo by railroad, but their advance is materially retarded by the inadequate means for crossing the river here, the ferry boats not being able to run and the ice not sufficiently strong to bear heavy weight.
> The weather is moderating again and the prospects for a speedy opening of the river are fair.
> General Price, the member elected from the Fifth Congressional district, left for Washington today.[44]
> No person will hereafter be allowed to leave the city until his baggage is inspected by the officers appointed for that purpose and the trunks sealed.
> Some of the papers are ventilating the antecedents of the newly appointed Senator from Missouri.[45]

After this letter, Knox was quiet for a week. The main news from Missouri was the move of troops southwest from Rolla and he was not there to report on it. The *Herald* republished bits from the *Missouri Democrat* on these movements datelined Rolla.[46] Although not named, these reports were from *Missouri Democrat* reporter William Fayel. One by one the regiments, led by Generals Osterhaus and Sigel, left the post at Rolla. On January 18, Knox again reported on a rumor:

> St. Louis, Jan. 18, 1862.
> A report has gained much currency here that Governor Gamble has resigned and gone to Washington and will there await his appointment by Acting Governor Hall to fill the seat of Trusten Polk in the Senate of the United States.[47]

A New Year 347

This rumor again was not true. On January 20, Knox sent a long letter to the *Herald* covering military movements, railroads, economics and politics. He was cheered by the prospect of action in the Southwest:[48]

> St. Louis, Mo., Jan. 20, 1862.
>
> In this department there are numerous indications that the army will soon see active service. On the 7th inst. General Halleck issued orders for all field batteries in the vicinity of St. Louis to be prepared as speedily as possible for a campaign. Among those to whom these orders were directed are four batteries of the First Missouri light artillery, commanded by Major Cavender and Major Lathrop. This regiment was the first one of Infantry raised in Missouri. It fought at Booneville and Wilson's Creek under General Lyon, and returned to St. Louis covered with glory, and with its ranks fearfully thinned by the terrible fire which it bravely withstood for hours. After its return to this city an order was issued for its formation into an artillery regiment, and it was speedily filled up with recruits from various parts of the West. It has been furnished with excellent equipments; its guns are rifled and of the newest pattern, and its drill has been most severe and complete. The batteries above referred to are ready to march at a moment's notice, and when in the field will do effective service.
>
> On Saturday last Colonel Totten, Chief of Artillery, ordered a review of several batteries in his charge, in order to give General Halleck an understanding of their condition. Thirty-four pieces passed in review in front of General Halleck's quarters, most of them being rifled ten and twenty-pounder Parrott guns, with an ample supply of ammunition wagons, caissons, forges, &c. Among the officers in various grades of command were Majors Cavender and Lathrop, and Captains Maurice, Murphy, Walker and Manter, and Lieutenants Barnes and Sokalski, all of whom fought at Wilson's Creek. The batteries all presented a fine appearance, and reflect great

credit upon the energy of Colonel Totten. All of them are ready to receive marching orders.

Rumors were strong that other movements toward Springfield were being made by troops based along the Pacific Railroad, west of Jefferson City. Knox tended to disbelieve these rumors because of the winter condition of the roads, both from Rolla and from Tipton and Sedalia. (He was too pessimistic about Curtis's determination.) He also commented on the rebels' situation:[49]

> The city is today full of rumors that the army is marching from Sedalia *en route* to overtake the fleeing rebel General Price. The army at that point has been in condition to move for several days; but it is hardly possible that it has made an advance, except as a feint at some point, or to scatter small congregations of rebels within striking distance of the railroad.
>
> The movement from Rolla of several thousand troops is looked upon as preliminary to a blow in the direction of Arkansas. At present they have halted on the Gasconade, opposite the camp of Colonel Carr's cavalry, and show no disposition to go forward.[50] General Price is near Springfield, with eight to fourteen thousand men and a good supply of artillery. McCullough is near Bentonville, Arkansas, with twelve thousand Arkansans and Indians. Price says that he will stand and show fight if he is attacked, but there is no certainty that he will make that promise good. The roads leading from the railroad terminus to Springfield are in bad condition and we shall hardly make a march thither unless there is a certainty that it will amount to something. Southeast Missouri from Ironton to the Arkansas line is quiet, with the exception of an occasional stir created by Jeff Thompson and his marauding bands.

North Missouri then came under Knox's scrutiny. Sterling Price had promised to return there from his base in Southwest Missouri and "free" the area. Recruits were trying to join his army, but the Missouri River remained a riverine obstacle. While the Union officers were sanguine about the situation, problems remained as Knox reported:

> Colonel Lewis Merrill, of the Merrill Horse, arrived a few evenings since from his command, in Columbia, near the North Missouri Railroad.[51] Colonel Merrill has, of late, been scouring the country around Columbia, and has scattered several bands of rebels that had been gathered in that vicinity, and were on their way to join Price's army. He says that for a long time the people of North Missouri firmly believed that General Price would join them in fulfillment of his promise in his proclamation, and that a concerted uprising was in accordance with that belief. A part of Colonel Merrill's regiment was in the skirmish at Silver Creek, and his men were the first to charge upon the rebel position.[52]
>
> The prisoners captured at the time of that affair were as thoroughly infatuated with a belief in the invincibility of Missourians as they well could be, and did not recover from their delusion some days after their capture. Colonel Merrill looks upon the war as ended in that section, provided vigorous blows are struck in the southwestern part of the State and down the Mississippi Valley.

Railroads also claimed Knox's attention. In the nation, the northern railroad system would prove to be one of the North's greatest assets. Overall, the Confederacy had only one third of the rail mileage of the North and there was little gauge standardization. Earlier, Knox had commented on how little business the railroads were doing in Missouri. Now, things had changed:[53]

> The railroads of Missouri are completely crowded with freight and passengers, principally on government account. The Pacific, in particular, is doing a thriving business, its depots in many instances being blocked for several days with accumulated freight. Not long since a gentleman was interrogating

the superintendent, Mr. McKissack, relative to the condition of the road. In reply to a question respecting its income, Mr. McKissack stated that, notwithstanding their losses from of bridges and other depredations of the rebels, the company was in a prosperous state, and, unlike many other railroads, had no desire or occasion for borrowing money. The North Missouri had suffered heavily by the recent destruction along its line; but it is proposed to make the counties in which the outrages were committed pay the expense.

Among the roads running to the East, the Ohio and Mississippi has a large share of business, on account of its directness, as it strikes out 340 miles from St. Louis on an almost direct line towards the rising sun. This route has furnished three men of note for the conduct of the war: Mr. McClellan, Mr. Biddle (an officer on General McClellan's staff) and another gentleman, whose name now escapes me, who is high in position on the Potomac.[54] Mr. Cohen, the present superintendent, commences the year with a display of commendable ability in railroad management. His last exploit was the transportation in one day of a cavalry regiment one thousand two hundred strong, over the entire length of the road, with their horses, tents, wagons and equipments.[sic] This labor required eight trains, and, when it is remembered that it was cone over a single track road, three hundred and forty miles long, without the derangement of a single regular train, those who are *au fait* in railroad matters will look upon it as quite an achievement.[55]

Knox then concluded his letter with an interesting miscellany of human interest information that would interest his Eastern readers-from cotton agriculture to local secessionists' taste in art to the river and weather:

The subject of cotton raising in Missouri and Southern Illinois is engrossing much attention in this region. The Illinois Central Railroad has lately been gathering information on the matter, and it finds that a large amount of cotton was produced in the country one hundred miles north of Cairo several years since, but that the culture was abandoned on account of its being unprofitable. Numerous certificates of persons engaged in the business have been produced, and will shortly be published. A few of them have already appeared.[56]

In the window of a print shop in this city a lithograph of Jeff. Davis and the principal officers in the rebel army was placed on exhibition last week. A call was at once made for duplicates, and within four days of the receipt of the picture several hundred have been sold and demand still continues. The St. Louis secessionists are having the lithographs framed, some of them in the most expensive style, and tonight many a parlor on Lucas place and Choteau avenue is ornamented with the portraits of the leaders of treason, done in Goupil's best style.[57]

The river is still choked with ice, though a few open spaces permit the passage of ferryboats. Night before last these boats were unable to run, and railway passengers arriving from the east were detained for twelve hours on the opposite shore, within full view of St. Louis, but unable to reach it. The continuance of ice in the river may have some little effect upon the contemplated forward movement. Present indications are that the channel will be clear within a week.

On January 23, Knox reported on an exchange of letters between Generals Sterling Price and Henry Halleck, mainly about the attacks on the railroads and prisoner treatment. Knox reproduced the letters without comment.[58] (They are to be found in the Appendix.) On the same day, Knox penned a report commenting on local events. He began with the machinations in the election of officers of the Mercantile Library. This note is in the endnotes.[59]

There was but little to report of military matters. Knox hinted of a campaign, but ignored the movements from Rolla. Perhaps the Frémont fiasco was still fresh in his mind. There was good news for one-armed Captain Sweeny:

> The lack of ostentation that has marked the career of General Halleck continues unabated. A vigorous campaign is now being prepared for, in what direction or at what time is known only to the commander.
>
> Captain T. W. Sweeny, of the regular army, better known as General Sweeny, commanding the three months volunteers in the southwest, has been made Colonel of the Fifty-second Illinois Volunteers, now ordered to Cairo. Captain conducted [sic] with great gallantry in the Mexican war, and during the campaign in the interior of Missouri. His appointment to command gives great satisfaction to his friends, and the regiment to which he is assigned can be certain of going where there is active work, if Colonel Sweeny can be allowed his way.

General Halleck announced further tightening of rules and regulations on secessionists related to their assessments to aid the refugees. On January 24, Knox reported these orders with a sense of satisfaction:[60]

> St. Louis, Jan. 24, 1862.
> Several of the secessionists of this city, who were recently assessed for the benefit of the Southwestern fugitives, by order of General Halleck, having failed to pay their assessments, their property has been seized for a day or two past under an execution to satisfy the assessment, with twenty-five percent additional, according to General Order No. 24.
>
> Yesterday Samuel Engler, a prominent merchant and one of those assessed, had a writ of replevin served on the Provost Marshall, for the property seized from him, whereupon he and his attorney, Nathaniel Cox, were arrested and lodged in the military prison.[61]
>
> General Halleck has issued a special order directing the Provost Marshal General to send Mr. Engler beyond the lines of Missouri, and to notify him not to return without

permission of the Commanding General, under the penalty of being punished according to the laws of war.

General Halleck also adds: Martial law having been declared in this city by authority of the President of the United States, all the civil authorities, of whatever name or office, are hereby notified that any attempt on their part to interfere with the execution of any order from these headquarters, or impede, molest, or trouble any officer duly appointed to carry such order into effect, will be regarded as a military offense, and punished accordingly. The Provost Marshal General will arrest each and every person, of whatever rank or office, who attempts in any way to interfere with the execution of any order issued from these headquarters. He will call upon the commanding officer of the Department of St. Louis for any military assistance he may require.[62]

Knox added a short note on January 25:[63]

St. Louis, Jan. 25, 1862.

Samuel Engler, the banished secessionist, was sent across the river under a guard this afternoon. His destination is unknown. His attorney has been released from military prison.

Attachments were served upon several other delinquent secessionists today.

General Henderson, the newly appointed Senator, left [for] Washington today.[64]

Judge James H. Burch announced himself a candidate for Governor at the August election.

On January 26, Knox wrote again from St. Louis with some news of an expedition to Benton, Bloomfield, and Dallas in Southeast Missouri. The main thrust of his note was to reproduce a special order from General Halleck that addressed loyalty problems and settled questions about the Chamber of Commerce and Mercantile Library Association:[65]

St. Louis, Jan. 26, 1862.

Official dispatches from Cape Girardeau state that the expedition which left that place a few days since for Benton and Bloomfield returned, having captured Lieut. Colonel Farmer, eleven other officers and sixty-eight privates of Jeff Thomson's command; also quite a number of arms, horses, saddles &c.[66]

The following special order will be issued in the morning:

Headquarters, Department of Missouri
St. Louis, Jan. 27, 1862.

The President, Secretary, Librarian, Directors and other officers of the Mercantile Association, the President, Secretary, Directors, and other officers of the Chamber of Commerce of this city, are required to take the oath of allegiance prescribed by article six, State ordinance of October 16, 1861.

1. Any of the above officers who shall neglect to file in the office of the Provost Marshal General, within ten days of date of this order the oath so prescribed, will be deemed to have resigned, and any who, neglecting to file the oath of allegiance within the time prescribed, shall attempt to exercise the functions of such office, he will be arrested for contempt of this order and punished according to the laws of war.

2. It is officially reported that carriages bearing the enemy's flag are in the habit of driving to the vicinity of the military prison in McDowell's College. The commanding officer of the prison guard will seize and take possession of any carriage bearing the enemy's flag, and the horses, carriages, and harness shall be confiscated.

3. It is officially reported that certain women are in the habit of approaching in the vicinity of the military prison, waving hostile flags for the purpose of insulting our troops and carrying on communication with prisoners

A New Year

of war. The commanding officer of the prison guard will arrest and place in confinement all women so offending.

4. Any carriage or other vehicle bearing a hostile flag in the city will be seized and confiscated. The city police and patrol guards are directed to arrest persons in vehicles under such flags; also, persons wearing or displaying a hostile flag in the city.

By order of

Major General Halleck.
N. H. McLean, Assistant Adjutant General.

A telegraph line is being constructed from Rolla westward.[67]

The treatment of General Sigel remained a problem for Knox. In St. Louis he saw and heard reports from other cities with large German immigrant populations of the affection which Sigel engendered in the immigrant population. Given, also, that Sigel had an ego problem which did not endear him to West Point graduates, considerable problems remained for General Halleck to try to solve. Halleck had read the reports of Sigel's work at Wilson's Creek as well as verbal reports from some officers that were not complementary. How much of this was credible and how much reflected professional or ethnic jealousy was undetermined. Knox's letter of January 27 expressed some of these concerns:[68]

St. Louis, Jan. 27, 1862.

General Sigel has been in St. Louis since Thursday last, in response to a request of General Halleck, and left this morning for Rolla, to take command of his division, now *en route* for Rolla. The report made some days since, and telegraphed all over the country, that General Sigel had no intention of resigning, but would remain in service, was very gratifying to his friends everywhere, but lacked the essential element of truth. General Sigel has not withdrawn his resignation, and will not do so until he has assurance that he can be justly and impartially treated.

Since he first entered the service he has been subjected to numerous annoyances at the hands of officers of American birth, prominent among whom are many of those attached to the regular army. The reasons that can be assigned for their malignity and hatred are that General Sigel is of foreign birth, is not a West Point graduate, displays military ability, and is popular with the people. I have listened many times to the vituperation of American officers against General Sigel, and can find no real reason for it other than those given above.[69]

About the end of November, after the army in General Frémont's command had returned to the line of the railroad, General Sigel came to this city and was confined to his room for three weeks by an attack of rheumatism. On December 21 he had sufficiently recovered to resume the command, and on that day reported for duty. General Halleck sent him to Rolla, with orders to organize the force there and prepare it for movement into the Southwest.

General Sigel at once obeyed orders, and after holding command for five days, and getting the organization fairly under way, was surprised at the appearance of General Curtis to take his place at the head of the army. As General Sigel had been three times in the Southwest under trying circumstances, and was then about ready to move with a more favorable prospect, he felt his treatment at that junction was hardly justifiable. Added to this was the fact that several regiments had been raised in his name, and with the promise of serving under him, had been placed in other commands.

On the 31st of December, General Sigel tendered his immediate and unconditional resignation through the proper channels, giving his reasons for so doing. On the 2nd of January General Halleck acknowledged the receipt of Gen. Sigel's resignation, and stated that Gen. Curtis had been assigned to command before Genl. Sigel reported for duty on the 21st. General Curtis previously informed Genl.

Sigel that he (Curtis) had been designated for command on the 24th, after Gen. Sigel had gone to Rolla. The discrepancy between these two statements has not yet been explained. Gen. Halleck, at the time of making this communication, requested Gen. Sigel to withdraw his resignation and remain in the service.

The *Official Records* show that there was some confusion on the part of General Halleck. On December 24, Halleck wrote to Sigel at Rolla: "You will assume command of all the troops at Rolla and vicinity, including the Fourth Division." And on the 25th he wrote: "Get all your troops ready for the field. The cavalry as soon as possible."[70] But also on December 25, in Special Orders No. 92, Halleck wrote: "Brig. Gen. S. R. Curtis is assigned to the command of the Southwestern District of Missouri, including the country south of the Osage and west of the Meramec River.[71] Sigel was ordered to command troops and Curtis to command the District – but the assignment was to command troops in either case. On December 29, Curtis reported to Halleck that he had arrived in Rolla and immediately met with Sigel, "wishing to treat the general with all possible courtesy by conferring with him before-hand," and had delayed assuming command. After the arrival by telegraph of Order 92, Curtis gave Sigel the date of his commission and showed him their relative positions in the Army Registers and then assumed command.[72]

Curtis apparently was acutely aware of Sigel's sensitivity. In the end, the relative dates of their commissions were the determining factor.[73] Continuing his report, Knox wrote:

> On the 8th of January Gen. Sigel replied to the letter of the 2nd, declining to withdraw his resignation, and giving additional reasons for doing so, among which was the statement that the plan of organization furnished by General Sigel had been received by General Halleck's Adjutant without eliciting any reply whatever. On the following day he sent another note to General Halleck, stating that he did not wish to have his personal matters interfere with any arrangements that

General Halleck might have made, and expressing his desire to receive and obey all orders until his resignation had been acted upon by the President. On the 11th, General Halleck replied to General Sigel's letter, denying having been the cause of the additional complaints of the letter, and in a postscript said he was happy to learn that General Sigel had no intention of quitting the service, adding that he had not sent the resignation of the latter to the President, as he hoped the matter might be amicably arranged.

The position of this unfortunate affair is that General Sigel, pressed upon hampered and annoyed in numerous ways, feels called upon, out of regard to his own honor, to tender his resignation. The resignation is sent through proper channels, but is stopped by General Halleck while on its way, and fails to reach the only authority by whom it can be acted upon. General Sigel wishes to remain in the service, as his whole heart is enlisted in the success of the flag under which he is fighting; but he feels that he can hardly do so, under the present circumstances, with a due regard for his personal honor. All that he asks and desires is that the command tendered him by General Halleck, and which he held for a few days, be again placed in his hands. Should this be done, he feels confident that if permitted to march into the Southwest he can make an end of the rebellion in that quarter.[74]

Knox then entered upon a totally different topic, the First Kansas infantry and its problems near Lexington. After the Battle of Wilson's Creek, the First Kansas had guarded Missouri railroads and was based at Tipton on the Pacific Railroad until it was sent to Lexington in December 1861:

The First Kansas regiment, which did such excellent service at the Wilson's Creek battle, is now stationed at Lexington, where it will probably remain during the entire winter. This regiment, since its arrival there, has been thoroughly examining the country around Lexington, and has captured some of the most noted desperadoes of that region. On the march thither some of the soldiers of the rear guard were shot from the bushes by concealed assailants, who always managed to escape. Deitzler, not approving of this mode of warfare, has seized all the wealthy secessionists of Lexington, and states by proclamation that, while he is ready and willing to meet his enemies in open fight, he will not have his men assassinated from places of concealment, and for every one hereafter so killed he will hang or shoot five of these hostages. As Colonel Deitzler is known as a man of his word, the rebels greatly fear him, and have entirely abandoned their murderous practice.[75]

The sending of troops to Cairo progresses slowly, in consequence of the ice blockade. The Thirteenth Missouri and a body of cavalry left this morning, by the Iron Mountain Railroad, for Sulfur Springs, thirty miles below here, where they will embark on the steamer *D. A. January* for Cairo. A shower last night, with thunder and lightning, has started the ice opposite this city, and the channel will soon be clear.

Knox sent a second, separate note to the *Herald* on the same day on the treason trials of the bridge burners.[76] In his note he reproduced part of just one case. From this letter, Knox's introductory words are sufficient. Transcripts of all the trials may be found in the *Official Records*:[77]

St. Louis, Mo., Jan. 27, 1862.
In the papers of this morning appeared General Order No. 20 of the current series, making nearly three columns of solid matter. It has reference to the late trials in North Missouri, under the direction of General Prentiss. Twenty-four persons have been tried, the most of them being charged with the recent railroad disturbances. Below I give a specimen of the report of the Commission.

Over the month of January, a stream of notes from Rolla, Otterville, Sedalia, and other points detailed the advance of General Curtis and his army towards Lebanon. The target was General Price and his men in winter quarters in Springfield. Knox went to Rolla and filed a report on January 9, but he was back in St. Louis on January 11. While Knox remained in St. Louis, advances from Rolla were reported on January 17, 18, 26, 27, 29, & February 2, 5, 6, 8, from Otterville, January 20, from Tipton February 3, and from Sedalia February 3. Given his restless spirit, it must have been difficult for Knox to remain in St. Louis, especially when his next report was about Commodore Andrew H. Foote and Brigadier General Grant capturing Fort Henry on the Tennessee River:[78]

St. Louis, Mo., Feb. 7, 1862.
St. Louis is today jubilant over the tidings of success at Ft. Henry. From numerous stores and business houses along Main and Second Streets the Union flag is displayed, and the drinking saloons are reaping a harvest of small silver from the numerous congratulatory cocktails imbibed by enthusiastic Union men. Those who wore long faces during the last week of July are happy today, while their opponents, who rejoiced over Bull Run, are now morose and disconsolate. "I can tell a Union man today as far as I can see him; his face is all upon a grin," was the remark made to me an hour since. Just as the Fort Henry victory was announced, your correspondent made a tour of Fourth Street, the Broadway of St. Louis. Union men were in the gayest humor imaginable, and saluted their friends with unwonted cordiality. Secessionists were gloomy and uncivil, and, compared with their visages, the face of the Laocoon is a picture of serenity.[79] While passing the store of a noted secession firm, I saw a newsboy enter the building, calling out, "Extra *Democrat* – All about the capture of Fort Henry." A moment after entering, he was ejected from the door, propelled by the boot of one of the proprietors. The elation of the loyal residents and the sadness of the disloyal commenced yesterday, long before we had any intimation of even a probability of success. Coleridge was right when he said:

A New Year

> *Often do the spirits*
> *Of great events stride on before the events,*
> *And in today already walks tomorrow.*[80]

In this letter, Knox then went on to discuss the situation of the Southwest refugees and other matters:

> The Southwest refugees now in St. Louis are at present domiciled in a large building just out of the busy portion of the city. Two thousand dollars have been distributed among them to relieve their wants, a part of it having been procured by subscription and the remainder being a portion of the amount raised by General Halleck's assessment upon the St. Louis secessionists. The utter destitution of some of these outcasts can be understood and appreciated only by an actual visit.
>
> One family arrived a few days since without a penny and destitute of clothing sufficient to make them comfortable. They owned a fine farm in Stone County in the Southwestern part of the State, well stocked and producing abundant crops for several years past. This they were compelled to abandon, and were permitted to bring away a single team for the transportation of a scant supply of household goods. They emigrated to Missouri from North Carolina, and consequently have no Eastern home to which they can return.
>
> One man, who came in about ten days since, owns an extensive hemp plantation in Saline County, near the farm of ex-Governor Jackson. His neighbors have nearly all followed in the wake of his fugacious Excellency, and adhere to the cause of the rebels. For months they have kept up a system of persecution against this Union citizen, and three weeks ago ended their assault by forcibly ejecting him from the county. All the products of his farm for the past year have been destroyed or used for the rebel army – his stock and

even the necessaries for the immediate wants of himself and his family not excepted.

Whenever these refugees from treason have friends in Illinois, or other of the Northern States, they are furnished with money and sent away. Forty were thus disposed of this morning. Upwards of sixty more are now domiciled here who have no relatives in the North, and must be cared for until the troubles are over and they can return to their homes. A much larger number is at Rolla, and there is quite a gathering at Sedalia and Otterville.

The bridge-burners of North Missouri next received Knox's attention – or rather, a delegation that came to St. Louis to plead their cause:

A delegation of North Missourians arrived here yesterday for the purpose of procuring a commutation of the sentences of the condemned bridge and railway destroyers in North Missouri. I am told that at an interview with General Halleck they earnestly represented the advantages of dealing gently with the erring, and suggested that an administration of the oath of allegiance would be sufficient punishment; the General was obdurate, and "didn't see it." He is determined to enforce the sentence of death, unless he receives positive orders to the contrary from Washington. We have dallied sufficiently with treason in Missouri and the only way to crush it is to carry on this war in earnest. General Halleck may be a little slow in his movements, but he is determined to put down the rebellion.[81]

Knox was a very competitive journalist. Although friendly with reporters from rival newspapers, the story was the most important and he enjoyed poking fun at the errors of major competitors, especially when he was "on the scene" and they were not:

I notice that the New York *Tribune* of the 5th instant discourses very learnedly upon the energy shown by General

A New Year

Frémont in his campaign in Missouri. In speaking of the present situation in this State, it speaks as follows:

"At Lebanon, then, it is clear, the scattered forces of Missouri are concentrating, and, of course, it can only be with one purpose, for Lebanon is only about thirty to thirty-five miles northeast of Springfield, and connected with it by rail."[82]

I have been several times over the route between Springfield and Lebanon, and have as yet been unable to find the faintest trace of a railroad. Springfield and Lebanon are full fifty miles apart, and the nearest point on any railroad is one hundred and thirteen miles from the former town and sixty-three from the latter.

The above is a specimen of Missouri geography and affairs generally that the *Tribune* has brought into play in its eloquent and learned dissertation on the Frémont question. In view of the general accuracy of the above, it would not be surprising if that decorous sheet should some morning give us a paragraph like this:

"*General McCook has followed up his success at the Dry Tortugas by investing San Francisco in flank and in front. When that fortress is captured he will attack Chicago on the upper left rear, while his gunboats descent the Amazon and blockade the mouth of the Rocky Mountains.*"

Would the readers of the *Tribune* consider themselves hoaxed on perusing the above, or would they receive it as Gospel truth?[83]

Knox concluded with bits of news and commentary on the situation as viewed from his advantageous St. Louis point of view:

Affairs in the interior are of no special importance. General Curtis at last accounts was at Lebanon, and it was rumored that General Davis's brigade had joined him there.[84] That they would advance to Springfield as soon as the roads permitted was highly probable. There was but little expectation that Price would stand and give battle. The roads beyond the railway are in frightful condition, being little more than continuous lines of mud.

The suggestion of General Halleck that business men in St. Louis would do well to take the oath of allegiance is being generally complied with. The *Republican* office today made a display of loyalty by flinging to the breeze a Union flag of great size but very thin texture. This is, I believe, the first time this paper has displayed Union colors since the outbreak of the rebellion. It is now the only daily paper in St. Louis that does not keep the Stars and Stripes at the head of its columns, and while professing to be loyal it condemns with its silence nearly every important movement of the government. Evidently force of circumstance, analogous to a child's fear of the switch, makes the *Republican* what it is.[85]

Although Knox had said, "Affairs in the interior are of no special importance," two days later he was on his way to Springfield.

Chapter 18

"Third Time's A Charm"

Thomas Knox had been there before. Twice he had traveled to Springfield, first with General Lyon for the 1861 Battle of Wilson's Creek and then again for Frémont's tragi-comic adventure. One must wonder what thoughts ran through his mind as he boarded the train for Rolla. There are no *Herald* reports of his trip to Springfield, but he did describe it with much "human interest" in Chapter 11, "Another Campaign in Missouri" in his 1865 book:[1]

> On the 9th of February, I left St. Louis to join General Curtis's army. Arriving at Rolla, I found the mud very deep, but was told the roads were in better condition a few miles to the west. With an attaché of the Missouri *Democrat*,[2] I started, on the morning of the 10th, to overtake the army, then reported at Lebanon, sixty-five miles distant. All my outfit for a two or three months' campaign, was strapped behind my saddle, or crowded into my saddle-bags. Travelling with a trunk is one of the delights unknown to army correspondents, especially to those in the Southwest. My companion carried an outfit similar to mine, with the exception of the saddle-bags and contents. I returned to Rolla eight weeks afterward, but he did not reach civilization till the following July.[3]
>
> From Rolla to Lebanon the roads were bad – muddy in the valleys of the streams, and on the higher ground frozen into inequalities like a gigantic rasp.
>
> Over this route our army of sixteen thousand men had slowly made its way, accomplishing what was then thought

next to impossible. I found the country had changed much in appearance since I passed through on my way to join General Lyon. Many houses had been burned and others deserted. The few people that remained confessed themselves almost destitute of food. Frequently we could not obtain entertainment for ourselves and horses, particularly the latter. The natives were suspicious of our character, as there was nothing in our dress indicating to which side we belonged. At such times, the cross-questioning we underwent was exceedingly amusing, though coupled with the knowledge that our lives were not entirely free from danger.

From Lebanon, we pushed on to Springfield, through a keen, piercing wind that swept from the northwest with unremitting steadiness. The night between those points was passed in a log-house with a single room, where ourselves and the family of six persons were lodged. In the bitter cold morning that followed, it was necessary to open the door to give us sufficient light to take breakfast, as the house could not boast of a window. The owner of the establishment said he had lived there eighteen years, and found it very comfortable. He tilled a small farm, and had earned sufficient money to purchase three slaves, who dwelt in a similar cabin, close beside his own, but not joining it. One of these slaves was cook and housemaid, and another found the care of four children enough for her attention. The third was a man upward of fifty years old, who acted as stable-keeper, and manager of the out-door work of the establishment.

The situation of this landholder struck me as peculiar, though his case was not a solitary one. A house of one room and with no window, a similar house for his human property, and a stable rudely constructed of small poles, with its sides offering as little protection against the wind and storms as an ordinary fence, were the only buildings he possessed. His furniture was in keeping with the buildings. Beds without sheets, a table without a cloth, some of the plates of tin and others of crockery – the former battered and the latter cracked – a less number of knives and forks than there were persons to be supplied, tin cups for drinking coffee, an old fruit-can for a sugar-bowl, and two teaspoons for the use of a large family, formed the most noticeable features. With such surroundings, he had invested three thousand dollars in negro property, and considered himself comfortably situated.

Knox's report to the *Herald* written on February 18 contains more information about Springfield and the rebels' occupation and retreat from the town:[4]

> Springfield, Mo., Feb. 18, 1862.
> Everything about the town at the time we arrived shows that the rebel army did not meditate departure until a few hours before they took up their line of march for Arkansas, the land of butternut breeches and bowie knives. On Wednesday morning a train of one hundred wagons – laden with clothing, tents, quartermaster and commissary stores – arrived from the South, and commenced unloading. The federal troops camped the night before at Marshfield, twenty-five miles east of this point, and at daybreak marched upon Springfield, as I detailed in my last letter. General Price was not correctly informed as to its strength, his scouts reporting that we numbered but two thousand five hundred, with little, if any, artillery. Under that impression he decided to make a stand here, and sent out a force from three to eight hundred strong to detain us in our advance and to give him time to post his army as he desired.
>
> In order to prepare for any emergency, he issued orders about noon for the train which had nearly discharged its freight to be again loaded and prepared for the road. About dark, many of his wagons moved out on the Fayetteville Road, and at a late hour in the night his army commenced its

retreat. The order for retreat must have been issued not far from midnight as it bears date on the 13th, and by dawn of that day the town had been completely evacuated. I send a copy of the order below.

A considerable quantity of quartermaster stores was left in the rebel warehouses, and is now in charge of Captain P. H. Sheridan, the Quartermaster of "our grand army of the Southwest."[5] General Price left in his headquarters numerous official papers and letters from various parties in the South, a few of which I append to this communication.

The most of them are unimportant, but strong in confirmation of the belief that there is a strong Union sentiment in Arkansas and Tennessee and other parts of the South. The adulation of General Price cropping out in all these letters is particularly refreshing. The disappointment of the rebels at the failure of Missouri to furnish the desired 50,000 for the patriot army of the South is evident in several of these documents. One letter which I have not given is from parties in Arkansas, who complain that Colonel Borland, the Solon of that State, has placed an embargo on every kind of provisions going South.[6]

The White and other rivers had been put into a state of blockade, and no boats were allowed to proceed "way down in Dixie" until they have been searched and found to contain no pork, corn, flour, or other material that can afford sustenance to the heroes of Arkansas militia. One pork dealer says he has purchased $12,000 worth of pork, and after preparing to send it to Memphis and New Orleans, has been refused to ship a single pound. He wants General Price to buy the same for the army of Missouri, and says he will take Missouri paper in payment, that being just as good as Confederate bonds. One of Price's intimate friends complains of Borland's embargo as "cruel, unwarrantable and outrageous." It seems that the dominions of Jeff. Davis have not yet become a terrestrial paradise.

Knox described the abandoned rebel camps in mostly glowing terms and also noted the rapidity of departure forced upon the rebels by Curtis's approaching army:

> The winter quarters erected by Price's army, and which they abandoned in complete order, will accommodate ten thousand men without being overcrowded. They consist of log and board structures, the former well-chinked with mud and clay, and the latter generally built right and comfortable. Most of them have a flooring of boards, and all are furnished with substantial brick fireplaces and chimneys, some of the largest buildings have two or three. Berths are arranged in tiers like those on steamboats or sleeping cars, and every portion of space is carefully economized. Some of these habitations are roofed with raw hides, and there are numerous chairs seated with the same material. In some of the camps these buildings are promiscuously dropped down, while in others they are arranged in streets and lanes, according to the highest style of urban regularity.
>
> The appearance of the cantonment attests to the haste of departure. There are cooking utensils containing the remains of the last meal, porkers lying dead on the ground with the fatal gash in their throats and the knife lying beside then, sheep partially flayed and disemboweled, dough mixed in the pans or poured on the ground, with the ripple marks still freshly distinct, and whiskey bottles whence the last drink has been drained, but in which the scent of the Bourbon is lingering still. The people of Springfield and the rebel sick left behind say they were deficient in tents, blankets, and clothing, and that they will suffer sadly from being driven from their comfortable quarters to bivouac in the open air. They fully expected to remain here the entire winter.

> Had we made a cavalry charge on them the afternoon of Wednesday, the 12th, we should doubtless have driven them forth with nothing to feed or shelter them. Had the army been thus scattered, the rebellion in Missouri would have received a severe blow.

Knox continued with news of some scouting and comments in praise of Sheridan's ability as a quartermaster and the fertility of Greene County:

> Lieutenant Colonel James K. Mills, commandant of the post, has today sent a small expedition to Mount Vernon, thirty-five miles distant, to capture a small party of rebels who have hoisted a Confederate flag on the Court House of the town. The party will not return before tomorrow night.[7]
>
> Notwithstanding the occupation of Springfield for nearly all the time since last July, Captains Sheridan and Winslow, the District and Post Quartermasters, have already contracted for ten thousand bushels of corn, at thirty cents per bushel, to be delivered at the rate of one thousand bushels per day. They have also secured wheat enough for supplying the entire army with flour, and have a sufficient number of mills in active operation. The above facts alone attest to the wonderful productiveness of Greene County.

Knox concluded his letter with copies of some of the letters found in General Price's abandoned headquarters. While these pieces were not written by Knox, they show his inquisitive nature and his desire to provide a look into the nature and thinking of General Price and the rebels. He began with Price's evacuation order:

> General Order No. 46
> Head-Quarters M. S. G.
> Springfield, February 13, 1862.
> The commanders of divisions will instanter, and without the least delay, see that their entire commands are

ready for movement at a moment's notice. By order of Major-General S. Price.

H. H. Brand, A. A. G.

Knox then presented a report of a rebel scout, noting, "His education was evidently neglected in his younger days."

Twenty-seven miles from Springfield, Jan. 10, 1862. General Price: The feds has left Lebanon at phillips mill yesterday. The same sorce says they are gon. I will knowe soon, and inform you of the fax in the cace. Those that left Lebanon yesterday left to meate Kerr's cavalry. This is reliable. Small scout this side Lebanon. They ley in the brush and scout in the nite. I send a man to you just from Roley [Rolla], captured on the rode. I think him to be a spey. Yours truly, Wm. Mankin.

BLANKETS NOT ABUNDANT IN THE CONFEDERACY –
HOW GEN. PRICE OBTAINED HIS UNIFORM

Memphis, Dec. 7, 1861.

General: The orders given me have all been executed, except the purchase of blankets, which we are unable to get. There are three or four thousand at the landing on White River, and a large quantity of carpet blankets and comforts, which may be used as a substitute. A train of forty wagons, loaded chiefly with those things – tents, equipments [sic], clothing and shoes – will start next week. Gen. Harding is now here. He has been generally disappointed about transportation. Be pleased to receive a major general's uniform, made according to Confederate States regulation, which is sent to you by Mr. J. M. Payne of New Orleans. With the highest respect, your obedient servant,

W. A. Broadwell, C. S. Agent.

To Major General Sterling Price, headquarters, Springfield, Mo.

ARMY MATTERS IN MEMPHIS – EXPLANATIONS OF PRICE'S RETREAT FROM OSCEOLA – A CORRUPT COURT AT RICHMOND

Memphis, Jan. 6, 1862.

Major General S. Price, Commanding M. S. G.

Dear General: I arrived here this morning, after a most tedious journey and I am happy to say that I meet with friends to our army without number, and all are willing to do more than they can for our success. Every department receives me with welcome and accommodation in the furtherance of the object of my visit. I will ship on tomorrow's packet for Jacksonport [Arkansas] many things for our army among them the sacks for Colonel Bricker and some buckshot molds for my department. The camp equipage for the Confederate camp I will have under contract tomorrow, and set forward as speedily as possible, when I tell you I will start in the morning for Richmond, I know you will say, "Damn it, he is just like all the balance" but I do assure you, General, that I have not the least curiosity or wish to go, but Major Anderson and Colonel Hunt of the Quartermaster and Ordinance departments advise to go immediately there. I will get a million and a half of G. D. caps in Nashville as I go along. I tell everyone who mentions your retreat that you only moved your camp to be more convenient to forage &c. I am satisfied that you have "enemies at court" in Richmond, and that if you could be cheated out of your just dues it would be done. There is unbounded enthusiasm for you here. With the most hearty hope of your success, I am, respectfully yours.

Thos. H. Price.[8]

THE REBELS WORKING THE GRANBY LEAD MINES TROOPS DESIRED FOR PROTECTION OF THE MINING PARTIES.

Granby, Jan. 4, 1862.

General: I have the pleasure to acknowledge your valued

favor of the 1st, proposing to station at this place sufficient force to render mining operations reliable and effective. At present, everything is unsettled and in confusion, and if convenient to send down a single company it will have the effect to restore quiet and facilitate the working of the mines, and I beg of you to do so. The company or any command you would wish to winter in this vicinity could, of course, be withdrawn and rendered available in any movement you may wish to make, and might receive, during the winter, considerable addition in the way of recruits. I understand there [is] abundance of provision in Lawrence County to subsist your entire command several months. With much respect, your obedient servant,

J. P. Broadwell,
Agent for working the Granby Lead Mines.
To Major General Price, commanding at Springfield.

Knox included another letter in his book that was not in his original letter that "revealed the treatment Union men were receiving in Arkansas":[9]

Dover, Pope Co. Arkansas
December 7, 1861

Major-General Price:
I wish to obtain a situation as surgeon in your army....Our men over the Boston Mountains are penning and hanging the mountain boys who oppose Southern men. They have in camp thirty, and in the Burrowville[10] jail seventy-two, and have sent twenty-seven to Little Rock. We will kill all we get, certain: every one is so many less. I hope you will soon get help enough to clear out the last one in your State. If you know them, they ought to be killed, as the older they grow the more stubborn they get.

Your most obedient servant,
James L. Adams.

In his book, Knox reported a bit more about General Price's hasty departure:

> In his departure, General Price had taken most of his personal property of any value. He left a very good array of desks and other appurtenances of his adjutant-general's office, which fell into General Curtis's hands. These articles were at once put into use by our officers, and remained in Springfield as trophies of our success. There was some war *materiel* at the foundries and temporary arsenals which the Rebels had established. One store full of supplies they left undisturbed. It was soon appropriated by Captain Sheridan.[11]

Knox's also used his book to comment on the march between Springfield and Pea Ridge:

> When it became certain the army would continue its march into Arkansas, myself and the *Democrat's* correspondent pushed forward to overtake it. Along the road we learned of the rapid retreat of the Rebels, and the equally rapid pursuit by our own forces. About twenty miles south of Springfield one of the natives came to his door to greet us. Learning to which army we belonged, he was very voluble in his efforts to explain the consternation of the Rebels. A half dozen of his neighbors were by his side, and joined in the hilarity of the occasion. I saw that something more than usual was the cause of their assembling, and inquired what it could be.
>
> "My wife died this morning, and my friends have come here to see me," was the answer I received from the proprietor of the house.
>
> Almost at the instant of completing the sentence, he burst into a laugh, and said, "It would have done you good to see how your folks captured a big drove of Price's cattle. The Rebs were driving them, doing all right, and your cavalry just came up and took them. It was rich, I tell you. Ha! ha!"
>
> Not knowing what condolence to offer a man who could he

so gay after the death of his wife. I bade him good-morning, and pushed on. He had not, as far as I could perceive, the single excuse of being intoxicated, and his display of vivacity appeared entirely genuine. In all my travels, I have never met his equal.

Up to the time of this campaign none of our armies had been into Arkansas. When General Curtis approached the line, the head of the column was halted, the regiments closed up, and the men brought their muskets to the "right shoulder shift" instead of the customary "at will" of the march. Two bands were sent to the front, where a small post marked the boundary, and were stationed by the roadside, one in either State. Close by them the National flag was unfurled. The bands struck up "The Arkansas Traveler," the order to advance was given, and, with many cheers in honor of the event the column moved onward. For several days "The Arkansas Traveler" was exceedingly popular with the entire command. On the night after crossing the line the news of the fall of Fort Donelson was received.[12]

Continuing the narrative of his travel from Springfield to Cross Hollows and Pea Ridge, Knox, as usual, included descriptions of the countryside and amusing anecdotes:

Soon after entering Arkansas on his retreat, General Price met General McCulloch moving northward to join him. With their forces united, they determined on making a stand against General Curtis, and, accordingly, halted near Sugar Creek. A little skirmish ensued, in which the Rebels gave way, the loss on either side being trifling. They did not stop until they reached Fayetteville. Their halt at that point was very brief.

At Cross Hollows, in Benton County, Arkansas, about two miles from the main road, there is one of the finest springs in the Southwest. It issues from the base of a rocky ledge, where the ravine is about three hundred yards wide, and forms the head of a large brook. Two small flouring mills are run during the entire year by the water from this spring. The water is at all times clear, cold, and pure, and is said never to vary in quantity.

Along the stream fed by this spring, the Rebels had established a cantonment for the Army of Northern Arkansas, and erected houses capable of containing ten or twelve thousand men. The cantonment was laid out with the regularity of a Western city. The houses were constructed of sawed lumber, and provided with substantial brick chimneys.

Of course, this establishment was abandoned when the Rebel army retreated. The buildings were set on fire, and all but a half-dozen of them consumed. When our cavalry reached the place, the rear-guard of the Rebels had been gone less than half an hour. There were about two hundred chickens running loose among the burning buildings. Our soldiers commenced killing them, and had slaughtered two-thirds of the lot when one of the officers discovered that they were game-cocks. This class of chickens not being considered edible, the killing was stopped and the balance of the flock saved. Afterward, while we lay in camp, they were made a source of much amusement. The cock-fights that took place in General Curtis's army would have done honor to Havana or Vera Cruz. Before we captured them, the birds were the property of the officers of a Louisiana regiment. We gave them the names of the Rebel leaders. It was an everyday affair for Beauregard, Van Dorn, and Price to be matched against Lee, Johnston, and Polk. I remember losing a small wager on Magruder against Breckinridge. I should have won if Breck had not torn the feathers from Mac's neck, and injured his right wing by a foul blow. I never backed Magruder after that.

Light-hearted travel was over. There were rumors of the approaching enemy. Outlying units were recalled to the main encampment and it was time to prepare for the battle. General Earl Van Dorn was now in command over McCulloch and Price. He had been sent by Richmond to bring order to the conflicts between Price and McCulloch. Van Dorn was exceedingly optimistic about his chances, writing to his wife, "I am now in for it, as the saying goes, to make a reputation and serve my country conspicuously or fail. I must not, shall not, do the latter. I must have St. Louis—then Huzza!"[13]

Chapter 19

Battle of Pea Ridge

There they were – the only two reporters on the scene at Pea Ridge, at what would be one of the key battles of the American Civil War.[1] Thomas Knox of the *New York Herald* and William Fayel of the St. Louis *Missouri Democrat* had chosen to follow the fortunes of General Samuel R. Curtis while other reporters who had followed Frémont to Springfield chose other paths to war news. From their base in St. Louis many of them saw the movements of General Grant and Commodore Foote southward from Cairo as more promising. Knox was not as close personally to General Curtis as he had been to General Lyon at Wilson's Creek, but he knew many of Curtis's officers and was able to freely circulate in the camp.

Once the battle was over, Knox and Fayel faced the problem of getting their stories to their editors. Knox and Fayel were not competitors even though they served different newspapers, and they probably compared their notes during the preparation of their dispatches. The roadblocks were immense – the battlefield itself and a dangerous road to Springfield. Was the telegraph line working? There were far too many words that needed to be written to send by telegraph, especially in light of the calls on the line for military communications. Letters must be written, but their carriage was problematical. What was the status of mail service between Springfield and Rolla, the first point where a letter could safely enter the mail service?

Short accounts, sent by telegraph appeared in the *Herald* beginning on March 11 under the blaring headline "ANOTHER BRILLIANT VICTORY":

<blockquote>
Washington, March 10, 1862

The President received to-night a dispatch from General Halleck announcing that after a three days' battle at Sugar
</blockquote>

Creek, in Arkansas, General Curtis had won a complete victory over the combined forces of the rebel leaders Van Dorn, McCulloch, Price and McIntosh. The Union loss is estimated at one thousand killed and wounded. The rebel loss is much greater.

The following is an official dispatch to Major General McClellan:

St. Louis, March 10, 1862

The army of the Southwest, under General Curtis, after three days hard fighting, has gained a most glorious victory over the combined forces of Van Dorn, McCulloch, Price and McIntosh.

Our loss in killed and wounded is estimated at *one thousand!*

That of the enemy was still larger.

Guns, flags, provisions, &c., were captured in large quantities. Our cavalry are in pursuit of the flying enemy.

H. W. Halleck, Major General.[2]

One day later, General Curtis's official report was printed in the *Herald* under the heading "THE GREAT FIGHT IN ARKANSAS."[3] An additional short note, unsigned, datelined, Springfield, March 11, appeared in the *Herald* on March 14 gave details on casualties, some of which was inaccurate.[4]

Finally, Knox's main report appeared in the March 19 *Herald*. It began with a descending series of what could be called "screaming" lead-ins:[5]

Pea Ridge, Benton County, Arkansas,
March 9, 1862.

The first battle in Arkansas since the outbreak of the rebellion has terminated favorably to the Union arms. After an engagement of fifteen hours, extending through the larger portion of two consecutive days, the rebel forces have been driven from the field, and the Stars and Stripes hoisted in triumph over the contested ground. Defeated and demoralized, the

THE GREAT BATTLE AT PEA RIDGE.

HIGHLY IMPORTANT FROM ARKANSAS.

Thirty Thousand Rebels Whipped by the Federal Troops.

TWO DAYS' ENGAGEMENT.

ATTACK AT THREE POINTS.

The First Day's Fighting Unfavorable to the Federal Arms.

A Night in Camp Before the Enemy's Lines.

SIGEL TO THE RESCUE.

MORNING OF THE 8TH OF MARCH.

IMPOSING LINE OF BATTLE.

The Rebel Position Shelled for Two Hours.

VAN DORN'S ARMY PUT TO FLIGHT.

Albert Pike's Aborigines Dispersed.

FIVE CANNON CAPTURED.

GENERAL CURTIS ORDERS A PURSUIT.

The Rebels Followed About Twelve Miles.

SCENES AND INCIDENTS OF THE BATTLE.

SPECIAL REPORT TO THE NEW YORK HERALD.

&c.   &c.   &c.

Confederate troops are in full retreat, and have been hotly pursued by a portion of our gallant army far beyond the confines of the State.[6]

PRELIMINARY MOVEMENTS OF THE WEEK.

Early in the past week, several small expeditions were sent out various directions for the purpose of capturing rebel bands said to be gathered in Southwestern Missouri and Northern Arkansas. One that proceeded to Pineville, Mo., arrived within a half mile of the object of its pursuit, but failed to bring on an engagement. The expedition returned safe to the camp of the army, crossing the route of the rebel forces but an hour before the latter reached the point of the roads' intersection. Another expedition, under Major Conrad,[7] consisted of six hundred infantry, with a section of artillery and one battalion of cavalry, proceeded to Maysville, near the line of the Indian nation, and failed to return in due season. At last accounts it was marching northward from Maysville to escape the rebel army, and was considered out of immediate danger. Still another, under Colonel Vandever, and accompanied by your correspondent, was sent to Huntsville, Madison County, with the object of capturing a portion of an Arkansas regiment said to be encamped there.[8] The rebel troops had left two days before our arrival, and the only prizes of importance were several men just returned from the rebel army. Two of these had been sent away on a previous morning, and gave the exciting intelligence that the whole rebel force, under General Van Dorn, about thirty thousand, was then marching to attack the Union camp. A messenger was at once sent to headquarters with this information, but he had scarcely left town before a dispatch bearer arrived from General Curtis making the same announcement, and ordering our immediate return. A forced march of forty-one miles was made to the camp of the main army, with but three halts of fifteen minutes each during the

Battles and Leaders of the Civil War, 1:322.

entire distance. The infantry, consisting of portions of the Ninth Iowa and Phelps' Twenty-fifth Missouri, was much fatigued by the long journey, but awoke on the morning of the battle refreshed and ready for the encounter. No troops ever fought better.

THE ENEMY ATTACK GENERAL SIGEL'S REAR GUARD.

On the 1st instant General Sigel moved his camp from Osage Springs to a point near Bentonville, in order to secure a better region for foraging purposes. About the same time Colonel Davis moved to Sugar Creek, while Colonel Carr remained at Cross Hollows. On receiving intelligence of the rebel advance, General Curtis decided to concentrate his forces at Sugar Creek, a short distance south of Pea Ridge, a good point of defense and abundantly supplied with water. On the 5th General Sigel received orders from General Curtis to join him at Pea Ridge, and on the 6th marched from Bentonville in obedience to those orders. His rear guard consisted of the Thirty-sixth Illinois infantry and a portion of the Second Missouri. Four rebel regiments of infantry and cavalry surrounded this rear guard and engaged it vigorously, but General Sigel, who had remained behind, succeeded in cutting his way through, with a loss of twenty-eight killed and wounded. A portion of Company B, of the Thirty-sixth Illinois, were captured during the encounter.

THE REBELS MOVING TO THE ATTACK.

The camp whence the rebels marched upon General Curtis, was situated on and near the Boston Mountains, about fifty miles from Pea Ridge. The rebel commander, General Van Dorn, ordered the men to take four days' cooked rations on the morning of the 5th and move forward to the encounter. As our camp at Sugar Creek was in its front a strong natural position and difficult of access on either flank, General Van

Dorn decided to make his attack in our rear, thus cutting off our line of supply and reinforcement. The Union position was on the main road from Springfield to Fayetteville, and General Van Dorn, in marching northward, left that road near the latter town and turned to the westward passing through Bentonville and entering the main road again near the State boundary, about eight miles north of Sugar Creek. A small force was left to make a feint upon our front, and a considerable body of Indians, under General Albert Pike, took positions about two miles on our right to divert attention from the main attack in the rear.

At this point, Knox broke into his narrative to enumerate the command structure of Curtis's Army of the Southwest and the supposed strength of the Confederate army. It is to be found in the endnotes.[9]

THE CAMP ON THE MORNING OF THE 7TH.

At the hour of revile on the morning of the 7th there was an unusual stir in the Union camp. Nearly every drum and fife that could be found was put into use, and the forest became vocal with martial noises. Orders had been issued to prepare rations for two days, to strike tents, load the wagons and prepare to move at any moment. At a little past seven I issued from the tent of a Colonel of a regiment prominent in the fight, and found his men drawn up in line and busy loading their guns, preparatory to marching to the field. This operation required but a short time, and after it was performed the order for movement was anxiously awaited. Passing through the principal portion of the camp, the troops were nearly all found occupied with similar duties, and everywhere anxious to meet the enemy they had marched so far to encounter.

GENERAL SIGEL ENGAGES THE ENEMY.

At about half past seven a scout arrived at headquarters,

reporting a strong force of the enemy posted on some hills and fields about three miles to the westward. In a few moments a messenger came in from the north (our rear) stating that the enemy was appearing on the hills and ridges near the junction of the Bentonville and Springfield roads, and about four miles from camp. As the reports indicated the force to the westward to be much larger. General Curtis ordered General Sigel, with his command (the first and second divisions), to proceed in that direction and dislodge and disperse the enemy. His troops were all in readiness, and a few moments found him on the way. About three miles from camp Colonel Osterhaus's division encountered what was supposed to be a small body of the rebels, posted on the edge of some timber and brushwood, and brought three guns to bear on them. After a few rounds of shell, grape and canister, the artillery was ordered to cease firing, and the Third Iowa Cavalry, which then accompanied Colonel Osterhaus, moved forward to complete the clearing of the timber. The supposition that few rebels were posted there was erroneous, for the woods swarmed with such numbers that the charge was at once broken and the Iowa cavalry driven back in disorder. The rebels followed up the cavalry in its retreat, and, taking advantage of the confusion, succeeded in capturing the three guns with which they had been shelled. Colonel Osterhaus brought up his Indiana regiments, and by a rapid succession of volleys of musketry, followed by a bayonet charge, covered the ground with dead Texans and Indians, and brought back the guns lost but a few moments before. General Sigel then came forward with the remainder of his command, and the force of rebels in the timber being strengthened at the same time, a vigorous action commenced.

 The rebels brought their artillery into position, and a duel of heavy guns ensued, ending with the rebels abandoning their position. A running fight next transpired, and a vigorous pursuit was kept up for two or three miles, the rebels fleeing toward the north in order to form a junction with the forces in our rear. General Sigel then abandoned the pursuit and returned to the camp of the army.

COLONEL DAVIS ADVANCED TO THE ATTACK.

About the time General Sigel came up with the rebels and commenced the action of the morning, a force consisting of two or three regiments of Arkansas infantry and a light battery appeared in front of Colonel Davis's position evidently inviting attack. Subsequent events show that this movement on the part of the enemy, together with the one upon General Sigel, were feints to prevent the concentration of our strength upon the rear where their grand attack was made.

For the time they were thus successful, and had their energy been equal to their strategy, it could hardly have failed of success. Colonel Davis responded to their invitation to battle and moved out for an encounter. A short but bloody contest, and the flight of the enemy by a circuitous route in the direction of their main force in our rear were the results of this movement. In this affair, as well as General Sigel's, many of the enemy remained scattered in the timber. In consequence of this, small parties and individuals attempting to visit the battle grounds later in the day were repeatedly fired upon. These guerrillas have not yet been completely driven out; but some of our cavalry are engaged in scouring the brush with a view to their expulsion.

COLONEL CARR'S DIVISION MOVES OUT.

Simultaneously with the departure of General Sigel to the westward, Colonel Carr's division was sent to our rear to engage the enemy in that quarter. From the position of the army on the night of the 6th to the Missouri line is about eight miles. The country here consists of level areas wooded with large timber, and generally but little underbrush. At intervals are large farms, with cleared fields for grain and cereals, some of them extending along the road for a half mile or more, and reaching away on each side for one to three miles. In places the general level is broken by gradual slopes with an occasional steep ascent, several with sharp angular fragments of stone, and having a scanty growth of low oak trees. West of the road and converging so as to strike it near the State line, is a high ridge, accessible at numerous points, and commanding the road to Bentonville, and also, in some places the battle ground of the 8th.

As the Missouri line neared, low hills appear sloping away to the north, but presenting an abrupt and precipitous face to the south. These hills are about two hundred feet in height, and two miles below the state boundary. They unite into a continuous double ridge, forming a narrow valley six miles in length, with steep and heavily timbered sides. The main road passes through this valley in a direction nearly due north. When McCulloch retreated from Missouri in September last, after his quarrel with Price, he ordered much of this timber to be felled across the way. To impede any pursuit, that might be made by the Union army. These obstructions the rebels themselves were compelled to move when they subsequently advanced to encounter Frémont. The valley is looked upon by all military engineers as a good position to hold against an enemy.

COMMENCING THE BATTLE OF THE 7TH.

Colonel Carr's division advanced up this road to a point about four miles from the State line. Colonel Dodge's brigade filed off upon a road leading to the east from the Elk Horn Hotel, and opened its battery upon the enemy, who was posted in a wood on a declivity in front. They were promptly replied to, and a brisk encounter of artillery and infantry speedily ensued. Colonel Vandever's brigade passed about half a mile beyond the hotel and took position on the left of the road. In front of them the ground descended to a dry ravine, and the opposite bank, which was somewhat abrupt and covered with low oaks, was held by the enemy. The Dubuque battery opened upon the rebels, and the scattering of some of the infantry of the latter showed that the guns were well aimed. The rebel batteries replied, and at the third fire a shell from their guns blew up one of the Union limber chests. It was about nine AM when the first gun was fired. Within fifteen minutes afterward the whole line of the division was fairly engaged. The explosion of the limber chest showed the rebels that their shots were well directed, and they appeared in large numbers, and poured in a terrific fire. Ten minutes after the blowing up of the limber chest another, belonging to the same battery, was exploded in like manner, badly burning Frank Thompson, one of the cannoneers. This explosion was a signal for a rush by the rebels upon the Union battery, and they succeeded in capturing one of the guns before they were driven back by the infantry. The enemy fell back to their cover leaving the ground strewn with their dead and wounded, who had fallen before the Iowa Ninth.

EXPERIENCE OF A LOOKER ON.

At the time of these occurrences your correspondent and a fellow journalist were standing in the road in front of the Elk Horn Hotel, where a good view was afforded. Shells which were thrown too high for effect upon Col. Vandever's brigade were just the elevation for the Elk Horn, and a rifled cannon projectile passing with a few feet, bursting twenty yards beyond me, rendered my notes of that moment somewhat difficult to decipher. Two companies of infantry were drawn up near the house awaiting moving orders. A shell burst in their midst, killing two men and wounding five others. Another struck in the yard, in the rear of the house, in its explosion shattering the leg of an old regular soldier in Quartermaster Carr's employ. Still another fell among some horse teams, frightening one into running away, directly up the road and over into the enemy's lines, where it was lost. In its flight several of our soldiers were run over, one being seriously and three or four slightly wounded. The drivers of some twenty or more wagons took fright, and started for the camp at full speed. Had it not been for the determined course of Quartermaster Carr, who, pistol in hand, brought them to a halt, a serious stampede would have been the result. A solid shot struck the house and passed completely through, injuring no one, as the family had taken shelter in the cellar. Long ago, at Wilson's Creek, I learned sufficient of the sound and substance of military projectiles to remove anything like novelty from the present scene, and accordingly sought a locality affording a fine view, but further removed from "the perilous edge of battle."[10]

COLONEL CARR FALLING BACK.

One hour's fighting in position on the slope accomplished nothing for Colonel Carr's division, except to reveal the presence of an immense force of the enemy preparing to charge upon the Union troops. As such a movement, with the rebels' overwhelming numbers, would be likely to lose us a battery, Colonel Carr withdrew to a better point, about a hundred yards to his rear. Here the fight was kept up for some time, the rebels repeatedly attempting to charge, but as often being driven back by the well-directed volleys from the Iowa infantry and the Missouri regiment. Colonel Phelps and Lieutenant Colonel Galligan of the Fourth Iowa, and Major Coyle and Adjutant Scott of the Ninth Iowa were wounded by a fire of musketry, and carried to the hospitals at the camp. Another charge was made by the rebels, in which they captured a second piece of artillery and a caisson limber. The ground after each of these charges was thickly strewn with their dead and dying, mingled too often with the bodies of the brave men who opposed them. The charges of the rebels were not made with the bayonet, but with double barreled shotguns, loaded with ball and ten buckshot. They discharged their pieces as they advanced, retaining most of their fire until within short range. The shotgun thus used is a terrific weapon, as the scattering of the charges renders it pretty certain to do execution without much regard to accuracy of aim. It was again necessary to fall back, and this time a stand was made near the hotel, and along the road leading to the east.

A GLOOMY PROSPECT.

The day had opened clear and still, and before the battle commenced, the purity of the atmosphere rendered every object on the hills and slopes distinctly visible. The smoke from the guns settled like a cloud on the field, and an hour after the beginning of the engagement the position of the enemy's was oftentimes only to be ascertained by the dull red flash at the moment of discharge. As the day advanced this cloud became more and more dense, and long before nightfall the contending masses of infantry were unable to discern each other except at very short range. Hour after hour passed away and still that one division was coping with a rebel force nearly quadruple its strength. They were driven back inch by inch, until they were only a mile and a half from the camp of the enemy.[11]

Messengers had been constantly going to headquarters, bearing appeals for assistance, but none could be sent them. Sigel and Davis had not returned from the forces they had been pursuing, and there had been nothing left in camp for its protection. "Two batteries and three regiments or sunset and darkness are the only alternatives for our safety," was the remark of Colonel Carr after his division for the third time fell back. About four PM General Asboth returned from his pursuit of the rebels to the westward, and immediately went with two infantry regiments and a battery to the aid of Colonel Carr.

The latter by that time had fallen back to an open field, little more than a mile from camp. The reinforcements thus received enabled him to hold his ground, and when night closed upon the conflict, and ended the carnage, the little division was still in position at that field. The lines of the contending armies during the night were not more than three hundred yards apart, and each party rested upon its arms and passed the long hours till dawn without lighting fires. The air was still, and conversations were carried on in low voices and whispers, through fear that ordinary tones would be overheard.

THE CAMP AT NIGHT.

In the main camp of the army everything was bustle and commotion. Coffee, bread and meat were prepared and sent out, with blankets and overcoats, for the comfort of those who had nobly fought during the day and were intending to renew the conflict at dawn. General Sigel and Col. Davis had returned and were making all preparation to throw their whole force to the aid of Col. Carr. The teams were still attached to the wagons, and the braying of the mules, never melodious, became doubly dismal and discordant. The poor animals had been without food for forty-eight hours and without water for twenty-four hours. They had been standing in harness since daybreak, and their usually hoarse tones gradually softened to a low, plaintive moan that was painful to hear.

Most of the officers were fearful of the results of the conflict on the morrow, since those of the day's battle had been so unfavorable. Some turned their thoughts upon escape; but saw not how it was to be accomplished, as our only lines of retreat to the north were completely cut off. Among the soldiers as they sat by the camp fires there was generally but one expression. "We must fight like heroes or surrender to the rebels. There is no falling safely back, as there was at Wilson Creek.

Our only alternative is desperate fighting, and we will all do our best."

AT HEADQUARTERS.

Around headquarters, most of the commanders passed a sleepless night. Though there were but few words spoken, nearly everyone felt that the following dawn would usher in our defeat. General Sigel brought his division into camp, where it was ready at call, and then calmly lay down to sleep. Colonel Davis moved his command at midnight, and anxiously awaited the coming light. The Commander-in-Chief was hopeful but fearful. Colonel Dodge and Colonel Vandever sent in for a fresh supply of ammunition, and at midnight visited the camp in person to swallow a cup of coffee and return to the field. Ambulances were in constant motion, bringing the wounded to the hospitals prepared for their reception, and surgeons were active in relieving the wants of the sufferers.

APPEARANCE OF THE MEN.

In the action of the day, the Iowa regiments had suffered fearfully. Nearly two hundred each had been the loss of the Iowa Fourth and Ninth, and the latter had not a single field officer fit for duty. Its Colonel was commanding a brigade, its Lieutenant-Colonel (Herron) was made prisoner while gallantly cheering his men, after losing a horse and receiving a severe wound, and its Major and Adjutant were disabled and in the hospital.[12] Still none of the men were despondent, but all were ready for the work of the morrow. From the camp of a German regiment, the notes of some plaintive air, possibly a love ditty, was wafted on the breeze in words unintelligible to my ear. It reminded me that long ago in the Crimea, on the night before storming of the Malakoff, the entire British army in the trenches before Sebastopol joined in singing a famous Scottish ballad, one of the sweetest ever known:

They sang of love and not of fame;
Forgot was Britain's glory,
Each heart recalled a different name,
But all sang Annie Laurie.[13]

MORNING OF THE FINAL DAY.

Daybreak and sunrise at last. Not the bright, clear sun that rose over Austerlitz and cheered Napoleon to his great victory, but a dull, copper-tinted globe, slowly pushing itself up through the murky cloud of cannon smoke that even the long hours of a winter night had not dispelled. The heavens soon became overcast, as if the elements foreshadowed an impending calamity. Every ear was open to catch the sound of the first dull boom of cannon, and every eye was watching for the first curling wraith of smoke that should usher in the contest of the 8th.

THE LINES OF BATTLE.

The fortune of the day was depending upon General Sigel, and that officer calmly, but carefully prepared his command for the conflict. Our whole force was concentrated to the north of our camp, and what, till then, had been our rear became our front. Colonel Carr's division was placed in the centre, occupying the road a short distance on either side. The enemy during the night had planted some of his batteries on an eminence, about two hundred feet high sloping away to the north, but precipitous on the side in our front.[14] Batteries and large bodies of infantry were posted at his right base of this hill and at the edge of some timber to its left. Infantry and cavalry, with a few guns, were posted on his extreme left beyond the road, and to oppose these Colonel Davis was sent to our extreme left. It was apparent that if we could dislodge the rebels from this hill the victory would be with our banners. With the skill of an expert in military science, General Sigel arranged his columns for the coming action. His foremost line was drawn up in battle array, with infantry, cavalry, and artillery all in their proper positions. At a suitable distance in the rear his reserves were placed, ready to be brought forward at any needed moment. A level, open field of great extent gave splendid opportunity for an imposing display. It had last been a cornfield, and the white and withered stalks were still on the ground, forming a fine background for the dark blue uniforms worn by our men. Throughout the morning skirmishing and light encounters had transpired with the portion of the enemy opposed to our centre and right, but on the left, not a gun was fired until the whole of General Sigel's command was in readiness.

OPENING OF THE GRAND BATTLE.

At a little past eight o'clock the decisive portion of the battle commenced. Along the entire line the cannoneers stood to their guns and at the word of command fire was opened. It was interesting to watch the movements of the artillerists in getting the range. Each gunner took a tree for his mark and tried upon it the effect of his first shell. "Too high," was the remark of a captain of a gun stationed near where I was standing. A turn of the elevating screw, a reload and another shot followed. "Still too high," and a second turn of the screw was made previous to another shot. "Just right this time," was the commentary on the direction of the third projectile. For the future, trees were not the objects aimed at. A brisk cannonade was kept up upwards of two hours with occasional intervals of five to fifteen minutes duration. The sharp booming of the six, twelve and eighteen pounders followed each other in rapid succession, and with such regularity that one could imagine that the huge dark object in the yellow field was an enormous organ on which a Mozart or a Verdi was executing one of his latest compositions.

TAKING A BATTERY.

The shot from the rebel batteries were well directed, but failed of execution equal to ours. Several guns were disabled and taken to the rear, and their places speedily supplied by others. During the cannonade, Colonel Carr's and Colonel Davis's divisions advanced slowly upon the enemy until they held the edge of the timber where the rebels had position in the morning. A battery of three guns in front of a wooded space on the left of the road at length became troublesome, and orders were issued for a bayonet charge to capture it. Just at this moment a gust of wind blew away the smoke from the front of the rebels, revealing their exact position. The Twelfth Missouri was designated the honor of taking the battery, and nobly acquitted themselves, advancing at the *pas de charge* under a terrible musketry fire, possessing themselves of the guns and holding them until their supports came up. Twelve of their men were killed in this charge and a large number wounded. Another gun was shortly after taken in the timber near by, and still another spiked piece on the extreme right of Davis's division.

REBEL STRENGTH WEAKENED.

After sustaining a heavy cannonade for two hours and a half the rebels showed signs of a desire to leave the ground. Their batteries were withdrawn from the hill and their infantry was fast melting away, large numbers of them, as we since learn, fleeing in terror at the fearful fire under which they had stood. The Eighteenth and Twenty-second Indiana regiments were ordered to charge, and did so in gallant style, but the rebels were too quick for the movement to succeed in taking the guns. Their infantry fled in disorder, and their artillerymen had barely the opportunity to attach their horses to the guns and move them from the field. It was useless to pursue with cavalry, the country being too densely wooded to admit using this arm of the service. The entire line moved forward to the support of the Indiana regiments, and up and down the entire length the air resounded with cheer upon cheer from our exultant troops. The enemy had been driven from his stronghold, and the victory was upon our banners.

THE REBEL'S FLIGHT AND GENERAL SIGEL'S PURSUIT.

General Sigel went in pursuit of the fleeing rebels, following their main body for twelve miles and capturing a considerable quantity of wagons, a load of powder and nearly a thousand stand of arms. They fled too rapidly to permit a capture of the entire force, and on the morning of the 9th, General Sigel's division returned to camp. A portion of the rebels fled to the eastward, felling timber across the road to prevent pursuit. Another portion turned to the westward, fleeing by way of Bentonville towards the sunny South. When last heard from they were in camp eight miles to the southward. A flag of truce came in today to arrange for burying the dead and making exchange of prisoners.

HOSPITAL SCENES.

The morning of the 8th I passed the hospital, where most of our wounded were carried on the previous night. Here lay dead officers and soldiers mingled indiscriminately together, most of them having died after or during amputations. Outside of the buildings were several legs and arms, the former with the stocking and occasionally a portion of the pantaloons still unremoved. A row of corpses lay in front of the principal hospital, and a number of attendants were busy in their removal. Each was covered with a blanket, and the utmost nonchalance was displayed in all their movements. "That's Captain ——," was a remark as a blanket was turned down from the face of a corpse, revealing at the same time the double barred shoulder strap. "That's private —— of

Company ——," or "That's a sergeant of —— regiment," and similar remarks were the only hospitable eulogiums as the column of dead was passed by. Whatever bravery and daring were shown when these death wounds were received was here unnoticed, the duties of the surgeon and his aides not requiring such knowledge. Satiated with these horrors, I turned away and hastened to the field, where the final battle was about commencing.

BATTLEFIELD HORRORS.

The appearance of the hill and woods shelled by General Sigel's division attests the terrific shower of missiles that fell upon them. Walking over the ground immediately after the flight of the enemy and the pursuit by our forces, I found it thickly strewn with dead and wounded, most of them having fallen by the deadly artillery projectiles. Tree after tree was shattered or perforated by shot and shell, and many were filled with grape and canister balls. One tree was pierced through and through by a solid shot, its top shivered by a shell and the base of its trunk scarred by seventeen canister and rifle balls. In one place lay the fragments of a battery wagon, wherein a shell had exploded, utterly destroying the wagon and killing two mules which had been its motive power. A ruined caisson and five cannon wheels were lying near it. Two dead artillerymen were stretched on the earth, each killed by a grapeshot, and by their side, was a third, gasping his last, with his side laid open by the fragment of a shell. On the hill, where the cannonade had been severe, trees, rocks and earth bore witness to its fierceness.

Fifteen wounded rebels lay in one group, and were piteously imploring each passerby for water and relief for their wounds. A few rods from them was another, whose arm had been torn off by a cannon shot, leaving the severed member on the ground a few feet distant. Near him was the dead body of a rebel whose legs and one arm had been shattered by a single shot. Behind a tree a few yards distant was stretched a corpse, with two thirds of its head blown away by the explosion of a shell, and near it a musket broken into three pieces. Still further along was the body of a rebel soldier, who had been killed by a grapeshot through the breast. A letter had fallen from his pocket, which, on examination, proved to be a long and well written love epistle from his betrothed in East Tennessee. It was addressed to Pleasant J. Williams, Churchill's Regiment, Fayetteville, Arkansas. Around him were all his dead and dying comrades, some stretched at full length upon the turf, and others contorted as it in extreme agony. The earth was thickly strewn with shot and fragments of shell.

THE WOODS ON FIRE.

The bursting of shells had set fire to the dry leaves on the ground, and the woods were burning in every direction. Efforts were made to remove the wounded before the flames should reach them, and nearly all were taken to places of safety. Several were afterwards found in secluded spots, some of them still alive, but horribly burned and blackened by the conflagration.

STRIPPING THE DEAD.

The rebels, in nearly every instance, removed the shoes from the dead and mortally wounded both of their own army and ours. Of all the corpses I saw I do not think one-twentieth had been left with their shoes untouched. In some cases pantaloons were taken and occasionally an overcoat or a blouse was missing. A large number of the killed among the rebels were shot through the head, while the majority of our dead were shot through the breast. The rebels, whenever it was possible, fired from cover; and as often as a head appeared from behind a tree or a bush it became a mark for our men. The Union troops generally stood in ranks, and, except when skirmishing, made no use of objects of protection.

AN INCIDENT.

Adjutant Sullivan, of the Third Illinois Cavalry, passed through the entire action unhurt. His horse was shot under him, but will probably recover from the wound. Adjutant Sullivan is the Sergeant Sullivan who received, in the charge at Dug Spring, in August last, five severe wounds, two of which were supposed to be mortal. The horse which was wounded yesterday is the same he rode at Dug Spring, and now carries fourteen balls received on that occasion.

REGIMENTAL AND INDIVIDUAL BRAVERY.

Where all the troops did well, it is difficult to particularize instances of special regimental valor. The Iowa infantry came from the field covered with blood and glory, and the two batteries from the same State are equally deserving of praise. The Twelfth Missouri was successful in a bayonet charge for the capture of a battery, and the Indiana regiments, by their determined bravery, more than trebly atoned for the unpleasant memories of Buena Vista.[15]

Colonel Hendricks, of the Twenty-second Indiana, was killed while gallantly leading his men in the action of the 7th, under Colonel Davis. Two of the German regiments illustrated the Teutonic love of music by singing one of the songs of Faderland [sic] while they stood under fire of the rebel batteries on the morning of the 8th. The Illinois regiments were not prominent in the action, with the exception of the Thirty-fifth, Colonel Wm. Smith (wounded),[16] and the Thirty-sixth, Colonel Greusel,[17] but they were all prompt to execute every order which they received. The Forty-fourth Illinois was in pursuit of the rebels and returned, bringing nearly a hundred prisoners and as many horses. Colonel Phelps,

Twenty-fifth Missouri, was prominent in the action of the 7th, and lost nearly thirty per cent of the number that went into battle.[18] Corporal J. H. Rowles, of Hayden's Dubuque Battery, was attached to one of the guns taken by the enemy. While the gunners were retreating he rushed back and spiked the piece, which was nearly surrounded by the rebels. He received a musket ball in each leg, and is now lying in the hospital. In a battle of such magnitude there were numerous deeds of individual daring and personal hardihood, rivaling the romantic exploits of the palmy days of chivalry, that will require days and weeks around the camp fires to learn their history.

CAVALRY USELESS – ITS LOSS.

The wooded nature of the country where the battle was fought rendered cavalry of relatively little value. The loss of the Third Illinois, the First Missouri and the Third Iowa was, nevertheless quite heavy. Lieutenant Colonel H. H. Trimble, of the Third Iowa, and Colonel C. A. Ellis of the First Missouri, were wounded, the former severely and the latter slightly.[19] The loss of rank and file of the cavalry in killed and wounded is about one-twentieth of their strength.

THE REBEL LOSS.

There is no data as yet by which we can estimate the loss of the enemy. Their dead and wounded on the ground were much more numerous than ours; at least one half or two thirds more. For ten miles on the road by which they retreated the houses were full of wounded. The whole line of buildings of the route to Keetsville is one grand hospital. Our entire loss is estimated at little more than a thousand, of whom about one-fourth are killed. The full returns will not be in for several days. A flag of truce which has just arrived in reference to the burial of the dead and exchange of prisoners, reports that Brigadier Generals McIntosh, Slack and McBride were killed.[20] By numerous prisoners we have a report that General McCulloch was also killed; but the redoubtable ranger has been slaughtered on so many occasions and afterwards, like the first husband of poor Pillicoddy's wife, turned up again, that we are all skeptical.[21] Perhaps Benjamin has been "gathered to his fathers," but nobody at present appears to see it.

AFTER THE BATTLE.

At present all is confusion with reference to the conflict and the various statistics connected with an engagement. We hardly know what we have accomplished, whether the enemy has fled, what is the extent of his calamity, his present position, his strength and his designs for the immediate future. Neither are we fully acquainted with our own condition, our casualties, our deeds of daring and our ability to again enter the arena and cope with an enemy nearly treble our strength. When the smoke shall have cleared away from the battlefield, and the clouds that now obscure it are dispelled by the clear sunshine, we can speak more definitely of its losses, its griefs, its instances of knightly bravery, its triumphs and its accomplished results.

Our number of killed, wounded and missing is not yet known, but it is estimated that our casualty list will not exceed a thousand. The reports will not be in for several days. Our heaviest loss was on the first day with Colonel Carr's division. Our lines sustained but little damage on the second day, notwithstanding the heavy artillery fire under which the stood for two hours.

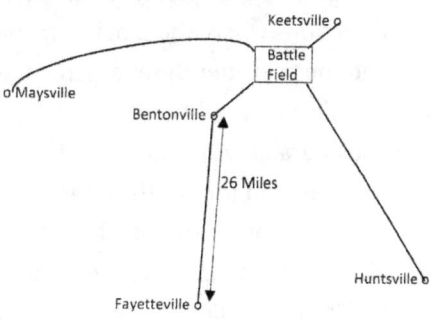

Map drawn by the author.

Thus ends Thomas Knox's 7500-word first report on the Battle of Pea Ridge, a record filled with vivid descriptions. The headings in this letter are Knox's. Two days later, on March 11, Knox wrote again from Pea Ridge.[22] In this letter he provided additional interesting vignettes, detailed the casualties, unit by unit, and presented a total figure. His casualty numbers are remarkably close to those presented by Shea and Hess.[23]

> Pea Ridge, Benton County, Ark., March 11, 1862.
> We have at length an opportunity to foot up our loss in the recent battle at this point. It is not as large as many had anticipated, and, considering the duration and severity of the engagement, does no particular credit to the skill of the enemy.
> The casualties in the various divisions are as follows:
> [There follows a long list of casualties by division and regiment.]
> The aggregate of our loss is supposed to be nearly as follows:
>
> | | | |
> |---|---|---|
> | Killed | 212 | (208)[24] |
> | Wounded | 926 | (989) |
> | Missing | 174 | (209) |
> | Total | 1312 | (1406) |
>
> The casualties of the enemy are not yet known; but information received from the rebel army shows that it was from three to eight hundred greater than ours. The country for miles in all directions where the rebels retreated is full of their wounded, and the field after the engagement was covered with rebel dead double the number of Union slain.[25] Their loss in officers is considerable. All statements from prisoners, wounded, spies, &c., confirm the death of McIntosh and Colonel McCulloch and most of them corroborate that of General McCulloch. General Slack and Colonel Clarkson are said to have fallen by Union missiles. Numerous Colonels, captains and lieutenants are said to be among the officers that were. [sic] Some of the wounded officers now in our lines speak of their men

as cowards of the worst description, and say that the loss of as many officers is owing to the cowardice of the men, necessitating the former constantly to expose themselves. The panic among the fleeing rebels was increased by the stories of Northern barbarity that have constantly been related by the officers to the rank and file. The roads were strewn with broken and disabled wagons, arms, provisions and various munitions of war. Several pieces of artillery were found a few days since with the woodwork of the carriages destroyed by fire and the guns carefully spiked. Two of them are bronze rifled twelve pounders, of new and beautiful patterns. The whole will be remounted as speedily as possible.

[ARKANSAS MILITIA.]

Colonel F. A. Rector's regiment of Arkansas militia was disbanded by order of the commanding officer on the afternoon subsequent to the battle.[26] Colonel Rector became disgusted and disheartened after the defeat, and, retreating about fourteen miles from the scene of action, ordered his men to stack their arms and disperse for their homes. Lieutenant Bradley, of Hayden's battery, yesterday went in search of these abandoned weapons, and, after a long and toilsome march, found them in a narrow ravine, stacked and without guard. Wagons sent out today to bring them in have just returned with upwards of 200 guns.

[BRAVERY.]

In the action of the 7th, a gun and caisson belonging to the Iowa First Battery became disabled, and were being abandoned by their gunners. Colonel Vandever ordered Captain Carpenter, of Company B, Ninth Iowa, to go forward with his company and remove them. Capt. Carpenter, under heavy fire from the enemy's infantry succeeded in the attempt and safely removed both the gun and caisson. Reaching the rear, it was noticed that there were some burning gun wads among several loaded shell and case shot, with their cartridges, in one of the caisson chests, momently threatening an explosion. Captain Carpenter ordered the burning wads to be removed and, with his own hands, aided in separating them from the deadly materials with which they were in close contact. By his promptness and coolness he saved all around from the consequences of a fearful explosion.

[THIEVERY.]

In nearly every instance where they fell into the hands of the enemy our dead and wounded were robbed of everything valuable about them. An artilleryman, named Yost, in Hayden's battery, was wounded and left upon the field at the time the battery was withdrawn, on the afternoon of the 7th. Seeing the enemy approaching, he took out his wallet, and, removing fifty dollars in Treasury notes, and placing them in his mouth, he returned to his pocket the wallet containing a small amount in silver and two or three postage stamps. A few moments later his wallet was taken by the rebels, but his fifty dollars remained untouched and are still in his possession.

[CASUALTIES AND INDIANS.]

Lieut. Perry Watts, of the Twenty-second Indiana, was slain by a ten pound cannon shot that previously killed two men and then lodged in his breast. Col. Hendricks, of the same regiment, was instantly killed by a rifle ball in the breast at the time the advance was made upon the Indians posted in the thicket. Colonel Hendricks was the only Union field officer killed in the battle.

The use of Indians in the late battle has raised a cry of indignation among our men that will not soon be hushed. Seven of the Indians are now prisoners in our camp and at first it was difficult to restrain our men in inflicting summary punishment upon them. In addition to the eight of the Third Iowa Cavalry that were scalped on the field, we have reports of several others scalped on other parts of the ground. It will be noticed that the report gives thirty-seven of that regiment killed and only eight wounded. This disparity arises from the fact that several that were left wounded on the ground were afterwards found pierced through and mutilated in the most horrid manner. This statement I provide, not upon hearsay, but from having been on the ground and seen with my own eyes what I have written. What will the response be, by the enlightened nations of Europe who have been contemplating a recognition of the Confederacy, to this mode of warfare?

[SUMMING UP.]

By subsequent developments I find that the affair of the 7th, on our right of that day, though short, was particularly hot during the time it lasted. Colonel Julius White, of the Thirty-seventh Illinois, commanding the Second Brigade of the Third Division, claims to have opened fire on that morning and to have withstood the brunt of the fight. It is estimated that ten thousand of the enemy attacked us in that quarter, and that General McCulloch was killed in the encounter. The fact of his death is not yet fully established.

The enemy at last accounts was about forty miles from this point, in full flight for Van Buren or Fort Smith. There appears to be no probability of a battle before we move to attack the discomfited rebels.

Subjoined is General Price's report of his retreat from Springfield. His confidence of the future as expressed in his last line, appears to have been misplaced.[27]

Knox wrote his letter from Pea Ridge on March 11. But it was probably not put into the mail service until he reached Rolla on March 17 and it did not see publication until March 23. On the same day he finished his letter, he set off for Rolla. On March 16, there was another report filed from Rolla, and certainly sent by telegraph, that was published by the *Herald* just one day later.²⁸ This report lacks the knowledge and information that Knox certainly had and presents other "information" that was untrue.

In his book he penned a parting comment:

> Half sick in consequence of the hardships of the campaign and satisfied there would be no more fighting of importance during the summer, I determined to go back to civilization. I returned to St. Louis by way of Springfield and Rolla. A wounded officer, Lieutenant-Colonel Herron (who afterward wore the stars of a major general), was my travelling companion. Six days of weary toil over rough and muddy roads brought us to the railway, within twelve hours of St. Louis. It was my last campaign in the region. From that day the war in the Southwest had its chief interest in the country east of the Great River.²⁹

Knox, *Camp-fire and Cotton-field*, facing 142

Chapter 20.

Other Times, Other Places

Knox wended his way back to St. Louis with the wounded Lieutenant-Colonel Herron. William Fayel, the *St. Louis Democrat* correspondent and the only other newsman with General Curtis, chose to remain on the battlefield and follow the fortunes of the Army of the Southwest.

When Knox arrived in St. Louis, he made a terrible discovery – he had been scooped! Two different news reports, one in the New York *Tribune* and the other in the New York *World* recounted the Battle of Pea Ridge. But no reporters from either newspaper had been there, not even close. Knox found that errors abounded in each story. It turned out that two reporters, Junius Henri Browne of the *Tribune* and Richard Colburn of the *World*, had apparently cooperated in the concoction of the stories.[1] Most correspondents, after the debacle of the Frémont campaign, had decided to follow the Grant campaign down the Mississippi. On returning to St. Louis after Grant's victories at Forts Henry on the Tennessee River and Donelson on the Cumberland River, Browne heard of the battle at Pea Ridge. He quickly took the train to Rolla and began gathering information to spin his tale. He knew the names of the commanders on both sides, of some of the units, and that Cherokees were among the rebel forces. The Cherokees were described in horrific terms, scalping and maiming and even, in their blood lust, attacking their Confederate allies. He also obtained information on the terrain from an "old countryman."

Browne and Colburn's vague descriptions of the battle were stirring – Colburn's was even written in the first person. Today, one would call the reports "purple prose" and smile, but at that time, it was deadly serious reporting. "'Follow me!' thundered Sigel, and his proud steed trampled an approaching rebel under his fiery feet," is a typical example.[2]

Knox, certainly chagrined, rested for a time in St. Louis but was drawn to the rapidly changing events downriver. While he was reporting on the Army of the Southwest, Forts Henry and Donelson had fallen and the Iron Banks fortification at Columbus, Kentucky, had been evacuated. In Missouri, New Madrid had fallen (March 14) and Island Number Ten's days were numbered. In St. Louis, Knox heard of the Battle of Shiloh (April 6–7) and the fall of Island Number Ten (April 8).

Thomas Knox could wait no longer. He made his way first to Cairo at the juncture of the Ohio and Mississippi Rivers and then up the Tennessee River to Pittsburg Landing three days after the Battle of Shiloh. After describing the devastation he found at Shiloh, he followed General Halleck's (in place of Grant) glacial move on Corinth. The Siege of Corinth was successful in that the city and rail junction was taken, but also a failure because Halleck had allowed General P. G. T. Beauregard and his army to escape. The siege went on and toward its conclusion he described a new order by General Halleck:

> Toward the end of the siege, General Halleck gave the journalists a sensation, by expelling them from his lines. The representatives of the Press held a meeting, and waited upon that officer, after the appearance of the order requiring their departure. They offered a protest, which was insolently rejected. We could not ascertain General Halleck's purpose in excluding us just as the campaign was closing, but concluded he desired we should not witness the end of the siege in which so much had been promised and so little accomplished. A week after our departure, General Beauregard evacuated Corinth, and our army took possession. The fruits of the victory were an empty village, a few hundred stragglers, and a small quantity of war *materiel*. The capture of Corinth terminated the offensive portion of the campaign. Our army occupied the line of the Memphis and Charleston Railway from Corinth to Memphis.[3]

Knox next returned to Cairo and followed the army and navy to Memphis. He viewed the naval Battle of Memphis and described Memphis and its occupation. The army organized the civilian administration of the city and, to control the editorial content of one Memphis newspaper, the Memphis *Argus*, named some overseers:

> Head-Quarters Third Division, Reserved Corps,
> Army of Tennessee, Memphis, June 17, 1862.
> Editors *Daily Argus*: As the closing of your office might be injurious to you pecuniarily, I send two gentlemen, Messrs. A. D. Richardson and Thos. W. Knox, both of ample experience, to take charge of the editorial department of your paper. The business management of your office will be left to you.
> Very respectfully,
> Lewis Wallace,
> General Third Division, Reserve Corps.[4]

Old friends, co-editors from Denver, now competitors representing the New York *Tribune* and the *New York Herald*, were given the job of writing the editorials. General Wallace had assured the owners of the *Argus* that control would be returned to them as soon as a Union paper was established in Memphis. It was not long before this occurred and Knox and Richardson were out of their editorial jobs.[5]

Meanwhile the war moved further southward towards Vicksburg and eastward toward Corinth and Holly Springs. After a short vacation and a respite from the heat and humidity Knox soon returned to his reporting. By December 1862, he was back with the river fleet.

But trouble followed him. General Sherman issued an order excluding all civilians, except such as were connected with the transports, and threatening to treat as a spy any person who should write accounts for publication which might give information to the enemy. Knox had a pass from General Grant to travel with Sherman but when he wrote an account of the failed attack at Chickasaw Bayou, his letter was intercepted by Sherman's staff. Knox traveled upriver to Cairo where he filed a second letter. Upon his return to Sherman's camp he was arrested as a spy and court-martialed. General Sherman had filed charges:

> First – Giving information to the enemy.
> Second – Being a spy.
> Third – Disobedience of orders.

The first and second charges were based on his published letter. The third referred to his accompanying the expedition without proper authority, and publishing a letter without official sanction. At his trial he was found innocent of the first two charges and guilty of the third. He was banished from Sherman's army. Reporter friends interceded with President Lincoln on his behalf.

Lincoln wrote a note:

> *Executive Mansion*
> *Washington March 20, 1863*
>
> *Whom it May Concern:*
> *Whereas it appears to my satisfaction that Thomas W. Knox, a correspondent of* The New York Herald, *has been, by the sentence of a court-martial, excluded from the Military Department under command of Major-General Grant, and also that General Thayer, president of the court-martial, which rendered the sentence, and Major-General McClernand, in command of a corps of that department, and many other respectable persons, are of opinion that Mr. Knox's offence was technical, rather than willfully wrong, and that the sentence should be revoked: Now, therefore, said sentence is hereby so far revoked as to allow Mr. Knox to return to General Grant's head-quarters, to remain if General Grant shall give his express assent; and to again leave the department, if General Grant shall refuse such assent.*
>
> *A. Lincoln.*[6]

Knox continued his reportorial career with the *Herald*, chronicling the war, and after the war became a travel writer. His memoir of his part in the Civil War, *Camp-fire and Cotton-field*, appeared in 1865 and was followed by a stream of biographies, travel works, many for a younger audience (the "Boy Travelers" series), histories, and a few fiction works, forty-six in all, appearing between 1865 and 1896.[7] He received the "Royal Order of the White Elephant of Siam" in 1883 for his *Boy Travelers in the Far East* account of travel in Siam and Java.[8] In 1894, Knox published *The Lost Army,* a fictionalized account of the Battle of Pea Ridge and the ensuing movements of General Curtis through Arkansas to Helena, on the Mississippi River.

Between his travels, Knox lived in New York at the Lotos Club, a gentleman's and literary society, and served as its secretary, 1880–1889.[9] He never married and upon his death in 1896 his estate was left to his sister and his housekeeper. His library was willed to Pembroke Academy in Pembroke, New Hampshire, but was lost in fire at the library a few years later.

A large memorial stone was erected in the Pembroke, New Hampshire, City Cemetery, but he was not buried there; his remains were cremated.[10]

Thomas W. Knox is mostly forgotten today, but he deserves to be remembered for his colorful, detailed, first-hand accounts of the first year of the Civil War in Missouri as reported by one of the first modern war correspondents.

(Findagrave.com)

Appendix

I. Proclamation[1]

MILITARY DEPARTMENT OF THE WEST,
Saint Louis, Mo., May 12, 1861.

I have just returned to this post and have assumed the military command of this department. No one can more deeply regret the deplorable state of things existing here than myself. The past cannot be recalled; I can only deal with the present and the future. I most anxiously desire to discharge the delicate and onerous duties devolved upon me so as to preserve the public peace. I shall carefully abstain from the exercise of any unnecessary powers and from all interference with the proper functions of the public officers of the State and city. I therefore call upon the public authorities and the people to aid me in preserving the public peace.

The military force stationed in this department by authority of the Government and now under my command will only be used in the last resort to preserve the peace. I trust I may be spared the necessity of resorting to martial law, but the public peace must be preserved and the lives and property of the people protected. Upon a careful review of my instructions I find I have no authority to change the location of the home guards. To avoid all cause of irritation and excitement if called upon to aid the local authorities in preserving the public peace I shall in preference make use of the Regular Army.

I ask the people to pursue their peaceable avocations, and to observe the laws and orders of their local authorities, and to abstain from the excitements of public meetings and heated discussions. My appeal I trust may not be in vain, and I pledge the faith of a soldier to the earnest discharge of my duty.

WM. S. HARNEY,
Brigadier-General, U. S. Army, Commanding Department.

II. Military Department of the West[2]

Saint Louis, May 14, 1861.

To the People of the State of Missouri:

On my return to the duties of the command of this department I find, greatly to my astonishment and mortification, a most extraordinary state of things existing in this State, deeply affecting the stability of the Government of the United States as well as the governmental and other interests of Missouri itself.

As a citizen of Missouri, owing allegiance to the United States, and having interests in common with you, I feel it my duty as well as privilege to extend a warning voice to my fellow- citizens against the common dangers that threaten us, and to appeal to your patriotism and sense of justice to exert all your moral power to avert them.

It is with regret that I feel it my duty to call your attention to the recent act of the general assembly of Missouri known as the "military bill," which is the result, no doubt, of the temporary excitement that now pervades the public mind. This bill cannot be regarded in any other light than an indirect secession ordinance, ignoring even the forms resorted to by other States. Manifestly, its most material provisions are in conflict with the Constitution and laws of the United States. To this extent it is a nullity, and cannot and ought not to be upheld or regarded by the good citizens of Missouri. There are obligations and duties resting upon the people of Missouri under the Constitution and laws of the United States which are paramount, and which I trust you will carefully consider and weigh well before you will allow yourselves to be carried out of the Union under the form of yielding obedience to this military bill, which is clearly in violation of your duties as citizens of the United States.

It must be apparent to every one who has taken a proper and unbiased view of the subject that, whatever may be the termination of the unfortunate condition of things in respect to the so-called Cotton States, Missouri must share the destiny of the Union. Her geographical position, her soil, productions, and, in short, all her material interests, point to this result. We cannot shut our eyes against this controlling fact. It is seen and its force is felt throughout the nation. So important is this regarded to the great interests of the country, that I venture to express the opinion that the whole power of the Government of the United States, if necessary, will be exerted to maintain Missouri in her present position in the Union. I express to you, in all frankness and sincerity, my own deliberate convictions, without assuming to speak for the Government of the United States, whose authority here and elsewhere I shall at all times and under all circumstances endeavor faithfully to uphold. I desire above all things most earnestly to invite my fellow-citizens dispassionately to consider their true interests as well as their true relation to the Government under which we live and to which we owe so much.

In this connection I desire to direct attention to one subject which, no doubt, will be made the pretext for more or less popular excitement. I allude to the recent transactions at Camp Jackson, near Saint Louis. It is not proper for me to comment upon the official conduct of my predecessor in command of this department, but it is right and proper for the people of Missouri to know that the main avenue of Camp Jackson, recently under command of General Frost, had the name of Davis, and a principal street of the same camp that of Beauregard, and that a body of men had been received into that camp by its commander which had been notoriously organized in the interests of the secessionists, the men openly wearing the dress and badge distinguishing the Army of the so-called Southern Confederacy. It is also a notorious fact that a quantity of arms had been received into the camp which were unlawfully taken from the United States Arsenal at Baton Rouge, and surreptitiously passed up the river in boxes marked "Marble."

Upon facts like these, and having in view what occurred at Liberty, the people can draw their own inferences, and it cannot be difficult for anyone to arrive at a correct conclusion as to the character and ultimate purpose of that encampment. No Government in the world would be entitled to respect that would tolerate for a moment such openly treasonable preparations. It is but simple justice, however, that I should state the fact that there were many good and loyal men in the camp who were in no manner responsible for its treasonable character.

Disclaiming as I do all desire or intention to interfere in any way with the prerogatives of the State of Missouri or with the functions of its executive or other authorities, yet, I regard it as my plain path of duty to express to the people, in respectful but at the same time decided language, that within the field and scope of my command and authority the supreme law of the land must and shall be maintained, and no subterfuges, whether in the forms of legislative acts or otherwise, can be permitted to harass or oppress the good and law-abiding people of Missouri. I shall exert my authority to protect their persons and property from violations of every kind, and I shall deem it my duty to suppress all unlawful combinations of men, whether formed under pretext of military organizations or otherwise.

WM. S. HARNEY,
Brigadier- General, U. S. Army, Commanding.

III. The Harney Price Agreement[3]

Saint Louis, Mo., May 21, 1861.

The undersigned, officers of the United States Government and of the government of the State of Missouri, for the purpose of removing misapprehensions and allaying public excitement, deem it proper to declare publicly that they have this day had a personal interview in this city, in which it has been mutually understood, without the semblance of dissent on either part, that each of them has no other than a common object equally interesting and important to every citizen of Missouri – that of restoring peace and good order to the people of the State in subordination to the laws of the General and State Governments. It being thus understood, there seems no reason why every citizen should not confide in the proper officers of the General and State Governments to restore quiet, and, as among the best means of offering no counter influences, we mutually recommend to all persons to respect each other's rights throughout the State, making no attempt to exercise unauthorized powers, as it is the determination of the proper authorities to suppress all unlawful proceedings, which can only disturb the public peace.

General Price, having by commission full authority over the militia of the State of Missouri, undertakes, with the sanction over the militia of the State, already declared, to direct the whole power of the State officers to maintain order within the State among the people thereof, and General Harney publicly declares that, this object being thus assured, he can have no occasion, as he has no wish, to make military movements, which might otherwise create excitements and jealousies which he most earnestly desires to avoid.

We, the undersigned, do therefore mutually enjoin upon the people of the State to attend to their civil business of whatsoever sort it may be, and it is to be hoped that the unquiet elements which have threatened so seriously to disturb the public peace may soon subside and be remembered only to be deplored.

STERLING PRICE,
Major-General Missouri State Guard.

WM. S. HARNEY,
Brigadier-General, Commanding.

IV. General Price's Address[4]

Gov. Price and the Missouri Militia

HEADQUARTERS MISSOURI GUARD
Jefferson City, June 4 1861

To the Brigadier Generals Commanding the Several Military Districts in Missouri

To correct misrepresentation and prevent all misunderstanding of my opinions and intentions in reference to the military trust confided to me by the government of Missouri, I desire to state to you and the public generally that my past and present position as a private citizen, as a member of our State Convention, and as a military commander, and my influence, have been exerted to prevent the transfer of the seat of war from the Atlantic States to our own State.

Having taken no steps towards dissolving our connection with the Federal Government, there was no reason whatever for disturbing the peace and tranquility of Missouri. I have therefore desired, and such I am authorized has been and still is the desire of the Chief Executive under whose orders I acted, that the people of Missouri should exercise the right to choose their own position in any contest which might be forced upon them unaided by any military force whatever. Their right to bear arms in defense of themselves and of their State cannot be questioned, secured as it is by both the constitution of the United States and of this State. For the purpose, therefore, of securing to the people of Missouri a free exercise of their undoubted rights, and with a view to preserve peace and order throughout the State, an agreement has been entered into between General Harney and myself, which I consider alike honorable to both parties and governments represented. The Federal Government, however, has thought proper to remove General Harney from the command of the Department of the West; but as the successor of General Harney will certainly consider himself and his government in honor bound to carry out this agreement in good faith, I feel assured that his removal should give no cause of uneasiness to our citizens for the security of their liberties and property. I intend on my part to adhere to it both in spirit and to the letter. The rumors in circulation that it is the intention of the officer now in command of this depot to disarm those of our citizens who do not agree in opinion with the administration in Washington, and put arms in the hands of those who in some localities of this State are supposed to sympathize with the views of the Federal Government, are, I trust, unfounded. The purpose of such a movement could not be misunderstood, and it would not only be a palpable violation of the agreement referred to, and an equally plain violation of our constitutional rights, but a gross indignity to the citizens of this State, which would be resisted to the last extremity.

My wish and hope is that the people of the State of Missouri be permitted in peace and security to decide upon their future course, and so far as my abilities can effect this object, it shall be accomplished.

The people of Missouri cannot be forced, under the terrors of a military invasion, into a position not of their own free choice. A million of such people as the citizens of Missouri were never yet subjugated, and if attempted, let no apprehensions be entertained of the result.

I enjoin upon you, gentlemen, to see that all citizens, of whatever opinion in politics or religion be protected in their persons and property.

STERLING PRICE
Major General Commanding.

V. Governor Jackson's Proclamation of June 12, 1861[5]

Jefferson City,
Thursday, June 12.

To the People of Missouri:

A series of unprovoked and unparalleled outrages have been inflicted on the peace and dignity of this Commonwealth and upon the rights and liberties of its people, by wicked and unprincipled men, professing to act under the authority of the United States Government. The solemn enactments of your Legislature have been nullified; your volunteer soldiers have been taken prisoners; your commerce with your sister States has been suspended; your trade with your own fellow-citizens has been, and is, subjected to increasing control of an armed soldiery; peaceful citizens have been imprisoned without warrant of law; unoffending and defenseless men, women and children have been ruthlessly shot down and murdered, and other unbearable indignities have been heaped upon your State and yourselves.

To all were outrages and indignities you have submitted with patriotic forbearance, which his only encouraged the perpetrators of these grievous wrongs to attempt still bolder and more daring usurpations.

It has been my earnest endeavor, under all these embarrassing circumstances, to maintain the peace of the State, and avert, if possible, from our borders the desolating effect of civil war. With that object in view I authorized Maj. Gen. Price, several weeks ago, to arrange with Gen. Harney, commanding the Federal forces in this State the terms of an agreement, by which the peace of the State might be preserved. They came, on the 21st of May, to an understanding, which was made public. The State authorities have labored faithfully to carry out the terms of that agreement. The Federal Government, on the other hand, not only manifested its strong disapprobation, of it by the instant dismissal of that distinguished officer, who, on its part, entered into it; but it at once began and has unintermittingly carried out a system of hostile operations in utter contempt of that agreement and in reckless disregard of its own pledged faith.

The acts have latterly portended revolution and civil war so unmistakably that I resulted to make one further effort to avert these dangers from you.

I therefore solicited an interview with Brig. Gen. Lyon, commanding the Federal army in Missouri. It was granted on the 11th inst., and waiving all questions of personal and official dignity, I went to St. Louis, accompanied by Major-Gen. Price.

We had an interview, on the 11th inst., with Gen. Lyon and Col. F. P. Blair, Jr., at which I submitted to them the following proposition: That I would disband the State Guard, and break up its organization; that I would disarm all the companies which had been ordered out by the State; that I would pledge myself not to attempt to reorganize the militia under the military bill; that no arms or munitions of war should be brought into the State; that I would protect all citizens equally in their rights, regardless of their political opinions; that I would repress all insurrectionary movements within the State; that I would repel all attempts made to invade it from whatever quarter and by whomsoever made, and that I would thus maintain a strict neutrality in the present unhappy contest, and preserve the peace of the State; and I further proposed that I would, if necessary, invoke the assistance of the United States troops to carry out these pledges. All this I propose to do upon condition that the Federal Government would undertake to disarm the Home Guards, which it has illegally organized and armed throughout the State, and pledge itself not to occupy with its troops any localities in the State not occupied by them at this time.

Nothing but the most earnest desire to avert the horrors of civil war from our beloved State could have tempted me to propose these humiliating terms. They were rejected by the Federal officers.

They demanded not only the disorganization and disarming of the State Militia, and the nullification of the Military Bill; but they refused to disarm their own Home Guard, and insisted that the Federal Government should enjoy the unrestricted right to move and station its troops throughout the State whenever and wherever that might, in the opinion of its officers, be necessary, either for the protection of loyal subjects of the Federal Government, or for repelling invasion, and they plainly announced that it was the intention of the Administration to take military occupation, under these pretexts, of the whole State, and reduce it, as avowed by Gen. Lyon himself, to the exact condition of Maryland.

The acceptance by me of these degrading terms, would not only have sullied the honor of Missouri, but would have aroused the indignation of every brave citizen, and precipitated the very conflict which it has been my aim to prevent. We refused to accede to them and the conference was broken up.

Fellow-citizens, all our efforts toward conciliation have failed. We can hope nothing for the justice or moderation of the agents of the Federal Government in this State. They are energetically hastening the execution of their bloody and revolutionary schemes for the inauguration of civil war in your midst; for the military occupation of your State by an armed band of lawless invaders; for the overthrow of your State Government and for the subversion of those liberties which the Government has always sought to protect; and they intend to exert their whole power to subjugate you, if possible, to the military despotism, which has usurped the powers of the Federal Government.

Now, therefore I, C. F. Jackson, Governor of the State of Missouri, do, in view of the foregoing facts, and by virtue of the powers vested in me by the Constitution and laws of this Commonwealth, issue this, my proclamation, calling the militia of the State, to the number of 50,000, into active service of the State, for the purpose of repelling such invasions, and for the protection of the lives, liberties and property of the citizens of this State, and I earnestly exhort all good citizens of Missouri to rally to the flag of their State for the protection of their endangered homes and firesides, and for the defense of their most sacred rights and dearest liberties.

In issuing this proclamation, I hold it to be my most solemn duty to remind you that Missouri is still one of the United States; that the Executive Department of the State Government does not arrogate to itself the power to disturb that relation. That power has been wisely vested in the Convention which will, at the proper time, express your sovereign will; and that meanwhile it is your duty to obey all constitutional requirements of the Federal Government. But it is equally my duty to advise you that your first allegiance is due to your own State, and that you are under no obligation whatever to obey the unconstitutional edicts of the military despotism which has introduced itself at Washington, nor submit to the infamous and degrading sway of its wicked minions in the State. No brave-hearted Missourian will obey the one or submit to the other. Rise, then, and drive out ignominiously the invaders who have dared to desecrate the soil which your labors have made fruitful, and which is consecrated by your homes.

CLAIBORNE F. JACKSON.

VI. Proclamation of General Lyon[6]

St. Louis, June 15.

[The following proclamation has just been issued in an extra *Democrat* to the people of Missouri.]

Prior to the proclamation issued by Governor Jackson, dated the 12th of June, it was well known to you that the Governor and Legislature sympathized in the revolutionary movement now in progress in this country; and had adopted every means in their power to effect a separation of this State from the General Government. For this purpose, parties of avowed secessionists have been organized into military companies throughout the State, with the full knowledge and approval of the Governor. The establishment of encampments in the State, at an unusual period of the year, and authorized for an indefinite period, could have had no other object in view than the concentrating of a large military force, to be subjected to the provisions of a military law, then in contemplation and subsequently passed; a bill, so offensive to all peaceful inhabitants, and so palpably unconstitutional, that it could be accepted by those only who were willing to conform to its extraordinary provision, for the purpose of effecting their cherished object, the disruption of the Federal Government. That bill provides for an obligation to the State on the part of all persons enrolled under its provisions, irrespective of any obligation to the United States; when the Constitution requires all State officers to take an oath of allegiance to the United States. This of itself is a repudiation of all authority of the General Government – whose Constitution is supreme law – on the part of State government, its officers, and such citizens as might choose to adopt the provisions of the bill; and coupled, as it was, on the part of the legislature and the governor with declarations hostile to its authority, and in sympathy with those who were arrayed in a condition of actual hostility against it, could leave no doubt of its object.

To carry out the provisions of this extraordinary law, the public schools were deprived of the funds necessary to the education of your children. Your asylums were even stripped of their means of support, and an additional onerous tax imposed on you. This bill, regarded as it has uniformly been by all loyal citizens of the United States, as having in direct view hostilities to the Federal Government, was so denounced by General Harney, who characterized it as a secession ordinance in his proclamation on the 14th May last. That proclamation doubtless gave rise to an interview between Gen. Harney and Gen. Price that resulted in an agreement which it was hoped would lead to the restoration of tranquility and good order in your State. That a repudiation of the military bill, and all efforts to organize the militia of the State under its provisions, was the basis of agreement, was shown, as well as by the proclamation of Gen. Harney, immediately preceding it, as by a certain paper submitted to Gen. Price, containing preliminary conditions to an interview with him.

[Here follows what was read to Gen. Price, published in the *Democrat* Wednesday last.]

This agreement failed to define specifically the terms of the peace or how far a suspension of the provisions of the military bill should form a part of it, though from express direction of Gen. Harney at the time of conference, as well as from the said paper a suspension of any action under the bill until there could be a judicial determination of its character by a competent tribunal, must in good faith be regarded as the fundamental basis of the negotiation.

Nevertheless, immediately after this arrangement, and up to the time the Governor issued his proclamation, complaints of attempts to execute provisions of this bill, by which most exasperating hardships have been imposed upon peaceful and loyal citizens, coupled with persecution and proscription of those opposed to its provisions, have been made to me, as commander of United States forces here, and have been carried to the authorities at Washington, with appeals for relief from Union men from all parts of the State, who have been abused, insulted, and, in some cases, driven from their homes. That relief I consider it to be the duty of a just government to use every exertion in its power to give. Upon this point the policy of the government is set forth in the following communication from the Department in Washington:

ADJUTANT GENERAL'S OFFICE,
Washington, May 27, 1861.

Brigadier General W. S. Harney, Commanding Department West of St. Louis:

Sir: The President observes with concern that notwithstanding the pledge of the State authorities to cooperate in preserving the peace of Missouri, that loyal citizens in great numbers continue to be driven from their homes. It is immaterial whether these outrages continue from inactivity or indisposition on the part of the State authorities to protect them. It is enough that they continue to devolve on you the duty of putting a stop to them summarily by force, under your command, to be aided by such troops as you may require from Kansas, Iowa and Illinois. The professions of loyalty to the Union by State authorities are not to be relied upon; they have already falsified their professions too often, and are far too committed to secession to be admitted to your confidence, and you can only be sure of their desisting from their wicked purposes when it is not in their power to prosecute them. You will therefore be unceasingly watchful of their movements, and not permit the clamor of their partizans [sic] and opponents to prevent you from checking every movement against the government. However disguised under the pretended State authority, the authority of the United States is paramount, and whenever it is apparent that movements, whether by color of State authority or not, is hostile, you will not hesitate to put it down.

Signed, L. THOMAS, Adjutant General.

It is my design to carry out these instructions in their letter and spirit. Their justice and propriety will be appreciated by all those who take an enlightened view of the relations of the citizens of Missouri to the General Government, nor can such policy be construed as at all disparaging to the rights or dignity of the State of Missouri, or as infringing in any sense upon the individual liberty of its citizens. The recent proclamation of Gov. Jackson, by which has set at defiance the authorities of the United States, and urged you to make war upon them, is but consummating his treasonable purposes, long indicted by his acts and expressed opinions, now manifest. If in suppressing these treasonable projects, carrying out the policy of the Government, and maintaining its dignity, as above indicated, hostilities should unfortunately occur, and unhappy consequences should follow, I would hope that all aggravation of those evils may be avoided, and that they may be diverted from the innocent and may fall only upon the hands of those by whom they have been provoked. In the discharge of my plain but onerous duties I shall look for the countenance and active cooperation of all good citizens, and I shall expect them to discountenance all illegal combinations or organizations, and to support and uphold, by every lawful means, the Federal Government, upon the maintenance of which depends their liberty and perfect enjoyment of all their rights.

Signed, N. LYON, Brig. Gen.,
U. S. Volunteers, Commanding.

VII. Proclamation of General Lyon[7]

To the People of Missouri:

Booneville, June 18, 1861.

Upon leaving the city of St. Louis, in consequence of war made by the Governor of this State against the Government of the United States, because I would not assume on its behalf to relinquish its duties and abdicate its rights of protecting loyal citizens from the oppression and cruelties of rebels in this State, I published an address to the people, in which I declared my intention to use the force under my command for no other purpose than the maintenance of the authority of the General Government, and the protection of the rights and property of all law-abiding citizens.

The State authorities, in violation of an agreement with General Harney, on the 21st of May last, had drawn together and organized upon a large scale the means of warfare, and, having made declaration of war, they abandoned the capital, issued orders for the destruction of the railroad bridges and telegraph lines, and proceeded to this point to put in execution their purposes toward the General Government. This devolved upon me the necessity of meeting this issue to the best of my ability, and accordingly I moved to this point with a portion of the force under my command, attacked and dispersed hostile forces gathered here by the Governor, and took possession of the camp equipage left and a considerable number of prisoners, most of them young and of immature age, who represent that they have been misled by fraud ingeniously devised and industriously circulated by designing leaders, who seek to devolve upon unreflecting and deluded followers the task of securing the object of their own false ambition.

Out of compassion for these misguided youths, and to correct impressions created by unscrupulous calumniators, I have liberated them, upon condition that they will not serve in the impending hostilities against the United States Government. I have done this in spite of the known facts that the leaders in the present rebellion, having long experienced the mildness of the General Government, still feel confident that this mildness cannot be overtaxed even by factious hostilities having in view its overthrow; but if, as in the case of the late Camp Jackson affair, this clemency shall still he misconstrued, it is proper to give warning that the Government cannot be always expected to indulge it to the compromise of its evident welfare.

Hearing that those plotting against the Government have falsely represented that the Government troops intended a forcible and violent invasion of Missouri for the purposes of military despotism and tyranny,

I hereby give notice to the people of this State that I shall scrupulously avoid all interferences with the business, rights, and property of every description recognized by the laws of this State, and belonging to law abiding citizens; but that it is equally my duty to maintain the paramount authority of the United States with such force as I have at my command, which will he retained only so long as opposition shall make it necessary; and that it is my wish, and shall be my purpose, to devolve any unavoidable rigor arising in this issue upon those only who provoke it.

All persons who, under the misapprehensions above mentioned, have taken up arms, or who are now preparing to do so, are invited to return to their homes, and relinquish their hostile attitude to the General Government, and are assured that they may do so without being molested for past occurrences.

N. LYON, Brigadier-General U. S. Vols., Com'g.

VIII. Proclamation of John Ross, Chief of the Cherokee Nation[8]

Jefferson City, June 24, 1861.

Several persons arrived here today from Southern Missouri, one of whom brings a proclamation issued by John Ross, of the Cherokee nation. Rev. T. O. Annay, a missionary among them left Tellfisho on the 5th of June and reports that Ben McCulloch and Albert Pike, of Arkansas, had been there, urging the chief to reconsider the position taken in his proclamation; but they failed in their object, and left for the Creek nation, hoping to get aid for the rebel cause. Captain Pike had an escort of seventy-five men.

Mr. Pierce [Price], paymaster of the Iowa regiments, was at Booneville.

The following is the proclamation in relation to the affairs pending among the people of the several States:

I, John Ross, principal Chief, hereby issue this my proclamation to the people of the Cherokee nation, reminding them of the obligation arising under their treaties with the United States, and urging them to the faithful observance of said treaties, and peace and friendship toward the people of all the States. The better to attain those important ends, I earnestly impress on all my fellow citizens the propriety of attending to their ordinary avocations, and to abstain from political discussions of the events transpiring in the States, and from partisan demonstrations in regard to the same.

They should not be alarmed with false reports thrown into circulation by designing men, but cultivate harmony among themselves, and observe strict neutrality between the States threatened with civil war. With these means alone can the Cherokee people hope to maintain their own soil and fireside spared from the hateful effects of devastating war. There has been no declaration of war between the opposing parties, and the conflict may yet be avoided with a compromise or a peaceable separation. The peculiar circumstance of their condition admonish the Cherokees to the exercise of prudence in regard to a state of affairs to the existence of which they have in no way contributed, and they should avoid the performance of any act, or the adoption of any policy calculated to destroy or endanger their territorial and civil rights. With an honest adherence to this course, they can give no just cause for aggression or invasion, nor any pretense for making their country the scene of military oppression, and will be in a situation to claim all their rights in the final adjustment that will take place between the several States.

For these reasons I earnestly urge on the Cherokee people the importance of non- interference with the people of the States, and the observance of unswerving neutrality between them. Trusting that God will not only keep from our own borders the desolation of war, but that He will, in His infinite mercy and honor stay its ravages among the brotherhood of the States.

Given under my hand at the executive office at Park Hill, this 17th day of May, 1861.

JOHN ROSS, Principal Chief.

IX. Proclamation of General Ben McCulloch, July 1, 1861[9]

Citizens of Arkansas

To defend your frontier, troops of Missouri are falling back upon you. If they are not sustained, your State will be invaded and your homes desolated. All that can arm themselves will rendezvous at Fayetteville, where they will await further orders. All those who have arms of the State, will march to the scene of action, or give their arms to those who will not desert their country in the hour of danger. All organized companies, whether cavalry or infantry, will report at Fayetteville, and will at once be formed into regiments and battalions.

The necessary subsistence stores will be forwarded from this post. Rally promptly, then, citizens of Arkansas, and let us drive this Northern horde back from whence they came.

BEN MCCULLOCH,
Brigadier General Commanding.

X. General Sweeny's Proclamation at Springfield, July 4, 1861[10]

To The Citizens of Southwest Missouri:

Your Governor has strove to cause the State to withdraw from the Union. Failing to accomplish this purpose by legislative enactment, he has already committed treason by levying war on the United States. He has endeavored to have you commit the same crime. Hence he has called for troops to enter the military service of the State – not to aid, but to oppose the government of the United States. The troops under my command are stationed in your midst by the proper authority of our government. They are among you not as enemies, but as friends and protectors of loyal citizens. Should an insurrection of your slaves take place, it would be my duty to suppress it, and I should use the force at my command for that purpose. It is my duty to protect all loyal citizens in the enjoyment and possession of all their property – slaves included. That duty shall be performed. I require all troops and armed men in this part of the State, now assembled, and which are arrayed against the government of the United States, to immediately disperse and return to their homes. If this should not be done without delay, those hordes of armed men will be taken prisoners or dispersed. I request every citizen who acknowledges he owes allegiance to the United States to aid me to prevent the shedding of blood and restore peace and quiet to this portion of the State. Those who have manifested a want of loyalty, either by word or act, toward the government of the United States, are requested to appear before me, or any officer in command of any post, or any detachment of troops under my command and take an oath of allegiance to our government. Gross misrepresentations of the oath, which has already been administered to many of your most respectable citizens, has been made. No loyal citizen will decline to take such an oath. It is the duty of every good citizen to bear allegiance to the government, and to support the constitution of the United States – not to encourage secessionism by word or act, and to obey all legal orders emanating from the constituted authorities of the land. No loyal citizen will bear arms against his government, or give aid and support to the enemies of the country. Such, in brief, are the obligations required. I assure you that the government of the United States will deal leniently, yet firmly, with all its citizens who have been misled, and who desire to maintain and preserve the best government ever devised by human wisdom.

T. W. SWEENY, U. S. A.
Brigadier General Commanding.

XI Judge Catron's Charge[11]

The charge was a lengthy document, occupying twenty pages of foolscap…its language in regard to treason – was the chief and leading feature of the paper – was to this effect:

1. That to constitute treason, there must be treasonable intent, as well as a treasonable overt act; and in order to make out treasonable intent and overt act, the part accused must have been leagued in a conspiracy to overthrow the government.
2. That there are certain constitutional guarantees, which passion nor the frenzy of the hour cannot touch; and among them is the right of expression and discussion and the freedom of the press.
3. That no sentiment, however hostile, can be held to be treasonable.
4. That the right of every citizen to bear arms is an inalienable right that cannot be infringed; and the fact of a citizen having arms, without

being in league with a hostile force, was not an act for which his liberty could be abridged.

5. That it is the duty of the Grand Jury to protect both the citizen and the government, and that they should not, on account of any fear, favor or affection, shrink from the discharge of that duty. As an arm of the judiciary, the Grand Jury should diligently inquire into all offenses brought to their knowledge, and bring to the bar of the United States Court all who have been guilty of unlawfully uniting against the government and the laws of the land.

XII. Franc Wilkie's Report on the Forsyth Action[12]

Springfield, Mo., July 24, 1861.

In my last, dated Saturday, I spoke of an expedition southward, and as I have just returned, I can give you full particulars. The command was under General Sweeney, and was composed of 1,200 men, 500 of whom were of the First Iowa Regiment under Lieutenant Colonel Merritt, Companies C and D, U. S. Dragoons, Captain Stanley and Lieutenant M. J. Kelley, one company of mounted Volunteers from Kansas, under Captain Wood, and a section of Captain Totten's Battery, under Lieutenant Sokalski. We had ten days' rations, and left with a view to break up a secession Camp at Forsyth, fifty-six miles from here, on the south side of the Ozark Mountains.

We left here about noon, and as the day was intensely hot, and many of the men had marched about eleven miles before reaching Springfield, the soldiers gave out by scores. Several, among whom was Lieutenant Marvin, of Company B, had sunstrokes; the dust was suffocating, and after marching seven miles, we camped on both sides of James Fork on White River. That night it rained as if the Indian Ocean had been upset on us – the thunder roared through the mountain tops as if ten thousand devils were howling from each peak, while the whole skies seemed for hours one incessant blaze of white ghastly flame. I generally enjoy quiet "family" thunder showers, but this was considered too much of what generally may be called a good thing, especially in the country. A hard shell Baptist Church served a majority of the men for protection; a hundred or so got in the covered bridge of the river, and a squad of reporters, enjoyed the hospitalities of the roof and fireside of an ardent secessionist in the vicinity, who rejoiced in the euphonic designation of Abner Dabbs.

The next morning (Sunday) it still rained – only a good deal harder – as if the Atlantic had been emptied into our Indian Ocean shower. We made fifteen miles that day, and halted, when for the first time since the night before, the rain "let up." That night I stayed with an old fellow of fifty-three, named James Vaughn, who owns a fine farm, and "heaps" of niggers right in the mountains. He had twelve children by his first wife, and now has another wife of twenty-two, who lately rejoiced the frosty-headed sire by presenting him with a couple of "tip top" first class babies. The much boasted of feat of Sarah, isn't so much ahead after all.

From this point to Forsyth it is thirty miles, along which on Monday our men pushed on with alacrity. The road lay down the mountains – now winding along a stupendous ridge, now skirting a ravine of dizzy depths, running up almost perpendicular ascents for miles or crossing mountain torrents, or running between vast heights and along the rocky channels of the dried up streams. At two PM we had reached a point four miles from Forsyth, where the cavalry halted to allow the infantry and artillery to come up. I rode half a mile and stopped at the house of an old woman, who asked which side I was on. I told her Price's (Price was the leader of one of the secession forces at Forsyth), when she said it was all right, and a few minutes after said that three men on foot just before passed on a run towards Forsyth. I communicated this to Captain Wood, who just then came up, and he instantly sent ten mounted men ahead to catch the fellows if possible. Not doubting they would give the alarm, Gen. Sweeney ordered the columns to advance. Companies C and D of Dragoons, under Captain Stanley, took the lead or rather followed the reporters of the New York *Herald*, Dubuque *Herald*, and the St. Louis *Democrat*, who spurred on in advance. After the Dragoons came the mounted Volunteers, then the Artillery and Infantry.

We started on a walk, and a half a mile ahead met two of the ten men coming back at the top of their horses' speed. One of them led a horse, upon which was strapped a young Missourian, while close behind came the other with a cocked revolver in one hand. They halted a moment; this fellow was one of three advanced pickets of the enemy; the other two had escaped and probably were in town ere this. The word was passed back to Gen. Sweeney, and in about five minutes came the order to advance. The road was down a steep ridge that terminated only at the town. Away we went, first a trot then a gallop, till the hills shook with the thundering tread of a squadron of five hundred horsemen dashing in column down the rocky descent. The stones and gravel flew, and so did we, and in next to no time we rounded a bend in the road that brought us in full sight of the town.

Thinking the Regulars might be aggrieved if the reporters kept ahead, I suggested to my quill-driving comrades that we should fall in behind them give them the first chance at the glory, and the bullets. This was consented to, Company C and D went ahead, Captain Wood advanced to the right of the Regulars, and then straight through a piece of timber, down through a cornfield, we charged at them. Swan Creek ran between us and the town, and a long time was spent in getting over, as the banks were thirty feet down and steep and the water breast high. However, companies C and D got across first, and formed on the other side, each man cocked his Sharpe's rifle and revolver, and then with a tremendous cheer the men dug their spurs into their horses and broke through the town.

From Swan Creek the land rises gently for three hundred yards to the centre of the village, and then slopes away gradually for a like distance to White River, which runs along the south side of the place. As the squadron reached the ridge, they caught sight of one hundred and fifty of the chivalry as they appeared in a woods lying some two hundred yards from the further bank of the river. The squadron galloped on towards the bank; I followed some six hundred yards behind, congratulating myself that I saw the chivalry "putting" for the timber that a battle wasn't so dangerous after all. Just then twe-r-r-r-r went a bullet straight from the direction I was going and close by my head, and the next instant it was tw-r-r-r-r tw-r-r-r tw-r-r-r-r-r, as if the whole air had suddenly become alive with invisible snakes or reptiles with peculiar hissing propensities. I drove in the spurs and put a substantial log house between myself and the bullets, satisfied to lose the beauty of the scene, providing I could avoid the necessity of meeting some of the leaden devils that were diving through the air as if vicious in their tendencies.

Off went the Dragoons from the horses, and as the Infantry advanced up to the bank and commenced a rapid fire upon the enemy, who, secured somewhat by the trees, were letting drive at us vigorously from the other side. Seventy-five or a hundred shots seemed sufficient for them, and they quit firing. I was standing on the north side of the log house, the enemy was on the south side of the river, to the east was a tremendous bluff. I was just congratulating myself upon my taste in selecting a house apparently so bullet proof, when whiz came a shower of bullets from the bluff. Here was a pretty fix! If I went round the house to get out of this fire, I should be exposed to the other, and there was no particular choice as to being shot at the gable end or in front of the house that stood near, a dilemma with neither horn preferable. Down went Captain Stanley's horse, shot through the lungs; another went tearing around with a ball in its leg; a third cut up some wild capers as a ball ploughed through its nose. And the men, too, seemed uncomfortable: one fellow did some tall swearing over a bullet hole that appeared "clean" through the calf of his leg; another was making wry faces over a similar orifice that suddenly went through his shoulders; a third unbuttoned his coat to find a half inch furrow ploughed straight across his chest. And I – well I expected it in the leg, head, back, arms, chest somewhere every second, and, I confess, just wished myself out of town, say a couple of miles. For about two minutes the bullets came spattering into the fences and tearing up the ground, when Captain Stanley gave the word to charge, The bugle rang out a few shrill notes, and the next instant Captain Stanley at the head of Co. D, and Lieutenant Kelly leading Co. C, breasted the bluff and rolled up it like a hurricane. Chivalry immediately betook itself to its heels, and "broke" for deeper timber, which, thank Heaven, was the last seen of them from that direction.

The Court House, a fine three story brick, stood in the centre of the town, and leading my horse into a blacksmith shop, I tied it, and walked into the Court House. The lower story was filled with benches and rifles, which the secessionists had abandoned in their hot haste. Accompanied by Captain Callaway of the Home Guards, and a Kansas Sergeant, we proceeded to the upper floor, which was filled with clothing. The Sergeant seated himself at a table, the Captain and I entered into a small talk, when – whang! For a second I thought the bluff had tipped over on the Court House, next that the comet had collided with mother earth, but finally concluded that somebody had sent a shell through the Court House. Through the dim media of flying brick and mortar I perceived the Captain bolting for the door; the Sergeant was getting himself unmixed from the bricks and table, in whose embraces he had rolled on the floor. Another second and I was doing "tall traveling" after Captain Callaway, only pausing the briefest part of a second to notice an immense opening in the wall, through which had broke the shell, passing between the Captain and myself, at about the height of our knees, and then tearing on had smashed through the partition beyond. Down stairs forty steps at a leap for all that I know, but not more than half down, myself in the rear, when again another tremendous whang, and something tore through just over my head, tearing things all to splinters, and sending me without further effort on my part, to the bottom of the stairway. I got up and dizzily staggered on and reached the door just as another shell tore through the lower story making kindling wood of a score of benches and burying itself in the south wall without exploding. I found a severe wound on the back of my head, from which the blood ran in streams, and for the moment supposed myself killed, as I felt so weak and unsteady – a mistake, however, as the writing of this letter (with a very sore head though) some thirty-six hours after will abundantly demonstrate.

But to return. About the time I entered the Court House the Artillery came up to a point in the road that overlooked the town, and Gen. Sweeney gave order to have the pieces brought to *bear* on the town. That was misunderstood by Lieutenant Sokalski, who supposed it was to *fire* on the town. Instantly he unlimbered his twelve-pound howitzer and sent three shells into the Court House before the mistake was discovered. Just then a body of secessionists made their appearance on the bluffs, and commenced a fire on the battery, which was flanked on the left by the Gov. Greys, under Captain F. Herron, and the Davenport Rifles, under Captain Wentz. Lieutenant Sokalski immediately put his twelve-pounder to a better use than firing shells at a reporter, by sending three charges of grape into the enemy, all of whom but four or five left instanter and have not since been visible. The four or five that staid, stay there yet if their friends have not carried them away.

And thus ended the "battle" or "affair," as the case may be. The Greys and Davenport Rifles were under fire for a few moments, and stood the initiation with perfect composure. The men were all anxious for a fight, for when the word was passed back to the Infantry to hurry op, they struck into double-quick and ran a distance of over three miles, notwithstanding that they had already traveled twenty-seven long and tedious miles the same day. Two men, one of whom was a Corporal, from some Iowa Companies, were away behind among the wagons when the head of the column began the attack. They were both lame and could scarcely bobble along, when word came back of the fighting in front; they tried to run, but broke down, and just then they passed an old, half-starved mule tied by a halter to the bushes. In a trice both were on her bare back, and the next instant were going down the column at as tremendous a gallop as their indifferent steed could be induced to afford at the suggestions of a well-plied cudgel and rope's end. In the sick wagon were a dozen or more men, completely used up; word came back that they were fighting ahead, and in a second half of them were out and on a dead run for the scene of the conflict. These and a dozen other similar instances which I might relate, will serve to show the spirit of our men, and their anxiety for a fight.

The result of our victory was the capture of two prisoners and a large amount of clothing, blankets, rifles, swords, and a quantity of lead which was fished up from a well into which it had been thrown by the secessionists just before leaving.

The operation is important, as it breaks up a force of four hundred men, who have been drilling for weeks at that place under Captains Price and Jackson, and who have created much disturbance in a large extent of country by their operations. If Gen. Sweeney had only made a detour with his cavalry and surrounded the town, he would have captured every soul; why he did not I am unable to state. I apprehend that Gen. Lyon will press for information on this point at an early opportunity.

The command remained till Tuesday noon, and then set out on its return, and will probably reach here by noon tomorrow. I left there at three PM yesterday, and came through to Springfield in six hours, bringing the intelligence of the skirmish.

The trip through is not one of great interest; the road is wholly through a mountainous country; the houses are far between; the inhabitants generally of a class but little above intelligent dogs; the married women mostly smoke, and a respectable minority chew tobacco, while five-sixths of the most interesting young ladies I saw were either smoking a short corn-cob pipe or nursing a baby – either operation being sufficient to destroy all the romance connected with a gentle Miss of sweet sixteen or thereabouts.

We lost two horses and had three men (without including myself) slightly wounded. The enemy lost five killed and thirteen wounded; among the former was supposed to be Jackson, their leader.

XIII. Frémont's Proclamation[3]

HEAD-QUARTERS OF THE WESTERN DEPARTMENT,
St. Louis, Aug. 31, 1861.

Circumstances, in my judgment, of sufficient urgency, render it necessary that the Commanding General of this Department should assume the administrative powers of the State. Its disorganized condition, the helplessness of the civil authority, the total insecurity of life, and the devastation of property by bands of murderers and marauders, who infest nearly every county in the State, and avail themselves of the public misfortunes and the vicinity of a hostile force to gratify private and neighborhood vengeance, and who find an enemy wherever they find plunder, finally demand the severest measures to repress the daily increasing crimes and outrages which are driving off the inhabitants and ruining the State.

In this condition the public safety and the success of our arms require unity of purpose, without let or hindrance, to the prompt administration of affairs. In order, therefore, to suppress disorders, to maintain, as far as now practicable, the public peace, and to give security and protection

Appendix

to the persons and property of loyal citizens, I do hereby extend and declare established martial law throughout the State of Missouri. The lines of the Army of occupation in this State are for the present declared to extend from Leavenworth, by way of the posts of Jefferson City, Rolla, and Ironton, to Cape Girardeau, on the Mississippi River. All persons who shall be taken with arms in their hands, within these lines, shall be tried by Court Martial, and, if found guilty, will be shot. The property, real and personal, of all persons in the State of Missouri, who shall take up arms against the United States, or who shall be directly proven to have taken active part with their enemies in the field, is declared to be confiscated to the public use, and their slaves, if any they have, are hereby declared free men.

All persons who shall be proven to have destroyed, after the publication of this order, railroad tracks, bridges or telegraphs, shall suffer the extreme penalty of the law.

All persons engaged in treasonable correspondence, in giving or procuring aid to the enemies of the United States, in disturbing the public tranquility by creating and circulating false reports or incendiary documents, are in their own interest warned that they are exposing themselves.

All persons who have been led away from their allegiance are required to return to their homes forthwith; any such absence without sufficient cause will be held to be presumptive evidence against them.

The object of this declaration is to place in the hands of the military authorities the power to give instantaneous effect to existing laws, and to supply such deficiencies as the conditions of war demand. But it is not intended to suspend the ordinary tribunals of the country, where the law will be administered by the civil officers in the usual manner and with their customary authority, while the same can be peaceably exercised.

The Commanding-General will labor vigilantly for the public welfare, and in his efforts for their safety hopes to obtain not only the acquiescence, but the active support of the people of the country.

(Signed) J. C. FRÉMONT,
Major-General Commanding.

XIV. Martial Law in Missouri: The Fall of Lexington[14]

We publish below the article of the *St. Louis Daily Evening News* on the "Fall of Lexington," for the publication of which its proprietor, Mr. Charles G. Ramsey, and editor, Mr. D. M. Grissom, were arrested and the paper suppressed. It seems that military authorities are willing enough to be praised, but cannot endure to be criticized by the newspapers. The *Evening News* is, and has always been, a staunch Union paper, and its statements in regard to the loss of Lexington are moderate compared with the utterances of the Press generally on that shameful affair:

Lexington is fallen. We write it with sorrow, for it is a heavy reverse to our arms in Missouri – the twin disaster to the reverse at Springfield, and, like that reverse, easily avoidable, had prompt steps been taken. The gallant garrison, under their heroic Irish commander after resisting with unflinching courage for six days, and repulsing the assaults of the quadruple force, beleaguered on every side, penned up within the narrow limits of earthwork defenses, wearied to exhaustion with incessant watching and fighting, was compelled, at last, to yield to that too more terrible to the brave soldier than bullet or bayonet – thirst – and surrender his courageous band as prisoners of war. He might, and no doubt would, have resisted longer, had not his supplies of water been cut off; but the intrenchments at Lexington were not supplied with wells and other conveniences of a stone fort, because they were not constructed with the design of resisting a week's siege. Hence, when the garrison was cut off from its supplies of water from the river and the wells in the vicinity, there was no alternative for the furnished men but a surrender. They are now in the hands of the enemy, who, by this triumph, secures possession of about 4,000 stand of arms, 700 cavalry horses, with their equipments, a considerable quantity of ammunition, several pieces of artillery, and the most important city of Western Missouri.

Col. Mulligan perhaps never dreamed of the possibility of not being reinforced. It never entered into his thoughts that with 40,000 friendly National troops within a few days' march of him, he could be neglected and left to the mercy of a besieging force for a whole week, and finally compelled to surrender for the want of the succor which could have been sent, and which, no doubt, he confidently presumed would be sent. It was with the confident conviction of being promptly supported that, when asked to surrender by Price on Sunday, the 15th, he answered with a ringing defiance, and instantly prepared for a desperate combat. He thought, that if he should hold out for three days – and he resolved that he would – he would be reinforced from the river, or the enemy attacked in the rear and forced to raise the siege.

But the heroic officer calculated too largely on the cooperation of the authorities at St. Louis. Price arrived at Warrensburgh, thirty-five miles from Lexington, two weeks ago, yesterday. Everybody knows that he was marching on Lexington, and that he would make a desperate attempt to take it.

But we cannot think that Price himself ever imagined he would be allowed leisurely to march to Lexington, surround the garrison, and beleaguer it for a whole week, without being disturbed in his amateur-like operations by any of the thirty or forty thousand National troops that were within a few days' march of him.

He, perhaps, never conjectured that he could, with a ragged, ill-armed, unpaid, half demoralized army, without a baggage train, and with a poor supply of war material, march all the way from Springfield over a rugged road, and attack and capture a Federal garrison, supported, or that ought to have been supported, by a department that has hundreds and thousands of tons or shot, shell, powder, cannon artillery, muskets and rifles, and that has command of all the rivers, all the railroads, and all the steamboats in the State, for the speedy transportation of men and material to any point of danger.

But so it is, and Price and Jackson and Parsons, in their exultations over their unlooked for victory, must feel even more surprise than we do, at being allowed to achieve it without interruption.

XV. Frémont's Staff, October, 1861[15]

Chief of Staff – Brigadier General A. Asboth. Hungarian. Came to St. Louis from New York with Frémont.

Assistant Adjutant General – Capt. Chauncey McKeeven. 1849 USMA. Later on staff of Gen. Samuel P. Heitzelman as Major. Later, assistant to Provost Marshall General in charge of mustering and disbursing. Brevetted Brig. Gen. March, 1865. Retired in 1893 with rank of Colonel.

Military Secretary and Senior Aide-de-camp – Col. J. H. Eaton. This was Joseph H. Eaton, West Point, 43/56 in Class of 1835. Fought in Mexican War. Continued service in Paymaster Dept. in Washington.

Chief Topographical Engineer – Col. John T. Fiala, One of the Hungarians. In the 1860 *Missouri Gazetteer* he was listed as "topographical engineer, living on Menard, between Marine & Park Avenues." Followed Frémont to Mountain Division. Took sick, recovered in Iowa. Died in CA in 1911.

Chief of Ordinance – Col. Gustav Waagner, Hungarian emigre. Served McClellan, sent to Cairo to train troops & build fortifications. Transferred to Frémont's Staff. Grant to Frémont, Sept. 22: "Col. Waagner, Chief of Ordinance, left here this evening in pursuance of orders telegraphed to him. His energy and ability have been of great service to me, particularly in directing reconnaissances, and his loss from this post will be felt."

Chief of Artillery – Col. Jas. Totten. Fought at Wilson's Creek, was retained on Halleck's staff as Lt. Col. Chief of Artillery.

Judge Advocate – Maj. R. M. Corwine. Went with Frémont to Ohio & WV. Dept. Judge Advocate in Cincinnati. Before the war, he was an attorney in Cincinnati.

Division Surgeon – Dr. T. Telkampe. Not in St. Louis Physicians list in 1860 *Missouri Gazetteer*. Theodore A. Telkampf was a New York doctor, probably a Frémont friend.

Assistant Surgeon – Dr. John Cooper. Went on to be in charge of hospitals in Alexandria, VA & New Orleans. Then assigned to 15th & 17th Army Corps. Invented ambulance dubbed, "Cooper's Pie Wagon."

Acting Assistant Quartermaster General – Major Robert Allen. Remained in Quartermaster Service, March 13, 1863, Brigadier General of Volunteers; Brevet Brig. General, Regular Army, July 4, 1864. Oct. 1861, "If the reckless Expenditures in this department are not checked by stronger arm than mine, the Quartermaster's Department will be wrecked in Missouri alone." He was retained on Halleck's staff as chief of Quartermaster Department. (Justus McKinstry had left his quartermaster post on being named Brigadier General, commanding one of Frémont's divisions.)

Assistant Quartermaster – Capt. E. M. Davis. Exposed as thief, "whose fraud in procuring military supplies was breathtakingly diverse."

Deputy Paymaster General – Lt. Col. T. P. Andrews. Was retained on Halleck's staff as chief of pay department.

Commander of Body Guard – Major Chas. Zagonyi.

Musical Director – Capt. A. Waldauer. St. Louis theater director, musician, composer, and one of the founders of the St. Louis Symphony Orchestra after the war.

Aides-de-Camp:

Col. Anselm Albert – aide to Chief of Staff. Formerly Lt. Col. to Sigel at Wilson's Creek.

Col. Gustav Koener. – Illinois (Belleville) politician, helped raise German volunteer regiments.

Col. J. P. C. Shanks. – Indiana radical abolitionist. Later: Dept. Of Mississippi, District of West Tennessee, Post of Columbus, KY, Commanded First Brigade of Cavalry Division as Colonel. Also Col. 7th Indiana Cavalry.

Col. John A. Gurley – From Ohio. Owned newspaper before election. Elected to represent Ohio in the U. S. House of Representatives, 1859–1863. Lincoln appointed him as first Governor of Arizona Terr., but he died before taking office.

Col. I. C. Woods – Aide-de-Camp and Director of Transportation. Also called "Chief Business manager" by Gurley in Oct. 1 letter to Lincoln. Gurley sent to Washington to ask for money, Woods requested $12 million. Contracts were not paid.

Col. R. N. Hudson – Owner & Editor, *Terre Haute Journal* after the war. In 1864 he organized an infantry regiment in Indiana.

Major James W. Savage – Aide-de-camp and Military "Registrator & Expeditor." Further data not found.

Major Frank J. White – Aide-de-camp. Commanded First Squadron of Prairie Scouts, took part troops took part in Zagonyi's charge.

Major William Dorsheimer – Aide-de-camp and Private Secretary. Returned to civilian life, wrote an article on Frémont's 100 days, which appeared in the *Atlantic Monthly*, Jan,–March, 1862.

Major B. Rush Plumley – Aide-de-camp, and Postal Director. Jewish. Later lived in Texas. Poet.

Captain J. R. Howard – Aide-de-camp and Private Secretary. From Brooklyn, old friend from California.

Captain Leonidas Haskell – Aide-de-camp and Police Director. Hungarian? Friend from California. One of the nest of thieves around Frémont. A contractor for mules as well as on his staff in California, at Fort Mason, San Francisco. Also friend of Jessie Benton Frémont. Leonidas Haskell was very politically active and well-connected as a "free-soiler." He helped develop the Black Point area and shaped the political thinking of the region. As one of the real estate developers of the Black Point neighborhood, he helped shape and direct the political leanings of this civilian community. At the outbreak of the Civil War in 1861, Black Point was taken over to expand Fort Mason. John Frémont returned to military service as commanding general of the Department of the West; his wife Jessie moved with him to St. Louis. The Frémont's neighbor and longtime friend, Leonidas Haskell, accompanied them to serve on his staff. Haskell remained with Frémont in West Virginia, and was promoted to Major & Asst. Chief of Cavalry.

Captain Joseph Reminfy – Hungarian. Otherwise, not found. May be spelled Reminyfi.

Lieutenant Joseph Mc Cullagh – Corresponding & Phonographic Secretary, also correspondent for *Cincinnati Inquirer*.

XVI. Frémont-Price Treaty[16]

HEADQUARTERS WESTERN DEPARTMENT,
Springfield, Mo., November 7, 1861.

Whereas, Maj. Gen. Sterling Price, commanding the Missouri State Guard, by letter dated at his headquarters, near Neosho, Mo., October 26, 1861, has expressed a desire to enter into some arrangement with Maj. Gen. John C. Frémont, commanding the forces of the United States, to facilitate the future exchange of prisoners of war released on parole; also that all persons heretofore arrested for the mere expression of political opinions may be released from confinement or parole; also that in future the war be confined exclusively to the armies in the field, and has authorized and empowered Maj. Henry W. Williams and D. Robert Barclay, Esq., to enter into such an arrangement in his behalf; and

Whereas, Maj. Gen. John C. Frémont concurs with Major-General Price:
Now therefore it is hereby stipulated and agreed by and between Maj. Gen. John C. Frémont and Maj. Gen. Sterling Price as follows, to wit:

First. A joint proclamation shall be issued signed by Major-General Frémont and Major-General Price in roper person in the following language, to wit:

Proclamation.

To All Peaceably Disposed Citizens of the State of Missouri Greeting:

Whereas, a solemn agreement has been entered into by and between Major-Generals Frémont and Price, respectively commanding antagonistic forces in the State of Missouri, to the effect that in the future arrests or forcible interference by armed or unarmed parties of citizens within the limits of said State for the mere entertainment or expression of political opinions shall hereafter cease; that families now broken up for such causes may be reunited, and that the war now progressing shall be exclusively confined to armies in the field;

Therefore be it known to all whom it may concern.

No arrests whatever on account of political opinions or for the merely private expression of the same shall hereafter be made within the limits of the State of Missouri, and all persons who may have been arrested and are now held to answer upon such charges only shall be forthwith released; but it is expressly declared that nothing in this proclamation shall be construed to bar or interfere with any of the usual and regular proceedings of the established courts under statutes and orders made and provided for such offenses.

All peaceably disposed citizens who may have been driven from their homes because of their political opinions or who may have left them from fear of force and violence are hereby advised and permitted to return upon the faith of our positive assurances that while so returning they shall receive protection from both the armies in the field wherever it can be given.

All bodies of armed men acting without the authority or recognition of the major-generals before named and not legitimately connected with the armies in the field are hereby ordered at once to disband.

Any violation of either of the foregoing articles shall subject the offender to the penalty of military law according to the nature of the offense. In testimony whereof the aforesaid Maj. Gen. John Charles Frémont, at Springfield, Mo., on this 1st day of November, A. D. 1861, and Maj. Gen. Sterling Price, at Cassville, Mo., on this 5th day of November, A. D. 1861, have hereunto set their hands and hereby mutually pledge their earnest efforts to the enforcement of the above articles of agreement according to their full tenor and effect to the best of their ability.

J. C. FRÉMONT,
Major-General, Commanding.

STERLING PRICE,
Major- General, Commanding.

HEADQUARTERS WESTERN DEPARTMENT,
Springfield, Mo., November 7, 1861.[16]

Maj. Gen. Sterling Price,
Commanding Forces at Cassville, Mo.

GENERAL: Referring to an agreement purporting to have been made between Major Generals Frémont and Price, respectively commanding antagonistic forces in the State of Missouri, to the effect that in future arrests or forcible interference by armed or unarmed parties of citizens within the limits of said State for the mere entertainment or expression of political opinions shall hereafter cease, that families now broken up for such causes may be reunited, and that the war now progressing shall be exclusively confined to armies in the field, I have to state that as general commanding the forces of the United States in this department I can in no manner recognize the agreement aforesaid or any of its provisions whether implied or direct, and that I can neither issue nor allow to be issued the joint proclamation purporting to have been signed by yourself and Maj. Gen. John C. Frémont on the 1st day of November, A. D. 1861.

Very respectfully, your obedient servant,

D. HUNTER,
Major General, Commanding.

XVII. McClellan's Instructions to Halleck[17]

HEADQUARTERS OF THE ARMY,
Washington, D. C., November 11, 1861.

GENERAL: In assigning you to the command of the Department of the Missouri, it is probably unnecessary for me to state that I have entrusted to you a duty which requires the utmost tact and decision. You have not merely the ordinary duties of a military commander to perform, but the far more difficult task of reducing chaos to order, of changing probably the majority of the personnel of the staff of the department, and of reducing to a point of economy, consistent with the interests and necessities of the

State, a system of reckless expenditure and fraud, perhaps unheard-of before in the history of the world.

You will find in your department many general and staff officers holding illegal commissions and appointments not recognized or approved by the President or Secretary of War. You will please at once inform these gentlemen of the nullity of their appointment, and see that no pay or allowances are issued to them until such time as commissions may be authorized by the President or Secretary of War.

If any of them give the slightest trouble, you will at once arrest them and send them, under guard, out of the limits of your department, informing them that if they return they will be placed in close confinement. You will please examine into the legality of the organization of the troops serving in the department. When you find any illegal, unusual, or improper organizations, you will give to the officers and men an opportunity to enter the legal military establishment under general laws and orders from the War Department, reporting in full to these headquarters any officer or organization that may decline.

You will please cause competent and reliable staff officers to examine all existing contracts immediately, and suspend all payments upon them until you receive the report in each case. Where there is the slightest doubt as to the propriety of the contract, you will be good enough to refer the matter with full explanation to these headquarters, stating in each case what would be a fair compensation for the services or materials rendered under the contract. Discontinue at once the reception of material or services under any doubtful contract. Arrest and bring to prompt trial all officers who have in any way violated their duty to the Government. In regard to the political conduct of affairs, you will please labor to impress upon the inhabitants of Missouri and the adjacent States that we are fighting solely for the integrity of the Union, to uphold the power of our National Government, and to restore to the nation the blessings of peace and good order.

With respect to military operations, it is probable, from the best information in my possession, that the interests of the Government will be best served by fortifying and holding in considerable strength Rolla, Sedalia, and other interior points, keeping strong patrols constantly moving from the terminal stations, and concentrating the mass of the troops on or near the Mississippi, prepared for such ulterior operations as the public interests may demand.

I would be glad to have you, make, as soon as possible, a personal inspection of all the important points in your department, and report the result to me. I cannot too strongly impress upon you the absolute necessity of keeping me constantly advised of the strength, condition, and location of your troops, together with all facts that will enable me to maintain that general direction of the armies of the United States which it is my purpose to exercise. I trust to you to maintain thorough organization, discipline, and economy throughout your department. Please inform me as soon as possible of everything relating to the gunboats now in process of construction as well as those completed.

The militia force authorized to be raised by the State of Missouri for its defense will be under your orders.

I am, general, &c.,

GEO. B. MCCLELLAN,
Major-General, Commanding U. S. Army.

XVIII. Hamilton Gamble, Calling State Militia into Service[18]

The powers of the civil authorities being insufficient to protect the lives and property of the citizens of the State, I, HAMILTON R. GAMBLE, Governor of the State of Missouri, do hereby call into the active service of the State, forty-two thousand men of the Militia of the State, assigning six thousand as the quota for each Military District, which is the same as a Congressional District. The force thus called into the service will be, as far as possible, a volunteer force, and will consist of ten thousand Cavalry, and thirty-two thousand Infantry. If the number volunteering should exceed this requisition, the excess will be held as a reserve corps. If there should be a deficiency, it may become necessary to resort to a draft. The Adjutant General will issue to the Division Inspectors of the several

Military Districts, the order necessary to carry this requisition into effect. The force called out will be for six months, unless peace in the State be sooner restored. Arms will be furnished as rapidly as they can be had.

Given under my hand and the seal of the State, at Jefferson City, this twenty-fourth day of August, in the year eighteen hundred and sixty-one.

H. R. GAMBLE.

By the Governor:
M. OLIVER, Secretary of State.

XIX. Letters Exchanged Between Generals Price and Halleck, January, 1862[19]

HEADQUARTERS MO. STATE GUARD,
Camp at Springfield, January 12, 1862.

Maj. Gen. H. W. HALLECK, Commanding U. S. Forces in the Western Department:

GENERAL: I have received information that, as major-general commanding in this department, you have either ordered or allowed the arrest of citizens in the pursuit of their usual and peaceful avocations; that men, officers and privates, belonging to this army have been taken prisoners on the Kansas border and conveyed to Fort Leavenworth, and as such, and for no other established offense or crime, have been shot. In some cases I have learned that my discharged soldiers have been seized whenever and wherever they have shown themselves, and that they have been by military coercion forced into a servitude unknown to international and civilized usages in such cases. I have obtained information that individuals and parties of men specially appointed and instructed by me to destroy railroads culverts and bridges, by tearing them up, burning, &c, have been arrested and subjected to a general court-martial for alleged crimes, which all the laws of warfare heretofore recognized by the civilized world have regarded as distinctly lawful and proper. I have learned that such persons, when tried, if convicted of the offense or offenses as stated, are viewed as lawful subjects for capital punishment.

These statements, brought to me in various ways, I cannot believe to be correct. It is upon this subject that I now propose to address you. It is necessary that we understand each other and have some guiding knowledge of that character of warfare which is to be waged by our respective Governments. This understanding should be given *at once*. It is desirable both by you and me. Both armies desire it, and the exigencies of the war demand that some certain rules should be the basis of our conduct and control. Delay is vital. It cannot be allowed. *We must understand each other.* Do you intend to continue the arrest of citizens engaged in their ordinary peaceful pursuits and treat them as traitors and rebels; if so, will you make exchanges with me for such as I may or will make for similar causes? Do you intend to regard members of this army as persons deserving death *whenever* and *wherever* they may be captured, or will you extend the recognized rights of prisoners of war by the code of the civilized world?

Do you regard – and state as such the law governing your army – the destruction of important roads, transportation facilities, &c., for military purposes, as the legal right of a belligerent power? Do you intend to regard men whom I have specially dispatched to destroy roads, burn bridges, tear up culverts, &c., as amenable to an enemy's court-martial, or will you have them to be tried as usual, by the proper authorities, according to the statutes of the State? It is vastly important to the interests of all parties concerned that these momentous issues should be determined. No man deplores the horrors of war more than I do; no one will sacrifice more to avert its desolating march. Each party must be heard. Each must have a kind of common protection. I am willing to afford this. It remains with you to decide the question with that frankness which attends your official communications. I await your reply.

I am, general, very respectfully, your obedient servant,
STERLING PRICE,
Major-General, Commanding Mo. S. G.

Saint Louis, *January 22, 1862.*

General Sterling Price, *Commanding, &c.*

GENERAL: Your letter, dated Springfield, January 12, is received. The troops of which you complain on the Kansas frontier and at Fort Leavenworth are not under my command. In regard to them I respectfully refer you to Maj. Gen. David Hunter, commanding Department of Kansas, headquarters at Fort Leavenworth.

You also complain that "individuals and parties of men specially appointed and instructed by you to destroy railroads, culverts, and bridges, by tearing them up, burning, &c., have been arrested and subjected to a general court-martial for alleged crimes." This statement is, in the main, correct. Where individuals and parties of men violate the laws of war they will be tried, and if found guilty will certainly be punished, whether acting under your "special appointment and instructions" or not. You must be aware, general, that no orders of yours can save from punishment spies, marauders, robbers, incendiaries, guerrilla bands, &c., who violate the laws of war. You cannot give immunity to crime. But let us fully understand each other on this point. If you send armed forces, wearing the garb of soldiers and duly organized and enrolled as legitimate belligerents, to destroy railroads, bridges, & c., as a military act, we shall kill them, if possible, in open warfare, or, if we capture them, we shall treat them as prisoners of war.

But it is well understood that you have sent numbers of your adherents, in the garb of peaceful citizens and under false pretenses, through our lines into Northern Missouri, to rob and destroy the property of Union men and to burn and destroy railroad bridges, thus endangering the lives of thousands, and this, too, without any military necessity or possible military advantage.

Moreover, peaceful citizens of Missouri, quietly working on their farms, have been instigated by your emissaries to take up arms as insurgents, and to rob and plunder and to commit arson and murder. They do not even act under the garb of soldiers, but under false pretenses and in the guise of peaceful citizens. You certainly will not pretend that men guilty of such crimes, although "specially appointed and instructed by you," are entitled to the rights and immunities of ordinary prisoners of war. If you do, will you refer me to a single authority on the laws of war which recognizes such a claim?

You may rest assured, general, that all prisoners of war not guilty of crime will be treated with all proper consideration and kindness. With the exception of being properly confined, they will be lodged and fed, and where necessary clothed, the same as our own troops. I am sorry to say that our prisoners who have come from your camps do not report such treatment on your part. They say that you gave them no rations, no clothing, no blankets, but left them to perish with want and cold. Moreover, it is believed that you subsist your troops by robbing and plundering the non-combatant Union inhabitants of the southwestern counties of this State. Thousands of poor families have fled to us for protection and support. They say that your troops robbed them of their provisions and clothing, carrying away their shoes and bedding, and even cutting cloth from their looms, and that you have driven women and children from their homes to starve and perish in the cold. I have not retaliated such conduct upon your adherents here as I have no intention of waging such a barbarous warfare; but I shall, whenever I can, punish such crimes, by whomsoever they may be committed.

I am daily expecting instructions respecting an exchange of prisoners of war. I will communicate with you on that subject as soon as they are received.

Very respectfully, your obedient servant,
H. W. HALLECK,
Major- General, Commanding Department.

Endnotes

Preface

1. The source of this quotation is uncertain, but variations of it appear as early as the 1940s in the *Washington Post.*
2. See for example the books by Adamson (1961), Gerteis (2001), McElroy (1909), Monaghan (1984), Parrish (1963), Peckham (1866), Rombauer (1909), Rowan (1983), Snead (1886), Winter (1994) and others. Multiple articles and short studies as well as theses have also appeared.
3. Knox, *Camp-fire and Cotton-field*, 3, 5.

Introduction

1. Alice L. Bates, "The History of the Telegraph in California," *Annual Publication of the Historical Society of Southern California* 9, no. 3 (1914), 185.
2. Junius Henri Browne, *Four Years in Secessia* (Hartford, CT: O. D. Case & Co., 1865), 13.
3. Ibid., 21.
4. J. Cutler Andrews, *The North Reports the Civil War* (Pittsburgh: University of Pittsburgh Press, 1955), 66.
5. His sister, Emily, in the 1850 census, was living in Northfield, NH, in the household of Cylas Green, a Methodist minister and his wife, who apparently ran a boarding school. In the 1855 Massachusetts State census, she is found married to James A. Chapman, a Methodist minister, and living in Blackstone, MA. They moved to Boston (1865), New York (1880), and in 1900, they were living in Greenland, Rockingham County, NH. He was a farmer, with a hired hand, apparently having retired from the ministry. In the 1910 census, she is living with

her unmarried daughter, Mattie in Philadelphia. She died, age 86, in 1915 and is buried in Greenland, NH.
6. 1850 Census records of Epsom, Merrimack County, NH. No other concrete information on his life between the death of his mother in 1840 and his activities as a journalist in 1860 was found.
7. Kingston Academy was established in 1819 under the patronage of the Methodist Church, and "men of influence and fame were among its pupils." After the Civil War, the school declined and disappeared. No record can be found of Thomas W. Knox at the school. Fellow journalists noted that he had been a teacher, but gave no specifics of where beyond "New England."
8. Louise Barry, ed. "Albert D. Richardson's Letters on the Pike's Peak Gold Region," *Kansas Historical Quarterly* 12, no. 1 (February 1943), 16.
9. Colorado Territory was established from the western portion of Kansas Territory on February 28, 1861.
10. The *Western Mountaineer* was published in Golden from December 7, 1859 to December 20, 1860. Center for Colorado & the West at Auraria Library: http://skyline.ucdenver.edu/record=b2000473~S0
11. *Rocky Mountain News Weekly*, March 6, 1872.
12. This piece is from "To Pike's Peak and Denver" that appeared in the August 1861 issue of *Knickerbocker's New York Monthly Magazine*. Quote from pp. 126–127.
13. Knox, *Camp-fire and Cotton-field*, 20.
14. Ibid., 21. This observation may have been true on election day, but the results infuriated St. Joseph's Mayor M. Jeff Thompson, a rabid secessionist. Turmoil in the town soon followed.
15. Ibid., 20.
16. Mitchel P. Roth, *Historical Dictionary of War Journalism* (Westport, CT: Greenwood Press, 1997), 367–376.
17. Franc B. Wilkie, *Pen and Powder* (Boston: Ticknor and Company, 1888), 23.

Chapter 1

1. Albert D. Richardson, *The Secret Service, the Field, the Dungeon and the Escape* (Hartford, CT: American Publishing Company, 1865), 125.; Knox, *Camp-fire and Cotton-field*, 24.
2. Richardson, *Secret Service*, 131.
3. Emmet Crozier, *Yankee Reporters, 1861–1865* (New York: Oxford University Press, 1956), 63. Crozier gives the date of May 15 without attribution. It is probable they arrived a few days earlier.
4. Knox, *Camp-fire and Cotton-field*, 25.
5. Ibid., 26.
6. *New York Herald*, May 17, 1861. Dispatch dated May 10.
7. William C. Winter, *The Civil War in St. Louis: A Guided Tour* (St. Louis: Missouri Historical Society, 1994), 36–37, 49–53. Captain Lyon had arrived with his company of men from Fort Leavenworth to reinforce the garrison at the Arsenal. He quickly made common cause with Frank Blair and other leading Unionists. Daniel Frost, Brigadier General of the State Militia had made common cause with Governor Claiborne Jackson, hoping to lead Missouri out of the Union.
8. *New York Herald*, May 12, 1861, 4.
9. Colonel John McNeil (1813–1891) led the 3rd Regiment U S. Reserve Corps Infantry. He later commanded in Northeast Missouri and was appointed brigadier general of volunteers to date from November 29, 1862. Colonel Egbert Brown (1816–1902) served as Lt. Col. of the 7th Missouri Volunteer Infantry Regiment. He was appointed brigadier general of volunteers to rank from November 29, 1862.
10. James Montgomery (1814–1871) of Kansas was an ardent abolitionist who wanted to drive all slavery out of his state. He also raided into Missouri. In November 1860, Missouri's Governor Robert M. Stewart (a "lame duck" who retained office until Claiborne Jackson, elected in August, 1860, was inaugurated on January 1, 1861) sent a "Southwest Expedition" of some 600 state militiamen, largely from St. Louis, to the border counties to suppress Montgomery's jay hawking raids. Simultaneously, federal troops led by Captain Nathaniel Lyon arrived

to attempt to capture Montgomery and Charles Jennison. Both were unsuccessful.
11. *New York Herald*, May 14, 1861.
12. Winter, 51.
13. *New York Herald*, May 14, 1861. Harney's proclamation of May 12 may be found in the Appendix.
14. Charles G. Stifel (1819–1900) a successful St. Louis brewer, began training men in his brewery in 1860 with muskets he purchased himself. He led the 5th Reserve Corps volunteers until resigning in early 1862 to return to his ailing brewery.
15. *New York Herald*, May 14, 1861.
16. *Harper's Weekly*, June 1, 1861. M. Hastings was Matthew Hastings, 1834–1919, a St. Louis painter and illustrator.
17. *New York Herald*, May 13, 1861.
18. Ibid., May 16, 1861.
19. Ibid., May 18, 1861. The State Tobacco Warehouse was located at 6th and Washington in St. Louis.
20. Ibid.
21. *New York Herald*, May 29, 1861.
22. Keevil's Corinthian Hall was a hat manufacturer located at 267–271 Broadway.
23. *New York Herald*, May 29, 1861.
24. Ibid.
25. Gibson, Charles D. and E. Kay Gibson, *Dictionary of Transports and Combatant Vessels, Steam and Sail, Employed by the Union Army*. vol. 1, *The Army's Navy Series* (Camden, ME: Ensign Press, 1995), 156.
26. *New York Herald*, May 24, 1861. Harlow's Landing was in Monroe County, Illinois.
27. *St. Louis Missouri Republican*, May 23, 1861.
28. Gibson, 61.
29. *New York Herald*. May 28.
30. *O.R.*, Series 1, vol. 3:374–375. The agreement is found in item III of the Appendix.
31. Ibid., 376.

32. Ibid., 377.
33. *New York Herald,* May 22, 1861.
34. Ezra Warner, *Generals in Blue* (Baton Rouge, LA: Louisiana State University Press. 1992), 287.
35. *O.R.,* Series 1, vol. 3:381.
36. *New York Herald,* May 26, 1861. Fear in St. Joseph was probably justified because St. Joseph had been a major source of pro-slavery manpower during the "bleeding Kansas" episodes of the 1850s. In 1861, St. Joseph's mayor was M. Jeff Thompson, an avid secessionist, who later served as a brigadier general in the Missouri State Guard.
37. Ibid.
38. Ibid.
39. Ibid.
40. Winter, 65.
41. *New York Herald.* May 29, 1861.
42. Ibid. This anecdote is repeated, almost word for word, in Richardson, *Secret Service,* 140.
43. *New York Herald,* May 29, 1861.
44. Ibid.
45. Ibid.
46. Ibid.
47. Ibid., May 31, 1861.
48. These were Captains Basil W. Duke and Joseph Kelly. Duke was one of the two representatives (along with Colton Greene) sent to New Orleans to obtain armaments from the captured Baton Rouge Arsenal. Joseph Kelly was captain of the Washington Blues militia company. Both men avoided capture at Camp Jackson as they had been detached to escort arms and ammunition to Jefferson City.
49. *New York Herald,* May 31, 1861.
50. Ibid.
51. Ibid., June 1, 1861.
52. Henry T. Blow (1817–1875) was a St. Louis businessman who sided with the Union and was a supporter of Frank Blair. Sedalia was the nearest rail point for Granby mines' lead shipments.

53. *New York Herald,* June 1, 1861.
54. Cherokee Nation, not Choctaw. John Ross (1790–1866) was the longest serving principal chief of the Cherokees. He was unsuccessful in healing the split within his nation, and Cherokee units fought on both sides during the war.
55. *New York Herald,* June 1, 1861.
56. Ibid.
57. Zouaves were patterned on French North African units known for their distinctive, colorful uniforms.
58. *New York Herald.* June 1, 1861.
59. Bird's Point was located in Missouri on the Mississippi River opposite Cairo, Illinois.
60. *New York Herald,* June 1, 1861. The *City of Louisiana* had been chartered for government service on May 26, 1861.
61. *New York Herald,* June 1, 1861.
62. William E. Parrish, *Frank Blair: Lincoln's Conservative* (Columbia, MO: University of Missouri Press, 1998), 106.

   Frank Blair sent a letter to Lincoln, explaining his decision to deliver the order to Harney. In part, it read:

   > We have conclusive evidence that extensive preparations within this State are on foot to raise and arm large forces to make war upon the United States Government. From every neighborhood in the central and southwest portion of the State men are drilling and arming, and both arms and men will speedily be brought to the State from Arkansas. A large number of wagons have been sent from Jefferson City to the southern part of the State to transport arms and other munitions of war. For the last ten days I have had most of my time occupied by persons from all parts of the State, who have come here expressly to give information of this state of facts, and ask the aid of the Government to protect Union men.
   >
   > Should these things be permitted longer to go on, the Union men would be crushed or driven out from all parts

of the State, and the State be completely given over to the hands of the rebels.

James Peckham, *Gen. Nathaniel Lyon and Missouri in 1861* (New York: American News Company, 1866), 223.

63. *New York Herald*, June 5, 1861, 8.
64. Ibid. Chillicothe was the county seat of Livingston County and was directly on the Hannibal & St. Joseph Railroad. General Slack was William Y. Slack (1816–1862) a Chillicothe lawyer who commanded a division in the Missouri State Guard. He died of wounds received at the Battle of Pea Ridge, Arkansas (March 7–8. 1862).
65. *New York Herald*, June 5, 1861. Dr. Joseph N. McDowell was a notorious Confederate sympathizer and proprietor of McDowell's Medical College, which was later seized and converted into the Gratiot Street Prison. See also Victoria Cosner and Lorelei Shannon, *Missouri's Mad Dr. McDowell: Confederates, Cadavers and Macabre Medicine* (Charleston, SC: The History Press, 2015).
66. *New York Herald*, June 7, 1861, 8. The anecdote of the pig refers to a book *Mr. Mathews at Home in His Youthful Days,* published in England in 1822.
67. *New York Herald*, June 7, 1861, 8.
68. *New York Herald*, June 6, 1861; *Missouri Republican*, June 5, 1861.
69. *New York Herald*, June 9, 1861.
70. Ibid., June 13, 1861.
71. Ibid., June 16, 1861.
72. This was Thomas L. Snead.
73. From John Gay's (1685–1732) "The Beggars Opera."
74. *New York Herald*, June 16, 1861.
75. Ibid.
76. Knox was fully justified in his criticism.

With the outbreak of the Civil War in 1861, Fort Leavenworth's arsenal and large stocks of military supplies made the post a valuable prize to Confederate sympathizers just across the river in Missouri. Fearing that his small command would be insufficient to protect the government property, the post commander, Captain William Steele, in April 1861 accepted the services of three small militia companies from the town of Leavenworth. Steele's plight was recognized by his superiors in St. Louis, who ordered Colonel D. S. Miles to bring several companies of infantry from Fort Kearny to augment the Fort Leavenworth garrison. Upon his arrival on April 29, 1861, Miles assumed command of the post and quickly discharged the local volunteers, believing his force to be sufficient to hold the post "against any rabble or detached secessionists" in the vicinity. Having secured Fort Leavenworth for the Union, Captain Steele resigned his commission in May and joined the Confederate Army, eventually attaining the rank of brigadier general.

http://dtic.mil/dtic/tr/fulltext/u2/a437828.pdf.

CHAPTER 2

1. *New York Herald,* June 14, 1861. See also Buel Leopard and Floyd C. Shoemaker, *The Messages and Proclamations of the Governors of the State of Missouri* (Columbia, MO: The State Historical Society of Missouri, 1922), 385.
2. All three were sidewheel steamboats. The *J. C. Swon* was built in Louisville in 1856; the *Iatan* in Cincinnati in 1858; and the *City of Louisiana* in Madison, IN, in 1857. See Frederick Way, Jr. *Way's Packet Directory, 1848–1983: Passenger Steamboats of the Mississippi River System since the Advent of Photography in Mid-continent America* (Athens, OH: Ohio University Press, 1983) for further details.
3. *New York Herald,* June 15, 1861.
4. St. Aubert is in Callaway County.
5. The *White Cloud* was a sidewheel wooden packet boat built at McKeesport, PA, in 1857. It was 200 ft. long, 35 ft. wide and drew 5 ½ ft. The steamer later served the Union Army. Gibson, 336. Way, 485.

6. *New York Herald*. June 15, 1861. Dodd's Island lies downriver from Jefferson City, opposite Bonnot's Mill.
7. *New York Herald*, June 16, 1861.

> Jefferson City, Mo. June 15, 1861.
> The capital of Missouri was taken possession of at two o'clock this afternoon, on the arrival of the steamer *Iatan*, by five companies of Colonel Blair's regiment of Missouri Volunteers, under command of Lieutenant Colonel Andrews, and a company of regular artillery, under Captain Totten, all under command of Brigadier General Lyon. The balance of the force remained on board the *J. C. Swon* until further orders.
>
> A company of regulars, under Major Serant, thoroughly searched the country for contraband articles, and found some wheels and other parts of artillery carriages.
>
> No violence was offered, but on the contrary, the boats containing the federal troops were received with enthusiastic cheers by a large concourse of the citizens.
>
> Governor Jackson and other leading secessionists left here on the steamer *White Cloud* at four o'clock on the afternoon of the 13th last. Much disappointment was manifested by the troops on finding that the enemy had fled. The officers, however, expressed no surprise, they having been previously informed of the evacuation.
>
> The troops under Lieutenant Colonel Andrews are now occupying the State House. One or two houses have been searched for secession flags, but none have been found.

No major by the name Serant has been found. This may be a misprint for Major Conant who was with the expedition.
8. *New York Herald*, June 20, 1861.
9. This is incorrect. Sigel was ordered up the Southwest Branch of the Pacific Railroad to the end of the line at Rolla.

10. Captain Barton Able, 1824–1877, was a noted river pilot and boat owner. He had sole charge of the boats in the Boonville Expedition. General Lyon had placed him in charge of the Transportation Department in St. Louis. In 1865 he was elected president of the Merchants' Exchange in St. Louis. See *The United States Biographical Dictionary and Portrait Gallery of Eminent and Self-Made Men*. 3:554–555.
11. Possibly a reference to Shakespeare:

> DUKE VINCENTIO Be not so hot; the duke
> Dare no more stretch this finger of mine than he
> Dare rack his own: his subject am I not,
> Nor here provincial. My business in this state
> Made me a looker on here in Vienna...
> *Measure for Measure*, Act 5, Scene 1

12. From Shakespeare, *Henry VIII*, Act 3, Scene 2.
13. Jefferson Davis had, on May 24, proclaimed June 13 to be a day of fasting and prayer.
14. The *McDowell* was the *Augustus McDowell*, built in St. Louis in 1860.
15. Knox, *Camp-fire and Cotton-field*, 45.
16. Orlando C. Richardson was not a regular staff artist for Harper's. He is found in the 1860 U.S. Census, living in the Sixth Ward of St. Louis, age 21, with the occupation "engineer." It is tempting to assume that this young man was working on one of the steamboats that carried the troops to Jefferson City.

Chapter 3

1. This steamboat was built in St. Louis in 1860 and after its capture continued to serve in the Union Army's "Navy," until it burned in St. Louis, October 27, 1862. Way, 33.
2. *New York Herald*, June 17, 1861.
3. Ibid., June 18, 1861.
4. Ibid., June 21, 1861.
5. Ibid., June 22, 1861.
6. Ibid., June 23, 1861. Knox's report in the *Herald* ran to 3072 words.

Lucien J. Barnes's *St. Louis Democrat* report as printed in the *New York Times* was 2760 words long. Both these reports were considered very accurate by Scott, Thiessen, and Dasovich in their report on battlefield archeology on the site of the battle (*The First Battle of Boonville, Cooper County, Missouri, June 17, 1861: Archeological and Historical Investigations* [St. Louis, MO: Heritage Identification and Preservation Foundation, 2009]). Other "civilian" reports were considered less reliable. The *St. Louis Missouri Republican,* a Democratic Party supporter, gave a scant 400-word report of the skirmish.

7. In many reports, the town receives alternate spellings, either Booneville or Boonville. The latter is the spelling accepted today.
8. The Southwest Expedition was an attempt to quiet the border troubles along the southern Missouri-Kansas border. In November 1860, Missouri Governor Stewart sent militia units from St. Louis and Jefferson City to try to suppress the Kansas Jayhawkers. The expedition was only marginally successful. https://www.sos.mo.gov/archives/soldiers/abstract.
9. Knox got this name wrong. This was Captain Johann D. Voerster. Robert J. Rombauer, *The Union Cause in St. Louis in 1861* (St. Louis: Nixon-Jones, 1909), 271.
10. This was Captain Benedict Schultz, Company I, 2nd Regiment Missouri Volunteer Infantry.
11. A Worm Fence is a zigzag fence consisting of interlocking rails supported by crossed poles — called also a snake fence or Virginia fence.
12. Knox called these men "German troops." They were, of course, American troops and German immigrants. They often called themselves "Deutsch," meaning German and to the rebels, Deutsch became "Dutch."
13. Donnybrook Fair was a fair that was held in Donnybrook, Dublin, Ireland from the 13th century until the 1850s. It became a slang term for a brawl or riot.
14. Named for George Graham Vest, 1830–1904, at the time was serving in the Missouri House of Representatives and was the author of the

"Vest Resolutions," which denounced coercion of the south. He later served in the Confederate House and Senate, and, after the war, served in the United States Senate from 1879 to 1903.

15. See note 9.
16. An informal definition of "trump" is "one who is reliable or admirable," a brick is an old fashioned noun for a man who is a "good sort" – solid, dependable. W. A. Pile was indeed a "trump" or a "brick." William Anderson Pile (1829–1889) was an ordained minister in the Methodist Episcopal Church. Chaplain Pile decided he preferred the military life. In July, 1862 he commanded Battery I of the 1st Missouri Light Artillery. He then transferred to the 33rd Missouri Infantry as lieutenant colonel, becoming its colonel in December, 1862. In December, 1863, he was promoted to brigadier general of volunteers. In the campaign against Mobile, he commanded the 1st Brigade of John P. Hawkins's Negro Division. He was brevetted major general for "gallant and meritorious service for the siege and capture of Fort Blakely, Alabama." Warner, *Generals in Blue*, 371–372.
17. See note 9.
18. Horace Brand of Cooper County was born in Kentucky, moved to Missouri in the 1850s, and in 1860 owned a farm and six slaves. After Boonville, he remained with the Missouri State Guard and then joined the Confederate service as a colonel. He was killed in 1863 in Arkansas.
19. The *H. D. Bacon* was built in Louisville in 1860. It was burned and lost in a major boat fire in St. Louis, October 27, 1862.
20. Knox is incorrect in part. The parole they gave was not to serve again until officially exchanged.
21. All three of these boats were taken into federal service.
22. Dr. Florence M. Cornyn served as a doctor at Boonville, but then raised a regiment, the 10th Missouri Cavalry, and served as its colonel. He was shot to death during an altercation with the regiment's deputy commander, Lieutenant Colonel William Bowen, August 10, 1863, in Corinth, MS. Cornyn is buried Calvary Cemetery in St. Louis. See also http://www.nps.gov/shil/upload/Cornyn.pdf.

23. Knox. *Camp-fire and Cotton-field*, 50.
24. *New York Herald,* June 21, 1861.
25. This was Cole Camp. The town was named after a site in Kentucky. By 1861 there was a significant population of Germans in the town with strong anti-slavery, pro-Union sentiments.
26. Knox continued his narrative with a description of an expedition to Tipton:

> Soon after the arrival of the command here yesterday, one company of the First regiment under the command of Lieutenant Murphy, took a trip to Tipton, where they captured fifty boxes of canister powder and made prisoner a conductor on the Pacific Railroad who had been conspicuous in aiding the rebels. He is now under guard in the depot and will probably be taken to Booneville.
>
> When the rebels left Florence yesterday, they took along as prisoners nearly all the able bodied men of the town, numbering some thirty. They were subjected to many iniquities both before and after their departure and it is unknown what disposition will be made of them.... Is not known, but they will doubtlessly be liberated at Warsaw.
>
> The feeling among the country people is very bitter against the rebels in consequence of their numerous depredations. In many instances they ransacked houses, taking whatever they pleased. Gen. Lyon's proclamation is removing much of the prejudice against the Union forces, and a good feeling will doubtless soon take the place of the fears so prevalent among the inhabitants. Gov. Jackson and his myrmidons have spread the story that the United States troops were coming to murder everybody, even to the women and children, and the un-reading country folk oftentimes exhibit the most unfeigned astonishment that we do not, at once, proceed to destroy them.
>
> Four of the leading gentlemen of Booneville have been

riding through Cooper and Morgan Counties, distributing copies of Lyon's proclamation. One of them has hitherto been a prominent supporter of Gov. Jackson. [Lyon's proclamation is to be found in the Appendix, also in the *New York Herald*, June 21, 1861 and in Peckham, 274.]

Col. Boernstein is to send troops in this direction, with a view to the occupation of some points on the railroad. A train will go from Syracuse tonight as far as Grass Creek, the point where the bridge was burned by Gov. Jackson, four miles above Jefferson City.

A gentleman has just arrived from Florence, having left two hours after the departure of our troops. He said that there were fears that the rebels will return tonight and burn the town, as they have made threats to that effect. Nearly all the property in Florence belongs to Union men.

Gen. Lyon and command were at Boonville yesterday, and will probably remain there for several days. Their next move is expected to be upon Lexington.

New York Herald, June 28, 1861.

27. Ibid., June 30, 1861.

Syracuse, Mo., June 23, 1861. Captain Totten's command is still here, but will probably return tonight to Booneville. It is impossible to get up a fight with the rebels since the affair of last Monday. They evidently intend to give the Union troops a wide berth in the future, notwithstanding their own boasted bravery and the doubts they pretend to have of Union courage. Hearing that Captain Totten's command was after them, they left Warsaw and proceeded farther south, and will not halt until they get to a safe spot in the southern portion of the State, among the Ozark mountains. At the time they left Warsaw, they had about three thousand men, with four pieces of artillery and horses enough to mount nearly all the men. There is a report here, but it cannot be traced to a reliable source, that, after leaving Warsaw, they fell in with Colonel Sigel's command, which left St. Louis at the time the expedition started up the Missouri, and were completely routed, leaving their cannon, and fleeing, with Governor Jackson at their head, toward the Kansas border. If they had a battle at all, it was probably with Col. Solomon's command, which is supposed to be in that region, though its exact whereabouts are not known to us here. If the rebels flee to the Kansas border, they will find Montgomery there ready to give them a warm reception. Sigel and Solomon will intercept them on the south, and the north is held by the Missouri river expedition and the Iowa and Illinois troops. They are, in fact, fairly hemmed in.

A report comes from Booneville that the rebels, 7,000 strong with sixteen pieces of iron cannon, are evacuating Lexington and heading for the South. They are fearing the approach of troops from above. There are now at Booneville about three thousand Union troops including the command of General Lyon and one thousand Iowa soldiers that arrived there yesterday in command of Colonel Beal. They will move up the river in a day or two and take possession of Lexington.

The prisoners taken by the rebels at Florence have been released. They were taken as far as Warsaw and were without food for twenty-four hours. The people everywhere complain of the outrages of the rebels.

"Colonel Beal" actually was Colonel John F. Bates. The 1st Iowa Volunteer Infantry Regiment was a 90-day unit created in response to Lincoln's call for volunteers. It was mustered in May 14 and mustered out August 20, after fighting at Wilson's Creek. A. A. Stuart, *Iowa Colonels and Regiments* (Des Moines, IA: Mills & Co., 1865), 22.

28. *New York Herald,* July 1, 1861.
29. Knox's letter continued:

> Rumors continue to come to our ears that Governor Jackson, after getting beyond Warsaw, fell in with Colonel Sigel's command and met with a defeat, but we cannot get the story confirmed. No attack has been made upon Cole Camp since the one of more than a week since. The Union men there are ready to take the field as soon as they can be supplied with arms, and Captain Cooke is now at Booneville to superintend the issuing of arms and ammunition to the [loyal] Home Guard of Cooper and Morgan counties. The rebels in their route through the Cole Camp region seized but few horses, the inhabitants on hearing of their approach secreting themselves with their horses, in the woods in places some distance from the road. The Florence prisoners that were released at Warsaw were required to take oath that they would not fight against the State of Missouri. Nothing was said about the government of the United States, and it is evident that Governor Jackson does not yet dare openly to favor secession. These prisoners were made to go on foot, in advance of a party of horsemen, for nearly fifty miles, and were allowed hardly anything to eat on the entire march. Before starting from Florence, the wives of some of these prisoners prepared dinners for their husbands, and, on being refused admission to the room where they were confined, sent in the food by the guards at the door. The guards, instead of delivering to the prisoners, ate the dinners themselves in the presence of those for whom they were intended. Nearly every house in Florence was plundered by Gov. Jackson's orders, and at the time of the visit of the Union troops a few days since, several families were destitute of provisions enough to furnish a single meal.

30. *New York Herald,* July 1, 1861.
31. Ibid.

> One hundred and fifty Home Guards in Booneville have taken the oath of allegiance to the United States and have received arms from General Lyon. Orders have not been issued for the disposal of the boats at Booneville, now in service of the government, during the time the expedition is absent. It is thought that one of them will remain there in charge of a company of Colonel Boernstein's regiment, while the remainder will go down the river to Jefferson City and the St. Louis Arsenal. The *D. A. January* will be kept plying on the Missouri river to keep that stream open until secession is fairly dead throughout the center of the State. Within a week, the Pacific Rail Road will again be in running order as far as Syracuse, and soon after, over its entire length. The Gasconade Bridge was finished yesterday and cars now run to Jefferson City with a single change at the Osage crossing. The bridge burning faction has probably received its quietus in the region now in charge of General Lyon and Colonel Boernstein, and order will reign there although it still does not in Warsaw.
>
> At Jefferson City yesterday, Colonel Boernstein arrested a stranger, who was making all haste to overtake Governor Jackson. He arrived in Jefferson night before last, and had engaged to give a man fifty dollars to carry him through to some point where he could see the Governor. He stated that Governor Jackson had pardoned a convict, now in the penitentiary, but for some cause the order for his release had not been received, and he was anxious to procure the precious document. His story was not considered by Colonel Boernstein as sufficiently plausible to admit of his going forward, and he was accordingly taken into custody. He was sent today to the St.

Louis Arsenal, and will be detained there till an investigation can be had.

The strictest discipline is enforced in General Lyon's command, and private property is everywhere respected. A day or two since one of the regulars entered the house of a rebel who was away from home with Jackson's forces, and stole therefrom a set of furs and a silk dress. The theft was reported, and upon the detection of the culprit, he was tied up and severely whipped. The stolen goods were returned, and the soldiers were warned against interfering in any way with private property. Among the rebels, thefts are a matter of commendation rather than reprimand, and no punishment, however slight, is made for the most extensive plunderings.

In Jefferson City and vicinity, Home Guards to the number of five hundred have been organized, and the most of them furnished with arms. They will probably be sufficient to hold Jefferson against the rebels, should the Union troops be removed. The latter at present remain there as a healthy precaution.

32. *New York Herald*, June 28, 1861.
33. John S. Phelps, (1814–1886), represented the 6th Missouri Congressional District in the House of Representatives from 1845–1863. He resigned his seat and served as colonel of a regiment that fought at Pea Ridge. He served as Missouri's 23rd governor 1877–1881.
34. Actually, Colonel John D. Stevenson (1821–1897). He was born in Virginia and was admitted to the bar there, but then moved to Missouri. Although a southerner, he sided with the Union and became colonel of the 7th Missouri Infantry on June 1, 1861. He led troops at Shiloh and Vicksburg. He remained in the army, eventually attaining the rank of brevet major general of volunteers. He was honorably discharged in 1870 and resumed his law practice in St. Louis. (Warner, *Generals in Blue*, 476–477). His command, the 7th Missouri, was not

a 90-day unit, but rather a three-year volunteer unit. See also: https://en.wikipedia.org/wiki/7th_Missouri_Volunteer_Infantry .

35. Actually Colonel Charles G. Stifel, 5th Regiment, United States Reserve Corps, Missouri Volunteers.

36. Knox is incorrect. Lieutenant Colonel Robert White served in the 5th Regiment United States Reserve Corps, Missouri Volunteers. A picture of him and a short biography can be found at http://www.civilwarmo.org/exhibits/means-war/faces-of-soldiers.

37. The Lexington foundry was that of William Morrison, who had built it in 1858 near the waterfront of the town. The Union troops did indeed destroy the foundry, but not nearly as completely as Knox colorfully described. It was burned, and later in 1861 at the Battle of Lexington Union troops used the ruins as shelter for sharpshooters. It was rebuilt in 1862, although probably not casting cannon for rebels, and was still in operation in 1881. *History of Lafayette County, Mo.* (St. Louis: Missouri Historical Company, 1881), 619.

38. *New York Herald*. July 2, 1861.

39. A good summary of the Battle of Boonville can be found at http://www.thecivilwarmuse.com/index.php?page=the-battle-of-boonville

40. Richardson, *Secret Service*, 151 .

41. Ibid., 152–154.

Chapter 4

1. *New York Herald*, July 8, 1861.

2. This proclamation of neutrality may be found in item VIII of the Appendix.

3. For McCulloch's Proclamation see item IX of the Appendix. The continuing rumors of McCulloch's location throughout Arkansas indicates both the respect for the Indian fighter and the lack of good, reliable information.

4. Copper was never mined to any extent in Missouri, although some small mining was tried in Shannon County. http://pubs.usgs.gov/bul/0267/report.pdf. It was probably expedient to keep even such

minor sources away from the Confederacy. Tennessee copper mining areas were overrun fairly early by Union forces.
5. This unit was three companies of the 3rd Regiment, United States Reserve Corps of Union Volunteers, organized for three months service. The remainder of this regiment served in a foray into Callaway County. The suggested marches are pure speculation made upon reading the attached map (which had many inaccuracies).
6. Col. Brown was B. Gratz Brown, a politician and one of Lyon's advisers before Camp Jackson, and his unit was the 4th Regiment, United States Reserve Corps, Union Volunteers. Colonel Solomon was Charles E. Salomon (sometimes spelled Soloman), who served as the county engineer before his war service. His was the 5th Regiment Infantry, Missouri Volunteers. Salomon had preceded Brown and occupied Springfield along with Col. Sigel in mid-June.
7. See note 34, chapter 3.
8. *The Missouri State Gazetteer and Business Directory* (St. Louis: Sutherland & McEvoy Publishers, 1860), 268–270.
9. "Sound on the goose" was a term often used during the Kansas troubles, meaning pro-slavery.
10. Nathaniel Paschall (1804–1866) was the editor of the *Missouri Republican*, which could trace its beginnings to 1810 and the *Missouri Gazette*, which became the *Republican* in the 1820s. Originally Whig in politics, it became associated with the Democratic Party upon the demise of the Whig Party in the 1850s. Paschall and the *Republican* endorsed Stephen Douglas for president in 1860.
11. Lyon was promoted from captain to brigadier general of volunteers, dating from May 17, 1861. There is no evidence or record of Lyon's appointment to Major General. (Warner, *Generals in Blue*, 286–287.)
12. Romans, 13:7.
13. James H. McBride (1814–1864) was a judge in Texas County, Missouri, before his appointment as brigadier general, 7th Division, Missouri State Guard. He fought with distinction at Wilson's Creek and Lexington, but was captured in February 1862, by General Curtis, south of Springfield, and later exchanged. He resigned his commission

in the MSG after Pea Ridge and remained in Arkansas to raise troops. He was temporarily appointed a general in the Confederate service by General Thomas C. Hindman, but resigned in September 1862, when the Confederate congress did not confirm his appointment. His health failed in 1864 and he died in Yell County, Arkansas, while en route to Texas. Bruce S. Allardice, *More Generals in Gray* (Baton Rouge, LA: Louisiana State University Press, 1995), 155–156; O.R., Series 2, vol. 1:166; Michael E. Banasik, ed., *Serving With Honor: The Diary of Captain Eathan Allen Pinnell of the Eighth Missouri Infantry (Confederate)* (Iowa City, IA: Camp Pope Bookshop, 1999), 389.
14. Aden Lowe (1827–1861) served as colonel, 3rd Infantry Regiment, 1st Division, Missouri State Guard. He was killed at the Battle of Fredericktown.
15. Colonel Chester Harding, Jr. (1827–1875) served as Gen. Lyon's assistant adjutant general and later led three different Missouri regiments. He was brevetted brigadier general at the end of the war.
16. O.R., Series 1, vol. 3:390.
17. Ibid., 406.

Chapter 5

1. *New York Herald*, July 10, 1861.
2. Ibid.

> The city was in condition yesterday to put down any attempts at insurrection. At the Arsenal the men were under arms or ready to fly to arms at a moment's warning, and no one was admitted inside the gate the entire day. The Home Guard were not negligent of their duty, and in case of trouble would have been on hand. The rebels concluded that the best thing for them to do was to keep quiet, and they accordingly conducted their festivities by muttering imprecations, swallowing bad liquor, and appearing in public with most lugubrious aspects. A few rebellious badges were worn, but not in crowded places,

and no flag save the old and well beloved Star Spangled Banner was seen throughout the day.

3. Ibid.

>   Last evening, I saw a man direct from the southwestern portion of the State. Sweeney's command, he says, is stretched from Rolla, the terminus of the southwest branch of the Pacific Railroad, through Springfield, Vernon and Neosho to the western line of Missouri, cutting off Jackson's escape into Arkansas. The Kansas troops are along the western border, and prevent the flight of our *ci-divant* [former or retired, ed.] Governor toward the land of the buffalo. General Lyon's forces are advancing from the north, and the situation of Governor Jackson is at present more interesting than enviable. His Fugacious Excellency was, on Wednesday, the 26th ult., encamped on Clear Creek, eight miles from Osceola and forty from Warsaw, waiting for that stream to go down and become fordable. He had with him one thousand men, six hundred guns, and three hundred horses and mules. [General James S.] Raines [Rains] was in Bates County, some forty miles south of Jackson, with four thousand men and four pieces of artillery, the same that were taken from Syracuse in the flight of the rebels. General Price was some ten miles west of Jackson, encamped with a body guard of two hundred and fifty men. He is quite unwell, not having yet recovered from his Booneville indisposition. All the stories about Jackson being in Memphis, Nashville and other cities east of the Mississippi river, are, without doubt, base fabrications. It was utterly impossible for him to have reached Memphis on the day he was reported there, after the time I saw and conversed with dozens of persons at Syracuse, several of whom had talked with, and all had seen the fugitive Governor but four hours before. I put down the present

stories concerning his whereabouts east of the great river in the same category. My informant of last night came from Jefferson City to Hermann with a man who was two days at Jackson's camp at Osceola, and gazed upon the haggard features of the late ruler of Missouri, and the information from this individual was the same as that gathered by the scouts from General Sweeney's command. Jackson took all the wheat at a large flouring mill on his route, and all the corn in possession of the farmers using it as forage for his horses. Groceries were opened in the absence of their owners, by aid of fence rails, and anything taken therefrom that could be of service to the army. Such a course was not ingratiating the rebel troops into the favor of the people, and everywhere the most bitter complaints are being made. Union men are gathering in various places, and would make quite a defense if they came furnished with arms. At Cedar City six hundred were thus assembled, anxiously looking for the advent of General Lyon with a supply of Minié muskets and ammunition. A clergyman in Dade County has ninety men at his house, whom he is maintaining at his own expense until they can get suitable weapons for going forth to the war. They will probably be furnished soon.

Captain Cooke received from General Lyon twenty-three boxes of guns for the Unionists of Cole Camp. They are to be taken to that place as the government troops march through, and are not trusted to the risks of transportation without a strong guard.

4. Ibid.

The bids for horses and mules at the Arsenal for use of the government were opened this morning. The contract is awarded to J. H. Bowen and A. S. Jones, as the lowest bidders – the former offering to furnish the kind of animals required at $119 each and the latter offering them at $119.50. The delivery is to take place immediately. [Bowen was John H. Bowen, the general agent for the Hannibal & St. Joseph RR in St. Louis. Jones was Asa S. Jones of the firm Jones and Sherman, attorneys, in St. Louis. Neither dealt in horses and mules directly, but had probably acted as agents for others in preparing bids.]

It is now a fixed fact that the July interest on the Missouri bonds will not be paid. All the efforts to prevent repudiation have proved futile. Another financial swindle, in the shape of notes of a denomination of less than $5, hitherto interdicted by the laws of the State, has lately been foisted upon the community. Although the bills promise the payment of the sums represented by their face on presentation at the counter, specie or anything like it is utterly refused. The issuing of the notes goes on as fast as possible, but many of the businessmen refuse to take them on any terms, and the railroads only receive them at a discount of from ten to fifteen per cent. The old remark, that "corporations have no souls," would seem to apply not only to the combined concern, but to the individual members of nearly all the institutions of St. Louis that make financial transactions their legitimate business.

Hon. John S. Phelps, of Springfield, Mo., representative in Congress for the 5th district, is expected in St. Louis tonight, *en route* for Washington. He will probably bring news of importance from Sweeney's command.

It will be recollected that J. R. Rogers, Paymaster General for the State of Missouri was arrested at Jefferson City by General Lyon, and the checks for the money for the Southwest expedition taken from his possession. Mr. Rogers was intending to divert the money from its original purpose, and use it in aid of Jackson's treasonable designs, and for some time refused to give up the

> payrolls, which by an oversight, were not captured at the time. He has since thought better of the matter, and has given up the documents to the proper authorities. The money has been drawn upon the checks. The payment of the demands of the officers and men of the Southwest expedition commenced today.

What Knox does not note is that many of the men of the Southwest Expedition were now in the service of the rebel Missouri State Guard and were with Governor Jackson. Others, however had been captured at Camp Jackson and were serving their paroles and probably were paid. Paroles were not lifted until the men were officially exchanged, which did not occur until November 1861. In addition, there were many Unionists in the Southwest Expedition who also must have been paid.

5. *New York Herald*, July 10, 1861.
6. The *Herald* carried the news of Frémont's appointment in its July 6 edition.
7. When the Convention of the State of Missouri, the historic one which decided that the state would not secede, adjourned, a committee was named that was empowered to recall the convention into session before the next regularly scheduled one of December 1861. Seven members, one from each Congressional District were named. In addition to the five who signed the recalling notice, there were J. R. Matson and J. P. Knott.
8. *New York Herald*, July 10, 1861.

> The object of summoning the Convention at this time is to take action relative to the extraordinary state of affairs in Missouri, almost in a condition of anarchy, her Governor literally a fugitive and emphatically a vagabond, her Lieutenant Governor missing and likely to be for some time yet, those of her State officers next in authority, unwilling to act, her treasury empty and all her financial resources at a low ebb, the situation of Missouri demands immediate attention. The Convention will have the duty

of appointing officers from the Governor down, in place of those absconded, and of putting the State affairs in the best possible order after the disasters the treasonable conduct of the runaway Jackson has brought upon it. It will probably appoint a provisional government for the State, the officers in it to have the same power and authority as those regularly elected by the people, and to hold their offices until the time when Governor Jackson's term of office would have expired had he remained at his post. After that, it is hoped the course of Missouri politics, unlike that of true love, will run smooth.

The men most talked of as candidates before the Convention for the provisional gubernatorial chair are Hon. John B. Henderson, of Pike County, and Hon. William A. Hall, of Clinton. The chances are in favor of the former. Both are sound Union men and are amply qualified to fill the position. The Convention will be Union by a considerable majority. Several rebel members are at present with Governor Jackson or have fled from Missouri to the warmer and more congenial clime of the South, and their places will remain vacant. Gen. Sterling Price and John B. Clark are among the missing ones, and the cause of secession, already weakened, will lose much by their absence. Ex-Governor R. M. Stewart, now editor of the St. Joseph *Journal*, is a member of the Convention and will do much toward putting the affairs of the State in order. In his issue of Friday was one of the ablest Union editorials that has yet been published in that part of the State. It thoroughly reviewed the course of the rebels of Missouri, and was particularly scathing on Governor Jackson.

9. *New York Herald*, July 10, 1861.
10. Francis W. Pickens was the governor of South Carolina, who approved his state's secession and the bombardment of Fort Sumter.
11. John Catron (1786–1865), originally from Kentucky, served as a

U.S. Supreme Court Justice, 1837–1865. Under the Judiciary Act of 1789, each justice was required to ride the circuit that was assigned to him. By the Civil War era, with the territorial expansion of the United States, "riding circuit" had become an onerous task. In addition, the propriety of hearing appeals from Circuit Court decisions Catron had participated in was raised. Actual Circuit riding was abolished in 1891.

12. *New York Herald*, July 10, 1861.

> The government has given orders for the stationing of a regiment at Cape Girardeau, one at Bloomfield, one at Rolla, and also one or two other points in the State which are not yet selected. A regiment from Caseyville, commanded by Colonel J. B. Wyman, arrived in this city yesterday, and at once left on the Pacific Railroad for the occupation of Rolla. The steamer *City of Alton* arrived at the Arsenal yesterday afternoon, bringing a regiment of Illinois volunteers from Alton, under the command of Colonel C. C. Marsh. It has not been decided whether they will proceed to Bloomfield or Cape Girardeau. The Illinois troops present a fine appearance and will give a good account of themselves when the time comes for fighting. The policy of the war managers in Missouri appears to be to anticipate every move that may be made on the part of the rebels. The State is now pretty thoroughly occupied in all directions by Union troops, and the rebels do not have the slightest hope of success unless by that long talked of invasion with an overwhelming force by means of Arkansas. In the southwest there are not far from 8000 Union volunteers, exclusive of several thousands of Home Guards, and well-armed and equipped, and provided with all means requisite for carrying the war into Arkansas and sweeping out secession from the semi-horse and semi-alligator State. Such now appears to be the intention of government. The southeast will soon be in the condition to take the

offensive. The northern and central portions of Missouri are quiet. There is much joy at the telegraphic statement that General Frémont is to have his headquarters at St. Louis. His presence will aid to settle the difficulties in this section of the west. With Frémont and Lyon to watch over them, the traitors of Missouri will be hushed to silence.

The payment of the Southwest expedition is now going on. There is much grumbling in secession circles at the summary process by which the money for that purpose was secured instead of being treasonably used by Governor Jackson.

Several prominent secessionists of St. Louis have disappeared of late. It is supposed they have gone to Memphis, or have joined their forces with those of Governor Jackson. The absence has somewhat diminished the crowd of Southern sympathizers that nightly gather in front of the Planters' House.

Col. John B. Wyman commanded the 13th Illinois and was killed at the battle of Chickasaw Bayou during the campaign for Vicksburg on December 28, 1862. Colonel C. Carroll Marsh's unit was the 20th Illinois.
13. Michael E. Banasik, "Wilkie, Franc Bangs." *The Biographical Dictionary of Iowa.* (Iowa City, IA: University of Iowa Press, 2009). http://uipress.lib.uiowa.edu/bdi/DetailsPage.aspx?id=407. The news article by Wilkie originally appeared in the *New York Times* of July 18 and was inscribed "On the Prairie, Mo., July 5, 1861."
14. *Harper's Weekly*, July 27, 1861.
15. Eugene F. Ware, *The Lyon Campaign in Missouri: A History of the First Iowa Infantry* (Topeka, KS: Crane & Co., 1907), 159.
16. The 3rd Regiment United States Reserve Corps, Missouri Volunteers.
17. The *State Journal* editor was Joseph W. Tucker, a "fire eater" secessionist originally from South Carolina.
18. *New York Herald*, July 13, 1861. A search of Tucker's office produced a letter from Governor Jackson, dated April 28, 1861, that was

treasonous in nature. with phrases such as, "we should not go out of the Union until the Legislature had time to arm the State to some extent, and place it in a proper position of defense." And, "who does not know that every sympathy of my heart is with the South?" And, "Let us then, prepare to make our exit. We should keep our own counsels." It is reproduced in Peckham, 287–289. A number of historians have considered this letter to be fabricated. The jury remains out. Col. McNeil was John McNeil, commander of the 3rd Regiment United States Reserve Corps, Missouri Volunteers, a ninety-day unit. He then became Colonel of the 2nd Missouri State Militia Cavalry. He is most remembered for the Palmyra Massacre.

19. Rombauer, 287. Tucker later created a roving army newspaper, the *Army Argus*. More information can be found on Tucker at http://www.civilwarstlouis.com/biographies/tuckers-war/.

20. *New York Herald*, July 14, 1861.

21. Ibid.

22. The Colonel was C. Carroll Marsh (not March). The 20th was sent to Cape Girardeau and went on to a distinguished career, fighting at Henry, Donelson, Shiloh and beyond. Frederick H. Dyer, *A Compendium of the War of the Rebellion* (Des Moines, IA: The Dyer Publishing Co., 1908), 1053.

23. The 13th remained at Rolla until it marched with Frémont to Springfield. Later it was with General Curtis at Pea Ridge. Dyer, 1050.

24. This skirmish at Valle Forge (not Valley Forge as Knox called it) never made into the *Official Records*. Valle Forge was an iron furnace on the plank road between Pilot Knob and Ste. Genevieve, a few miles east of Farmington. The forge was established in 1854, when iron ore was carried there from Pilot Knob, and finished iron was sent to Ste. Genevieve. With the arrival of the Iron Mountain Railroad at Pilot Knob in 1858, business declined and the forge closed in 1863. Among the owners was the Valle family of St. Genevieve. Campbell, 496.

25. *New York Herald*, July 14, 1861.

26. Peckham, 294; Thomas L. Snead, *The Fight for Missouri* (New York: Charles Scribner's Sons, 1886), 224. Also Rombauer (in 1909), 281.

David C. Hinze and Karen Farnham's book on Carthage is the best, most comprehensive study of the battle.
27. McDonald County, the furthest southwest county in Missouri.
28. Catron had voted with the majority in the Dred Scott case.
29. The *New York Times* of July 13, 1861, in an article titled "A Loyal Judge," began with, "The country will read with much pleasure the accounts, from St. Louis, of Judge Catron's unflinching fidelity to the Constitution and Union." Chief elements of the charge were summarized in the *New York Herald* of July 14, 1861, and are presented in item XI of the Appendix,
30. *New York Herald*, July 14, 1861. The proclamation can be found in full in item X of the Appendix.
31. *Anzeiger* was *Anzeiger des Westens* (Gazette of the West), the first German newspaper in St. Louis, founded in 1835. Henry Boernstein became its editor in 1850. The *Anzeiger* was strongly pro-Union. The paper's staff suffered with the coming of the war due to enlistments (including Boernstein), and it suspended publication in February 1863.
32. The St. Louis Custom House was located at Third & Olive in 1861.
33. *New York Herald*, July 18, 1861.
34. Ibid.
35. Ibid.
36. Thomas C. Reynolds, *Sterling Price and the Confederacy*, ed. Robert G. Schultz (St. Louis: Missouri History Museum Press, 2009), 32–33.
37. John S. Bowen (1830–1863) ultimately became a major general in the Confederate Army. He fought at Shiloh, Second Corinth, and Vicksburg. He died of dysentery shortly after the surrender of Vicksburg.
38. This is incorrect. Brig. General Daniel Frost led the expedition.
39. *New York Herald*, July 18, 1861.
40. Ibid.

> The war has affected business so much in this region, that all the railroads leading to the East from this city have withdrawn one of their trains, and now run only one train per day. Formerly, there were six different through trains

for New York from St. Louis, but now we have only three. The reason given is simple – hard times. No patronage and no money to pay expenses.

A desperate effort is being made to force the circulation of Ben Wood's paper [the *New York Daily News*] and the evening luminary that belches forth treason to a few hundred readers daily. It is a failure. Until lately these papers were utterly unknown in St. Louis and a small circulation has been obtained among rebels, and the papers in question stare one in the face at every newsdealer's, the *Herald* outsells the two combined twenty to one.

41. *New York Herald*, July 18, 1861.
42. Ibid., July 6, 11, 12, 13, 1861.
43. Winter, 71.

Chapter 6

1. Knox, *Camp-fire and Cotton-field*, 56.
2. *New York Herald*, July 22, 1861.
3. See note 13, chapter 4.
4. John B. Wyman (1817–1862) was killed while leading his troops at the battle of Chickasaw Bayou, MS.
5. The Sons of Temperance was a brotherhood of men who promoted the temperance movement and mutual support. The group was founded in 1842 in New York City. It began spreading rapidly during the 1840s throughout the United States and was in many ways a fraternal organization.
6. Knox, *Camp-fire and Cotton-field*, 56.
7. *New York Herald*, July 27, 1861.
8. Knox, *Camp-fire and Cotton-field*, 59–60.
9. *New York Herald*, July 27, 1861.
10. 5th Regiment Infantry, Missouri Volunteers.
11. 3rd Regiment, United States Reserve Corps, Missouri Volunteers.
12. B. Gratz Brown's 4th Regiment United States Reserve Corps, Missouri

Volunteers. The war was proving to be much longer than expected, and 90-day units were becoming a real problem. Brown (1826–1885) did not continue a military career beyond his command of the ninety-day unit.

13. *New York Herald,* July 27, 1861.
14. Ibid.
15. On May 3, 1861, President Lincoln issued a proclamation for volunteers for three-year service; this effectively ended 90-day enlistments. *O.R.,* Series 3, vol. 1:145–146.
16. Camp Walker was near Maysville, west of Bentonville and near the Arkansas/Oklahoma state line.
17. *New York Herald,* July 27, 1861.

> The reports from Carthage still represent the rebel loss at the time of the battle with Colonel Sigel as not far from seven hundred. I think their loss must have been not less than three or four hundred, making all reasonable deductions for the growth of stories. Colonel Sigel is receiving great praise for the ability shown on the 5th, and all our officers would be proud of a similar success. He remarked in my hearing yesterday "Had I been provided with regulars, instead of volunteers, I would have formed a solid column at the time Jackson's mounted men on the wings advanced, and supported by my artillery would have marched straight to the enemy's centre. My men were brave and fought like heroes, but they might have been frightened at seeing the enemy's wings behind them. If they had been regulars I would certainly have done it, for I know how to depend on them always." Colonel Sigel is of slight frame, a pleasing countenance, with the German features strongly shown, possesses a fine musical voice and has nothing of the brusque manners that too often display themselves in the military man. He is "every inch a soldier" and enjoys the esteem of all who know him.

> Unlike Marius of old, Governor Jackson did not long remain sitting among the ruins of Carthage, but on the same night of Sigel's retreat to Sarcoxie made good his departure towards the south. Fifteen hundred troops from Tennessee are reported to have reached Forsythe, a landing on the White river, intending to reinforce Jackson. [*Not true.*] General Sweeney leaves this afternoon with two thousand men for that point. It is hardly expected that the enemy will stay for a fight, but we can at any rate frighten them a little.

The actual number of casualties at the battle of Carthage remains a mystery. Reports vary widely, but probably the number used by the National Park Service – 200 State Guard and 44 Union – is as good as any. There is no way to separate killed from wounded. Burchett spends ten pages discussing casualties without reaching a firm conclusion (Kenneth E. Burchett, *The Battle of Carthage, Missouri* [Jefferson, NC: McFarland & Co., 2013]).

The reference to "Marius of old" is taken from Plutarch's *Lives of the Noble Greek and Romans*. Roman General Caius Marius was banished to exile after a power struggle with Sulla and is said to have sat among the ruins of Carthage – previously destroyed by the Romans – contemplating his fate.

18. *New York Herald*, July 27, 1861.
19. Isaac F. Shepard (1816–1889) attained the rank of brigadier general and fought at Wilson's Creek, Arkansas Post, and Vicksburg. Warner, *Generals in Blue*, 435–436.
20. David S. Stanley (1828–1902) attained the rank of major general. He fought at Wilson's Creek, New Madrid, Iuka, Corinth, Chattanooga, and Franklin. After the war, he remained in the army serving on the Indian frontier. Warner, *Generals in Blue*, 470–471.
21. Knox and Barnes were "old campaigners" from the Boonville battle, and Franc Wilkie had traveled with the 1st Iowa Infantry, marching through Missouri from Hannibal to Springfield.
22. Two corrections are needed in Knox's narrative. Lyon was never

named a major general, and Thomas Sweeny did not spell his name "Sweeney." (Knox uses Sweeney and Sweeny interchangeably.) Forsyth today is spelled without a final "e."
23. This accessibility at this time of the year is highly doubtful. Normal head of navigation for the White River was Jacksonport or Batesville. Forsyth was attainable by light-draft steamboats only in the spring when the river was at its highest.
24. Lieutenant George O. Sokalski (1839–1867), was the first Polish-American graduate of West Point, in 1861. During the war he rose to the rank of lieutenant colonel.
25. Captain Samuel N. Wood, of the Kansas Rangers, later served in the 6th Missouri Cavalry, rising to the rank of lieutenant colonel.
26. Lieutenant Colonel William H. Merritt, 1st Iowa Infantry.
27. Colonel Robert Byington Mitchell, 2nd Kansas Infantry. He was badly wounded at the Battle of Wilson's Creek.
28. *New York Herald*, July 31, 1861.
29. Franc B. Wilkie, *The Iowa First: Letters from the War* (Dubuque, IA: The Herald Book and Job Establishment, 1861), 89.
30. Taney City. Today known as Taneyville.
31. *New York Herald*, July 31, 1861.
32. Ibid.
33. Wilkie, *Iowa First*, 91–92.
34. Mills was later colonel of the 24th Missouri Infantry Regiment.
35. *New York Herald*, July 31, 1861.
36. *O.R.*, Series 1, vol. 3:44–45.

Chapter 7

1. Knox, *Camp-fire and Cotton-field*, 61.
2. Ibid., 62.
3. Brig. General Ben McCullough (1811–1862) fought at San Jacinto in the fight for Texas independence and served with honor in the Mexican War under General Zachary Taylor. He fought Native Americans and raised regiments for the Civil War. As a brigadier general, he

commanded Arkansas troops at Wilson's Creek, and was killed in the Battle of Pea Ridge. Warner, *Generals in Gray*, 200. Colonel Louis Hébert (1820–1901) graduated 3rd in the West Point class of 1845, but later left the army. He raised the 3rd Louisiana Infantry and marched north to support McCulloch. He fought at Wilson's Creek and later was captured at Pea Ridge. Warner, *Generals in Gray*, 130.

4. Wilkie (under the pen name Galway), *New York Times*, August 12, 1861.
5. This was Wilson Creek, the actual name of the waterway in southeast Missouri. The creek was generally known as "Wilson's Creek" after the battle, especially by Northern participants. It will be referred to as such for the sake of convenience in this book, except where "Wilson Creek" appears in quoted material.
6. *New York Herald*, August 12, 1861.
7. Major Ferdinand W. Cronenbold served in the 5th Regiment Infantry, Missouri Volunteers, Colonel Salomon's Regiment, a ninety-day unit.
8. *New York Herald*, August 12, 1861.
9. Ibid.
10. Knox, *Camp-fire and Cotton-field*, 64–66.
11. *New York Herald*, August 12, 1861. *Harper's Weekly*, August 24, 1861.
12. Balaklava refers to the "Charge of the Light Brigade," a poem by Alfred, Lord Tennyson about the October 25, 1854, light cavalry charge during the Crimean War.
13. Ibid.
14. McCulla's Farm represents a small problem. The area was also known as McCulla's Store and apparently housed the Curran Post Office. McCulla was no relation to Ben McCulloch, the Confederate General.
15. *O.R.*, Series 1, vol. 3:47.
16. Actually, the name was McCulla as in Lyon's report.
17. *New York Herald*, August 12, 1861.
18. Ibid.
19. Ibid.
20. Ibid.
21. Ibid.

Chapter 8

1. Union casualties, killed, wounded, and missing were 1347 or 24.8% of Lyon's army and of these, 285 were killed (5.2%). The larger Confederate force suffered a similar number of casualties, 1232, or 10.2%. Of these 277 were killed (2.3%).
2. *New York Herald*, August 14, 1861.
3. Ibid., August 15, 1861.
4. Dr. Melcher was the assistant surgeon for Salomon's 5th Regiment of Missouri Volunteers.
5. *New York Herald*, August 19, 1861.
6. Dug Springs skirmish.
7. *New York Herald*, August 19, 1861.
8. Ibid.
9. Ibid.
10. Ibid.
11. Ibid.

> "Where is Sigel?" had been passing from lip to lip for an hour before this attack, and he had been anxiously looked for at the very point where the rebel infantry, bearing the Secession flag, had made their appearance. As we had not heard from him since the night previous, save by the reports of his cannon, we were uncertain as to his fate, and fearful that we might fire upon him should he approach, as we did not know from what quarter to expect him. Our cannon ammunition was nearly exhausted, and several companies of infantry had expended their last round of cartridges. Major Sturgis (who took command after General Lyon's death) ordered a retreat and the whole army took up its line of match for Springfield. Ambulances were ordered back with a flag of truce to gather up the dead and wounded. The flag was received by General McCulloch and Colonel McIntosh, and by nine P. M., the ambulances returned,

bringing all that could be found. The battle commenced a few minutes past six A. M. and the retreat was ordered at eleven. With but a few intervals the batteries on both sides were in constant action throughout the whole day, and there were few minutes when the roll of musketry could not be heard.

To understand Colonel Siegel's position it will be necessary to explain more fully the situation of the rebel camp. Wilson's Creek has a general southerly direction; but at a farm called McNary's it makes a sharp bend to the east, follows an easterly course for two and a half miles, and then bends suddenly to the south. The Fayetteville Road crosses the creek about a mile and three-fourths below the upper bend. The rebel camp extended three miles along the creek, two and a half in an easterly direction, and a quarter of a mile above the upper bend towards the north, and the same distance below the lower bend towards the south. General Lyon's attack was made on the western side, just above the upper bend. Colonel Sigel marched from Springfield down (going south) the Fayetteville road, left that road four miles this side of Wilson's creek, and turned to his left, went around the rebel camp, came into the same road two miles beyond Wilson's Creek, and marched up the Fayetteville road toward the enemy's camp. Some who saw his command coming, about daylight, from the direction of Arkansas, walked out to meet him, not dreaming of the approach of the Union forces on that side. These he allowed to get within his lines, and made prisoners of them before they discovered their mistake. He fell upon their camp at the road, routed them and took possession, planting his cannon in the camp and playing upon them from that position. He found and took possession of the private papers of General McCulloch, and one of his Lieutenants was fortunate enough to secure a bag of gold. Colonel Sigel was so severely pressed that he had to abandon the camp and take a position on the hill where he served his artillery efficiently and brought his infantry into active use. A concentrated fire was made upon his battery, killing many of his artillerymen and nearly all his horses. A dash of infantry and cavalry was then made, and five of his six cannon fell into possession of the rebels. The infantry and cavalry came so hard upon him as to compel him to retreat, which he did bringing away nearly two hundred prisoners. His command was badly cut up and he found it impossible make a junction with the main column.

The last assault on the main column was made just after the retreat of Colonel Sigel and the cannon which played upon us on the right were the five that were captured. At one time, had a vigorous move been made on our part, the rebel battery might have been taken.

12. The best current estimates for troop strength are Union 5,430 and Confederate 12,120. William Garrett Piston and Richard W. Hatcher, III, *Wilson's Creek: The Second Battle of the Civil War and the Men Who Fought It* (Chapel Hill, NC: University of North Carolina Press, 2000), 337–338.
13. Alexis Mudd, originally from the 3rd Regiment Infantry Volunteers. He served as A. C. S. (assistant commissary of subsistence) in Sweeny's Brigade. He was one of the founders of the Republican Party in Missouri.
14. "Private" Grant of the 1st Iowa was First Sergeant William S. Grant, age 49 at enlistment. When the 1st Iowa was mustered out on August 21, he reenlisted in the 11th Iowa and became captain of Company A of that regiment.
15. Knox, *Camp-fire and Cotton-field*, 67–80.
16. "How Sleep the Brave," by English poet William Collins, 1721–1759.
17. A recorded performance can be found in *Rebel in the Woods: Civil*

War Songs from the Western Border, by Cathy Barton, Dave Para, and Bob Dyer.

Chapter 9

1. Many of the details portray the life of a war correspondent as well as the context of rural life.
2. The *Missouri State Gazetteer* of 1860 lists two hotels in Lebanon (population 400), the Lebanon House and the Washington House. One may have escaped Knox's attention or have closed.
3. At that time, Knox was with General Samuel R. Curtis's Army of the Southwest, advancing to Springfield and ultimately, Pea Ridge.
4. This was in Waynesville. The building has been restored as the "Old Stagecoach Stop."
5. "Mudsill" refers to "The 'Mudsill' Theory," by Senator James Henry Hammond of South Carolina, from a speech he made before the U.S. Senate, March 4, 1858. In all social systems there must be a class to do the menial duties, to perform the drudgery of life. That is, a class requiring but a low order of intellect and but little skill. Its requisites are vigor, docility, fidelity. The term derives from a mudsill, the lowest threshold that supports the foundation for a building.

    The Confederacy did establish a patent office and inventions were registered. See H. Jackson Knight, *Confederate Invention: The Story of the Confederate States Patent Office and Its Inventors* (Baton Rouge: Louisiana State University Press, 2011).
6. *New York Herald*, August 19, 1861.
7. *New York Times*, August 15, 1861.

    ST. LOUIS, Mo., Wednesday, Aug. 14.

    The following proclamation has just been issued:

    HEAD-QUARTERS, WESTERN DEPARTMENT, ST. LOUIS,
    Aug. 14, 1861.

    I hereby declare and establish martial law in the City and County of St. Louis. Major J. McKinstry, United States

Army, is appointed Provost-Marshal. All orders and regulations issued by him will be respected and obeyed accordingly.

(Signed) J. C. Frémont,
Major-General Commanding.

8. Justus McKinstry (1814–1897) carried the distinction as the only general officer to be cashiered during the war. He had risen through the Quartermaster Corps, a place that made it easy for him to profit. He was charged with and convicted of "neglect and violation of duty, to the prejudice of good order and military discipline." (Warner, *Generals in Blue*, 303). A recent biography of McKinstry, by John K. Driscoll, is entitled *Rogue: A Biography of Civil War General Justus McKinstry* (Jefferson, NC: McFarland & Co., 2005).
9. Dr. McKellog is not to be found in the *Missouri State Gazetteer* of 1860 in St. Louis. The closest name may a dentist, Henry McKellope.
10. John A. Brownlee (1819–1861) arrived in St. Louis in 1839, worked as a dry goods clerk, eventually owning the dry goods company, Brownlee, Homer & Co. He was also president of the Merchants' Bank of St. Louis and the Millers and Manufacturers Insurance Co. His arrest was due to his being the president of the St. Louis Police Board, a group created by Governor Jackson to give the State control of the City Police. He died October 11, 1861.
11. *New York Herald*, August 23, 1861.
12. Frank Blair, a colonel of volunteers, had not officially resigned from his seat in the House of Representatives. He was replaced by Col. George Lippitt Andrews (1828–1920). Andrews entered the army in 1861 as a lieutenant colonel in the 1st Missouri Volunteer Infantry. After the Battle of Wilson's Creek, in which he was wounded and had his horse killed under him, he was commissioned as major of the 17th U.S. Infantry, and served thereafter in the Army of the Potomac, receiving two brevets for gallantry; he was promoted to lieutenant colonel in the 13th U.S. Infantry, in 1864, and colonel in the 25th U.S. Infantry in 1871; after the war he served on frontier service with his regiment, in Dakota, Montana, Arizona, and Texas. He was

Superintendent of Indian Affairs for Arizona, 1869–1871. He is buried at Arlington National Cemetery. William H. Powell and Edward Shippen, *Officers of the Army and Navy Who Served in the Civil War* (Philadelphia: L. R. Hamersly & Co., 1892), 12.

13. Total casualties 313 out of 725 = 43%.

14. Total casualties 159 out of 825 = 19%.

15. Dr. William H. White (1824–1880), of Iowa City, IA, served first in the 1st Iowa Infantry Regiment at Wilson's Creek and later with the 22nd Iowa in the Vicksburg Campaign. https://www.findagrave.com/cgi-bin/fg.cgi?page=gr&GRid=87508577&ref=acom

16. *New York Herald*, August 29, 1861.

17. In 1845 the Methodist Episcopal Church in the United States split into two separate church organizations – North and South. In 1854, the Methodist Episcopal Church- South struck out from their *Methodist Discipline* the chapter against slavery. The *St. Louis Christian Advocate* under its editor, Dr. David R. McAnally, staunchly represented the South branch of Methodism.

18. Information on these generals may be found in Allardice, *More Generals in Gray* (McBride, 155; Rains, 190; Clark, 59; and Hughes, 132).

19. Richard C. Peterson, Kip A. Lindberg, James E. McGhee, and Keith I. Daleen, *Sterling Price's Lieutenants: A Guide to the Officers and Organization of the Missouri State Guard, 1861–1865*. Revised Edition. (Independence, MO: Two Trails Publishing, 1997), 320.

20. Richard Hanson Weightman, 1818–1861. Born, Washington, DC, expelled from West Point for a knife fight. New Mexico Territorial Delegate to Congress, 1851–1853. Newspaper editor in Albuquerque; killed F. X. Aubry in a bar fight there. Moved to Kansas; involved in troubles there. Moved to Independence, MO; elected colonel (not general) of 1st Regiment Cavalry, 8th Division, Missouri State Guard. Led a brigade at Wilson's Creek. See Peterson, 320; http://bioguide.congress.gov/scripts/biodisplay.pl?index=W000255

21. *New York Herald*, August 29, 1861.

22. Named for Captain Cary Gratz, Company F, 1st Missouri Volunteers,

who was killed at Wilson's Creek. He was a commission merchant in St. Louis (1860 Census), from an old Kentucky and Philadelphia family and cousin to Frank Blair.
23. Captain Emmett MacDonald, 1837–1863, fought at Wilson's Creek, Lexington, and Pea Ridge. He raised a cavalry unit in Arkansas and led it in General Marmaduke's raid into southwest Missouri. He was killed at Hartsville, MO, January 11, 1863, during that raid.
24. *New York Herald*, September 9, 1861.
25. Robert Patterson (1792–1881) was appointed major general of Pennsylvania volunteers, commanding the Department of Pennsylvania and the Army of the Shenandoah. He failed to stop Confederate General Joseph E. Johnston from joining forces with P. G. T. Beauregard at the First Battle of Bull Run. He is still blamed for this historic Union defeat. He was mustered out of the army in late July 1861.
26. See note 13, chapter 4.

Chapter 10

1. *New York Herald*, August 23, 1861.
2. General Benjamin M. Prentiss (1819–1901) practiced law in Quincy, Illinois, until his appointment as colonel of the 10th Illinois infantry in April 1861. In August 1861, he was appointed brigadier general of volunteers to date from May 17, 1861. He was supplanted at Pilot Knob by Brigadier General Grant. He fought at Shiloh in 1862 and at Helena in 1863. He resigned in 1863 and returned to his law practice in Quincy.
3. The 1st Nebraska Infantry served in their first assignment at Pilot Knob, but saw little action there. In February 1862, they were sent to join General Grant's forces in Kentucky.
4. Col. Friedrich Hecker (1811–1881) commanded the 24th Illinois Infantry regiment at Pilot Knob. He resigned his command in December 1861, but later commanded the 82nd Illinois Regiment, which fought in the Eastern theater.
5. William Joseph Hardee, 1815–1873 first commanded in Arkansas.

His rumored attack on Pilot Knob never materialized. He was called to serve east of the Mississippi by General A. S. Johnston. See Warner, *Generals in Gray*, 124

6. A mounted sentry positioned beyond an army's outposts to observe the movements of the enemy.
7. *New York Herald*, August 29, 1861.
8. Solon Borland (1808–1864) of Arkansas was a newspaper editor, senator, doctor and officer in the Mexican War. He served in recruitment (3rd Arkansas) and served in Northeast Arkansas as colonel at Pitman's Ferry and Pocahontas, directing troop deployment and supplies. He resigned from Confederate service in June 1862.
9. Now a ghost town west of Sikeston in Stoddard County.
10. The region that Knox describes is today called the "Bootheel" of Missouri. The rivers are the St. Francis rivers. It was said that the lead mines in Missouri in the Potosi region had sent up to the Galena Illinois lead mines whole hordes of uncouth ruffians, from which it was inferred that Missouri had taken a "Puke," and had vomited forth to the upper lead mines, all her worse population. From thenceforth, the Missourians were called "Pukes."
11. In 1861, the Cairo & Fulton Railroad existed only in the minds of its promoters. Construction did not begin until 1871.
12. New York *Herald*, August 26, 1861.
13. Actually, these three towns abut one another and are within three miles of one another.

Chapter 11

1. *O.R.*, Series 1, vol. 3:467. *New York Times* and *New York Herald*, September 1, 1861.
2. In a letter to his friend Orville H. Browning (1806–1881), senator from Illinois (1861–1863) who had been appointed by Governor Yates to fill the balance of Stephen Douglas's term after Douglas died (June 3, 1861), Lincoln wrote of Frémont's emancipation order:

  No doubt the thing was popular in some quarters, and

would have been more so if it had been a general declaration of emancipation. The Kentucky Legislature would not budge till that proclamation was modified; and Gen. Anderson telegraphed me that on the news of Gen. Frémont having actually issued deeds of manumission, a whole company of our Volunteers threw down their arms and disbanded. I was so assured, as to think it probable, that the very arms we had furnished Kentucky would be turned against us. I think to lose Kentucky is nearly the same as to lose the whole game. Kentucky gone, we can not hold Missouri, nor, as I think, Maryland. These all against us, and the job on our hands is too large for us. We would as well consent to separation at once, including the surrender of this capitol."

Collected Works of Abraham Lincoln, https://quod.lib.umich.edu/l/lincoln/lincoln4/1:1003.1?rgn=div2;view=fulltext.

3. *O.R.*, Series 1, vol. 3:469
4. Ibid.
5. *New York Herald*, September 9, 1861.
6. After Wilson's Creek, the 2nd Kansas Infantry served in northeast Missouri, August 30–September 7. They traveled by steamboat to Hannibal and skirmished at Paris on September 2; Shelbina, September 4; Iatan, September 4; Captured St. Joseph, September 13. Dyer, 1187; http://www.kansasguardmuseum.com/?page_id=1968.
7. James Wilson Alexander MacDonald, a New York artist who had lived in St. Louis from 1844 until after the Civil War.
8. Prince Napoleon, 1822–1891, was the first cousin of Napoleon III, ruler of France at the time of the American Civil War. He visited in the United States between July 27 and September 25.
9. Captain W. H. Kidd is not found in the Missouri military records. It is possible that he was an Arkansas officer.
10. Dr. E. C. Franklin appears in the 1860 *Missouri Gazetteer* as a Homeopathic Physician at 79 Pine, St. Louis.

11. The Indiana units in Western Virginia were 90-day units, unlike these three year regiments.
12. Actually a courtesy title of Major. Smith had been in charge of the consolidated telegraph offices of the four telegraphic lines serving St. Louis with offices at 10 Chestnut. See the 1860 *Missouri Gazetteer* and Plum.
13. On September 30, 1861, the *New York Times* published a report from Fort Scott dated September 5, about the relatively minor skirmish.
14. *New York Herald*, September 14, 1861.

> All sorts of reports are in circulation relative to General Frémont and the visit of Postmaster Blair and Quartermaster General Meigs to St. Louis. These reports are not only current here, but are telegraphed all over the country. I have ascertained the facts in the case. The gravest difficulty at St. Louis was personal, between General Frémont and Colonel Frank P. Blair, Jr. It arose from different causes, and was manifested on various occasions, public and private. Confident hopes are entertained that it has now been substantially adjusted.
>
> Complaints are made, from sources which have received consideration, against General Frémont, for alleged inaccessibility to persons having important business with him, and an indisposition to co-operate cordially with the State officials. It is probable that the ground for such dissatisfaction will be removed. General Frémont's proclamation, which was written and promulgated without consultation with anybody, will be modified to a certain extent by the President. He requires, or requests, General Frémont, in a letter already written, to be made public in a few days, to interpret his proclamation so as to make it accord with the law of Congress passed at the recent session. This is the substance. I do not undertake to give yet his language, but my authority for all these statements is the highest that the case admits of.

> The relations between President Lincoln and General Frémont continue amicable. The President sent Postmaster General Blair out to St. Louis as a friend of General Frémont's. Quartermaster General Meigs went on other business – simply to investigate the Quartermaster's Department there. No other charges, except those mentioned, which have any weight at all with the President, have been made against General Frémont.
>
> Mrs. Frémont left Washington in good spirits today, on her return to St. Louis.

15. Pamela Herr and Mary Lee Spence, eds. *The Letters of Jessie Benton Frémont* (Urbana, IL: University of Illinois Press, 1993), 264. *O.R.*, Series 1, vol. 3:477.
16. Herr and Spence, 264–267.
17. *O.R.*, Series 1, vol. 3:485–486.
18. Herr and Spence, 269.
19. Ibid., 267–271.
20. *New York Herald*, September 14, 1861.
21. Benton Barracks is today's Fairgrounds Park, located in the northern part of St. Louis City.
22. *New York Herald*, September 14, 1861. There were a considerable number of problems with the postal service in Missouri. Post offices were closed and post routes were often robbed by guerrillas. For many small towns, postal service did not resume until after the war was over.
23. *New York Herald*, September 14, 1861. It was not until November 1861 that the "Missouri State Militia" (MSM) was officially established. Therefore such an offer, made in September, was probably meaningless.
24. Martin Green (1815–1863) was a brigadier general of the Missouri State Guard and raised units in Northeast Missouri. He became a brigadier general in the Confederate Army and was killed by a Union sharpshooter during the siege of Vicksburg. Warner, *Generals in Gray*, 116–117.
25. See note 19, chapter 3. The boat was captured by Confederates at

Glasgow and used to transport men across the Missouri River to join General Price.

26. Washington had ordered General Frémont to send 5,000 of his men eastward to Washington. *O.R.*, Series 1, vol. 3:491.
27. *New York Herald*, September 25, 1861.
28. Ibid.
29. This statement is only partly true. North Missouri was free of organized rebel units (such as Green's), but there were many small attacks on the railroad and severing of telegraph lines by individuals or small groups.
30. *New York Herald*, September 25, 1861.
31. Ibid.
32. Knox here refers to the arrest of Frank Blair by General Frémont on charges of "insidious & dishonorable efforts to bring my authority into contempt with the Government" on September 18. (Parrish, *Frank Blair*, 124). Blair was released from arrest a few days later. In releasing Blair, Frémont wrote that he had made the arrest because Blair and his family had impaired the efficiency of the Department. The hot-tempered Blair then threatened to file countercharges against Frémont. Frémont had Blair rearrested. Washington's doubts about Frémont's ability to lead and govern were increasing.
33. This refers to the apparent affliction of General Price at the Battle of Boonville.
34. McKinstry was promoted to brigadier general of volunteers on September 2, 1861.
35. *New York Herald* September 26, 1861.
36. Ibid.
37. *New York Herald*, September 26, 1861. *New York Times*, September 27, 1861. The *Times* reprint of the editorial is to be found in item XIV of the Appendix.
38. *New York Herald*, September 28, 1861.
39. The *St. Louis Evening News* was listed in the 1860 *Missouri State Gazetteer and Business Directory* (p. 268). "Published daily, tri-weekly and weekly, by the proprietors, C. G. Ramsey & Co., at the office, No.

76 North Third street. Abram S. Mitchell and Daniel N. Grissom, editors. Terms, daily, $8; tri-weekly, $4; weekly, $1."
40. Dennis K. Boman, *Lincoln and Citizens' Rights in Civil War Missouri* (Baton Rouge, LA: Louisiana State University Press, 2011), 48.
41. Franc Wilkie in *Pen and Powder*, 49–51, gives an amusing account of his efforts to see Frémont upon his arrival in St. Louis.
42. *New York Herald*, September 29, 1861
43. Ibid., October 5, 1861.

Chapter 12

1. Knox, *Camp-fire and Cotton-field*, 95–98.
2. Browne, 28.
3. George W. Beaman (1837–1917) was born and educated in Vermont. He enlisted as a private in the 3rd Regiment, Missouri U.S. Reserve Corps in May 1861, a three-month regiment, and took part in the capture of Camp Jackson. From August 1861 to March 1862, he was a correspondent for the *Missouri Democrat*, and reported on Frémont's southwest Missouri campaign, and later U.S. Grant's battles at Forts Henry and Donelson. He was appointed from Missouri into the Navy as Acting Assistant Paymaster, U.S. Navy, on March 5, 1862. He remained in the Navy in the paymaster service until retirement in 1899.
4. Jules Michelet's *L'Amour* (1859) was a treatise on love, marriage, and celibacy in bachelorhood.
5. Richardson, *The Secret Service*, 189–193.
6. This must have been Knox, given Wilkie's description of him at Springfield.
7. *New York Herald*, October 4, 1861.
8. *New York Herald*, October 8, 1861.
9. There are several steamboats with the name *Emma* in *Way's Packet Directory*, but it is not possible to distinguish which one is mentioned here.
10. Philip St. George Cooke (1809–1895) did indeed become a brigadier

general in November 1861, but he did not serve under Frémont. Instead, the 2nd Dragoons, renamed the 2nd Cavalry, served in guarding the Washington area. After minimal success in the Peninsula Campaign, he was shunted aside from active service for the rest of the war. He retired in 1873.
11. Possibly from Charles A. Goodrich, *Great Events in the History of North and South America* (Hartford, CT: House & Brown, 1854).
12. Frémont named this encampment Camp Lily after his daughter, Elizabeth Benton "Lily" Frémont (1842–1919).
13. The *New Era* was a center wheel snagboat built in 1856. She was enlarged and converted to a gunboat, the *Essex*.
14. *New York Herald*, October 8, 1861.
15. Ibid., October 9, 1861.
16. Ibid.
17. Ibid., October 10, 1861.
18. Ibid.
19. The Blair family had been friends and political promoters of Frémont over the years. Frémont received the nomination for president by the newly formed Republican Party at least in part to Blair family influence. As a mark of this close relationship, their fifth child was named Francis Preston Frémont (1855–1931).
20. *New York Herald*, October 16, 1861

Chapter 13

1. Samuel R. Curtis (1805–1866), an 1831 graduate of West Point, served as colonel of the 2nd Iowa Infantry and was promoted to brigadier general of volunteers to rank from May 17, 1861. Warner, *Generals in Blue*, 107–108.
2. Richardson, *Secret Service,* 196.
3. Franz Sigel (1824–1902) received military training in Germany. He was a professor at the German-American Institute in St. Louis, not at a university. He became Director of St. Louis Public Schools in 1860.

He was named brigadier general on August 7, to rank from May 17. Warner, *Generals in Blue*, 447–448.

4. David Hunter (1802–1886) graduated from West Point in 1822. He was an early Lincoln protégé. Warner, *Generals in Blue*, 243–244.

5. John Pope (1822–1892) also graduated from West Point in 1842. He was appointed brigadier general of volunteers on June 14, 1861, to rank from May 17. Warner, *Generals in Blue*, 376–377.

6. Alexander Asboth (1811–1868) was appointed brigadier general and chief of staff by Frémont, but that appointment was not recognized. His official appointment did not come until March 21, 1862. Warner, *Generals in Blue*, 11–12.

7. Justus McKinstry (1814–1897) graduated from West Point in 1838. He was another brigadier appointment by Frémont. It was never confirmed by the Senate. Warner, *Generals in Blue*, 303–304.

8. Quoted in Charles C. Clayton, *Little Mac: Joseph McCullagh of the St. Louis Globe-Democrat* (Carbondale, IL: Southern Illinois University Press, 1969), 9.

9. *New York Herald*, October 18, 1861.

10. Apparently at this time Knox was not aware of or chose not to mention the real reason for Cameron's visit.

11. Egbert B. Brown (1816–1902), although not trained militarily, effectively fought guerrillas in Missouri and was appointed brigadier general of volunteers to date from November 29, 1862. Warner, *Generals in Blue*, 48

12. Actually, the Missouri Legislature met at Neosho and enacted the secession ordinance on October 30, 1861, and Governor Jackson signed it the next day. Questions remain whether or not a quorum was present.

13. Spanish for a herd of horses or mules.

14. *New York Herald*, October 18, 1861.

15. Ibid., October 22, 1861.

16. Ibid., November 1, 1861.

17. James H. "Jim" Lane (1814–1866) was a fighter in "Bloody Kansas" prior to the Civil War. When Kansas achieved statehood, he was

elected to the U.S. Senate. In addition, he raised a brigade of "Jayhawkers" (3rd, 4th, and 5th Kansas Volunteers), known as "Lane's Brigade" or the Kansas Brigade. He carried the title of brigadier general of volunteers. On September 23, 1861, his "Jayhawkers" sacked Osceola, MO, an unauthorized act. Osceola was plundered and burned to the ground, and nine local citizens were executed. Lane was reelected in 1865, but committed suicide in 1866.
18. Knox, *Camp-fire and Cotton-field*, 99.
19. Ibid., 100.
20. *New York Herald* , November 3, 1861.
21. Ibid., November 6, 1861.
22. Colonel Albert Sidney Johnston led the Utah Expedition to put down an imagined Mormon rebellion against the United States. There were no real battles or significant casualties, and a peaceful resolution of differences was obtained. Johnston did not come to Missouri.
23. *O.R.,* Series 1, vol. 3:553, 559.

Chapter 14

1. General David Hunter resigned from the Army in 1836 and rejoined in 1842 as captain and paymaster. He had settled in Illinois and was a close friend of Lincoln. On August 13, 1861, he was appointed major general of volunteers. He outranked all other major generals except Nathaniel Banks, John Dix, and Benjamin Butler. He commanded a regiment at First Bull Run, where he was wounded. Upon recovery, he was posted as second in command to Frémont in the Western Department.
2. Charges were made against McKinstry in Mexico City in 1848 and in San Diego in 1853 for financial improprieties. These resurfaced in 1862. See *Report of the Joint Committee on the Conduct of the War*. House of Representatives, 37th Congress, 3rd Session; and G. E. Rule, "Justus McKinstry and His Enemies," http://www.civilwarstlouis.com/articles/justus-mckinstry-enemies/.
3. Haskell was an old friend of both J. C. Frémont and his wife, Jessie

Benton Frémont, from San Francisco. All twenty-eight of Frémont's staff as listed in the *New York Herald* of November 7, 1861, are to be found in item XV of the Appendix.

4. *Report of the Joint Committee on the Conduct of the War.* III. Department of the West.
5. Ibid., 14.
6. *New York Herald*, November 7, 1861.
7. Ibid.
8. Ibid.
9. Ibid., November 16, 1861.
10. James H. Phinney from Pennsylvania served as assistant paymaster on Frémont's staff. Later he served the same role in the Northwest Department, based in St. Paul, MN. In 1865, he was brevetted lieutenant colonel.
11. Colonel John B. Wyman was never a brigadier general. He died on December 28, 1862, while leading his regiment, the 13th Illinois, at the Battle of Chickasaw Bayou.
12. *New York Herald*, November 19, 1861.
13. Ibid.
14. Ibid.
15. Halleck was appointed on November 9 and assumed command on November 19. *O.R.*, Series 1, vol. 3:567.
16. *New York Herald*, November 19, 1861.
17. Ibid.
18. Grenville M. Dodge (1831–1916) began as commander of the 4th Iowa Infantry and went on to lead a brigade at Pea Ridge and the XVI Corps in the Atlanta Campaign, rising to the rank of major general. After the war he was appointed chief engineer of the Union Pacific Railroad. Warner, *Generals in Blue*, 128.
19. Sempronius Hamilton Boyd (1828–1892) raised the 24th Missouri Infantry from men around Springfield and served as its colonel. He later served in the U.S. House of Representatives. http://bioguide.congress.gov/scripts/biodisplay.pl?index=B000720.
20. The *New York World* was established in 1860 as a penny paper with

a basically religious orientation. It supported Abraham Lincoln's prosecution of the Civil War and his other policies, but it lost money and was later sold to a consortium of New York City Democrats. In 1861, it still had a religious orientation.
21. *New York Herald*. November 19, 1861.
22. General Hunter was officially named to command on October 24 (*O.R.*, Series 1, vol. 3:553), but did not assume command in Springfield until November 3 (*O.R.*, Series 1, vol. 3:561). General Halleck was named to replace Hunter on November 9 (*O.R.*, Series 1, vol. 3:567) and assumed command in St. Louis on November 19 (*O.R.*, Series 1, vol. 8:369).

Chapter 15

1. *New York Herald*, November 16, 1861.
2. Henry Halleck (1815–1872) served in California where he knew Frémont. After his time in Missouri, he was promoted to general-in-chief and served Lincoln in an advisory capacity. When Grant became general-in-chief, Halleck served as his chief of staff. Schuyler Hamilton (1822–1903), Halleck's assistant chief of staff was also Halleck's brother-in-law. He was named brigadier general of volunteers to date from November 12, 1861.
3. *New York Herald*, November 26, 1861. "Colonel Price" was Lieutenant Colonel John H. Price, who was captured at Springfield on October 25, 1861. (*O.R.*, Series 2, vol. 1:552–553.) He was supposedly exchanged on November 2 by an agreement between Frémont and Sterling Price. However, on taking command, General Hunter rescinded the agreement and Colonel Price was brought to St. Louis and exchanged later. This unlucky colonel was recaptured at the Battle of Pea Ridge.
4. *New York Herald*. November 26, 1861.
5. *O.R.*, Series 1, vol. 5:37–38. The full text can be found in item XVII of the Appendix.
6. Harney, Lyon, Frémont, Hunter, and now Halleck.
7. See note 17, chapter 13.

8. *New York Herald,* November 26, 1861.
9. Ibid.
10. See Driscoll, *Rogue.*
11. John M. Schofield (1831–1906) served forty-six years in the army rising to the rank of lieutenant general. From 1888 to 1895 he was commanding general of the army. He also served from June 1868 to March 1869 as interim secretary of war.
12. James Totten (1818–1871) was named brigadier general of Missouri militia February 12, 1862, and brevetted brigadier general in March 1865. He was noted for his extensive vocabulary of profanity.
13. *New York Herald*, November 26, 1861. The reference to "Captain Billy Mulligan" is unclear. Billy Mulligan was a street tough or "bruiser" in the 1850s–60s in New York and California. Perhaps Knox has mistaken this Mulligan with Colonel James Mulligan who was captured at Lexington.
14. Way, 437. The sidewheel, wood-hulled *Sunshine*, a packet of 354 tons, was built in Pennsylvania in 1860 and entered Missouri River service in September, 1861. Way states she, "had some hot times. Confederates captured her at Glasgow, MO, and required her to transport their troops across. The 38th Indiana Regiment on the *Des Moines, Iatan, White Cloud* and *War Eagle* recovered her." This story differs from Knox's. Perhaps there were two incidents.
15. Charles R. Jennison (1834–1884), also known as Doc Jennison was an abolitionist active in the "Bloody Kansas" troubles prior to the Civil War. He served as colonel of the 7th Kansas Cavalry which was also known as Jennison's Jayhawkers. Sometimes they were called "redlegs" because of their red leggings. This unit, like Lane's was not above bushwhacking and banditry.
16. Way, 374. The *Platte Valley* was a sidewheel packet built in 1857 in Indiana and was taken over for U.S. transport service during the war. (It had been in the St. Louis-Vicksburg trade.)
17. Price's Landing is located in Scott County at the juncture of Highways N and NN, about seven miles north of Sikeston on Highway N.
18. *New York Herald*, November 26, 1861.
19. Ibid.

20. Ibid., November 22, 1861.
21. *O.R.*, Series 1, vol. 8:370. This order did not appear *per se* in Knox's letter.
22. *New York Herald*, November 22, 1861.
23. John F. Marszalek, *Sherman's Other War: The General the Civil War Press* (Kent, OH: Kent State University Press, 1999), 111–112. Charles Sumner (1811–1874) was a senator from Massachusetts, and George Washington Julian (1817–1899) was a congressman from Indiana.
24. *O.R.*, Series 1, vol. 8:382.
25. *New York Herald*, December 4, 1861.
26. This was First Lieutenant Henry Hescock of the 1st Regiment Artillery Volunteers. He enlisted April 22, 1861. He was promoted to captain on September 26, 1862, to rank from January 25, 1862.
27. George R. Smith (1804–1879) was the founder of Sedalia and was named by Governor Hamilton Gamble as adjutant general of the 6-month Missouri militia being formed.
28. This was the Missouri State Militia (MSM). These were state militia, enrolled and commanded by state officers, under the control of the governor of the state. Their charter was to fight for the Union within the borders of the state and not leave the state. They were financed by the Federal Government.
29. John Y. Simon, ed. *The Papers of Ulysses S. Grant*, 32 vols. (Carbondale, IL: Southern Illinois University Press, 1967–2012), 3:279 .
30. Horace Greeley, editor of the *New York Tribune* and staunch abolitionist, strongly favored Frémont, and was very angry over his removal from command in Missouri.
31. *New York Herald*, December 4, 1861.
32. Generals Frémont and Price executed an agreement relating to treatment of civilians and guerrilla warfare and promising prompt military justice to offenders. Frémont signed on November 1, Price on November 5, and the agreement was announced on November 7. On the same day, the new commander, General Hunter, refused to recognize the agreement and refused to allow publication. See *O.R.*, Series 2, vol. 1:559, 561. The texts may be found in the Appendix.

33. The *Benton* was not one of Eads's gunboats built at Carondelet or Mound City. Rather, it was a converted snag boat owned by Eads. It was 202 ft. long, 72 ft. wide and drew 9 ft. Original armament was fourteen guns. See Angus Konstam, *Union River Ironclad 1861–65*, New Vanguard 56 (Osceola, WI: Osprey Publishing, 2002), 7.
34. Dunleith was the original name for East Dubuque, Illinois.
35. *New York Herald*, December 10, 1861.
36. Ibid.
37. These four paragraphs should remind us that, in addition his military training, Halleck also was an attorney and had been a partner in a successful practice in San Francisco before the war.
38. Dorothea Dix visited St. Louis and was instrumental along with Jessie Frémont in formation of the Western Sanitary Commission. The founders were James E. Yeatman, lawyer, banker & founder of the Mercantile Library, who served as Chairman, John B. Johnson, MD, who served as Medical Director, William Greenleaf Eliot, D. D., Pastor of the First Unitarian Church of St. Louis and co-founder of Washington University, and attorneys George Partridge and Carlos S. Greeley. See Jacob G. Forman, *The Western Sanitary Commission* (St. Louis: R. P. Studley & Co., 1864).
39. Henry W. Williams was not the mayor of St. Louis, but rather the president of the State and County Assessors in St. Louis.
40. The exact message that Knox is referring to is unclear, but most likely it is the "First Annual Message" released on December 3, two days before Knox's letter. See http://www.presidency.ucsb.edu/ws/index.php?pid=29502.
41. "Chappelle" was Lieutenant Colonel William C. Chappell, of the staff of Jeff Thompson's 1st Division Missouri State Guard. He was detained at Cairo and not allowed to "go after" Thompson's wife in St. Joseph. Further correspondence ensued, and it was reported that Jeff Thompson's wife was a resident of the "lunatic asylum" in St. Louis under the care of the Sisters of Charity. (*O.R.*, Series 2, vol. 1:525–528).
42. *New York Herald*, December 10, 1861.
43. Peter V. Daniel (not Daniels), 1784–1860, was a very conservative

Supreme Court justice from Virginia, appointed by Martin Van Buren in 1841. He strongly favored slavery.

44. A discussion on financing the Civil War can be found at: http://abrahamlincolnsclassroom.org/abraham-lincoln-in-depth/abraham-lincoln-and-civil-war-finance/

45. Evans Rogers, $16,200; Beman Crickard, 10,650; Goodwin & Anderson, 10,000; Stephen D. Gore, 4,000; Tony Neiderweisser, 1,000; David McFarland, 1,000; Augustus Adams, 1,000; L. H. Long, U.S. Army, 1,000; Mary A. Bailey, 1,000; Isaac V. W. Dutcher, 500; Solomon Smith, 200; Saml. A. Gaylord, 100; Robt. L. Whitney, 250; Jas. R. Peterson, 100; Agnes E. Williams, 150; Galusha Anderson, 750; J. Hinckley, 600; Sarah B. Morris, 300; John C. Krom, 200; C. M. Kosner, 600; Martin Carmody, 350; Isaac Comstock, 100; G. A. Hawley, 800; Aaron Blake, 200; Phillip Catieny, 100; Danl. Koliko, 600; Louis Duncan, 500; John Tilden, 100; J. F. Wentzel, 900; Sidney Burbank, 400; John Hinckley, 150; John P. Hawkins, 850; James A. Hearn, 600; G. Anderson, 800; Sophia D. Slawson, 100; J. S. Hinckley, 300; P. H. Jacquith, 600; Martha E. Crooks, 200; N. B. Williams, 400; Clinton B. Fisk, 50; Jannette B. Fisk, 50; Charles A. Fisk, 50; Mary C. Fisk, 50; William R. Carver, 50; A. M. Gardner, 50; Rev. D. Dimond, 50; Rudolph Bonde, 50; Susan E. Gardner, 50; Henry Begeman, 50; Rev. H. A. Nelson, 50; Jane Hutton, 50; Grace L. Hazard, 50. The total of this list amounted to $59,000.

46. The Confederate Congress admitted Missouri to the Confederacy on November 28, 1861.

47. *Journal of the Missouri State Convention*, October 1861, 10–16. The State Convention body was the *de facto* legislature of the State of Missouri. Provisional Governor Hamilton Gamble effectively ran the state, at least those areas under Union control.

48. *O.R.*, Series 1, vol. 8:414,

49. *New York Herald*, December 10, 1861.

50. Ibid., December 13, 1861.

St. Louis, December 8, 1861

There is a strong undercurrent of feeling among the secessionists of this city that something is going to happen of an unusual nature. Yesterday, the merchants of change were talking quite extensively of a rumor that General Halleck intends to issue an order this week requiring every able bodied male resident of the city between the ages of eighteen and forty-five to be enrolled as a Home Guard for the defense of the city, and to subscribe an oath of allegiance to the United States government.

If this rumor should turn out true, the question may be asked how the secesh learned the fact in advance of loyal citizens. Upon inquiry, it appears likely that some such order will be issued. The secesh obtain their information through leaky Union vessels, who are constantly consorting with rebel friends in public barrooms and in hotels. When anything important is ascertained, it is duly reported around among the secesh and not unfrequently the Union men of this city obtain interesting information of the designs of our military men from rebel sympathizers sooner than from any other source. The fact that the secesh are expecting an order for a home guard to issue from General Halleck's headquarters taken with other circumstances, is tolerably good evidence that such a scheme is meditated.

General Halleck has lately given proof that he is thoroughly in earnest. Without display or ostentation, without a Hungarian barricade or mock philanthropy on the negro question – he is all the time industriously engaged in forwarding preparations to make good his brief speech several nights ago in front of the Planters' House, that he intends driving every hostile flag out of Missouri.

His business hours are admirably arranged. There is a time allotted to all classes of business – a time for military reports, a time for citizens to bring information, a time to hear complaints, and a time to consider all applications. Not the least important of General Halleck's acts is an order to admit any person having pressing business or important information concerning the enemy to his presence at any hour, day or night. Everything about his office works like a charm. There is no waiting hours in anterooms, subject to the caprices of a private secretary; in short, General Halleck has the united affection of the army and the people already.

51. *New York Herald*, December 10, 1861.
52. The 1860 *Missouri State Gazetteer* listed 32 printing houses in St. Louis.
53. "Ever Be Happy" or the pirate's farewell ballad, from 1849. See https://www.loc.gov/resource/sm1849.461380.0/?sp=2
54. This song appears in Frank Moore's *Rebellion Record*, Poetry and Incidents Section, 4:19. There is no attribution as to source or location. One must wonder if Moore, working in New York, came across this song in the *New York Herald* of December 13, 1861.
55. *New York Herald*, December 13, 1861.
56. S. Gordon was Silas (or Si) Gordon (1835–1888). He and his men were implicated in the September 3 Platte Bridge railroad tragedy. At Bee Creek, in November, two federal soldiers were killed in a skirmish. In December after another skirmish, the town of Platte City was burned by the Union troops in retaliation. Gordon joined the Missouri State Guard and fought at Pea Ridge, Iuka, and Corinth. Later he returned to guerrilla activities in Platte County and finally retired to Texas, where Gordonville was named for him.
57. The commander of the 50th Illinois was Moses Bane, not William.

Chapter 16

1. *New York Herald*, December 19, 1861.
2. In the 1860 *Missouri State Gazetteer*, Thomas Souper was listed as "insurance and collecting agent," located at 29 Chestnut St.
3. The reference to Judge Goode presents a problem. George W. Goode

had died in June 1860! However, his wife, Fanny, had maintained ownership of the farm and perhaps she had made the statement from "Judge Goode's Farm."
4. Samuel M. Pook (1804–1878), a naval architect, assisted in the design and construction of the gunboats, using the talent and experience of James B. Eads.
5. There is no *Sam Gates* listed in *Way's Packet Directory*. There is, however, a *Sam Gaty*.
6. Child, Pratt & Fox, hardware dealers, was located at 139 & 141 North Main St. in St. Louis. They are found in *Kennedy's 1860 St. Louis City Directory*. https://www.rollanet.org/~bdoerr/1860Cy-Dir/1860CD-C.htm#C
7. *New York Herald*, December 13, 1861.
8. The full text of General Orders No. 24 may be found in the *O.R.*, Series 1, vol. 8:431–432.
9. *New York Herald*, December 14, 1861. The required oath of allegiance was soon applied to other professions.
10. Ibid., December 16, 1861.
11. Senator Trusten Polk (1811–1876) was expelled from the United States Senate on January 10, 1862. He then served as a colonel in the Confederate Army. Bruce S. Allardice, *Confederate Colonels: A Biographical Register* (Columbia, MO: University of Missouri Press, 2008), 309; http://bioguide.congress.gov/scripts/biodisplay.pl?index=P000411
12. *New York Herald*, December 16, 1861.

> The case of the negro contraband who stands in the extraordinary position of being claimed as a chattel by a pretended British subject while claiming himself to be a subject of Great Britain, is assuming interesting proportions. The English Consul, J. Edward Wilkins, is thoroughly interested in solving the riddle how one British subject can be the slave or another.
>
> On the 10th the negro and his pretended master were brought to St. Louis by General Halleck's order, and as

soon as messengers who have been dispatched to Chicago and Canada to hunt up evidence, have returned, the matter will be investigated with all the formalities of a high court before the Consul.

There is a touch of romance in the case which may make it notorious. The negro says he was born in Canada. His mother who still resides there, was a fugitive from Virginia. The boy (he is about twenty years old) came to St. Louis, and worked, at the age of twelve, on the farm of Judge Goode, on the Meramec River, in this county, for his board and clothes. He had a chance to go on a steamboat and obtain wages; but fearing Goode would belie his name and treat him otherwise than well, he ran away. The next account finds him in Canada again, and then in Chicago as a waiter and house servant. He says he has an uncle and half-brother in Chicago. From the latter place he came to this State with one of the Illinois regiments; was spirited away from this city by Wheelan, under a pretense that he was going to the interior to buy mules for the government; but as soon as he was beyond the Union lines, Wheelan clapped handcuffs upon him and started for the Arkansas line. The boy endeavored to escape, but Wheelan chained him to an ox wagon where he was found by Captain Wood, of the Kansas Rangers.

The undoubtedly true part of the boy's narrative is that which traces him from Judge Goode's farm to Canada and back to Missouri. One of the most extraordinary features of the case is the declaration of the boy that his mother resides at the present time near Windsor, Canada, and of his pretended master (Wheelan), that the boy's mother is now living with Judge Goode's family. It would not be supposed that such a case as this would be allowed to go against the negro for the want of friends but nevertheless such is the fact. The efforts of the British Consul to determine truthfully whether the boy was born in British possessions are prompted solely by a desire to mete out exact justice. Beyond that the negro boy's case is hopeless unless Wheelan is proved a secessionist, in which case it is probable the darkey will have a good start in the race when both master and slave are set free.

13. This is probably a misprint for *Iatan*. No *Liaten* is found in *Way's Packet Directory*.
14. In the 1860 *Missouri State Gazetteer*, Child, Pratt & Co. were listed as "importers and jobbers of hardware, cutlery, guns and the only agents for Herring's safes and Colt's fire arms. 139 & 141 Main."
15. Oak Hall Clothing was located in Philadelphia and was founded by John Wanamaker and Nathan Brown in 1861.
16. *New York Herald*, December 24, 1861.
17. Ibid.
18. Ibid., December 25, 1861.
19. A full tabulation of the losses was attached as an appendix to the *Journal of the Senate of the State of Missouri*, 23rd Session (1865) and amounted to, by the Railroad's calculation, $71,466.
20. Colonel Robertson served in the 6th Division of the Missouri State Guard, leading the 3rd Infantry Regiment. He was exchanged at Vicksburg in the summer of 1862.
21. Leslie Anders, "The Blackwater Incident," *Missouri Historical Review* 88 (July 1994), 416–429."
22. *New York Herald*, December 28, 1861.
23. Dr. Joseph Nash McDowell ran a medical college in St. Louis. He was an eccentric, opinionated bigot. He hated all immigrants, especially Catholic immigrants. He was a staunch member of the American, or "Know Nothing" Party. See Cosner and Shannon, "*Missouri's Mad Doctor McDowell*."
24. This was not "Bill" but rather Ebenezer "Ben" Magoffin. For the full story see "Escape From Alton Prison: 1862," http://madison.illinois-genweb.org/prison_magoffin_escape.html.

25. Colonel Thomas A. Marshall (1817–1873) commanded the 1st Regiment Illinois Volunteer Cavalry.
26. *New York Herald*, December 28, 1861. Transcripts of many of these trials are to be found in the *O.R.*, Series 2, vol. 1:284–494.
27. Actually, General Price established his winter camp in Springfield.
28. Thomas Jefferson McKean (1810–1870) was briefly in charge of prisoner of war camps in Missouri, and was appointed a brigadier general in the Union Army on November 21. McKean commanded at Jefferson City from December to March 1862. Warner, *Generals in Blue*, 301.
29. Jefferson C. Davis served as a First Lieutenant at Fort Moultrie in Charleston, SC, harbor and was among those withdrawn into Fort Sumter before its surrender.
30. *O.R.*, Series 1, vol. 8:38–40.
31. *New York Herald*, December 31, 1861.
32. John B. Henderson, (1826–1913) was commissioned as brigadier general in the Missouri State Militia (MSM). He was stationed in Northeast Missouri as part of the force to suppress guerrilla activity against the railroads. He was appointed to succeed Trusten Polk on January 17, 1862, and in August 1862 was elected to a full, six-year term. Henderson co-authored and co-sponsored the Thirteenth Amendment to the United States Constitution that permanently prohibited slavery in the United States.
33. *O.R.*, Series 1, vol. 8:473. Brigadier General Curtis took command of the Post at Rolla and, as senior in rank to General Sigel, reported directly to Halleck.
34. *New York Herald*, December 31, 1861. *O.R.*, Series 1, vol. 8. 473.
35. *O.R.*, Series 1, vol. 8:473.

Chapter 17

1. *New York Herald*, January 4, 1862. On January 5, the *Herald* published the long list of prisoners.
2. Ibid., January 3, 1862. *O.R.*, Series 1, 8:475. Knox mixed first names in

his report. It was Colonel Jefferson F. Jones who was captured, paroled, and later arrested. His story can be found in Griffin Frost, *Camp and Prison Journal* (Iowa City, IA: Camp Pope Bookshop, 1994), 289–292; Peterson, 151; and Carolyn Bartels, *The Forgotten Men, Missouri State Guard* (Independence, MO: Two Trails Publishing, 1995), 188–189. Owens was probably Captain J. Owens, regimental quartermaster, 1st Cavalry Regiment, 4th Division, Missouri State Guard. Peterson, 197; Bartels, 280.

3. Audrain not Adrian.
4. The story was covered in the Missouri *Republican* for January 3, 5, and 6, 1862. The total amount embezzled was $28,685.38.
5. *New York Herald,* January 12, 1862.
6. From: *A Handbook of Hygiene and Sanitary Science* (1889): "In the severe type of the disease, known as black measles, there is generally haemorrhage from the mucous surfaces, and death may occur before the rash is thrown out. As everyone knows, black measles is extremely fatal."
7. Actually, Price was hoping to make his winter encampment at Springfield since winter campaigns were very rare.
8. Judge Krum was John M. Krum, a former mayor, a director of Washington University and professor at St. Louis Law School. Reverdy Johnson was a defense counsel in Washington who defended Sanford (Dred Scott case), Major General Fitz John Porter at his court martial, and Mary Suratt in the Lincoln assassination.
9. Alexander Cummings of Philadelphia used his influence for appointment as a special purchasing agent for the War Department. His $2,000,000 budget was a model for waste, profiteering, and stupidity.
10. This was the beginning of protracted troubles with Siegel. He had performed well at Carthage against heavy odds, did poorly at Wilson's Creek, and would do well again at Pea Ridge in March 1862. But he was a divisive influence and did not fare well in the Eastern Theater at Sharpsburg, Fredericksburg, or New Market. He resigned on May 4, 1865.
11. See Robert G. Schultz, *The March to the River: From the Battle of Pea*

Ridge to Helena, Spring 1862 (Iowa City, IA: Camp Pope Publishing, 2014), 20.

12. *New York Herald,* January 9, 1862.

St. Louis, January 3, 1862.

Yesterday afternoon Gen. Sigel tendered his resignation to the proper authorities in this department, who have referred the whole matter to Washington. The resignation was sent from Rolla, at which post Gen. Sigel had been in command until relieved a few days ago by Gen. Curtis. There is not the least ill feeling between Generals Sigel and Curtis, all the trouble being with the headquarters in this city. Friends of the former claim that in view of the efficiency he has shown since the commencement of the war and his ability to control the German element, which is very large in the Western army, his treatment of late has been unfair. They contend that his removal from the command at Rolla, at a time when matters bid fair to be interesting, were not a proper return for his services.

Per contra, the commander of a department has full right to do just as he pleases in all matters of a military nature within the district over which he has authority. Attempts are being made to induce General Sigel to withdraw his resignation and remain in the service, as he is too valuable to be spared at the present juncture.

The *morceau* for the quidnunc today is the rumor that General Halleck has been called from this department to command upon the Potomac. The effect of his removal at this time would be exceedingly unfavorable as the Western public generally feel that we have had changes enough already.

Our first commander was General Harney, who was superseded by the lamented Lyon. General Frémont, after a hundred days spent in the midst of reckless extravagance and unpardonable blunders, disappeared from the martial firmament, and his loss supplied by General Hunter. The latter officer at present commands the Department of Kansas, leaving us with our fifth in less than twice as many months.

General Halleck displays much military skill and shows himself far superior in strategy to the rebel General Price, who could outmaneuver General Frémont with the utmost ease. He has gained a thorough knowledge of Missouri and her wants, an acquirement of no small magnitude. Quiet and unostentatious in his manner, a diligent worker, and unsurrounded by a kid-gloved bodyguard to render him difficult of access, he is universally popular throughout his department.

13. *New York Herald*, January 9, 1862. Scott's "Anaconda" plan envisioned a naval blockade of all Confederate ports and an attack down the Mississippi River to split the Confederate States. A newspaper cartoon envisioned a giant snake squeezing the Confederacy from all directions.
14. *New York Herald*, January 9, 1862.
15. Captain Sweeney appears as Capt. Robert W. Swynne, *O.R.*, Series 1, vol. 8:35; and in Peterson, 127, as Robert W. Swinney.
16. Sam Weller was a worldly cockney character in Charles Dickens's *Pickwick Papers*.
17. *New York Herald*, January 12, 1862.
18. This was the Battle of Mount Zion Church. *History of Boone County, Missouri* (St. Louis: Western Historical Co., 1882), 412.
19. See note 2.
20. *New York Herald*, January 12, 1862.
21. A short history of this prison may be found at: https://www.battlefields.org/visit/heritage-sites/alton-military-prison-site.
22. *New York Herald*, January 12, 1862.
23. Ibid.
24. The Palmyra trials of John C. Tompkins, William J. Forshey, John Patton, Richard B. Crowder, George M. Pulliam, and Thomas S. Foster appear in *O.R.*, Series 2, vol. 1:374–402. All were found guilty and

sentenced to death. The sentences were confirmed by General Halleck. Later, they were commuted to imprisonment at Alton.

25. *New York Herald*, January 12, 1862.
26. Ibid.

> General Halleck is evincing his military wisdom by making strict rules for officers of the army, and of which there can be no evasion. On his arrival here in November, the policy he at once adopted showed that a change was to take place in the administration of affairs in the Western Department, and that order and discipline would be the substitute for the chaos and confusion of Frémont's reign.
>
> First came the order for all officers to return to their commands and report for duty. This sent many back to their places, but did not entirely clear the city. Next came an order that all officers found on the street without passes after nine o'clock P. M. would be liable to arrest. Passes were comparatively easy to obtain, and this order did not perfect the work. Within the past few days the clearing out process has been made complete by the promulgation of an order that officers on the streets, without proper passes at any time are liable to arrest, and materially restricting the issuing of passes by the proper authorities.
>
> General Halleck does not receive visitors with the urbanity characteristic of General Frémont; but he does what is far better: he keeps all branches of his army under the best possible discipline, and promptly meets the exigencies of his department.
>
> General Order No. 24 relating to the assessment of a tax of $10,000 upon the property of St. Louis secessionists for the support of the Southwest refugees, has not been suspended as was at first reported. Ten days have been added for compliance with the order, for what reason I cannot ascertain.

27. Ibid., January 19, 1862.

28. *Missouri Republican,* January 9, 1862.

> Special Orders, No. 18. The absence of one of the Board of Assessors appointed by General Orders, No. 21, ... a new Board is hereby appointed to consist of Colonel George Thorn, Colonel B. G. Farrar, Charles Borg, Esq., Franklin A. Dick, Esq., and Samuel H. Gardner, Esq.

The original member absent was Gen. Samuel Curtis, now at Rolla.

29. *New York Herald*, January 19, 1862.
30. The St. Louis Chamber of Commerce was located in the Merchant's Exchange Building at Main & Market Streets. In 1860, the officers included R. M. Funkhouser, President; Charles L. Tucker, and John T. Douglas, Vice-Presidents; and Wm. B. Baker, Secretary/Treasurer. Funkhouser was a banker; Tucker, a miller; Douglas, a rope (hemp) maker; Baker, proprietor of the Merchant Exchange Reporter & Prices Current publications.
31. *O.R.,* Series 1, vol. 8:472.
32. *New York Herald*, January 11, 1862.
33. Ibid., January 15, 1862.
34. Curtis seemed to manage men differently than Frémont. Curtis sent a note of approval to Carr for his timely movement. *O.R.,* Series 1, 8:484. The "camp on the Gasconade" was on the Osage Fork of the Gasconade. Today it would be near mile marker 145 on Interstate 44.
35. Jennison had rampaged through Missouri in the fall of 1861. The towns of Pleasant Hill, Dayton, and Columbus had been burned and looted. Halleck, in a report to McClellan, wrote, "The conduct of the forces under Lane and Jennison has done more for the enemy in this state that could have been accomplished by 20,000 of his own army." (*O.R.,* Series 1, vol. 8:449.)
36. *O.R.,* Series 1, vol. 8:471.
37. *New York Herald,* January 15, 1862.
38. Today known as Pacific, in Franklin County, MO.
39. *New York Herald*, January 16, 1862.
40. This quote may be from *Warwick Castle,* an 1815 novel by a "Miss Prickett."

41. *New York Herald*, January 16, 1862.

A serious rupture has occurred in the St. Louis Chamber of Commerce. At the annual elections, a few evenings since, the secession members endeavored to control the affairs, and elect officers of their own stripe, turning out those of Union sentiments and choosing in their places persons who adore the three-barred flag. The Union men became indignant and withdrew. Yesterday, they met and organized the Union Merchants Exchange, at the store room of L. W. Patchin & Co., corner of Main and Elm Streets. [[This Commission Merchant had its main offices at 138 & 139 Levee on the riverfront.] This firm offered to give the use of the rooms rent free, and an enthusiastic member donated a fine flag, which is to be permanently hoisted over the building. One hundred and fifty firms and individuals put down their names on the new list, paying on the spot the fee of $10 each. Today they meet for permanent organization and choice of officers. The Committee on Permanent Organization yesterday made the following report:

1. That all good, loyal Union men of St. Louis, engaged in mercantile or manufacturing pursuits, who desire to become members of the Union Exchange be and they are hereby requested to come forward and signify their intention by giving their names to the Secretary of this meeting.

2. That this body will proceed to the permanent organization of the Union Merchants Exchange of St. Louis, by the permanent officers for the ensuing year, at twelve o'clock, noon, on Saturday, the 11th inst., and that each member be required to pay the sum of ten dollars to the Secretary *pro tem* before casting his vote.

3. That the President appoint a committee of five

persons, whose duty it shall be to prepare suitable rules and regulations for the government of this Exchange.

4. That your present committee be continued for the purpose of procuring rooms for the permanent occupancy of this Exchange

The report of the committee was received and adopted by acclamation.

James Archer tendered to the Exchange a flag of the Union, to be displayed from the rooms on Saturday the 11th inst.

H. M. Woodward proposed to an iron safe in rooms free of rent.

The meeting passed a vote of thanks to Messrs. James H. Lucas, L. W. Patchin & Co., Teichman & Co., Wattenberg Bush & Co., James Archer and H. M. Woodward for their generous courtesies to this body.

Parties desiring membership in the Union Merchants Exchange were then invited to make application to the Secretary.

One hundred and fifty firms enrolled their names, when the Exchange adjourned to meet at eleven o'clock on Saturday the 11th inst., election of permanent officers to take place at twelve o'clock.

Judges of Election – Clinton B. Fisk, Alexander H. Smith and Henry S. Reed.

The Secretary will be present at the Union Exchange rooms at ten o'clock on Saturday morning to receive additional names and fees for membership.

List of members will be published in the city papers of Monday morning January 13, 1862.

S. M. Edgell, President
Clinton B. Fisk, Secretary

42. *New York Herald*, January 18, 1862.

43. Robert Wilson, of Andrew County, was vice president of the First Session of the Missouri Constitutional Convention, and with the absence of Sterling Price, who had been president, was elected unanimously president of the Second Session in July, 1861. William E. Parrish, *Turbulent Partnership: Missouri and the Union, 1861–1865* (Columbia, MO: University of Missouri Press, 1963), 4, 35, 87.
44. This was Thomas Lawson Price (1809–1870), probably the richest man in Jefferson City. He held slaves, but was a staunch Unionist. Lincoln named him brigadier general of volunteers and he commanded the post at Jefferson City until his election. He was not related to Sterling Price.
45. Since two appointments were made for the two Senate seats, it is unclear which new senator that Knox is referring to. Most likely it was Robert Wilson. *New York Herald*, January 18, 1862.
46. *New York Herald,* January 17, 18, 20, 1862.
47. Ibid., January 19, 1862.
48. Ibid., January 26, 1861.
49. Ibid.
50. This is incorrect. On January 23, Halleck ordered Curtis to advance to Lebanon. *O.R.,* Series 1, vol. 8:516.
51. Colonel Lewis Merrill (1834–1896) graduated from West Point in 1855. From 1856 to 1858 he served in Kansas, trying to suppress the fighting between pro- and anti-slavery factions. In August 1861 he was promoted to colonel of volunteers, commanding the 2nd Missouri Cavalry Volunteers. In 1861–62 his command actively scoured North Missouri suppressing guerrilla activity and rebel recruitment.
52. This skirmish is better known as the battle of Roan's Tan Yard.
53. *New York Herald,* January 26, 1862.
54. Knox is being coy. Abraham Lincoln served as counsel for the Illinois Central.
55. 340 miles is the distance from East St. Louis to Cincinnati.
56. Northern cotton mills were desperate for cotton, and alternative production areas were sought. In peacetime, such attempts could not compete with southern slave labor.

57. Goupil & Cie. was a Paris-based print company specializing in providing art reproductions and lithographs to the middle-class market. They had a branch in New York City. Lucas Place and Chouteau Avenue were elite neighborhoods.
58. *New York Herald*, January 25, 1862.
59. Ibid., January 27, 1862. The Mercantile Library was the oldest library west of the Mississippi River. Membership was by subscription. It supported the business community and had hosted the Convention that decided that Missouri would remain in the Union.

St. Louis, Mo., January 23, 1862.

The annual election of Officers of the Mercantile Library Association took place on Tuesday evening last. The number of members belonging to the association is ordinarily from three to four hundred; but on this election an aggregate of fifteen hundred votes were cast. The officers of last year were decidedly secession, and the Librarian and other employees of the concern were violent in their utterances of treason.

The Union members desired a change in the sentiment of the managing Board, and made arrangements to run a thoroughly Union ticket. The secessionists played a deep game by nominating a ticket on which were the names of several Union men, but with a majority against the latter. They then, through their mouthpiece, the *Republican*, talked loudly about the wrong of introducing "politics" into the management of the association, and persuaded quite a number of weak kneed Union men to agree with them. The Union men on the ticket of course did not work against it, and their influence and aid, combined with that of the secseshers, told heavily against the Union ticket. The officers voted for were as follows:-

Secession Ticket

President – John R. Beach*

Vice President – Charles Miller

Treasurer – John E. Yore
Recording Secretary – Henry C. Marston*
Corresponding Secretary – Charles L. Thompson
Directors – William A. Moffett, James A. Wilgus,* Henry Senter,* O. B. Filley,* George W. Parker, J. R. Lionberger, Joseph M. Hanson.

Those with a star annexed to their names are Union men. Below is the

Unconditional Union Ticket

President – Albert Pearce, of Henning & Woodruff
Vice President – Isidor Busch, of Busch & Taussig
Treasurer – E. D. Jones, Cashier Exchange Bank
Recording Secretary – John Proctor Smith, with Humphreys, Taylor & Co.
Corresponding Secretary – Charles H. Howland
Directors – William H. Benton of Pomeroy & Benton, Chauncey I. Filley, Daniel Gilchrist with Toomer Kimbrough & Co., Carlos S. Greeley, of Greeley & Gales, S. Rich of Rich & Co., Eben Richards, Jr., of Christopher & Richards, Henry R. Whitmore with Quartermaster.[sic]

The utmost exertions were put forth by both parties but the secessionists had the advantage of discrimination in their favor by the old officers. Who are made, ex officio, judges of the claim of parties to membership, added to the causes above mentioned, the Union men were beaten. During the day, upwards of a thousand new members were added to the association. The treasury was made glad by the influx of nearly $3,000. By the laws of the association the polls are required to be open at twelve o'clock and to close at nine o'clock P. M. Heretofore the custom has been to allow every man within the room at nine o'clock P. M. to vote, the door being closed to prevent further ingress. When nine o'clock arrived, the order was given to shut the doors, and it was promptly obeyed. On looking at the gathered crowd, it was noticed by the committee in charge of the polls that three-fourths of the waiting voters were Union members, and it was accordingly decided to close the polls and cut off further voting. The vote on the Union ticket was six hundred and twenty-five, and on the secession ticket eight hundred and seventy. Yesterday morning the *Democrat* was sorrowful over the result whilst the *Republican* was jubilant.

The result of this election reveals the secession feeling in St. Louis to a greater extent than has been exhibited by any previous event. The loyal citizens are quite crestfallen, as they had of late deluded themselves into the belief that St. Louis was rapidly becoming overwhelmingly loyal. The finale of the affair has shown them their error.

60. *New York Herald,* January 26, 1862.
61. Samuel Engler was listed in *Kennedy's 1860 City Directory* as a lard oil manufacturer. A writ of replevin is a prejudgment process ordering the seizure or attachment of alleged illegally taken or wrongfully withheld property, to be held in the U.S. Marshal's custody or that of another designated official, under order and supervision of the court, until the court determines otherwise.
62. This Martial Law is that declared by General Frémont in August 1861.
63. *New York Herald,* January 26, 1862.
64. See note 32, chapter 16.
65. *New York Herald*, January 27, 1862.
66. Lieutenant Colonel Benjamin James Farmer had formed the "Bloomfield Southern Guards" and had fought at Fredericktown on October 21 as part of Jeff Thompson's 1st Division, 2nd Infantry Regiment, Missouri State Guard. This regiment was mustered out in early January before his capture. Peterson, 77, 79, 82.
67. A telegraph line already stretched from Rolla to Springfield and beyond. Perhaps this was a reconstruction.
68. *New York Herald*, February 5, 1862.

69. These were not the only reasons for concern about General Sigel. Verbal and written reports were given to General Halleck by a number of officers, including Major Sturgis of Wilson's Creek fame, questioning Sigel's competence.
70. *O.R.,* Series 1, vol. 8:460, 461.
71. Ibid., 462.
72. Ibid., 471.
73. Promotion lists proved critical to resolving the command dispute between Curtis and Sigel. Curtis had been promoted to brigadier general on May 17, 1861 while Sigel's promotion came on August 7, to rank from May 17. This placed him in the May 17 promotion list, but below Curtis. Rank depended first on date and then on position within the list.
74. A complete portrayal of these incidents can be found in Stephen D. Engle, *Yankee Dutchman: The Life of Franz Sigel* (Fayetteville, AR: University of Arkansas Press, 1993), 90–99.
75. These events received greater mention in the *Rebellion Record,* vol. 4, Diary pp. 7–9. Deitzler was George Washington Deitzler (1826–1884). He had participated in the Kansas "troubles" since 1855. He raised the 1st Kansas Regiment and became its colonel. He was promoted to brigadier general and fought in the Vicksburg Campaign. Warner, *Generals in Blue,* 116–117.
76. *New York Herald*, February 5, 1862.
77. *O.R.,* Series 2, vol. 1:282–504
78. *New York Herald*, February 12, 1862.
79. An icon of Hellenistic art, the figurative Greek sculpture known as the *Laocoon Group*, or *Laocoon and His Sons*, is a monumental statue which is on display in the Vatican Museums, Rome. It is a marble copy of bronze sculpture, which, according to the Roman writer Pliny the Elder (23–79 CE), depicted the Trojan priest Laocoon and his two sons Antiphas and Thymbraeus being killed by giant snakes, as described by the Roman poet Virgil (70 BCE–19 CE) in his epic poem the *Aeneid*.

80. From Samuel Taylor Coleridge's translation of Friedrich Schiller's *Wallenstein*, Part II, Act 5, Scene 1.
81. These death sentences were not carried out. On February 20, 1862, in General Orders No. 44, Halleck commuted the death sentences to confinement at Alton (Illinois) Prison. But he also threatened that if further destruction occurred, the death sentences could be reinstated. *O.R.*, Series 1, vol. 8:561.
82. This can be attributed in part on the *Tribune's* reliance on overly ambitious maps prepared by railroad speculators and builders who often made very small distinctions between actual and proposed routes. The *Tribune* had no reporter on scene in St. Louis.
83. *New York Herald*, February 12, 1862.
84. While Davis was promoted to the rank of brigadier general on May 3, 1862, to date from December 18, 1861, he was still a colonel at the time of Pea Ridge.
85. *New York Herald*, February 12, 1862.

Chapter 18

1. Knox, *Camp-fire and Cotton-field*, 121–126.
2. This was William Fayel.
3. Fayel chose to remain with Curtis and the Army of the Southwest and its campaign through Arkansas that ended in Helena in July 1862.
4. *New York Herald*, February 27, 1862.
5. Phil Sheridan (1831–1888) later left the quartermaster service and made his fame in the cavalry. Warner, *Generals in Blue*, 437–439.
6. Solon Borland was a controversial figure in Arkansas politics who had many enemies. At the beginning of the war, Governor Henry M. Rector appointed him a commander of the Arkansas State Militia, but he was replaced by the Arkansas secession convention a month later. Later he commanded in northeast Arkansas, near Pocahontas. He helped to raise the 3rd Arkansas Cavalry which elected him colonel, but when the unit was sent to the east, Borland remained in Arkansas.

In his position as militia commander in north Arkansas, he ordered an embargo on goods to end price speculation.
7. *O.R.*, Series 1, vol. 8:64. Thirty men of the 3rd Iowa Cavalry succeeded in their mission, capturing five prisoners and restoring the Stars and Stripes to the courthouse. Mills served with the 24th Missouri Volunteer Infantry, becoming its colonel in 1863.
8. Thomas H. Price (1829–1883) was a cousin of Sterling Price and was a lawyer in Brunswick, Chariton County, near the home of Sterling Price. Later in the war Major Price served as a munitions expert in the plant at Selma, Alabama.
9. *Camp-fire and Cotton-field*, 125.
10. Burrowsville, now Marshall, Searcy County, Arkansas.
11. *Camp-fire and Cotton-field*, 125.
12. Ibid., 127.
13. Arthur B. Carter, *Tarnished Cavalier: Major General Earl Van Dorn* (Knoxville, TN: University of Tennessee Press, 1999), 42.

Chapter 19

1. The best study of the Battle of Pea Ridge is William L. Shea and Earl J. Hess, *Pea Ridge: Civil War Campaign in the West* (Chapel Hill, NC: University of North Carolina Press, 1992).
2. *New York Herald*, March 11, 1862.
3. Ibid., March 12, 1862. This report is also to be found in *O.R.*, Series 1, vol. 8:191–193.
4. Ibid., March 14, 1862. The author of this report is unknown.
5. Ibid., March 19, 1862. The various section headings in this account are those placed there by copy editor.
6. It was unlikely that any pursuit beyond the borders of Arkansas occurred, except into Missouri.
7. Major Joseph Conrad of the 3rd Missouri Infantry. *O.R.*, Series 1, vol. 8:278.
8. This expedition to Huntsville was extensively covered by Knox in his book, 131–133:

I accompanied an expedition, commanded by Colonel Vandever, of the 9th Iowa, to the town of Huntsville, thirty-five miles distant. Our march occupied two days, and resulted in the occupation of the town and the dispersal of a small camp of Rebels. We had no fighting, scarcely a shot being fired in anger. The inhabitants did not greet us very cordially, though some of them professed Union sentiments.

In this town of Huntsville, the best friend of the Union was the keeper of a whisky-shop. This man desired to look at some of our money, but declined to take it. An officer procured a canteen of whisky and tendered a Treasury note in payment. The note was refused, with a request for either gold or Rebel paper.

The officer then exhibited a large sheet of "promises to pay," which he had procured in Fayetteville a few days before, and asked how they would answer.

"That is just what I want," said the whisky vendor.

The officer called his attention to the fact that the notes had no signatures.

"That don't make any difference," was the reply; "nobody will know whether they are signed or not and they are just as good, anyhow."

I was a listener to the conversation, and at this juncture proffered a pair of scissors to assist in dividing the notes. It took but a short time to cut off enough "money" to pay for twenty canteens of the worst whisky I ever saw.

At Huntsville we made a few prisoners, who said they were on their way from Price's army to Forsyth, Missouri. They gave us the important information that the Rebel army, thirty thousand strong, was on the Boston Mountains the day previous; and on the very day of our arrival at Huntsville, it was to begin its advance toward our front. These men, and some others, had been sent away because they had no weapons with which to enter the fight.

Immediately on learning this, Colonel Vandever dispatched a courier to General Curtis, and prepared to set out on his return to the main army. We marched six miles before nightfall, and at midnight, while we were endeavouring to sleep, a courier joined us from the commander-in-chief. He brought orders for us to make our way back with all possible speed, as the Rebel army was advancing in full force.

At two o'clock we broke camp, and, with only one halt of an hour, made a forced march of forty-one miles, joining the main column at ten o'clock at night. I doubt if there were many occasions during the war where better marching was done by infantry than on that day. Of course, the soldiers were much fatigued, but were ready, on the following day to take active part in the battle.

9. The listing of brigades and divisions has a few inaccuracies, but is overall quite good. See Shea and Hess, 331–339.

THE UNION STRENGTH:
The Union forces engaged in the battle were as follows: Commander-In-Chief Brigadier General Samuel R. Curtis.
1ST DIVISION
Colonel Osterhaus Commanding.
    36th Illinois Infantry.
    12th Missouri Infantry.
    17th Missouri Infantry.
    Battalion 3rd Missouri Infantry.
    Two battalions Benton Hussars (cavalry).
    One battalion 39th Illinois Cavalry [36th Infantry].
    Battery A, Capt. Welfrey, six guns.
    Battery B, six guns [4th Ohio Light Artillery].

1st Brigade
Colonel Coler Commanding.
    25th Illinois Infantry.
    44th Illinois Infantry.
2nd Brigade
Colonel Greusel Commanding.

2ND DIVISION
Brigadier General Asboth, Commanding.
1st Brigade
Colonel Schaefer, Commanding.
    2nd Missouri Infantry.
    2nd Ohio Battery (six guns), Lieutenant Chapman.
2nd Brigade
Colonel Joliat, Commanding.
    15th Missouri Infantry.
    Capt. Elbert's Flying Battery (six guns).
    6th Missouri Cavalry, Col. Wright.
    Battalion 4th Missouri Cavalry, Major Meszaros.
General Sigel commanded the 1st and 2nd divisions, thus filling the position of Field Marshal.

3RD DIVISION
Colo. Jeff. C. Davis, Commanding.
1st Brigade
Col. Barton [Benton], Commanding.
    8th Indiana Infantry.
    22nd Indiana Infantry.
    18th Indiana Infantry.
    Indiana Battery, six guns.
2nd Brigade
Col. White, Commanding.
    37th Illinois Infantry.
    9th Missouri Infantry.
    Battery, four guns.

[The 9th Missouri has been placed on the list of Illinois regiments, and now ranks as the "Fifty-ninth Illinois."]

4TH DIVISION

Colonel Carr, Commanding.

1st Brigade

Colonel Dodge, Commanding.

    4th Iowa Infantry.

    35th Illinois Infantry.

    1st Iowa Battery, Captain Jones, six guns.

2nd Brigade

Colonel Vandever, Commanding.

    9th Iowa Infantry.

    25th Missouri Infantry (Phelps's regiment).

    3rd Illinois Cavalry.

    Dubuque Battery, Captain Hayden, six guns.

The following were not brigaded:

    3rd Iowa Cavalry, two battalions, Colonel Bussey.

    Mountain Howitzer Battery, four guns, Capt. Stevens.

    Battalion of Cavalry, General Curtis's body guard, Major W. D. Bowen.

But few of the above regiments were full, many of them having left considerable numbers of sick at Rolla and Lebanon. The aggregate number of effective men in the federal army on the morning of the battle it would not be prudent to mention, but it is much smaller than generally supposed.

THE CONFEDERATE STRENGTH.

The rebel army, from reports of spies and prisoners, is estimated as follows:

Commander-in-Chief Major General Earl Van Dorn

Missouri troops, under Brig. General Price, about 9,000.

Arkansas, Louisiana and Texas troops, under Brigadier General McCulloch, about 13,000.

Choctaw, Cherokee, Chickasaw and other Indian troops,

with two white regiments under Brigadier General Pike, about 7,000.

Estimated aggregate of rebel army under General Van Dorn 30,000.

10. From John Milton's *Paradise Lost*.
11. Surely this is a misprint. They were only a mile and a half from Curtis's headquarters.
12. Knox exaggerates, but only slightly. Per Shea and Hess, the 9th Iowa suffered more casualties than any other Union unit, a total of 218 (38 killed, 176 wounded, 4 missing); the 4th Iowa was second, with a total of 160 (18 killed, 139 wounded, 3 missing). Shea and Hess, 335.
13. From "The Song of the Camp," by Bayard Taylor, American poet, 1825–1878.
14. This was Pea Ridge, the namesake for the battle.
15. Knox is referring to the service of the Indiana Brigade at the Battle of Buena Vista, in the Mexican War (February 22–23, 1847).
16. This was Colonel Gustavus A. Smith (1820–1885). He was severely wounded, but survived. He was promoted to brigadier general in August 1862, but the Senate failed to act on his nomination. Warner, *Generals in Blue*, 458–459.
17. Colonel Nicholas Gruesel (1817–1896) was later breveted brigadier general.
18. This was not the 25th Missouri. Colonel John S. Phelps (1814–1886) organized the regiment which bore his name in September–December 1861. It was raised at Rolla, largely of Union refugees from southwestern Missouri. By special arrangement with the Federal Government, the regiment was classified as an independent unit of Missouri Volunteer Infantry. It bore no numerical designation. The members enlisted for a term of six months rather than the customary three years. After service at Rolla, the regiment joined the Army of Southwest Missouri in February 1862. It saw action at Pea Ridge, losing twenty-five officers and men killed. The unit was mustered out in May 1862. http://shsmo.org/manuscripts/rolla/r0272.pdf
19. Henry Hoffman Trimble, (1827–1911) of the 3rd Iowa Cavalry was

severely wounded in the face and received medical discharge with his injury that would trouble him the rest of his life. Col. Calvin A. Ellis (unk.–1895) did not fare so well as a soldier. In March 1862 he was charged with numerous violations of the Articles of War, including "beastly intoxication." The controversial officer was mustered out of service on April 2, 1862, before a court martial could be convened.

20. William Y. Slack (1816–1862) died of his wounds March 21. Warner, *Generals in Gray*, 278. James H. McBride (1814–1864) was not at Pea Ridge but some of the units he had commanded in the Missouri State Guard were.
21. J. Madison Morton's *Poor Pillicoddy,* a farce in one act. The play was composed before 1850 and presented in New York and Boston in the 1850s.
22. *New York Herald*, March 23, 1862.
23. Shea and Hess, 331–334. For additional accounts of the aftermath of the battle, see Schultz, *The March to the River,* Chapters 2 and 3.
24. Numbers in parentheses are from the Civil War Sites Advisory Commission, mainly based on Shea and Hess. http://civilwarlandscapes.org/cwla/cwsac/ar001.htm; the figures from Knox two days after the battle are amazingly close to much later numbers.
25. There are no exact figures for Confederate casualties. General Van Dorn's numbers are highly suspect and, for a number of reasons, not accurate. Estimates vary from a total of 2000–2500 (National Park Service) to 4,600 (Civil War Sites Advisory Commission).
26. This was the 17th Arkansas regiment, Colonel Frank A. Rector (1829–1874) commanding. The regiment was not disbanded but did receive considerable opprobrium for its abandonment of its colors on the battlefield, and it was reorganized.
27. This report to Governor Jackson is not attached, but may be found in *O.R.*, Series 1, vol. 8, 756–757. The "last line" Knox refers to reads: "Governor, we are confident of the future."
28. *New York Herald*, March 17, 1862.
29. Knox, *Camp-fire and Cotton-field,* 145–146.

Chapter 20

1. An excellent description of the fraudulent news stories can be found in David Bosse, "'The Enemy Were Falling like Autumn Leaves.' Fraudulent Newspaper Reports of the Battle of Pea Ridge," *The Arkansas Historical Quarterly* 54 (Autumn 1995), 359–375.
2. Wilkie, *Pen and Powder*, 127.
3. Knox, *Camp-fire and Cotton-field*, 166–167.
4. Ibid., 190. Andrews, 250.
5. Knox, *Camp-fire and Cotton-field*, 192–193.
6. Ibid., 253–260. The entire transcript of this trial is to be found at Southern Illinois University Library, Carbondale, IL. http://archives.lib.siu.edu/?p=collections/findingaid&id=2274&q=. The opening page, in Knox's handwriting reads:

   > In December of 1862 I accompanied the Vicksburg expedition by authority of Major Genl Grant. I wrote a history of its operations, for publication in the *New York Herald*. The expedition was a complete failure, and the officer who led it was much chagrined at the publication of the story of his disaster. In revenge he caused me to be arrested and tried as a spy, the court being composed, at his direction, of officers under his command. He failed to establish anything against me upon the main charges, but succeeded in showing a violation of an Army regulation, practically obsolete, and no where enforced. This volume contains the record of the trial.

7. Donald Ross and James J. Schramer, *American Travel Writers, 1850–1915*. Vol. 189, Dictionary of Literary Biography (Detroit, MI: Gale Research, 1998), 238, article by James A. Wren.
8. This medal resides in the Thomas W. Knox Collection at the Southern Illinois University Library.
9. *New York Times*, January 7, 1896.
10. This memorial stone is readily visible from the street and reads: "Thomas W. Knox, 1835–1896, Author and Traveler." On the reverse

of the stone are the names of his mother and father, but they are buried elsewhere in this cemetery.

Appendix

1. *The War of the Rebellion: A Compilation of the Official Records of the Union and Confederate Armies,* 128 vols. (Washington, 1880–1901), Series 1, vol. 3:370. Hereafter cited as O.R.
2. Ibid., 371–372.
3. Ibid., 375.
4. *New York Herald,* June 6, 1861.
5. Ibid., June 14, 1861.
6. *St. Louis Democrat,* June 15, 1861.
7. Two versions of this proclamation appeared. The one printed here appeared in the *New York Herald* on June 18, 1861. The one that appeared in Peckham, 274, had a few different wordings, but the overall content was the same.
8. *New York Herald,* June 27, 1861.
9. *New York Herald,* July 8, 1861.
10. *New York Herald,* July 14, 1861.
11. *New York Herald,* July 14, 1861.
12. Wilkie, *The Iowa First,* 89–93
13. Both the *New York Times* and the *New York Herald* published Frémont's Proclamation on September 1, 1861. It is also found in the *Official Records,* Series 1, vol. 3: 466–467.
14. *St. Louis Evening News,* September 23, 1861.
15. Names and titles only were listed in the *New York Herald,* November 7, 1861. The author researched other sources for additional biographical information.
16. O.R., Series 2, vol. 1:558–559.
17. O.R., Series 1, vol. 5:37–38.
18. From the *Appendix of the Journal of the Senate,* p. 134.
19. O.R., Series 1, vol. 8:496–497, 514–515.

Bibliography

Government Documents:

Journal of the Missouri State Convention Held at the City of St. Louis, October 1861. St. Louis: Geo. Knapp & Co., 1861.

Journal of the Senate of the State of Missouri at the Regular Session of the 23rd General Assembly. Jefferson City, MO: W. A. Curry, Public Printer, 1865.

Proceedings of the Courts of Inquiry and Courts-Martial in the Case of Justus McKinstry. House of Representatives, 37th Congress, 2nd Session. Ex. Doc. No. 144.

Report of the Joint Committee on the Conduct of the War. House of Representatives, 37th Congress, 3rd Session. Rep. Co. No. 108.

Register of the Officers of the United States Military Academy, at West Point, N.Y., from March 16, 1802, to January 1, 1890. Third Edition. In four Volumes.

United States War Department. *The War of the Rebellion. A Compilation of the Official Records of the Union and Confederate Armies.* 128 Volumes. Washington DC: U.S. Government Printing Office, 1880–1901.

Newspapers:

Harper's Weekly.

New York Herald.

New York Times.

New York Tribune.

Rocky Mountain News (Denver, CO).

St. Louis Evening News.

St. Louis Daily Missouri Democrat.

St. Louis Daily Missouri Republican.

Books and Articles:

Adamson, Hans C. *Rebellion in Missouri. Nathaniel Lyon and His Army of the West.* Philadelphia: Chilton Co., 1961.

Allardice, Bruce S. *Confederate Colonels: A Biographical Register.* Columbia, MO: University of Missouri Press, 2008.

———. *More Generals in Gray.* Baton Rouge, LA: Louisiana State University Press, 1995.

Ambrose, Stephen E. *Halleck, Lincoln's Chief of Staff.* Baton Rouge, LA: Louisiana State University Press, 1990.

Anders, Curt. *Henry Halleck's War.* Carmel, IN: Guild Press of Indiana, Inc., 2000.

Anders, Leslie. "The Blackwater Incident." *Missouri Historical Review* 88 (July 1994): 416–429.

Anderson, Galusha. *A Border City during the Civil War.* Boston: Little, Brown & Co., 1908.

Andrews, J. Cutler. *The North Reports the Civil War.* Pittsburgh: University of Pittsburgh Press, 1955.

Banasik, Michael E., ed. *Confederate Tales of the War in the Trans-Mississippi, Part One, 1861.* Iowa City, IA: Camp Pope Publishing, 2010.

———. *Serving With Honor: The Diary of Captain Eathan Allen Pinnell of the Eighth Missouri Infantry (Confederate).* Iowa City, IA: Camp Pope Bookshop, 1999.

Barry, Louise, ed. "Albert D. Richardson's Letters on the Pike's Peak Gold Region." *Kansas Historical Quarterly* 12, no. 1 (February 1943): 14–57.

Bartels, Carolyn. *The Forgotten Men, Missouri State Guard.* Independence, MO: Two Trails Publishing, 1995.

Bates, Alice L. "The History of the Telegraph in California." *Annual Publication of the Historical Society of Southern California* 9, no. 3 (1914): 181–187.

The Biographical Dictionary of Iowa. Iowa City, IA: The University of Iowa Press, 2009.

Boernstein, Henry. *Memoirs of a Nobody. The Missouri Years of an Austrian Radical, 1849–1866.* Trans. Steven Rowan. St. Louis: Missouri Historical Society Press, 1997.

Boman, Dennis K. *Lincoln and Citizens' Rights in Civil War Missouri.* Baton Rouge, LA: Louisiana State University Press, 2011.

Bosse, David. "'The Enemy Were Falling Like Autumn Leaves.' Fraudulent Newspaper Reports of the Battle of Pea Ridge." *The Arkansas Historical Quarterly* 54 (Autumn 1995): 359–375.

Bostick, Douglas W. *The Confederacy's Secret Weapon, The Civil War Illustrations of Frank Vizetelly.* Charleston, SC: The History Press, 2009.

Brooksher, William R. *Bloody Hill, The Civil War Battle of Wilson's Creek.* Washington: Brassey's, 1995.

Browne, Junius Henri. *Four Years in Secessia.* Hartford, CT: O. D. Case & Co., 1865.

Brugioni, Dino. *The Civil War in Missouri As Seen from the Capitol City.* Jefferson City, MO: Summers Publishing, 1987.

Burchett, Kenneth E. *The Battle of Carthage, Missouri.* Jefferson, NC: McFarland & Co., 2013.

Campbell, R. A. *Campbell's Gazetteer of Missouri.* St. Louis: R. A. Campbell, 1875.

Carter, Arthur B. *Tarnished Cavalier: Major General Earl Van Dorn.* Knoxville, TN: University of Tennessee Press, 1999.

Castel, Albert. *Civil War Kansas.* Lawrence, KS: University Press of Kansas, 1997.

Clayton, Charles C. *Little Mac: Joseph McCullagh of the St. Louis Globe-Democrat.* Carbondale, IL: Southern Illinois University Press, 1969.

Coffin, Charles C. *My Days and Nights on the Battlefield.* Leonaur Books, 2009.

Coffin, Charles C. *The Boys of '61.* Leonaur Books, 2011.

Collins, Robert. *Jim Lane: Scoundrel, Statesman, Kansan.* Gretna, LA.: Pelican Publishing Co., 2007.

Crozier, Emmet. *Yankee Reporters, 1861–1865.* New York: Oxford University Press, 1956.

Cosner, Victoria and Lorelei Shannon. *Missouri's Mad Dr. McDowell: Confederates, Cadavers and Macabre Medicine.* Charleston, SC: The History Press, 2015.

Cullum, George W. *Biographical Register of the Officers and Graduates of the U.S. Military Academy at West Point, N.Y., From Its Establishment, in 1802 to 1890.* Boston: Houghton-Mifflin Co., 1891.

Driscoll, John K. *Rogue: A Biography of Civil War General Justus McKinstry.* Jefferson, NC: McFarland & Co., 2005.

Dyer, Frederick H. *A Compendium of the War of the Rebellion.* Des Moines, IA: The Dyer Publishing Co., 1908. Reprint. Dayton, OH: Morningside Press, 1994.

Eicher, John H. and David J. Eicher. *Civil War High Commands.* Stanford, CA: Stanford University Press, 2001.

Bibliography 541

Engle, Stephen D. *Yankee Dutchman: The Life of Franz Sigel*. Fayetteville, AR: University of Arkansas Press, 1993.

Fiske, Stephen. *Off-hand Portraits of Prominent New Yorkers*. New York: Geo. R. Lockwood & Son., 1884. (Knox is to be found on pp. 222-228.)

Forman, Jacob G. *The Western Sanitary Commission*. St. Louis: R. P. Studley & Co., 1864.

Frost, Griffin. *Camp and Prison Journal*. Iowa City, IA: Camp Pope Bookshop, 1994.

Gerteis, Louis S. *Civil War St. Louis*. Lawrence, KS: University Press of Kansas, 2001.

Gibson, Charles D. and E. Kay Gibson. *Dictionary of Transports and Combatant Vessels, Steam and Sail, Employed by the Union Army*. Vol. 1, *The Army's Navy Series*. Camden, ME: Ensign Press, 1995.

Gott, Kendall D. *Where the South Lost the War: An Analysis of the Fort Henry-Fort Donelson Campaign February 1862*. Mechanicsburg, PA: Stackpole Books, 2003.

Grasso, Christopher, ed. *Bloody Engagements: John R. Kelso's Civil War*. New Haven: Yale University Press, 2017.

Harding, Samuel B. *Life of George R. Smith, Founder of Sedalia, MO*. Sedalia, MO: N.p., 1904.

Harris, Brayton. *War News: Blue & Gray in Black & White, Newspapers in the Civil War*. Lexington, KY: N.p., 2010.

Herr, Pamela and Mary Lee Spence, eds. *The Letters of Jessie Benton Frémont*. Urbana, IL: University of Illinois Press, 1993.

Hinze, David C. and Karen Farnham. *The Battle of Carthage: Border War in Southwest Missouri, July 5, 1861*. Gretna, LA: Pelican Publishing Co., 2004.

History of Boone County, Missouri. St. Louis: Western Historical Co., 1882.

History of Greene County, Missouri. Chicago: Goodspeed Bros., 1893.

History of Lafayette County, Mo. St. Louis: Missouri Historical Company, 1881.

Holland, J. G. *Scribner's Monthly, An Illustrated Magazine for the People.* New York, NY: Scribner & Co., 1874.

Hubble, Martin J. *Personal Reminiscences and Fragments of The Early History of Springfield and Greene County, Missouri: Related By Pioneers and Their Descendants at Old Settlers' Dinners Given at the Home of Capt. Martin J. Hubble, March 31, 1907, 1908, 1909, 1910, 1911.* Springfield, MO: Inland Printing, 1914.

Johnson, Robert U. and Clarence Buel. *Battles and Leaders of the Civil War.* 4 vols. New York. The Century Co. 1887–1888. Reprint. Secaucus, NJ: Castle Books, 1991.

Knight, H. Jackson. *Confederate Invention. The Story of the Confederate States Patent Office and Its Inventors.* Baton Rouge: Louisiana State University Press, 2011.

Knox, Thomas W. *Backsheesh! Or Life and Adventures in the Orient.* Hartford, CT: A. D. Worthington & Co., Publishers, 1875.

———. *Camp-fire and Cotton-field: Southern Adventure in Time of War. Life with the Union Armies and Residence on a Louisiana Plantation.* New York: Blelock & Co. 1865.

———. *The Lost Army.* New York: The Merriam Co., 1894.

———. "To Pike's Peak and Denver." *Knickerbocker's New York Monthly Magazine* 58 (August 1861): 115–128.

Konstam, Angus. *Union River Ironclad 1861–65.* New Vanguard 56. Osceola, WI: Osprey Publishing, 2002.

Leopard, Buel and Floyd C. Shoemaker. *The Messages and Proclamations of the Governors of the State of Missouri.* Columbia, MO: The State Historical Society of Missouri, 1922.

McElroy, John. *The Struggle for Missouri*. Washington, DC: National Tribune Co., 1909.

Marszalek, John F. *Sherman's Other War: The General the Civil War Press*. Kent, OH: Kent State University Press, 1999.

———. *Commander of All Lincoln's Armies: A Life of General Henry W. Halleck*. Cambridge, MA: Belknap Press (Harvard University Press), 2004.

Miller, Edward A. *Lincoln's Abolitionist General: The Biography of David Hunter*. Columbia, SC: University of South Carolina Press, 1997.

The Missouri State Gazetteer and Business Directory. St. Louis: Sutherland & McEvoy Publishers, 1860.

Monaghan, Jay. *Civil War on the Western Border, 1854–1865*. Boston: Little, Brown, 1955. Reprint. Lincoln, NE: University of Nebraska Press, Bison Books, 1984.

Moore, Frank, ed. *The Rebellion Record: A Diary of American Events*. 12 vols. New York: G. P. Putnam, 1862.

Mott, Frank Luther. *American Journalism, A History: 1690–1960*. New York: The MacMillan Company, 1962.

Nevins, Allan. *Frémont, Pathmarker of the West*. Lincoln, NE: University of Nebraska Press, Bison Books, 1992.

Parrish, William E. *Frank Blair: Lincoln's Conservative*. Columbia, MO: University of Missouri Press, 1998.

———. *Turbulent Partnership: Missouri and the Union, 1861–1865*. Columbia, MO: University of Missouri Press, 1963.

Patrick, Jeffrey L. *Campaign for Wilson's Creek: The Fight for Missouri Begins*. Buffalo Gap, TX: McWhiney Foundation Press, 2011.

Peckham, James. *Gen. Nathaniel Lyon and Missouri in 1861*. New York: American News Company, 1866.

Perry, James M. *A Bohemian Brigade: The Civil War Correspondents.* New York: John Wiley & Sons, 2000.

Peterson, Richard C., Kip A. Lindberg, James E. McGhee, and Keith I. Daleen. *Sterling Price's Lieutenants: A Guide to the Officers and Organization of the Missouri State Guard, 1861–1865.* Revised Edition. Independence, MO: Two Trails Publishing, 1997.

Phillips, Christopher. *Damned Yankee: The Life of General Nathaniel Lyon.* Columbia, MO: University of Missouri Press, 1990.

———. *Missouri's Confederate: Claiborne Fox Jackson and the Creation of Southern Identity in the Border West.* Columbia, MO: University of Missouri Press, 2000.

Piston, William Garrett and Richard W. Hatcher, III. *Wilson's Creek: The Second Battle of the Civil War and the Men Who Fought It.* Chapel Hill, NC: University of North Carolina Press, 2000.

Plum, William R. *The Military Telegraph during the Civil War in the United States.* Chicago: Jansen, McClurg & Co., 1882.

Powell, William H. and Edward Shippen. *Officers of the Army and Navy Who Served in the Civil War.* Philadelphia: L. R. Hamersly & Co., 1892.

Reynolds, Thomas C. *Sterling Price and the Confederacy.* Edited by Robert G. Schultz. St. Louis: Missouri History Museum Press, 2009.

Richardson, Albert D. *The Secret Service, the Field, the Dungeon and the Escape.* Hartford, CT: American Publishing Company, 1865.

———. *Beyond the Mississippi: From the Great River to the Great Ocean.* Hartford, CT: American Publishing Co., 1867.

Risley, Ford. *Civil War Journalism.* Santa Barbara, CA: Praeger, 2012.

Rombauer, Robert J. *The Union Cause in St. Louis in 1861.* St. Louis: Nixon-Jones, 1909.

Ross, Donald and James J. Schramer. *American Travel Writers,*

1850–1915. Vol. 189, *Dictionary of Literary Biography.* Detroit, MI: Gale Research,1998.

Roth, Mitchel P. *Historical Dictionary of War Journalism.* Westport, CT: Greenwood Press, 1997.

———. *The Encyclopedia of War Journalism, 1807–2010.* Amenia, NY: Grey House Publishing, 2010.

Rowan, Steven, ed. *Germans for a Free Missouri: Translations from the St. Louis Radical Press, 1857–1862.* Columbia, MO: University of Missouri Press, 1983.

Sachsman, David B., et al., eds. *Words at War: The Civil War and American Journalism.* West Lafayette, IN: Purdue University Press, 2008.

Schrantz, Ward L. *Jasper County in the Civil War.* Carthage, MO: The Carthage Press, 1923.

Schultz, Robert G. *The March to the River: From the Battle of Pea Ridge to Helena, Spring 1862.* Iowa City, IA: Camp Pope Publishing, 2014.

Scott, Douglas D., Thomas D. Thiessen, and Steve J. Dasovich. *The First Battle of Boonville,Cooper County, Missouri, June 17, 1861: Archeological and Historical Investigations.* St. Louis, MO: Heritage Identification and Preservation Foundation, 2009.

Shea, William L. and Earl J. Hess. *Pea Ridge: Civil War Campaign in the West.* Chapel Hill, NC: University of North Carolina Press, 1992.

Shoemaker, F. C. and Buel Leopard. *The Messages and Proclamations of the Governors of the State of Missouri.* Vol. 3. Columbia, MO: The State Historical Society of Missouri, 1922.

Simon, John Y., ed. *The Papers of Ulysses S. Grant.* 32 vols. Carbondale, IL: Southern Illinois University Press, 1967–2012.

Snead, Thomas L. *The Fight for Missouri.* New York: Charles Scribner's Sons, 1886. Reprint. Independence, MO: Two Trails Publishing, 1997.

Starr, Louis M. *The Civil War's Bohemian Brigade.* New York: A. A. Knopf, 1954.

Stuart, A. A. *Iowa Colonels and Regiments.* Des Moines, IA: Mills & Co., 1865. Reprint. Salem, MA: Higginson Book Co., 1998.

United States Biographical Dictionary and Portrait Gallery of Eminent and Self-Made Men. New York: United States Biographical Publishing Co., 1878.

Weisberger, Bernard A. *Reporters for the Union.* Boston: Little, Brown & Co., 1953.

Ware, Eugene F. *The Lyon Campaign in Missouri. A History of the First Iowa Infantry.* Topeka, KS: Crane & Co., 1907. Reprint. Iowa City, IA: Camp Pope Bookshop, 1991.

Warner, Ezra. *Generals in Blue.* Baton Rouge, LA: Louisiana State University Press. 1992.

———. *Generals in Gray.* Baton Rouge, LA. Louisiana State University Press. 1987.

Way, Frederick, Jr. *Way's Packet Directory, 1848–1983: Passenger Steamboats of the Mississippi River System since the Advent of Photography in Mid-continent America.* Athens, OH: Ohio University Press, 1983.

Wilkie, Franc B. *The Iowa First: Letters from the War.* Dubuque, IA: The Herald Book and Job Establishment, 1861.

———. *Thirty-five Years of Journalism.* Chicago: F. J. Schulte & Co., 1891.

———. *Pen and Powder.* Boston: Ticknor and Company, 1888.

Winter, William C. *The Civil War in St. Louis, A Guided Tour.* St. Louis: Missouri Historical Society, 1994.

Woodward, Ashbel. *Life of General Lyon.* Hartford, CT: Case, Lockwood & Co., 1862.

Theses and Dissertations:

Sale, Sara Lee. *Governor Claiborne Fox Jackson and His Role in the Secession Movement in Missouri, 1861.* Warrensburg, MO. Central Missouri State University. MA Thesis. 1979.

Websites:

2nd Kansas Infantry
http://www.kansasguardmuseum.com/?page_id=1968

Abraham Lincoln and Civil War Finance
http://abrahamlincolnsclassroom.org/abraham-lincoln-in-depth/abraham-lincoln-and-civil-war-finance/

Alton Military Prison
https://www.battlefields.org/visit/heritage-sites/alton-military-prison-site

The American Presidency Project: Abraham Lincoln, First Annual Message, December 3, 1861
http://www.presidency.ucsb.edu/ws/index.php?pid=29502

A Brief History of Fort Leavenworth, 1827–1983
http://dtic.mil/dtic/tr/fulltext/u2/a437828.pdf

Abstract of Wars & Military Engagements: War of 1812 through World War I
https://www.sos.mo.gov/archives/soldiers/abstract

Battle of Boonville
http://www.thecivilwarmuse.com/index.php?page=the-battle-of-boonville

Battle of Mount Zion Church (Boone County, MO)
https://en.wikipedia.org/wiki/Battle_of_Mount_Zion_Church

Biographical Directory of the United States Congress:
 Sempronius H. Boyd
   http://bioguide.congress.gov/scripts/biodisplay.pl?index=B000720

Trusten Polk
   http://bioguide.congress.gov/scripts/biodisplay.pl?index=P000411

Richard H. Weightman
   http://bioguide.congress.gov/scripts/biodisplay.pl?index=W000255

The Civil War in Missouri: Faces of Soldiers
http://www.civilwarmo.org/exhibits/means-war/faces-of-soldiers

Civil War Sites Advisory Commission, Battle Summaries: Pea Ridge
http://civilwarlandscapes.org/cwla/cwsac/ar001.htm

Colorado Newspapers
Center for Colorado and the West at Auraria Library. http://skyline.ucdenver.edu/record=b2000473~S0

Collected Works of Abraham Lincoln, Vol. 4.
http://quod.lib.umich.edu/l/lincoln/lincoln4?view=toc

The Copper Deposits of Missouri
http://pubs.usgs.gov/bul/0267/report.pdf

"Escape From Alton Prison: 1862"
https://madison.illinoisgenweb.org/prison_magoffin_escape.html

"Ever Be Happy" or the Pirate's Farewell Ballad
https://www.loc.gov/resource/sm1849.461380.0/?sp=2

Find a Grave:
   Thomas W. Knox
      https://www.findagrave.com/memorial/20484672/thomas-w-knox

   William White
      https://www.findagrave.com/cgi-bin/fg.cgi?page=gr&GRid=87508577&ref=acom

Kennedy's 1860 St. Louis City Directory
https://www.rollanet.org/~bdoerr/1860CyDir/1860CD-C.htm#C

Knox, Thomas W.
http://en.wikipedia.org/wiki/Thomas_W._Knox

McKinstry, Justus.
http://www.civilwarstlouis.com/articles/justus-mckinstry-enemies/

Phelps's Regiment
http://shsmo.org/manuscripts/rolla/r0272.pdf

Richardson, Albert D.
https://en.wikipedia.org/wiki/Albert_D._Richardson

Thomas W. Knox Collection, 1863–1915, Southern Illinois University Special Collections Research Center
https://archives.lib.siu.edu/?p=collections/findingaid&id=2274&q=

Tucker's War
http://www.civilwarstlouis.com/biographies/tuckers-war/

"Union officers in Corinth fight each other, 1 dies"
https://www.nps.gov/shil/upload/Cornyn.pdf

Wilkie, Franc Bangs.
The Biographical Dictionary of Iowa. http://uipress.lib.uiowa.edu/bdi/DetailsPage.aspx?id=407

Zagonyi, Charles.
http://www.ozarkscivilwar.org/archives/354

Index

Able, Bart 35, 36, 185, 461
Adams, Augustus 508
Adams, James L. 373
Albert, Anselm 441
Allen, Robert 440–441
Alton Prison, IL 333, 334, 518, 527
Anderson, G. 508
Anderson, Galusha 508
Anderson, Major—— 372
Anderson, Robert 495
Andrews, George L. 35, 39–40, 79, 101, 114, 122, 133, 144, 160, 460, 491
Andrews, T. P. 441
Annay, T. O. 426
Archer, James 521
Asboth, Alexander 221, 222, 225, 229, 247, 248, 256, 257, 264, 317, 390, 439, 501, 531
Aubrey, F. X. 166–167, 492
Axtell, Stephen D. 325

Backoff (Backof), Frank 101
Bailey, Mary A. 508
Baker, James 308, 320
Baker, Wm. B. 519
Bane, Moses 292, 510
Banks, Nathaniel P. 80, 502
Barclay, D. Robert 443
Barnes, Lucien J. 65, 105, 347, 462, 484
Bates, Edward 285, 287
Bates, John F. 61, 62, 84, 101, 122, 133, 466
Battles and Skirmishes
  Antietam, MD 515
  Arkansas Post, AR 484
  Atlanta, GA 503
  Belmont, MO x
  Boonville, MO xvi, 44–65, 64–65, 76, 223, 470
  Carthage, MO x, 87–89, 91, 103, 105, 114, 483–484, 515
  Chattanooga, TN 484
  Chickasaw Bayou, MS xxii, 409, 479, 482, 503
  Cole Camp, MO 58–59, 232, 464, 467, 474
  Corinth, MS (Battle of) 481, 484, 510
  Corinth, MS (Seige of) 408
  Dug Springs, MO xvi, 118–120, 125, 399
  First Bull Run, VA 127, 141, 312, 360, 493, 502
  Forsyth, MO 105–111, 430–436
  Fort Blakely, AL 463
  Fort Donelson, TN 407, 408, 480, 499
  Fort Henry, TN 360, 407, 408, 480, 499
  Fort Scott, KS 188, 193
  Franklin, TN 484
  Fredericksburg, VA 515
  Fredericktown, MO x, 242, 267, 284, 472, 525
  Helena, AR 493
  Island Number Ten, MO 408
  Iuka, MS 484, 510
  Lexington, MO x, 192–193, 195–196, 199, 202–203, 438–439, 470, 471, 493
  McCulla's Farm, MO 121–124, 486
  Memphis, TN 409

Index 551

Mount Zion Church, MO 331–332, 517
New Madrid, MO 408
New Market, VA 515
Pea Ridge, AR xvii, 378–406, 407, 458, 469, 472, 480, 486, 490, 493, 503, 504, 510, 515, 527, 528, 534
Pilot Knob, MO 493, 494
Shelbina, MO 184, 495
Shiloh, TN 408, 469, 480, 481, 493
Springfield, MO (Zagonyi's Charge) 230, 244–245, 275, 442
Valle Forge 87, 480
Vicksburg, MS 469, 481, 484, 492, 497, 526, 535
Wilson's Creek, MO xvi, 127–147, 171–172, 207, 249, 250, 252, 267, 333, 355, 358, 365, 391, 471, 484, 485, 486, 491, 492, 493, 495, 515, 526
Beach, John R. 523
Beaman, George W. 209, 499
Beauregard, P. G. T. 376, 408, 414, 493
Begeman, Henry 508
Belt, Henry B. 274
Bennett, James Gordon xxi
Benton, William H. 524
Benton, William P. 531
Biddle,—— 350
Bittinger, Joseph L. 292
Blair, Frank xvi, 9, 10, 13, 14, 16, 24, 29, 35, 47, 55, 77, 160, 188–192, 198, 202–203, 206, 285–287, 419, 454, 456, 457–458, 460, 491–492, 496
  controversy with General Fremont 216–219, 498
Blair, Montgomery 13, 188–191, 191, 198
Blake, Aaron 508
Blandowski, Constantin 15
Bland, Peter E. 71–72
Blow, Henry T. 22, 456

Boernstein, Henry 9, 10, 35, 42, 45, 47, 55, 65, 465, 468, 481
Boester (Voerster), Johann D. 47, 50, 52, 462
Bonde, Rudolph 508
Borg, Charles 300, 519
Borland, Solon 177, 368, 494, 527–528
Bowen, John H. 475
Bowen, John S. 92–93, 481
Bowen, William D. 342, 463, 532
Boyd, Sempronius H. 261, 503
Brackett, Betsy Critchett xvii
Brackett, William xvii
Bradley, Jerome 403
Brand, H. H. 371
Brand, Horace T. 52, 143, 463
Bricker, Colonel—— 372
Broadwell, J. P. 373
Broadwell, W. A. 371
Brown, Alonzo J. 144
Brown, B. Gratz 70, 79, 101–102, 346, 471, 482
Brown, Egbert B. 3, 225–226, 454, 501
Brown, J. B. 17–19
Brown, John (lieutenant, First Missouri) 144
Brown, Nathan 513
Browne, Junius Henri xiii–xiv, 207, 209–210, 407
Browning, Orville H. 494
Brownlee, John A. 159, 165, 166, 491
Bruce, Joshua P. 13
Buell, Don Carlos 345
Burbank, Sidney 508
Burch, James H. 353
Burke, Patrick E. 48, 51, 144
Busch, Isidor 524
Bussey, Cyrus 532
Butler, Benjamin F. 80, 502
Butterworth, Lieutenant—— 324

Cadwallader, George 80

Callaway, Captain—— 109–110, 433–434
Cameron, Simon 219–220, 224, 226, 228–229, 246, 501
Campbell, Hugh 293
Camp Jackson Massacre xvi, 1, 2–11, 15, 25, 32, 38, 53, 55, 78, 91, 93, 113, 114, 158, 200, 273, 274, 282, 283, 286, 302, 303, 414, 425, 456, 471, 476, 499
Carmody, Martin 508
Carpenter, Don A. 403–404
Carr, Eugene A. 248, **322**, 323, 341, 342, 345, 348, 383, 386–387, 388–390, 390–391, 391, 393, 395, 401, 519, 532
Carver, William R. 508
Catieny, Phillip 508
Catron. John 84, 90–91, 429, 429–430, 477, 478, 481–482
Cavender, John S. 48, 144, 347
Chapman, James A. 452
Chappell, William C. 284–285, 507
Chipman, N. P. 341
Clark, John B. 166, 477, 492
Coffee, John T. 90
Cohen,—— 350
Colburn, Richard T. 209, 407
Cole, Nelson 41, 48, 49, 69, 144
Coleridge, Samuel Taylor 527
Coler, William N. 531
Comstock, Isaac 508
Conant, Horace A. 29, 40, 105, 460
Conrad, Joseph 381, 528
Cooke (Cook), Abel H. W. 58–59, 467, 474
Cooke, Philip St. George 214, 499–500
Coolidge, M. W. 55
Cooper, John 440
Cornyn, Florence M 54, 59, 163, 463
Corwine, Richard M. 440
Cox, Nathaniel 352

Coyle, William H. 389
Crickard, Beman 508
Critchett, Jane Wallace xvii
Critchett, Sally xvii
Cronenbold, Ferdinand W. 115, 125, 486
Crooks, Martha E. 508
Crowder, Richard B. 517
Cummings, Alexander 327, 515
Curry (Curley), Thomas 62
Curtis, Samuel R. 221, 295, 300, 316, **317**, 322, 323, 328, 329, 337, 341, 343, 348, 356, 359, 363, 365, 369, 374, 375, 376, 378, 379, 381, 383, 385, 407, 411, 471, 480, 490, 500, 514, 516, 519, 522, 526, 527, 530, 532

Dabbs, Abner 106, 431
Daniel, Peter V. 285, 507–508
Davis, David 293
Davis, Dr.—— 145
Davis, E. M. 441
Davis, Jefferson C. (Union general) 308, 315, 363, 383, 386, 390, 391, 392–393, 393, 395, 399, 514, 527, 531
Davis, Jefferson F. (Confederate president) 40, 73, 82, 92, 164, 195, 255, 284, 288, 321, 330, 337, 351, 369, 414, 461
Deitzler, George W. 122, 133, 138, 144, 359, 526
Devlin, Private—— 125
Dickens, Charles 517
Dick, Franklin A. 519
Dimond, Rev. D. 508
Dix, Dorothea 507
Dix, John 502
Dodge, Grenville M. **261**, 297, 317, 387, 392, 503, 532
Dorsheimer, William 442
Dougherty, Private—— 125

Index

Douglas, John T. 519
Douglas, Stephen 471, 494
Dubois, John V. D. 114, 122, 123, 133, 135, 136, 137, 139, 216
Duke, Basil 20, 456
Duncan, Louis 508
Dutcher, Isaac V. W. 508

Eads, James B. 190, 297, 507, 511
Eaton, Joseph H. 440
Edgar, George P. 312
Edgell, S. M. 521
Elbert, Gustavus M. 531
Eliot, William G. 282, 507
Ellis, Calvin A. 400, 534
Engler, Samuel 352, 353, 525

Farmer, Benjamin J. 354, 525–526
Faron, Lieutenant—— 5
Farrar, Benjamin 288, 300, 320
Farrar, Bernard G. 519
Fayel, William 346, 378, 407, 527
Fiala, John T. 440
Filley, O. B. 524
Fisk, Charles A. 508
Fisk, Clinton B. 508, 521
Fisk, Jannette B. 508
Fisk, Mary C. 508
Foote, Andrew H. 360, 378
Forshey, William J. 517
Foster, Thomas S. 517
Franklin, Edward C. 90, 145, 146, 185–186, 495
Franklin, H. B. 73
Franz, Captain—— 11
Frémont, Francis Preston 500
Frémont, Jessie Benton 80, 93–94, 188–189, 442, 497, 502–503, 507
Frémont, John C. 80, 83, 84, 86, 87, 159, 162, 163, 175, 180–181, 183–184, 185, 186, 187, 188, 189, 190, 191, 194, 197, 198, 199, 200, 201, 202, 203, 204, 205, 206, 207, 214, 215, 216, 217, 218, 219, 220, 221, 222, 223, 224, 226, 227, 228, 229, 230, 231, 233, 235, 236, 237, 238, 239, 240, 241, 243, 244, 245, 254, 255, 259, 261, 262, 265, 268, 269, 272, 275, 276, 282, 292, 303, 304, 314, 326, 337, 340, 341, 344, 351, 356, 363, 365, 378, 387, 407, 436–437, 439, 439–443, 443–445, 476, 479, 480, 491, 494, 495, 496, 497, 498, 499, 500, 501, 502, 503, 504, 506, 507, 516, 517, 518, 519, 525, 536
  arrives in St. Louis 80, 93–94
  declares martial law in Missouri 183–184, 185–186, 188–189, 194, 197
  declares martial law in St. Louis 158, 490
  declines to reinforce Lyon at Springfield 113, 127, 162–163
  dismissal and departure from the army 246–252
  takes the field for southwest Missouri 205–206
Frost, Daniel M. 2, 166, 283, 414, 454, 481
Fry, Private—— 125
Funkhouser, R. M. 519

Galligan, John 389
Gamble, Hamilton R. xvii, 191–192, 273, 285, 287, 288, 346, 447, 447–448, 506, 508
Gantt, Thomas T. 83
Gardner, A. M. 508
Gardner, Samuel H. 519
Gardner, Susan E. 508
Gaylord, Saml. A. 508
Gilbert, Charles C. 135, 144
Givens (Gibbons), John A. 125
Glover, Major—— 316
Glover, Samuel T. 285

Goode, George W. 297, 302, 510–511, 512
Gordon, Silas 292, 510
Gore, Stephen D. 508
Gottshalk, Frederick 144
Granger, Gordon 122, 139
Grant, Corporal—— 145
Grant, Ulysses S. xxii, 268, 269, 273–274, 360, 378, 407, 408, 409, 410, 440, 493, 499, 504, 535
Grant, William S. 145, 489
Gratiot Street Prison. *See* McDowell's Medical College
Gratz, Cary 144, 169, 492–493
Greeley, Carlos S. 282, 507, 524
Greeley, Horace xviii, 506, 507
Green, Cylas 452
Greene, Colton 456
Greene, David B. 198
Green, James S. 345
Green, Martin 184, 193, 196, 497, 498
Greusel, Nicholas 399, 531
Griffin, William 47
Grissom, D. M. 203–205, 438, 499
Groesbeck, John 334
Gurley, John A. 441

Halleck, Henry W. 260, 263, 264–266, **265**, 269, 270, 271, 272, 273, 274, 275, 279, 280, 282, 283, 286, 288, 289, 292, 293, 295, 297, 298, 301, 302, 303, 305, 306, 308, 310, 314, 315, 316, 317, 321, 326, 327, 329, 331, 332, 334, 335, 337, 338, 341, 347, 351, 352, 353, 355, 356, 357, 358, 361, 362, 364, 378, 379, 408, 440, 441, 445–447, 448–451, 503, 504, 507, 509, 510, 511, 514, 516, 517, 518, 519, 522, 526, 527
    assesses St. Louis secessionists for the benefit of Union refugees 306, 335–336, 361, 518
    bars fugitive slaves from Federal lines 270–271
    controversy over General Sigel's resignation 355–358
    meets with British consul 295
    orders rebel property to be made available to fugitive Missouri Unionists 280–282
    orders St. Louis city officials to take oath of allegiance 288–289, 354–355, 364
    orders summary execution for bridge burners 306
    places river commerce under Union military control 301
    replaces General Hunter 263
Hall, Willard Preble 285, 346
Hall, William A. 477
Hamilton, Schuyler 264, 504
Hammond, James Henry 490
Hanson, Joseph M. 524
Hardee, William J. 131, 168, 175–176, 180, 194, 371, 493–494
Harding, Chester, Jr. 78, 79, 273, 472
Hare, Lieutenant—— 39
Harney-Price Agreement 11–12, 16, 20, 21, 24, 25, 27, 77, 418–419
Harney, William S. 6, 11, **12**, 13, 14, 16, 17, 19, 20, 21, 24, 25, 26, 27, 28, 29, 30, 31, 77, 80, 412, 415, 416, 417, 418, 422, 423, 425, 455, 457, 504, 516
Harris, Major—— 309
Haskell, Leonidas 241–242, 246, 442, 502–503
Hastings, Matthew 7, 455
Hatch, Reuben B. 180
Hawkins, John P. 463, 508
Hawley, G. A. 508
Hayden, Mortimer M. 400, 403, 404, 532
Hazard, Grace L. 508
Hearn, James A. 508
Hébert, Louis **113**, 486

Index

Hecker, Friedrich 71, 175, 493
Heitzelman, Samuel P. 440
Henderson, John B. 319, 345, 353, 477, 514
Hendricks, John A. 399, 404
Herron, Francis J. 144, 344, 392, 406, 407, 434
Hescock, Henry 273, 506
Hinckley, J. 508
Hinckley, John 508
Hinckley, J. S. 508
Hinderman (Halderman), John A. 144
Hindman, Thomas C. 472
Holman, John 248
Holt, Joseph 293, 305
Hough, Warwick 46
Howard, J. R. 442
Howland, Charles H. 524
Hudson, Frederick xxi
Hudson, R. N. 247, 248, 251, 442
Hughes, James R. 313
Hughes, John T. 166, 492
Hunt, Colonel—— 372
Hunter, David 198, 215, 216, 221, 222, 225, **246**, 246–254, 256, 257, 259, 262, 263, 264, 266, 283, 338, 445, 450, 501, 502, 504, 506, 517
Hurlbut, Stephen A. 196
Hutton, Jane 508

Jackson, Captain—— 4
Jackson, Claiborne Fox xvi, 10, 13, 14, 17, 18, 21, 22, 22–23, 23, 24, 26, 27, 28–32, 33–34, 35, 37, 38, 53, 58, 60, 62, 64, 69, 72, 73, 74, 76, 77, 79, 80, 81, 83, 87, 88, 89, 91, 93, 102, 103, 104, 105, 121, 223, 227, 235, 252, 254, 255, 288, 302, 312, 333, 361, 418–421, 435, 454, 460, 464, 465, 466, 467, 468, 473, 475, 476, 477, 479, 483, 484, 491, 501, 534
Jacobs,—— 120–121, 125

Jacquith, P. H. 508
Jayne, Dr. —— 17
Jennison, Charles R. 268, 283, 342, 455, 505, 519
Jennison's Jayhawkers. *See* 7th Kansas Cavalry
Johnson, John B. 282, 507
Johnson, Reverdy 327, 515
Johnson, Waldo P. 286, 345–346
Johnston, Albert Sidney 244, 245, 494, 502
Johnston, Joseph E. 172, 493
Joliat, Francis J. 531
Jones, Asa S. 474
Jones, E. D. 524
Jones, Jefferson F. 324, 325, 515
Josephs, Major—— 292
Julian, George W. 271, 506

Keim, William H. 80
Kelly, Joseph 20, 34, 456
Kelly, Michael J. 119–120, 125, 430, 433
Kelton, John C. 198, 301, 309–310
Kerr,—— 371
Kiburtz, Jacob 55
Kidd, W. H. 185–186, 495
Knott, J. P. 476
Knox, Emily xvii, 452–453
Knox, Nehemiah xvii
Knox, Thomas W.
  arrested as a spy by General Sherman 409–410
  birth and early life xvii–xviii
  death and burial 411
  friendship with Nathaniel Lyon 131–133, 146
  newspaperman in Kansas Territory (Colorado) xviii–xx
  physical description by Franc Wilkie xxi–xxii
Koener, Gustav 441
Koliko, Danl. 508

Kosner, C. M. 508
Krom, John C. 508
Krum, John M. 327, 515

Lane, James H. "Jim" 65, 193, 198, 231, 242, 243, 267, 501–502, 505, 519
Leach, J. H. 236–237
Leighton, George E. 283, 309
Lincoln, Abraham xii, xiii, xx, 9, 12, 13, 40, 183, 184, 185, 188, 189, 191, 221, 234, 236, 260, 284, 287, 288, 337, 410, 441, 442, 457, 466, 483, 494, 495, 497, 501, 502, 504, 515, 522
Lionberger, J. R. 524
Long, L. H. 508
Lothrop, Warren L. 35, 47, 114, 133, 136, 347
Lovejoy, Owen 247, 248, 251
Lovie, Henri 209
Lowe, Aiden 78, 472
Lucas, James H. 521
Lusk, W. H. 37, 40
Lyon, Nathaniel xvi, xvii, 2, 5, 9, 11, 13, 14, 24, 25, 28–32, 33–34, 35–43, 44, 45, 46, 47, 49, 51, 52, 53, 54, **56**, 57, 60, 61, 62, 63, 64, 65, 67, 72, 77, 79–80, 80, 81, 84, 86, 87, 90, 95, 96, 100, 103, 104, 105, 106, 112, 113–114, **114**, 115, 119, 121, 123, 124, 127, 129–134, 138–139, 141, 145, 146, 148, 157–158, 159–160, 161, 162–163, 166, 170, 205, 223, 228, 249, 312, 342, 347, 365, 366, 378, 421–424, 424–426, 435, 454, 460, 461, 464, 465, 466, 468–469, 471, 472, 484, 488, 516
   death at Wilson's Creek 138–139
   Planter's House conference 28–30, 419–420

MacDonald, Emmett 169, 493

MacDonald, J. W. A. 185, 495
Magoffin, Beriah 313
Magoffin, Ebenezer "Ben" 313, 323, 513
Magree,—— 309
Mankin, Wm. 371
Mansfield, Joseph K. 80
Manter, Francis H. 347
March (Marsh), C. Carroll 87, 480
Marmaduke, John S. 44, 47, 52, 493
Marshall, Thomas A. 313, 514
Marsh, C. Carroll 478, 479, 480
Marston, Henry C. 524
Marvin, William E. 430
Mason, Alexander L. 144
Matson, J. R. 476
Maurice, Thomas D. 48, 347
McAnally, David R. 492
McBride, James H. 77–78, 95–96, 166, 172–173, 400, 471–472, 492, 534
McClellan, George B. 80, 168, 265, 271, 293, 327, 350, 379, 440, 445–447, 519
McClernand, John A. 410
McClurg, J. W. 83
McCormack, James. R. 83
McCullagh, Joseph B. 209
McCulloch, Ben 61, 68, 73, 80, 91, 104, **113**, 114, 115, 124, 127, 130, 162, 165, 169, 171, 172, 178, 180, 199, 227, 230, 238, 248, 252–253, 255, 271, 272, 276, 279, 348, 375, 379, 401, 402, 405, 426, 427–428, 470, 485, 486, 487, 488, 532
McCulloch, Robert 50
McDonald, Emmett 4, 169
McDowell, Irvin 80
McDowell, Joseph N. 25, 310, 458, 513
McDowell's Medical College (Gratiot Street Prison) 308, 310–311, 314, 319–321, 323–324, 334–335, 354, 458, 517

Index

McFarland, David 508
McIntosh, James M. 161, 379, 400, 402, 487
McKean, Thomas J. 315, 514
McKeeven, Chauncey 440
McKeever, Chauncey 217
McKellog, Dr.—— 158–159, 491
McKellope, Henry 491
McKinstry, Justus 158, 159, 164, 184, 187, 194, 198, 204, 215, 216, 221, 222, 224, 225, 229, 246, 247, 267, 298, 325, 326, 327, 441, 490, 491, 498, 501, 502
McKissack,—— 350
McLean, N. H. 355
McLivane, Private—— 125
McMichael, William 270
McNeil, John 3, 69, 86, 101, 454, 480–481
Meigs, Montgomery C. 189, 191, 293, 496, 497
Melcher, Samuel H. 145, 162, 487
Merrill, Lewis 254, 349, 522
Merritt, Thomas 196–197
Merritt, William H. 106, 430, 485
Meszaros, Emeric 531
Miles, D. S. 459
Military units
  Confederate
    Arkansas
      3rd Cavalry 527
      17th Infantry 534
    Louisiana
      3rd Infantry 486
    Missouri
      Missouri State Guard (MSG) xvi–xvii, 20, 21, 25, 44, 80, 166, 282, 456, 471–472, 472, 492, 513, 515, 525, 534
      Missouri State Militia (aka Missouri Volunteer Militia) xvi, 2
      Southwest Battalion 3, 4, 5. *See* *also* Southwest Expedition
  Union
    Illinois
      2nd Light Artillery 531
      1st Cavalry 313, 514
      3rd Cavalry 399, 400, 532
      10th Infantry 493
      11th Infantry 72
      13th Infantry 71, 87, 96, 479, 480, 503
      14th Infantry 71, 168
      15th Infantry 71, 168
      16th Infantry 71, 292
      17th Infantry 71
      18th Infantry 72
      20th Infantry 71, 87, 479, 480
      21st Infantry 71
      22nd Infantry 71
      24th Infantry (Hecker's German Jaeger Volunteers) 71, 493
      25th Infantry 531
      35th Infantry 399, 532
      36th Infantry 383, 399, 530
      37th Infantry 405, 531
      44th Infantry 399, 531
      50th Infantry 292, 510
      66th Infantry (Birge's Western Sharpshooters) 307, 319
      82nd Infantry 493
    Indiana
      1st Battery, Light Artillery 531
      7th Cavalry 441
      8th Infantry 531
      11th Infantry 187
      18th Infantry 395, 531
      22nd Infantry 395, 399, 404, 531
      24th Infantry 311
      25th Infantry 308–309, 317
      38th Infantry 505
    Iowa
      1st Battery Light Artillery 403, 532

3rd Battery Light Artillery
(Hayden's Dubuque Battery)
388, 400, 403, 404, 532
3rd Cavalry 385, 400, 405, 528, 532, 533
1st Infantry 59, 61, 62, 65, 70, 72, 84–85, 101, 106, 114, 122, 130, 133, 136, 138–139, 144, 147, 160, 163–164, 199, 430, 466–467, 484, 485, 489, 492
2nd Infantry 71, 72, 308–310, 320, 324, 500
3rd Infantry 71, 331
4th Infantry 317, 389, 392, 503, 532, 533
5th Infantry 297
9th Infantry 344, 383, 388, 389, 392, 403, 529, 532, 533
11th Infantry 489
13th Infantry 304
22nd Infantry 492

Kansas
  7th Cavalry ("Jennison's Jayhawkers") 505
  1st Infantry 101, 122, 133, 136–137, 138, 144, 194–195, 358–359, 526
  2nd Infantry 101, 106, 114, 122, 133, 136–137, 144, 170, 184, 485, 495
  3rd Infantry 502
  4th Infantry 502
  5th Infantry 502

Missouri
  1st Flying Battery 531
  1st Light Artillery 273, 347, 463, 506
  Backof's Battalion (artillery) 101
  Welfley's Independent Battery 530
  1st Cavalry 400
  2nd Cavalry (Merrill Horse) 348, 522
  4th Cavalry (Fremont Hussars) 531
  5th Cavalry (Benton Hussars) 530
  6th Cavalry 485, 531
  10th Cavalry 463
  1st Infantry 35–42, 51, **58**, 72, 100, 114, 122, 130, 133, 135–136, 141, 142, 144, 147, 160, 163, 169, 194–195, 198, 491, 492
  1st Regiment, U.S. Reserve Corps 71
  2nd Infantry 35, 45, 48, 63, 72, 133, 383, 462, 531
  2nd Regiment, U.S. Reserve Corps 71
  3rd Infantry 35, 114, 489, 528, 530
  3rd Regiment, U.S. Reserve Corps 86, 454, 471, 479, 482
  4th Infantry 23
  4th Regiment, U.S. Reserve Corps 471, 482
  5th Infantry 90, 114, 471, 482, 486, 487
  5th Regiment, U.S. Reverve Corps 63, 455, 470
  6th Infantry 71
  7th Infantry 62, 163, 454, 469–470
  9th Infantry (59th Illinois) 198, 531
  10th Infantry 331
  12th Infantry 395, 399, 530
  13th Infantry 359
  15th Infantry 531
  17th Infantry 530
  24th Infantry 485, 503, 528
  25th Infantry 383, 399–400, 532, 533–534
  33rd Infantry 463

Index

Holman's Battalion of
  Sharpshooters 248
Home Guard xvi–xvii, 3, 7,
  8, 72, 106, 115, 129, 133,
  135, 153, 154, 162, 170, 188,
  419–420, 467, 468–469, 472,
  478, 509
Missouri State Militia (MSM)
  506
Nebraska
  1st Infantry 175, 227, 493
Ohio
  2nd Independent Battery, Light
    Artillery 531
  4th Independent Battery, Light
    Artillery 530
  39th Infantry 334
  81st Infantry 331
U.S. Regulars
  4th Artillery 114, 133
  1st Cavalry 119–120, 122
  2nd Cavalry 214
  1st Infantry 114, 133
  2nd Infantry 114, 133, 500
  11th Infantry 315
  13th Infantry 491
  17th Infantry 491
  18th Infantry 279
  25th Infantry 491
Wisconsin
  8th Infantry 318
  11th Infantry 318
Miller, Charles 523
Miller, Madison 49
Miller, Private—— 125
Mills, James K. 110, 370, 485, 528
Missouri Constitutional Convention
  of 1861-1863 xx–xxi, 83–84,
  288–289, 416, 421, 476–477, 508,
  522–524, 523–525
Missouri Military Bill 28, 30, 413, 420
Mitchell, Abram S. 499
Mitchell, Robert B. 106, 114, 122, 133,
  144, 485
Moffett, William A. 524
Montgomery, James 4, 71, 74, 92, 171,
  188, 454–455, 466
Morrison, William 470
Morris, Sarah B. 508
Mudd, Alexis 145, 489
Mulligan, James A. 205, 313, 438–439,
  505
Murphy, David 347, 464

Napoléon, Prince Joseph Charles Paul
  Bonaparte 185, 495
Neiderweisser, Tony 508
Nelson, H. A. 508

Oliver, Mordecai 448
Osterhaus, Peter J. 133, 135, 346, 385,
  530
Owens, Jeff 324, 325, 332, 515

Parker, George W. 524
Parsons, Mosby M. 52, 53, 439
Partridge, George 282, 507
Paschall, Nathaniel 77, 471
Patchin, L. W. 520–521
Patterson, Robert 80, 172, 493
Patton, John 517
Payne, J. M. 371
Peabody, Everett 193
Pearce, Albert 524
Peckham, James 89
Peterson, Jas. R. 508
Phelps, John S. 62, 161, 256, 338, 383,
  389, 399–400, 469, 475, 532, 533
Phinney, James H. 255, 503
Pickens, Francis W. 84, 477
Pike, Albert xix, 75, 231, 319, 380,
  384, 426, 533
Pike, Captain—— 231
Pile, William A. 51, 463
Pillow, Gideon J. 177
Planter's House Conference 28–31, 33

Plumley, B. Rush 442
Plummer, Joseph B. 114, 119, 133, 135, 144, 242
Polk, Leonidas 273–274
Polk, Trusten 285–287, 289, 301–302, 345, 346, 511, 514
Pollock, James 17
Pook, Samuel M. 297, 511
Pope, John 196, 221, 222, 225, 247, 250, 264, 293, 308, 315, 316, 327, 329, 343, 373, 501, 515, 516
Porter, Fitz John 515
Prentiss, Benjamin M. 72, 168, 174–175, 176, 178, 180, 272, 292, 315, 331, 359, 493
Price, Hiram 426
Price, John H. 264, 504
Price, Sterling **12**, 17, 24, 26–28, 27, 28–32, 33, 38, 39, 52, 53, **57**, 60, 69, 76, 83, 87, 88, 104, 113, 114, 125, 127, 130, 162, 165, 171–172, 193, 195, 196, 204, 208, 214–215, 222, 223, 227, 229, 230, 231, 238, 245, 255, 256, 257, 258, 269, 271, 272, 275–276, 279, 282, 283, 284, 288, 302, 303, 304, 306, 314, 315, 316, 317, 326, 331, 332, 333, 334, 341, 342, 348, 349, 351, 360, 364, 367, 368, 369, 370–374, 405, 416–418, 418, 422, 431, 435, 439, 443–445, 448–451, 473, 477, 498, 506, 514, 515, 522, 528, 529, 532
Price, Thomas H. 372, 528
Price, Thomas L. 39, 40, 346, 522
Prince, Captain—— 71
Pulliam, George M. 517
Pursell, William 144

Quarles, William 55

Rains, James S. 80, 88, 103, 104, 115, 121, 123, 166, 171, 473, 492
Ramsey, Charles G. 203–205, 438, 498

Rector, Frank A. 403, 534
Rector, Henry M. 527–528
Reed, Henry S. 521
Reminfy, Joseph 443
Reynolds, Thomas C. 24, 92
Richards, Eben, Jr. 524
Richardson, Albert D. xviii–xx, xix, 1, 56, 65, 85, 207, 209, 210–216, 221–222, 238, 239, 409
Richardson, Henry 47, 50
Richardson, Orlando C. 43, 56, 461
Rich, S. 524
Robertson, Franklin S. 308, 513
Rogers, Evans 508
Rogers, J. R. 46, 475
Ross, John 22, 68, 426–427, 457
Rowles, David H. 400

Savage, James W. 442
Schaffer, Gustavus A. 114, 133
Schaffer (Shaefer), Frederick 47, 531
Schiller, Friedrich 527
Schofield, John M. 267, 273, 319, 324, 325, 326, 331, 332, 505
Schultz, Benedict 47, 462
Schutte, Captain—— 47
Scott, Major—— 230
Scott, Winfield 40, 217
Senter, Henry 524
Seward, William H. 206
Shanks, John P. C. 251, 441
Shepard, Isaac F. 105, 484
Sheridan, Phil 368, 370, 374, 527
Sherman, William T. xxii, 287, 409–410
Sigel, Franz 10, 35, 61, 62, 70, 74, 79, 81, 84, 87, 88, 89, 90, 91, 101, 103, 105, 114, 122, 129–131, 133, 138, 140, 141, 143, 145, 148, 158, 160, 171, 216, 221, 224, 225, 229, 230, 237, 243, 256, 257, 260, 276, 280, 317, 325, 328, 329, 333, 336, 337, 338, 343, 344, 346, 355, 356, 357,

358, 383, 384, 385, 386, 390, 391, 392, 393–394, 396, 397, 408, 441, 460, 466, 467, 471, 483, 487–489, 488, 500–501, 514, 516, 526, 531
Simplot, Alexander A. 94, 209, 215, 222, 236, 245, 298
Simpson, —— 41
Slack, William Y. 25, 400, 402, 458, 534
Slawson, Sophia D. 508
Sliefer, Charles G.. *See* Stifel, Charles G.
Smith, Alexander H. 521
Smith, Dr.—— 145
Smith, George H. 188, 496
Smith, George R. 229, 273, 506
Smith, Gustavus A. 399, 533
Smith, John Proctor 524
Smith, Robert F. 292
Smith, Solomon 508
Snead, Thomas L. 89, 458
Sokalski, George O. 106, 109, 347, 430, 434, 485
Solomon (Salomon), Charles E. 61, 70, 74, 79, 88, 90, 101, 114, 122, 162, 466, 471, 486, 487
Souper, Thomas W. 296–297, 510
Southwest Expedition 46, 92, 454, 462, 476–477, 479–480
Stanley, David S. 105, 106, 107, 108, 109, 430, 431, 433, 484
Starks, Colonel—— 247, 248
Steamships and Gunboats
 Augustus McDowell 40, 44, 45–46, 49, 50, 52, 461
 Benton 278, 507–508
 City of Alton 478
 City of Louisiana 11, 23, 33, 35, 42, 45, 51, 457, 459
 D. A. January 59, 63, 185, 359, 468
 Emma 214, 499
 H. D. Bacon 52, 463
 Iatan 11, 33, 35, 39, 40, 42, **43**, 46, 303, 459, 460, 495, 505, 513
 J. C. Swon 11, 25, 33, 35, 37, 38, 39, 40, 42, 44, 45, 63, 78, 459, 460
 New Era 216, 500
 North Star 93–94
 Platte Valley 268, 505
 Sam Gaty 36, 298, 511
 Sunshine 54, 193, 268, 505
 War Eagle 54, 505
 White Cloud 34, 38, 459, 460, 505
Steele, Frederick 114, 119, 133, 313, 315
Steele, William 459
Stevenson, John D. 62, 71, 72, 163, 168, 469, 469–470
Stewart, Charles 17
Stewart, Robert M. 13, 454, 462, 477
Stifel, Charles G. 6, 72, 455, 470
Stokes, Private—— 125
Sturgis, Samuel D. 62, 90, 101, 114, 120, 122, 129, 130, 138, 141, 160, 169, 193, 198, 201, 216, 222, 231, 243, 264, 277, 487, 526
Sullivan, Thomas W. 120, 125, 399
Sully, Major—— 71
Sumner, Charles 271, 506
Suratt, Mary 515
Sweeny, Thomas W. 61, 65, 80, 81, 83, 84, 87–88, 89, 90, 91, 95, 101, 102, 103, 105, 106, 107, 110, **111**, 112, 138, 144, 145, 169, 185, 216, 274, 330, 352, 428–429, 430, 431, 432, 434, 435, 473, 474, 484–485, 485, 489
Swynne (Sweeny), Robert W. 330, 517

Taylor, Daniel G. 7
Taylor, Zachary 485
Telkampf, Theodore A. 440
Thayer, John M. 410
Thomas, Lorenzo 246, 424
Thompson, Charles L. 524
Thompson, Francis M. 388

Thompson, John A. 279–280
Thompson, M. Jeff 24, 175–176, 242, 268, 284–285, 310, 318, 348, 354, 453, 456, 507, 525
Thorn, George 519
Tilden, John 508
Tindall, J. T. 83
Tompkins, John C. 517
Totten, James 35, 47, 48, 49, 58, 59, 60, 72, 106, 114, 119, 122, 127, 129, 133, 134–135, 137, 139, 142, 171, 194, 195, 216, 223, 267, 347, 348, 430, 440, 460, 465, 505
Treaty of Ghent xii
Trimble, Henry H. 400, 533–534
Tucker, Charles L. 519
Tucker, Joseph W. 84, 87, 479, 480
Turnlee (Turnley), Parmenas T. 198
Tuttle, James M. 71

Underground Railroad 296–297

Van Buren, Martin 508
Vandever, William 381, 387, 388, 392, 403, 529–530, 532
Van Dorn, Earl 376, 377, 379, 381, 383–384, 532, 533, 534, 540
Vest, George G. 462–463

Waagner, Gustav 440
Waldauer, August 441
Wallace, Lew 187, 409
Wanamaker, John 513
Ware, Eugene 86
Watts, Perry 404
Weightman, Richard H. 166, 167, 492
Welker, Frederick 347
Weller, Sam 330, 517
Wentz, Augustus 434
Wentzel, J. F. 508
Western Sanitary Commission 507

Wheelan,—— 296–297, 512–513
White, Frank J. 242, 245, 268, 442
White, Julius 405, 531
White, Robert 63, 470
White, William 163, 492–493
Whitney, Robt. L. 508
Wilgus, James A. 524
Wilkie, Franc B. xvi, xxi–xxii, 85–86, 105, 106, 109, 114, 116, 148, 157, 207, 209, 222–223, 430, 479, 484, 486, 499
Wilkins, J. Edward 294–297, 511
Williams, Agnes E. 508
Williams, Edward C. 80
Williams, Henry W. 283, 443, 507
Williams, N. B. 508
Williams, Nelson G. 196
Williams, Pleasant J. 398
Wilson, Robert 83, 346, 522
Winslow, Frederick S. 370
Wolff, Christian D. 90
Wood, Ben 482
Wood, Samuel N. 106, 107, 109, 137, 144, 296–297, 430, 432, 485
Woods, I. C. 441–442
Woodward, H. M. 521
Wright, Clark 135, 342, 531
Wyman, John B. 95–96, 168–169, **255**, 255–257, 264, 478, 479, 482, 503

Yates, Richard 494
Yates, Theodore 38, 46, 48, 51, 52, 55, 144
Yeatman, James E. 282, 507
Yore, John E. 524
Yost, Jacob 404

Zagonyi, Charles 230, 243, 245, 441, 442

www.ingramcontent.com/pod-product-compliance
Lightning Source LLC
Chambersburg PA
CBHW070157240426
43671CB00007B/474